DEEP SPACE

DEEP SPACE

COLIN A. RONAN

CRESCENT BOOKS
NEW YORK

This 1987 edition published by Crescent Books,
distributed by Crown Publishers, Inc., 225 Park
Avenue South, New York, New York 10003

Editor: James Somerville
Art Direction: David Pearce
Design: Michael Keates
Picture Research: Janet Croall
Typesetting: Input Typesetting Limited
Reproduction by F. E. Burman Limited, London

Made by Roxby Astronomy Limited
A division of Roxby Press Ltd.

Library of Congress Cataloging-in-Publication Data

Ronan, Colin A.
Deep space.

Reprint. Originally published: New York: Macmillan, 1982.
Includes index.
1. Cosmology. 2. Outer space. I. Title.
QB981.R65 1987   523.1   87-19925
ISBN 0-517-65421-0
h g f e d c b a

Printed and bound in Yugoslavia

CONTENTS

CONTENTS

ACKNOWLEDGEMENTS

I should like especially to thank Mr. Storm Dunlop for all his preliminary work on suggesting appropriate illustrations for the book. I would also like to thank those who supplied helpful information, especially Professor Malcolm Longair, Dr. Russell Cannon, Dr. Susan Wyckoff, Dr. David L. Meier, Dr. Sidney Fox and Dr. Nick Wrigley.
Colin A. Ronan

The author and publishers would also like to thank the following people for help with illustrations.

Mr. H. Arnold of Space Frontiers Ltd., Mr. Dennis di Cicco, Dr. Sidney Fox, Kitt Peak National Observatory for the original drawings of the telescopes, p. 26/27, Mrs. E. Lake and Mr. Hingley of the Royal Astronomical Society, Mr. Hadley & Mr. Waldron of the Royal Observatory Edinburgh, Dr. Stanley Miller, Mr. D. Smith, Mr. Salim Patel of the Science Photo Library, Professor J. Weber, Dr. W. Wrigley.

Photographs
J. Allan Cash 8 above.
Ann Ronan Picture Library 14 below, 42 above, 113 below.
Mr. Ron Arbour 40, 151 above.
Anglo-Australian Observatory 166.
Anglo-Australian Telescope Board 62/63, photo courtesy D. F. Malin, 190.
Association of Universities for Research & Astronomy Inc., the Kitt Peak National Observatory 15, 24 below, 31 above, 52 above, 69, 71, 73, 74 below, 86, 88, 90, 91, 96 below, 100 below left & right, 101 left & right, 106, 121, 126 below, 161 above, 162, 163, 168.
Australian Information Service 109.
Bell Laboratories, Courtesy of, 154
Biofotos 179 below
Mr. Paul Brierley 178/9
British Astronomical Association 40/41, 42 below
British Museum (Natural History) 115, 175 right.
Elaine Brown & Dr. N. G. Wrigley, Medical Research Council 176 above.
Bruce Coleman Ltd. 170 above.
Camera Press Ltd. 131 above left.
CERN 169.
Mr. Dennis di Cicco 70, 114 below right.
Mr. J. Dix/Planetarium National Maritime Museum 112/113.
European Space Administration 33

below, 114 below left.
Dr. Sidney Fox, 176 below
Fox Photos Ltd. 28, 130/131.
Griffith Observatory 61 above, courtesy Lois Cohen.
Hale Observatories 11 above, 14 above left & right, 18, 19 left & right, 51 below left, 56/57, 58, 74 above, 76 top, left & right, 78 above, 87 right, 89, 92, 98 below 99, 119 above, 120 above, 122, 124.
Michael Holford Library 146 left, 146 right Michael Holford/British Museum.
Jet Propulsion Laboratory 51 right
Dr. Edward Kibblewhite 24 above.
La Recherche Magazine 199
Leiden Observatory 93 right, 161 below.
Lick Observatory 35 left, 64, 66 below, 96 above, 104 centre, 120 below, 137, 172, 173 above & below, 184 right, 186.
Professor M. Longair 108.
Lowell Observatory 49 below, left & right
Mr. Fred J. Maroon 1979, 9 above.
Max Planck Institut für Radioastronomie 29 left.
Dr. David Meier 158
Dr. Stanley Miller 180 right.
Mount Tambourine Observatory 150, courtesy Mr. A. Page.
Mount Wilson Observatory 157, 198.
NASA 8 below, 22, 38 above & below, 39 below, 44 above, 50 below, 129, 155, 165, 188 above, 192, 193, 200/201, 203 left.
National Radio Astronomy Observatory New Mexico 29 right, 134 below right, 151 below.
Mr. A. Page 13 above, 52 below.
Mr. P. J. E. Peebles 107 above.
Perkin-Elmer Corporation 36 below, 36/37, 127
Mr. R. Pilsbury 180 left.
Popperfoto 171 left.
Mr. H. B. Ridley 131 centre right.
Royal Astronomical Society, Courtesy of, 113 above, 133 below, 145 below, 148 left.
Royal Greenwich Observatory 27 below left, 31 below, 134 left & right above.
Royal Observatory Edinburgh 25 above & below, 28 right, 60, 66 top, 67 above, 79, 81 right, 87 left, 100 above, 102, 103 above & below, 104 top, 175 left.
Rutherford Appleton Laboratory, courtesy Dr. J. J. Thresher 139.
Science Photo Library 30 above, courtesy Kitt Peak, 30 below courtesy Drs. Dunford/Boksenberg, 34

courtesy CERN 54 above, 66 centre, 85 above, 114 above, 118, 119 below, courtesy Kitt Peak, 126 above, 131 above right, 179 above.
Seaphot 170 below
Smithsonian Institution 27 below right, 32, 33 above, 78 below, 81 left, 85 below, 94 below, 107 below.
Space Frontiers Ltd. 36 above, 50 above, 201, 203 right.
Prof. H. Spinrad, University of California, Berkeley 104 below.
Sproul Observatory 76 centre, 116, 184 left.
Tass 188/189 below.
Trans-Time Inc. 200
United Kingdom Atomic Energy Authority 136
University of California San Diego, Dr. Stanley Miller 180 right.
University of Cambridge, High Resolution Electron Microscope, courtesy Dr. D. Smith, 142, 143.
University of Cambridge, Mullard radio Astronomy Observatory 44 below, 93 left.
University College Los Angeles, Prof. P. B. Price 164.
University of Hawaii 28 left.
US Naval Observatory, Washington 49 above.
Professor J. Weber 35 right.
Wells Cathedral, Courtesy Dean & Chapter 148 right.
World Data Center A 132/3 above, 182, 183 above & below, 189 above.
Dr. Susan Wyckoff 21, 94/95 above.
Yerkes Observatory 72 left, 76 below.
Zentralbibliothek, Zürich 149.

Artwork
Ian Craig, Dave Eaton, Ted Hammond, Edwina Keene, Aziz Khan, Simon Roulstone, Jeff Ridge, Peter Roziki, John Thompson, John Woodcock.

Artwork based on existing sources is acknowledged as follows:
Aerodynamic Phenomena in Stellar Atmosphere – Academic Press London 18 below
The American Astronomical Society 81 left
Black Holes and Warped Space Time by W. J. Kaufmann 111, W. H. Freeman, San Francisco 79 below
Cosmos 77 by Adolf Schaller
The Hamlyn Encyclopaedia of Astronomy 59 below
Kerr & Westerhout, Universities of Sydney & Leiden 57 centre
Scientific American 56/57 bottom, 128 right, 141 above, 156/157 bottom, 159, 163, 181, 192/193 below

CHAPTER 1
THE SCALE OF SPACE

In this book we shall journey into the farthest depths of space. The distances we shall travel are almost unbelievable in their immensity, and we shall have to use special ways of describing them.

The scale of space is so immense that before considering it at all, we need to get an idea of the scale of things nearer home. Indeed, there is a vast range in the size of things even on the Earth itself.

The scale we shall use to describe these is the metric scale – the scale of millimetres, centimetres, metres and kilometres – because this is used by scientists the world over. This is due to the fact that the metric scale is as convenient when it comes to measuring the very small as it is for the very large. With it we can describe the sizes of atoms or the wavelength of light or even the most minute creatures known to us.

For instance, the size of the smallest things – atoms – which consist of a nucleus surrounded by one or more orbiting electrons, is so minute that their diameters are no more than about two ten millionths of a millimetre. We can write this as 0.0000002 mm or, better still, by the 'index method' as 2×10^{-7}, the 10^{-7} meaning the seventh place of decimals after the decimal point. This index method of writing numbers saves a lot of trouble, not only because it is quicker to write, but also because it shows the number at a glance without any need to start counting zeros. This principle goes for large numbers as well. Thus, one million is 10^6, which is easier to recognize than 1,000,000. But the system really comes into its own when we consider very large numbers like 10^{13} or 10^{24}, which we shall need when we come to talk about the distances of the stars.

The range of sizes of things on the Earth is not only vast; it is almost unbelievable. The nucleus of an atom has a diameter of no more than 10^{-12} mm while an atom itself, as we have seen, is only 2×10^{-7} mm across. Atoms, as we shall see later on, are

usually grouped together into molecules, yet these too are very small. They can only be seen with an electron-microscope which uses electrons instead of light-waves because light-waves are too large and pass round the molecules. Yet light-waves themselves are very small; the shortest we can see are only 4×10^{-6} mm long.

Everyday things we see around us are very much larger. The thickness of a letter in this book is about one third of a millimetre ($3 \times$

10^{-1} mm). A page of this book is over 20 cm wide, and it is measurements like the last with which we are most familiar. Our bodies are almost a couple of metres tall, and we travel distances measured in kilometres. If we go abroad to other countries we may go for thousands of kilometres, and if we should be fortunate enough to voyage right round the world, our journey would take us some 40,000 km (4×10^4 km).

The range millimetres to kilometres describes things on Earth

above left
The Great Pyramid of Khufu, which stands almost 146 metres high, and covers an area of 5.6 hectares.

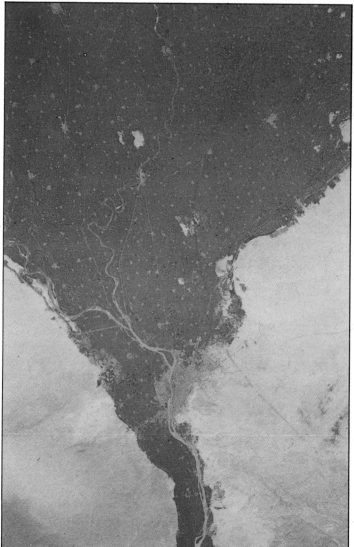

left
In this photograph from an orbiting spacecraft, the Great Pyramid is too small to see as an individual object.

very well, but then it should. The whole metric system was devised to do just this; to give precision to everyday measurements. The basic unit, the metre, is based on the size of the Earth; one metre was defined in the 1790s as one ten millionth (1×10^{-7}) of the distance between the north pole and the equator. (We do not use that definition now; instead we use a more precise one based on the wavelength of light.) The metre and its multiples has proved to be a very useful system of measurement, but as will become evident, when we start going into deep space, it becomes totally inadequate as far as distances are concerned. It is too Earth-bound. Yet it is still useful in measuring how dense gas clouds are in space or the energy which stars emit.

Nevertheless, even though it will not do for deep space distances, the metric scale does allow us to get a sense of proportion at the beginning of our journey into space. Let us start with the tiniest thing of all, the size of an atomic nucleus. Its diameter is 10^{-12} mm. If we compare that with the Earth, we find that the Earth is 10^{22} times larger; a range of ten thousand million million million to one. What a vast difference this is, almost impossible to imagine. Yet you can perhaps get some idea of it when you realize that one letter of the text you are now reading is ten thousand million (10^{10}) times bigger than an atom and another hundred thousand times larger than a nucleus. But the Earth is ten thousand million (10^{10}) times bigger than the letter. So, roughly speaking, a letter in this book is half way in size between an atom and the Earth.

Or we can look at it all another way. Start with a grain of sand. This is a million times larger than an atom. Now take a good handful of sand; this will contain something like a million grains. (If you have ever wondered what a million is like, now you have an example. But look carefully at the handful; the grains are *very* small and there really is a vast number of them.)

Next compare these things with ourselves. A grown person is something like 30 times larger than a handful of sand and, of course, immense compared with a single sand grain. But large though we are compared with grains or even handfuls of sand, we are dwarfed when we stand next to a giant structure like the Great Pyramid of the Egyptian king Khufu. This vast observatory-tomb, the world's largest single structure, was built some four and a half thousand years ago and is more than 80 times taller than an average man. It would also need 1500 people standing shoulder to shoulder to surround it.

Yet even the vast pyramid of Khufu becomes much less significant if we fly far above it; it almost merges into the general picture of the area. Go up between 160 and 330 km above the Earth's surface as the astronauts Cooper and Conrad did in 1965 in Gemini V, and the pyramid has shrunk away until it is too small to see. Higher still, at 900 km, the orbiting Landsat satellite merely produces a living map; the giant pyramid is no more. In a photograph from space of the whole Earth (on which the pyramid occupies a mere thirty thousand millionths (3×10^{-10}) of the disc) it would not show up even under a microscope. To us the pyramid is gigantic, to the Earth it is submicroscopic; yet the Earth is a small body astronomically speaking. It is all a matter of scale.

above
The three Great Pyramids of Egypt, near the ancient city of Memphis and close to the Nile, as seen from the air.

The Earth from space. Here, the Great Pyramid would be too small to detect with a powerful microscope.

NEAR SPACE

The Moon – our nearest neighbour in space – is a mere 384,400 km away. This is a distance equal to travelling round the Earth almost ten times, but it is only a tiny step into the depths of space.

The distance to the Moon was calculated long before astronauts visited it. Observations against the background of the stars, made at the same instant from two locations, gives us the Moon's 'parallax' from which its actual distance is computed. This is a time-honoured system but it has now been supplanted because the astronauts placed mirrors on the lunar surface. These reflect laser beams from Earth and allow the Moon's position to be calculated to the nearest few centimetres. Yet whatever method we use, the Moon, our own natural satellite, is still very close to us.

A small world, a little more than one third the size of the Earth, the Moon is nevertheless a large satellite for the Earth to have. With the exception of Pluto, none of the other planets orbiting the Sun have such relatively large companion bodies; at the most they are one tenth the size of their primary body (the body round which they orbit), and usually less. Yet some of these satellites are larger than our Moon, the biggest being Ganymede – which orbits round Jupiter and is one and a half times bigger. So what we find is that our Earth itself is not all that large a body. On the other hand compared with its nearest neighbours in space it is the same in size or a little bigger. About equal in size to Venus (the Earth is actually some 600 km larger in diameter), it is 2½ times larger than Mercury and just over 1⅜ times as big as Mars. Thus within a radius of 92 million kilometres the bodies we encounter are all of the same general size; none exceeds 12,756 km in diameter, and none is smaller than 3,500 km, including our own Moon. All have solid surfaces on which spacecraft can land.

It is when we come to measuring the distances of these nearby bodies that we have to begin thinking in terms of larger distances than we are accustomed to on Earth. The Moon's distance is equivalent to travelling ten times round the Earth, but the distance of Venus when it comes closest to the Earth is almost 108 times further off. To travel to the Moon in 1969 in an Apollo spacecraft took astronauts three days; to travel to Venus at the same speed would take 324 days or almost eleven months, yet Venus is comparatively near. Mars is the next nearest planet, and a journey there in the Apollo spacecraft would take 1 year 8 months. To Mercury it would take almost two years. So we see that the distances even to the nearer planets are immense by earthly standards.

Yet once we leave our immediate surroundings in the Solar System and

move further out to the more distant planets orbiting the Sun, distances increase enormously. The nearer planets really do seem comparatively close at hand. For if we bypass the little lumps of orbiting rock we call the asteroids and go on

Diameter of Sun (1,392,530 km)

Earth 12,756 km diameter

Orbit of Moon (768,800 km)

The Sun is so large that it would swallow up the Earth and surrounding space to a point out beyond the Moon's orbit.

to Jupiter, travelling all the way at the same speed as the astronauts did in Apollo, our journey would take no less than 13½ years. (Of course unmanned spacecraft can do the journey much faster).

Jupiter at its nearest lies at a distance of about 588 million kilometres, or more than 1,530 times the distance of the Moon, or 14,673 times round the Earth. The other distant planets – Saturn, Uranus, Neptune and Pluto – are a very great deal further off still. Apollo speeds would take us 30½ years to get to Saturn, over 61 to reach Uranus, 96 years to Neptune and something like 126 years to Pluto.

The best way to get a scale of the Solar System is to find how long light or radio waves would take to cover the distance. On this scale the Moon is only 1.28 seconds away, Mars a mere 4.3 minutes, and Jupiter 35 minutes. Saturn is 1.2 hours, and that is the time TV pictures from Voyagers 1 and 2 took to reach us back on Earth. The rest of the planets are Uranus 2½ hours, Neptune 4

hours and Pluto over 5 hours.

Except for Pluto the sizes of the outer planets are immense compared with the Earth. Jupiter is more than 11 times larger in diameter; it could contain 1,323 Earths packed inside it. Saturn, Uranus and Neptune are not so big but all are far larger than our Earth – Saturn 9½ times, Uranus 4 and Neptune 3.9. Yet all these planets, even giant Jupiter, are dwarfed by the Sun.

Lying at an average distance of 149.6 million kilometres, light from the Sun takes 8.3 minutes to reach us – so we never see the Sun as it *is* but as it *was* 8 minutes 19 seconds ago. Its distance is great, certainly – 390 times further than the Moon – but most surprising of all is its size. The Sun has a diameter of over 1¼ million kilometres, so large that it could swallow up 1,300,000 planets the size of our Earth. If we could put the Earth at its centre then the Moon in its orbit would fit comfortably inside with almost 320,000 km to spare; in fact almost twice.

So we find that, even the nearby Solar System distances are large by Earthbound standards, and we see that the Earth itself is by no means one of the largest bodies. As we go deeper into space we shall find even these distances dwarfed almost out of recognition.

The Earth, Jupiter, and part of the Sun (there is not room to show all of it) to the same scale. The Earth is a solid body, but Jupiter is mainly gas, and the Sun wholly so.

INTO DEEP SPACE

Even in our own Galaxy, the stars are surprisingly distant compared with the planets and the Sun. Enormous though the Sun seems in comparison with the Earth, it is really not a large star at all.

Once we have passed Pluto, leaving behind the planets of the Solar System, we find ourselves out in deep space. Our distance is now about six thousand million (6×10^9) kilometres; travelling at the speed of light we are over 5½ hours out from Earth. Around us space is empty, yet strange though it may seem, we may not yet have left the Solar System. From time to time comets are observed which have such elongated orbits round the Sun that they will not return again for hundreds or even thousands of years. Some astronomers think that there is a vast spherical cloud of cometary material enveloping the whole Solar System. This lies, they believe, between 1½ and 15 million million kilometres away – so far that travelling with the speed of light it would still take about 58 days to reach its inner boundary and 1½ years to get to its outer rim. Those who take this view believe that sometimes a passing star causes a gravitational upheaval in the cloud, and so triggers off the despatch of a comet from the cloud towards the Sun; then, and only then, can we on Earth observe the comet. At all events, once we have travelled the 15 million million kilometres we have left the Solar System and are out in the depths of interstellar space.

We now move in a seemingly empty space. Looking back at the Sun we find it is not the bright hot globe we are used to seeing in the sky, but has dwindled until it has become just a very bright star. As we move still further into space the Sun loses more of its brilliance, yet we still meet with no other bodies. We seem to be utterly alone.

Not until we have left the Solar System and the cloud of comets far behind; not until we have travelled another 26 million million kilometres do we come close to another star. So even if we left the Earth at the speed of light, after travelling for a whole year we should only find ourselves in the cloud of cometary material. After two years we should be in empty space beyond the last boundaries of the Solar System; after another year we should still be travelling alone. The beginning of our fourth year would find us still in isolation. Not until we have been going for another four months should we arrive at a star, the triple star α Centauri.

We have now travelled what seems a great distance. If we laid out a scale model in a living room, where the diagonal from one far corner to the other is, say, five metres, the result is surprising. If, α Centauri is in one far corner and the Sun in the other, then the outer boundary of the comet cloud would be 1.8 metres from the Sun; the inner boundary only 18 cm. Yet the distances being represented are so vast that Pluto would be less then ¾ mm from the Sun, which would only be the size of a single atom. We must come to terms with such vast distances because so far we are only at the very edge of interstellar space. However, experience shows that it

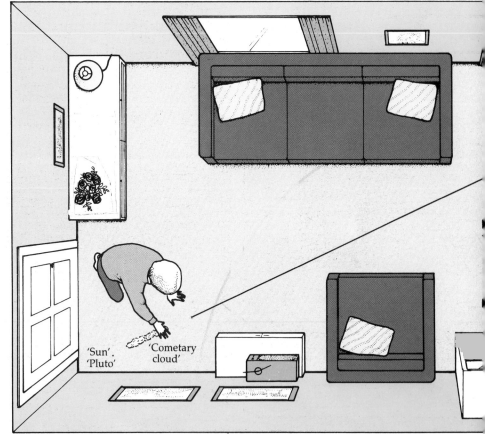

above A scale model in a living room of the distances from the Sun to Pluto (0.7 mm or a grain of sugar) to the cometary cloud (18 cm to 1.8 m) and then on to α Centauri (5m).

below The supergiant star Antares which is large enough to swallow up the Sun and the inner planets of the Solar System well beyond the orbit of Mars.

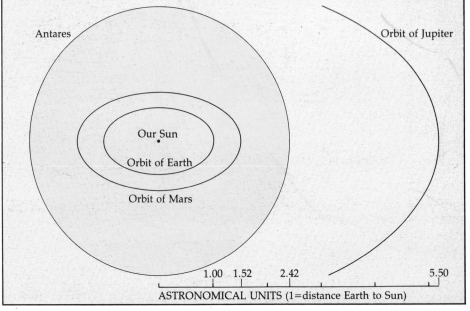

Antares — Orbit of Jupiter — Our Sun — Orbit of Earth — Orbit of Mars

1.00 1.52 2.42 5.50
ASTRONOMICAL UNITS (1=distance Earth to Sun)

does not take long to become accustomed to them.

The α Centauri star system lies 1.3 parsecs or 4.3 light-years away (one parsec equals 3.26 light years) yet it has the nearest stars to us in deep space. Other stars are even further off and, in fact, something like four or so light-years separates one star from another, at least in the volume of space occupied by the Sun and the nearby stars. The α Centauri star system can only be seen by observers living in the Earth's southern hemisphere. It consists of one bright star of a type rather like our Sun, another which is a little redder and is about 3½ times dimmer, and the third, sometimes called 'Proxima' Centauri — a red star more than 6,300 times dimmer still. The three stars orbit each other.

Interestingly enough, the brightest of the three was the first star to have its distance measured; this was done by Thomas Henderson between 1832 and 1833 when he was observing at the Cape of Good Hope in South Africa. But Henderson was a very cautious man, and he did not make his results public at once. He waited until they could be confirmed by a colleague, but by the time this had happened Friedrich Bessel had already announced his measurement of the distance of the star 61 Cygni, which lies 3.4 parsecs away.

Multiple stars like α Centauri and binary systems, where only two stars are in orbit around each other, are quite common. Of the 40 nearest stars to the Sun, two are multiples, and nine are binaries; these include 61 Cygni and the brightest star in the sky – Sirius – which is 23 times brighter than our Sun, but whose companion is 184,000 times dimmer.

Stars vary in size, and if we travelled out in the direction of Scorpius for 520 years, we should come to Antares or α Scorpii, a very bright but very red star. This is a red supergiant star, and though each square centimetre of its surface is much dimmer than an equivalent area of the surface of the Sun, its total brightness is over 8,000 times greater. This is because of its very large size (it has much more surface to shine), for the diameter of Antares is 560 times bigger than the Sun (i.e. 763 million kilometres). If Antares lay at the centre of our Solar System it would swallow up the Earth and Mars, though it would not reach out as far as the orbit of Jupiter. Antares is one of a number of colossal red supergiant stars. Betelgeuse (α Orionis) is another – you can see it in the 'left' shoulder of Orion. It is a variable star and continually changes in size from between 600 and 900 times the Sun's diameter.

So we find that stars come in all kinds of sizes with some of them occupying an immense volume. Yet all of them are grouped together in one vast island in space. We see some of the boundaries of this island when we look up at the Milky Way, and for this reason it has been given the name The Galaxy (Greek *galaxias*, milky). Our own Sun lies some way from the middle; probably at a distance of about 10,000 parsecs (33,000 light-years) from the true centre. Certainly, the Galaxy is vast; its thickness towards the centre, where it bulges, is at least 3,000 parsecs (10,000 light-years) and its diameter some 30,000 parsecs (100,000 light-years). We are now getting to very large distances indeed, yet our Galaxy is not unique. It is only one of millions upon millions of other galaxies which lie further out in yet deeper space.

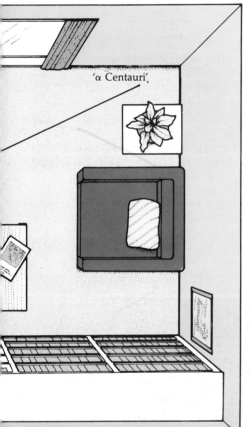

'α Centauri'

below The position of Antares in our own Galaxy. It is located in a spiral arm far from the centre.

above α and β Centauri photographed by Arthur Page. (β is 114 times farther away than α).

A UNIVERSE OF GALAXIES

Space is populated with countless other galaxies besides our own. Galaxies in their millions, stretching as far as telescopes can see, are the occupants of deepest space.

It was the astronomer William Herschel who, two hundred years ago in the late eighteenth century, began to count the number of stars in the sky. His 'gages' as he called them, showed him that there were more stars in some regions of the sky than in others. He then put forward the idea that our Sun and all the other stars are part of a large 'island' in space. But was this theory correct? Was there just empty space outside our star island? More observations made by later generations of astronomers showed that there were some puzzling features. On the one hand there were the clouds of gas or 'nebulae', which Herschel had discovered, on the other there were great spherical or 'globular' clusters

of stars and spirally shaped nebulae. Were these all part of our continent, too, or were they separate?

Harlow Shapley, a young American astronomer, discovered that the globular clusters of stars did not seem to be part of the island, but opinion was divided over the spiral nebulae. In the early years of the twentieth century, using large American telescopes and, from 1918, the world's then largest and newest telescope, the '100-inch' (2.5-metre) on Mount Wilson in California, photographs of the spirals were taken and measured under a microscope. The astronomer who measured them was Adriaan van Maanen, a Dutchman working at Mount Wilson, and he claimed that by comparing photographs taken a few years apart he could detect an actual rotation in some of the spirals. He argued that they must be inside our island because, if they were outside (and therefore very distant) this movement would mean such a high speed of rotation that the nebula would tear itself apart.

However, later studies, mainly by the American astronomer Edwin Hubble, made it clear that no rotation had been observed. Hubble had detected stars in the spirals that

showed they really were distant objects, lying well outside our own star island. In fact the universe was composed of millions upon millions of star islands.

How had van Maanen made his mistake? The answer seems to be not that he had faked his results – he was, after all, a very honest man – but that the measurements he was trying to detect were so small that they were about as large as the errors of the equipment he was using. What van Maanen thought was a shift due to rotation was a shift of the photograph itself or of his microscope eyepiece.

At all events we now know for certain that the spiral nebulae and some other nebulae as well lie far outside our own star island. We now recognize this fact by no longer calling them nebulae – a term which we keep for clouds of gas inside our own Galaxy – but instead call them galaxies. They are vast, just as our own Galaxy is vast, for they all contain millions upon millions of stars, and the distances between them really do begin to beggar our imagination.

As we have seen, setting off from Earth at the speed of light, we should have to travel for over four

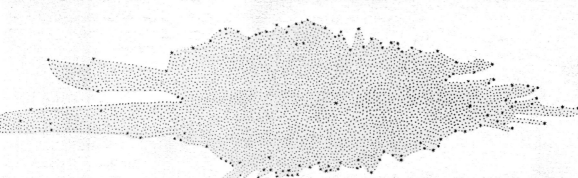

far left
The spiral galaxy NGC 5364 in the constellation Virgo, photographed with the 200-inch (5-m) Hale telescope.

left
This photograph taken with the 100-inch (2.5-m) Hale telescope. It shows part of the Andromeda Galaxy (M31) as separate stars. On the left is a companion galaxy.

right
This large cluster of galaxies in the Coma Berenices constellation was photographed by the four-metre telescope at Kitt Peak National Observatory.

left
William Herschel's drawing of our star island, derived from his star counts over the sky. He thought the Sun lay near the centre.

years to reach the next nearest star to the Sun. Then, as we move out into deep space, we travel distances of many light-years before we reach other stars, some of which dwarf our own Sun and even parts of the Solar System. Yet if we set out travelling, say, towards the constellation Dorado (The Swordfish) in the southern skies, and go close to the star δ Doradus, a bluish-white star some 27½ times brighter than our own Sun, we shall then have gone 100 parsecs. But if we continue on and on until we have gone more than sixty times this distance, only then shall we approach the outer boundary of our own Galaxy. When we have travelled some 15,000 parsecs then, and only then, shall we have reached an edge, and approached intergalactic space.

Yet although we have now left the main body of our Galaxy we still have a long way to go until we reach another galaxy. In fact we have to travel an additional 46,000 parsecs before we come to the Larger Magellanic Cloud, so named because in 1520 the explorer Ferdinand Magellan and his ship's crew were the first to notice and chart this cloudy looking object. We now know it to be a galaxy and recent studies show that it seems to be a kind of spiral with a great amount of material running across its central regions. Containing stars, dust and gas, it spreads out over 3,000 parsecs in space. A further 10,000 parsecs away in a slightly different direction – we should have to make for the constellation Tucana (The Toucan) – lies the Smaller Magellanic Cloud, which is only about half the size of the larger cloud. We have now travelled 63,000 parsecs into space, but we have hardly touched the fringe of intergalactic space. Indeed we can consider the Magellanic Clouds as satellite or companion galaxies to our own.

The nearest very large galaxy to our own is the great galaxy in Andromeda, known as M31 (because it is number 31 in the catalogue of nebulous looking objects published in 1774 by the French astronomer Charles Messier). This is a vast spiral galaxy like our own, though it seems not quite as big. Its diameter is about 50,000 parsecs, so it is over half as large again as our Galaxy. It also has two small companions. Yet although it is the next nearest large galaxy to us, the distance of M31 is no less than 690,000 parsecs (2¼ million light-years away) though now we are at distances too far for us to be precise, even to a parsec.

We are now reaching really large distances, yet we have only moved a comparatively little way into intergalactic space, for astronomers have found that our own Galaxy and the Andromeda Galaxy (M31) are both members of a local group of galaxies. This contains at least 30 galaxies, some large and many small, which all lie within a distance of about one megaparsec (a million parsecs). However, groups or clusters of galaxies are not unusual, many are now known, some of them containing several thousand separate galaxies. After our Local Group, the next nearest is the cluster of galaxies in Virgo (the Maiden), which has some 2,500 members. This lies at a distance of 20 megaparsecs.

For all its great distance, the Virgo cluster is not all that far off in space. Some galaxies are known which lie hundreds and even thousands of millions of light-years into space. How far they go astronomers cannot tell, but one galaxy at least has been discovered at a distance estimated at three thousand million parsecs. Truly galaxies extend as far as observations can take us.

MEASURING DISTANCES IN SPACE

Measuring distances in space is not easy. Traditional methods can only give us the distances of our nearest neighbours. Other systems had to be devised to calculate distances in deep space.

When we came to talk about the distance of the Moon (page 10) we found that the way astronomers used to do this was to observe the Moon simultaneously from two different places on Earth. It is this principle that surveyors have used for centuries to measure the distance of places they could not reach – across the other side of a river, for instance. From two given positions they measure the angle between the distant object and the even more distant background. Knowing – or measuring – the actual distance between the two places, and subtracting the two angles they have measured, it is possible to determine the distance by simple trigonometry. In the case of a moving object like the Moon, observations from both observatories must be made at the same time (or a special calculation done to allow for any time difference there is). But can we apply the lunar distance method to the stars?

We can apply the principle, but not precisely the same method because the stars are so far away that places on the Earth's surface are too close together to give us an angle which is large enough to be measured. The solution is to make observations from only one observatory, and then to wait for the Earth to carry the observatory to the other side of its orbit, before making the observation again. This gives a separation between observing positions – a base-line – of twice the Earth-to-Sun distance, or 299 million kilometres. Even so, this very long base-line still only gives very small angles. The angle, which gives the shift of the star measured against the background of more distant stars, is only something like 1⅝ arc seconds, and as one arc second is 1/60th of one arc minute which is itself 1/60th of a degree, this angle is miniscule. Half this angle is used in calculating

distance and is known as the star's parallax.

So what astronomers measure in order to find the distances of the nearer stars is an angle. Thus they find that the nearest star, α Centauri, has a parallax of 0.76 arc seconds; converting this to a distance tells us that it is 4.3 light-years away. But to compare distances astronomers do not need to convert to light-years; they can save themselves time by merely comparing angles. Indeed, for distances astronomers usually use the terms parsec and megaparsec. One parsec is that distance at which a star would have a parallax of one *second* of an arc. No star is as near as this, but that does not matter because all we are after is a comparison of angles. Because the distance in parsecs is equal to one divided by the parallax, a star of parallax 0.5 would lie at 1/0.5, or two parsecs. A megaparsec is one million parsecs.

How useful this scheme is immediately becomes obvious. For example, α Centauri has a parallax of 0.76 arc seconds, so its distance is 1.3 parsecs, while the star Lalande 21185 has a parallax of 0.377 arc seconds and thus a distance of 2.6 parsecs.

The direct angle measuring method for determining stellar distances, using the Earth's orbit as base-line, is known as 'trigonometrical parallax', but it is only of use for nearer stars. Beyond 100 parsecs (some 300 light-years) the angles become too small to measure with sufficient accuracy. This method will therefore only give the distances of some 8,000 stars. What is to be done, then, for more distant stars?

One way out of this difficulty is to determine what have become known as 'cluster parallaxes'. Here, astronomers make use of the fact that some clusters of stars – the Pleiades or the Hyades, for example – are moving relative to the Sun. All the stars of such a cluster are moving with the same speed and appear to us on Earth as if they are converging on a particular point in space, just as cars on a motorway appear to converge into the distance.

Now the technique of distance measurement here is to find how the cluster shifts across the background of more distant stars and compare this with the true space velocity of the stars. (The true velocity is found by measuring the movement directly away from us of the stars and knowing the position of the converging point of the cluster.) This method is, of course, limited to clusters and is only accurate up to

distances of something like 800 parsecs (2,600 light-years). Some other method is required for the majority of other stars.

The alternative to ordinary parallax measurements and to cluster parallax depends on finding how truly bright particular stars are. Observation immediately tells us how bright a star appears to be but, of course, not its true brightness. The further off it is, the dimmer it will seem to be. For instance, the bright star Sirius appears over 13 thousand million (13×10^9) times dimmer than our Sun, but this is only because it is 2.6 parsecs away; its true brightness is 22½ times greater than the Sun's. We know how brightness drops off with distance, so if we know the true brightness of a star as well as its apparent brightness, we could calculate the star's distance. But how can we tell the true brightness of a star without knowing its distance?

The answer to this was found by examining a diagram devised in 1914 by two astronomers, the Dane Ejnar Hertzsprung and the American Henry Norris Russell. This Hertzsprung-Russell or 'HR' diagram shows the relationship of true brightness compared with spectral class. Spectral class refers to the kind of spectrum a star shows when its light is spread out into a coloured band or spectrum. The class is determined by the dark lines which lie across the colours of the spectrum, their number and positions giving a clue to the star's temperature, and thus its colour. The true brightness is given on the diagram in 'absolute magnitudes'. This is a measure of the magnitude (i.e. the brightness) a star would have if it were only ten parsecs away.

What the HR diagram shows is that the hotter (and bluer) most stars are, the brighter they really are; the cooler and redder they happen to be, the dimmer they are. There are some exceptions – the red supergiants are one – but the 'main sequence' of stars follow the general rule. So we now have a new way to determine distance. Observing a star's spectrum gives us its spectral class and the HR diagram then gives its absolute magnitude. Direct observation provides us with the apparent magnitude – the brightness we see. By comparing the two – apparent magnitude and absolute magnitude – and knowing how brightness drops with distance, we can easily calculate the star's distance. This method of measuring distance is known as 'spectroscopic parallax'.

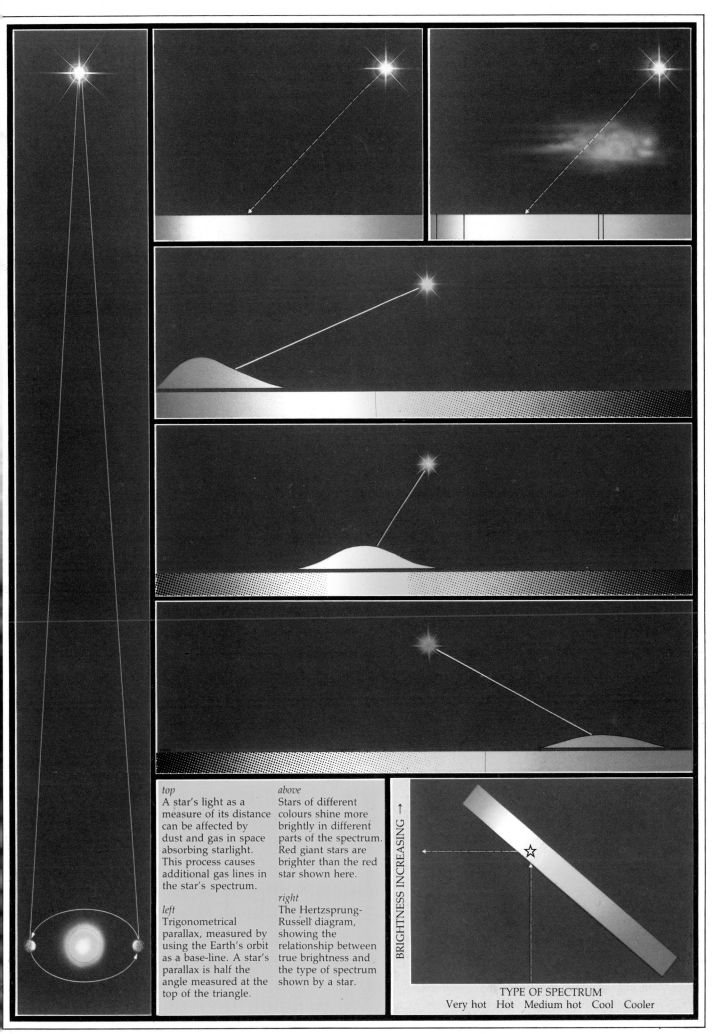

top
A star's light as a measure of its distance can be affected by dust and gas in space absorbing starlight. This process causes additional gas lines in the star's spectrum.

left
Trigonometrical parallax, measured by using the Earth's orbit as a base-line. A star's parallax is half the angle measured at the top of the triangle.

above
Stars of different colours shine more brightly in different parts of the spectrum. Red giant stars are brighter than the red star shown here.

right
The Hertzsprung-Russell diagram, showing the relationship between true brightness and the type of spectrum shown by a star.

BRIGHTNESS INCREASING →

TYPE OF SPECTRUM
Very hot   Hot   Medium hot   Cool   Cooler

CELESTIAL LIGHTHOUSES

By examining the changing light from variable stars, astronomers have found that some can be used as distance indicators – natural lighthouses in space.

Lighthouses on Earth are built near the shore as a guide to mariners, who recognize them both by their brightness and by the pattern of flashes that they emit. There are natural lighthouses in deep space which also display changing patterns of light, and it is from such patterns that astronomers can recognize them and calculate their distances.

More than seventy years ago, the Harvard University Observatory had an out-station, a second observatory, at Arequipa in Peru, from which the stars of the southern hemisphere skies could be observed. Here, a large number of photographs had been taken of the two Magellanic Clouds (page 102). These look for all the world as if they are pieces broken off from the Milky Way – though this is not what they really are – and back at Harvard the photographs were examined in great detail by an astronomer called Henrietta Leavitt. She found that she could detect variable stars (stars which vary in brightness) in the Clouds and that many of these were variables of a particular kind. These had very short periods of variation, ranging from no more than a few days to a few weeks at the most. By a painstaking comparison of the photographs, she was able, in 1908, to announce that the Clouds contained between them no less than 1777 variables.

What was so important about Miss Leavitt's work was her realization that, to put it in her own words, '. . . the brighter variables have the longer periods'. Four years of further detailed study of all the variables, not only the brighter ones, led her to claim that 'A remarkable relation between the brightness of these variables and the length of their periods will be noticed'; it was this observation that led to the stars being used as celestial lighthouses. For what Henrietta Leavitt had discovered was that the real brightness of the very short period variables depended on the period itself. The longer the period, the brighter the star really was. For

example, one with a period of one day was 179 times brighter than our Sun, whilst one with a period of 10 days was 449 times brighter, and a variable with a period of 30 days outshone our Sun 1355 times.

Miss Leavitt did not know the true brightness (absolute magnitude) of these stars at first; all she had to go on was the apparent brightness (apparent magnitude). But as the stars were all at approximately the same distance she was able to conclude that there was a real relationship between period of variation and true brightness in stars of this type. The type soon became known as Cepheids because their

light-curves – the charts of the way brightness varied during the whole period of change – were similar to those of the star δ Cephei.

Later on, in more recent times, it has been discovered that there are two kinds of Cepheids, each having slightly different values for period of variation and brightness. It has also been found that there is a different brightness-period relationship for variables with extremely short periods – those which are measured in hours rather than days – but the important thing is that there is still a relationship nonetheless. These are known as RR Lyrae variables.

Henrietta Leavitt's discovery was

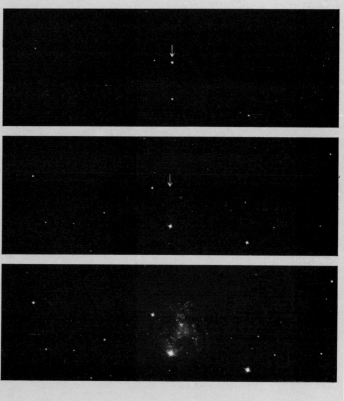

right
A supernova explosion in a distant galaxy (IC 4182 in Virgo). The top photograph was taken in 1937, the supernova was at its brightest but the exposure was too short to show the galaxy. The middle photo taken in 1938 shows that the supernova has become faint; vestiges of the galaxy can just be seen. The bottom photo taken in 1942 shows no remains of the supernova even though a long exposure shows up the galaxy. These photographs were taken by the 100-inch (2.5m) telescope at Mount Palomar.

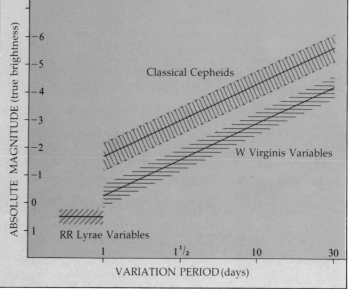

left
A graph comparing absolute magnitude with period of variation for Cepheids. The 'Classical Cepheids' are massive, young stars; the W Virginis type are far less massive and much older stars. The RR Lyrae variables are found in globular clusters (page 58). All have the same magnitude, and are excellent distance indicators.

a crucial one, for if the distance of some Cepheid variables could be measured, the rest could be used as lighthouses. Their periods would be measures of their true brightness; knowing this and knowing how bright they appear, their distances could be calculated. The method is like spectroscopic parallax (page 17) but the period of variation is used instead of the star's spectrum. Of course, one has first to find the distance of some Cepheids so that a scale between true brightness and period can be worked out, but fortunately some Cepheids are comparatively close to us in space; close enough for their distances to be directly determined by measuring their parallax angles. Admittedly some errors were made to begin with – before the two classes of Cepheids were known, for instance – but the method is a useful one for astronomers. For whereas straightforward parallax methods only take us out to 100 parsecs (330 light-years) and spectroscopic methods to a little more than 10,000 parsecs (33,000 light-years), Cepheid variables can deal with distances out to around four million parsecs — well into intergalactic space.

What happens when we want to go further still? What other stars, if any, can help us? The answer lies in exploding stars, the so-called novae and supernovae. Novae are stars which suddenly flare up in brightness once or more during their lifetime. The increase in brightness may be anything between 100 and a million times. Probably most of these stars are binaries – pairs of stars orbiting round one another – in which one of the pair is a very dense collapsed star known as a 'white dwarf' (page 79), and the other a large red star on its way to becoming a red giant. The flare-up occurs when material from the large red member of the pair falls on to the white dwarf and suddenly burns up. However, some novae may just be caused by dust and gas falling on to a single star, pulled towards it by gravity. At all events, in both cases hot bright gas will eventually be thrown into space, and by measuring the rate at which this gas moves towards us, we know how fast the whole shell of gas is moving. Knowing the speed of expansion of the shell of gas and by measuring the change in apparent size of the gas cloud over a period of time (a period of many years) it is possible to calculate the distance of the star. Such measurements can take the astronomer out to at least ten million parsecs, or 2½ times further than Cepheids can do.

Supernova explosions, when an entire star rather than just some of its material is thrown outwards into space, cause a vast increase of brightness. Indeed, typical supernovae show increases in brightness of a hundred million (10^8) times. These outbursts can be detected in galaxies lying up to about 400 million (4×10^8) parsecs or some 1300 million light-years away, and so carry the astronomer even further out into intergalactic space. Unfortunately, though, supernova explosions do not happen all that frequently. Most astronomers think that, on the average, they occur once every 200 years in a galaxy like our own. This means that we should not expect to see supernovae flaring up all over space, nor in most of the galaxies we observe.

Nevertheless there are such a great number of galaxies in space that we should expect to observe supernova explosions in at least a few, and this has in fact happened. And when they are observed, they do enable astronomers to get a measure of distance to the particular galaxies in which they occur, and so make it possible to check up on the other methods used for the distance determination of far-off galaxies.

Fig. 1

Fig. 2

above Two Cepheid variables (*Figs 1 and 2*) in the Andromeda Galaxy (M31). The stars lie between the pairs of broken lines, and the variation is obvious. (The brighter stars are from our own Galaxy.)

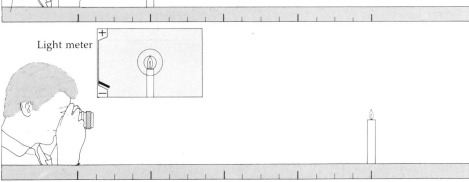

Light meter

Light meter

A photographic lightmeter built into a camera will demonstrate that light intensity varies in proportion to the square of the distance. For example, a candle 16 units away appears only 1÷4² or one-sixteenth as bright as it does at 4 units.

REDSHIFT DISTANCES

By observing how far lines in the spectrum are shifted towards the red, astronomers can obtain an idea of the distance of bodies far out in deepest space.

If you hear a police car or an ambulance coming close to you and then moving away, you will notice a change in the sound of its siren. As the vehicle approaches, the siren wails at a particular pitch and then, as it moves away, it wails at a different pitch. In brief, the sounds appear at a higher pitch as the vehicle approaches and a lower pitch as it moves away. Yet really the siren is wailing at the same pitch all the time. To the driver of the vehicle the sound of the siren never changes; he does not notice any change in pitch. Why does this happen?

The reason the siren's pitch seems to change to someone who is not riding on the vehicle is because the sound waves it sends us change in frequency. Every sound we hear is due to vibrations travelling through the air, and its pitch depends on how frequently these vibrations reach our ears. If, then, the sounds come from a moving vehicle, the frequency with which they reach our ears will alter according to the direction in which the vehicle is travelling. When it is coming towards us, each vibration starts off a little closer than the one before it. As each has a shorter distance to travel, we receive it sooner than we should have done if the vehicle had been standing still. So the vibrations will arrive more frequently from an approaching vehicle, and as higher frequency means higher pitch, we hear a higher pitched note from the siren than does the driver. The opposite happens when the vehicle moves away from us. Then the vibrations have further to go to, and the interval between them is lengthened. In other words, the frequency drops, and we hear a lower pitched sound.

Of course you cannot hear sounds from the stars because there is no air to carry them across space, but the basic principle – the way the frequency of a wave changes if the source emitting it is moving towards us or away from us – is the same. Frequency increases if the source is

coming towards us and drops if the source is receding into the distance. And this principle is true not only of sound waves, but of waves of every kind. Because light travels as waves, we should expect this to happen to starlight, and so it does.

The first man to point out that we should expect both sound frequencies and light frequencies to change when bodies are moving towards us or away from us was the

Austrian scientist Johann Christian Doppler. He announced his ideas in 1842, and claimed that as far as light was concerned, motion away from us would make the light being emitted redder in colour. This is because red light has a longer wavelength – and thus a lower frequency – than light of other colours.

Conversely, motion towards us would raise the frequency and shorten the wavelength, thus making

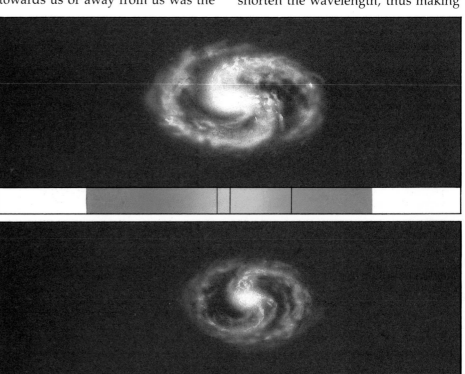

above The diagrams illustrate the principle that the more distant a galaxy is, the greater the redshift in its spectrum. The lower galaxy has a similar spectrum to the upper galaxy, but the lines are shifted further towards the red. (The dotted lines are the position of the lines in the spectrum of the galaxy in the top diagram.)

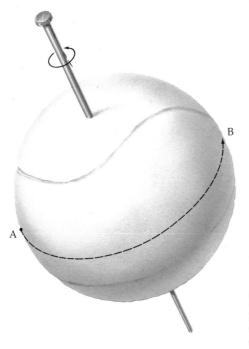

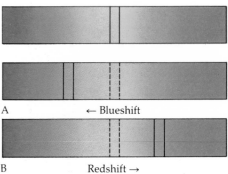

A   ← Blueshift

B   Redshift →

left If you rotate a tennis ball with a knitting needle through its axis, then one side (A) moves towards you as the other side (B) moves away. If the ball had a shining surface, A would display a blueshift and B a redshift compared with light from the centre of the ball.

the light seem bluer (because blue light is a short wavelength, high frequency vibration). However, Doppler made a slight mistake over light from the stars, because he believed they were all white in colour; in other words they radiated equally in every colour of the spectrum. This led him to claim that the colours of the stars were an effect due to their motions towards us or away from us.

It was the French scientist Armand Hippolyte Fizeau who, six years later in 1848, realized that because stars also shine at frequencies beyond the range of the visible coloured spectrum – in ultraviolet and infrared rays, for example – that what we observe would not be a change in colour but a shift of the lines in the spectrum. A motion towards us would cause a shift towards the blue end: motion

away from us would lead to a redshift of the lines. As Fizeau does not seem to have known about Doppler's work, his discovery of the correct result was quite independent. Perhaps, then, we should call it the Fizeau shift and not by its customary name, the Doppler shift.

The redshift and blueshift effect can be seen in action on the Sun. The Sun is rotating, as a telescope clearly shows, and because of this, one side of the Sun is moving towards us and the other side moving away. If the Sun's sides are observed with a spectroscope, the one moving towards us displays a shift of lines to the blue end of the spectrum, whilst the other side, which is moving away, shows a redshift. So Fizeau was certainly correct.

Redshifts indicate motion away from us, but how can they be used for determining distances in space? The answer to this question lies in two basic facts. The first is that the amount of the shift – how far into the red the lines are moved – is a measure of the speed at which the body is moving away from us. The greater the speed, the larger the shift. The second fact is that, strange though it may seem (and this is discussed more fully on pages 118 to 125) all distant galaxies are moving away from us. They all display redshifts. And not only this, but in the case of those near enough for us to measure their distances by, say, the appearance of a supernova or the presence of Cepheid variables, it is clear that the further off a galaxy is, the faster it is receding, and so the greater its redshift. So by measuring the amount of redshift, astronomers can obtain a measure of distance.

This redshift measure of distance can be applied to any far-off celestial object which sends enough radiation for us to spread it out into a spectrum, and it is a powerful method for probing into very deep space. But there is still some doubt about precisely how the redshift increases with distance (page 122) and so the method, while fine for comparing distances, cannot be used to give measurements absolutely correct to within a few light-years. All the same, we can get a good idea of the distances of galaxies by this method, and it is found that they extend out at least to some 3,000 million (3×10^9) parsecs (almost ten thousand million light-years), while it may well be that recent redshift measurements of quasars (page 94) have taken astronomers out to still greater distances than this.

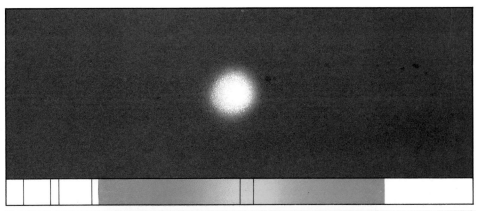

above Similar redshifts to those of a galaxy are seen in a quasar, though they are much greater. Two quasars are compared here, the upper one is nearer than the lower one. The dotted lines show the vast shifts observed, which are typical of all quasars.

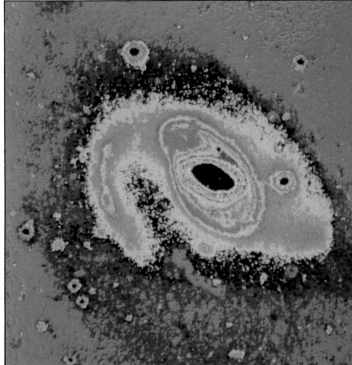

right A 'false colour' photograph taken with an electronographic camera (page 30) of the spiral galaxy NGC 4319 showing redshifts. The different colours indicate different speeds of recession.

CHAPTER 2
PROBING INTO SPACE

The invention of the telescope made a vast difference to Man's knowledge of space. Today elaborate telescopes are used together with satellites and space probes to fathom the deepest regions of the universe.

In the very earliest times, Man's only way of probing space was to use his eyes; as a result his universe was limited to the stars he could see on a clear dark night. He would have been able to see out into space as far as the great spiral galaxy in Andromeda which is six hundred thousand parsecs or two million light-years away (though he did not know it at the time – determination of its distance is a twentieth-century discovery). To early astronomers, the galaxy was no more than a hazy star.

A little more than 370 years ago, the telescope was first used in astronomy and it became possible to examine the heavens in more detail. Astronomers began to map the surface of the Moon, examine the planets, and chart stars they had never seen before because they had been too dim to be detected with the eye alone. The discoveries they made are now history, but all the same they underline the great advantages of the instrument.

First of all a telescope allows the observer to see more detail in distant objects than is possible with the eye alone. This is because a telescope magnifies a distant scene, making everything appear larger, so that detail which was too small to pick out or even to detect at all now becomes visible. The amount of detail that can be seen depends on the magnification, but the magnification that can be used basically depends on the telescope's aperture. The larger the front lens or main mirror of a telescope – the part of the instrument which gathers in the light from outer space – the greater the magnifying power that can be used. So the power of a telescope to detect or 'resolve' detail depends on its aperture; double that and you double the power to pick out detail.

Secondly, a telescope allows you to see dimmer things than you can without it. This is because even a small telescope collects more light than the human eye can do. And since the amount of light gathered depends on the area of the front lens or main mirror, double the telescope aperture and you raise the light-gathering power by 2×2 i.e. four times; treble it and the light-gathering power goes up 3×3 or nine times. So the larger the aperture, the greater a telescope's ability to show up dim objects and therefore the further into space it can penetrate. Today the large telescopes used by astronomers are all 'reflectors' because mirrors can be made larger than lenses; most are from two to five metres in diameter, though still larger instruments are being planned.

Of course to be really useful, a telescope must be manageable; it must be possible to point it anywhere in the sky and to follow the stars automatically as they move across the sky due to the Earth's rotation on its axis. To carry the large telescopes now in use, mountings have to be heavy and call for high-precision engineering. In modern observatories the control of the whole instrument is electronic.

However, an optical telescope is limited in the information about deep space that it can provide. Astronomers now know that stars and other celestial objects radiate at wavelengths longer than we can see – in the infrared and radio wave regions – and also in wavelengths shorter than we can see – in the ultraviolet, X-ray and gamma-ray regions. To observe in these wavelengths means using special equipment. Infrared observations can be made with an optical reflecting telescope using special detectors, but for full effectiveness a specially designed infrared telescope is needed, since the time on optical telescopes is fully taken up with optical work. What is more, infrared telescopes work best on extremely high ground, preferably above water vapour, which absorbs the infrared. Modern optical telescopes are always now placed on mountainous sites so that they are in clear, relatively dust-free and cloudless air, away from city lights, but often they are still not high enough for infrared.

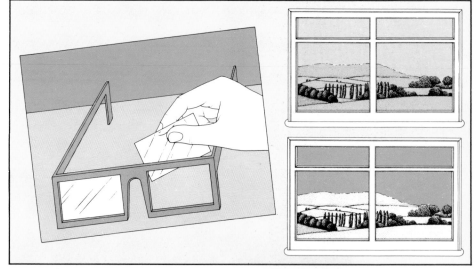

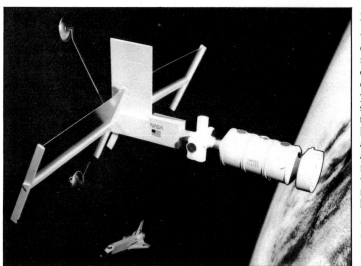

above
The way the world looks depends on what radiation reaches us – the countryside looks different through yellow-tinted spectacles, because they cut out all blue light. The Earth's atmosphere (*right*) also acts like a filter cutting out very short wavelength radiation – not blue light.

left
A proposed permanently manned space station.

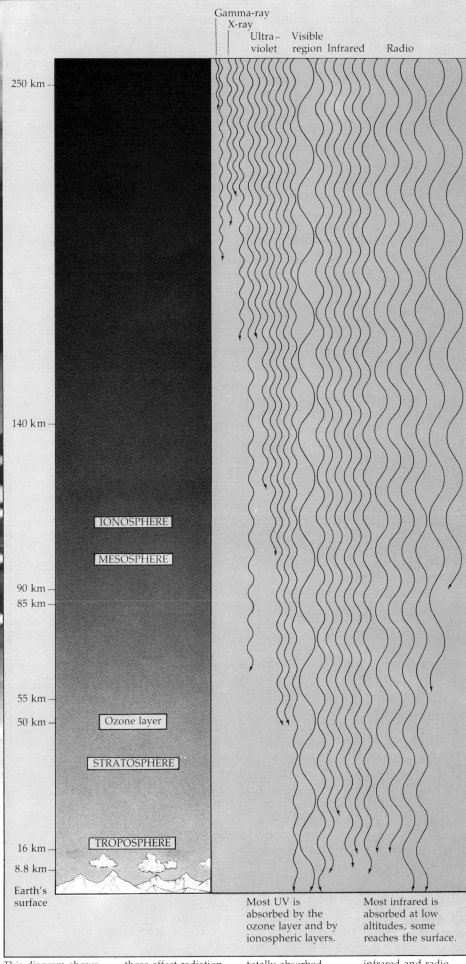

Gamma-ray
X-ray
Ultra– Visible
violet   region Infrared   Radio

250 km —

140 km —

IONOSPHERE

MESOSPHERE

90 km —
85 km —

55 km —
50 km —   Ozone layer

STRATOSPHERE

TROPOSPHERE

16 km —
8.8 km —
Earth's
surface

Most UV is
absorbed by the
ozone layer and by
ionospheric layers.

Most infrared is
absorbed at low
altitudes, some
reaches the surface.

This diagram shows
the various layers of
the Earth's atmosphere
(*above*, *left*) and how

these affect radiation
at various wavelengths
(*right*). The shortest
wavelengths are

totally absorbed,
a little ultraviolet gets
through and so does
light. There are also

infrared and radio
'windows' that allow
some wavelengths to
reach the ground.

Radio telescopes can be built on low ground, which is just as well as they have to be very large in aperture because the wavelength of radio waves is so long compared with those of light. What is more, they are often used in pairs either at the same observatory or in conjunction with radio telescopes at other observatories. In this way they can detect very fine detail in radio sources deep in space. Neither infrared nor radio telescopes can make use of all the information coming to them from space, because the atmosphere absorbs some infrared and radio radiation. All the same, like optical telescopes, both can do a vast amount of work from their Earth-based sites and, at the present time, space probes have to be reserved for observations which cannot be made from the ground. Yet what can be achieved, even sending a high-flying balloon carrying an optical telescope up 30 km or so above the ground to photograph detail on the Sun, makes it clear that space telescopes could be very useful indeed.

Once we go to the very short wavelength end of the spectrum, the Earth's atmosphere represents a serious problem. A small amount of ultraviolet can penetrate – that is the wavelength which make us sunburned – but most cannot, and no X-rays nor gamma-rays can get through. The only way to observe them is to go above the atmosphere, at least 160 km above the Earth's surface. Some useful observations in ultraviolet and pictures in ordinary light free from the worst effects of moving air can be made, launching a telescope fixed to a high-flying balloon – this will rise some 30 kilometres above the ground – but for the extreme ultraviolet, X-rays and gamma-rays only rockets or artificial satellites will do. Rockets carrying small payloads up to 160 kg and more were used thirty years ago but now the technique of putting satellites into orbit round the Earth has proved to be far more satisfactory.

To study the atomic particles that are coming from space, the so-called 'cosmic rays' (page 32) – though they are not rays at all – high-flying balloons carrying special detectors can do a lot, though space probes can do even more. So, clearly, observing from beyond the Earth's atmosphere is an important way of probing deep space. But it is not the only way. Earth-based optical, infrared and radio observations are also vital to get a complete picture.

OPTICAL TELESCOPES

Optical telescopes are still the chief tool used by astronomers for probing deep into space. But modern telescopes, some of which are linked to computers, are much more powerful than those used in the past.

Modern telescopes are masterpieces of optical science and practical engineering, though they are based on the same principles devised by telescope makers three and a half centuries ago. This is because a telescope is essentially a device for collecting light, and then bringing that light to a 'focus' where it forms an 'image' of a distant scene. This image is then examined by a lens – the 'eyepiece' – or used to take a photograph or feed other equipment for studying the incoming light.

The earliest telescopes were 'refractors'. These telescopes have a large two-component lens at the front to collect the light. But there are practical limits to the size of a large double lens, and the biggest refractor ever used in astronomy was built in 1898. It is at Yerkes Observatory in the United States and has an aperture of just over one metre (40 inches). Like all refractors it has a long focal length – its tube being almost 19 metres (62 feet) long – an additional disadvantage.

Astronomers now use reflectors. A reflector has a large mirror at the rear end of its tube to collect and focus the incoming light. The top surface of the mirror is coated with a shiny reflecting surface – usually aluminium – so the light does not have to travel through the mirror at all. This means that the mirror need not even be made of glass, and nowadays it is usually made of a special ceramic material which hardly changes its shape at all, even over a wide range of temperatures such as are met with on mountain-top observatories. Mirrors can be made to very large sizes and although six metres is the present largest diameter, plans are being drawn up for a ten metre reflector in the United States.

What happens to the light after it has been reflected by the main mirror

depends on the kind of observations to be made. Some observations require a long focal length, some a shorter focal length and some require heavy and bulky equipment attached to the telescope. Deep space photographs are often taken at the short focus point – the 'prime focus' – at the top of the tube, the place where the main mirror brings light to focus by itself. Long-focus observations are taken at the bottom of the tube, behind the main mirror. In this case the light from the main mirror is reflected by a convex (bulging) small secondary mirror down the tube and through a hole in the centre of the main mirror. This hole does, it is true, remove a little of the reflecting surface of the main

mirror, but the prime focus or the secondary mirror blots this area out anyway. This design was originally suggested by Cassegrain, a seventeenth century French scientist, and observing from below the mirror in this way is still known as observing at the Cassegrain focus. In either case the total length of the telescope tube is only about half that of a similar aperture refractor.

When an astronomer wants to place a very heavy spectroscope (for spreading out starlight into a spectrum) or some other bulky equipment on the telescope, additional small mirrors are used to bring the light out to a particular place on the telescope mounting. By rotating the additional mirrors as the

above One of the most modern of all astronomical photograph measuring machines, at Cambridge University, England, designed by Edward Kibblewhite. The photograph analysis section is shown here. In the centre is a micro-computer.

The large, modern four-metre reflector at the Cerro Tololo Inter–American Observatory at Chile. The spiky vanes fold down to form a cover over the main mirror.

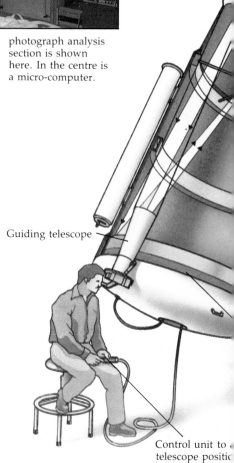

A cutaway section of a large Schmidt telescope for taking wide-angle pictures of the sky.

Guiding telescope

Control unit to telescope positio

telescope moves, the light can be made to come out always at one fixed place, wherever the telescope is pointing. This is called the coudé or 'elbow' focus because of the way the light path is turned by the secondary mirror. The coudé focus is used with an equatorial mounting, where the telescope only has to pivot around one direction or axis to follow stars across the sky. But most large modern telescopes now being built are put on an 'altazimuth' mounting because it is so very much less expensive to construct. Here the telescope moves up and down in altitude and round sideways in azimuth, and needs two continuous movements to follow the stars. In the past such a mounting was

inconvenient, but now computer control can readily cope with both movements. Big heavy equipment can also be fixed to such a mounting and remain in one position wherever the telescope is pointing. This is done by putting it at one end of the altitude axis and carrying it round with the telescope in azimuth. This is known as the Nasmyth focus, named after the engineer James Nasmyth.

Large optical telescopes can only view a small area of the sky at a time. And the longer the focus being used, the smaller that area is. But magnifying power and focal length are not the only reasons why their useful field of view is small. There is an additional reason, which is that to give first-class pictures the main

mirror must be curved to the shape of a parabola, making it deeper in the centre and shallower near the edge. This is the best way to bring rays from every part of the mirror to focus at the same point. Yet while a parabola-shaped mirror works excellently for objects straight ahead in the direction the telescope is pointing, it does not work well over a wide field. To get a wide field needs a spherically shaped mirror because this is equally curved all over. Yet if we use a spherically shaped mirror we get spherical aberration, so the light will not all be brought to the same focus; that is the very reason a parabolically shaped mirror was used in the first place. Is there any way out of this quandary?

The problem was solved in the 1930s by an Estonian optician, Bernhard Schmidt. What he did was to use a main spherical mirror with a thin single lens in front of it. This thin lens, which is a little smaller in diameter than the mirror, bends the light entering the telescope so that it falls on the mirror and is reflected as if the mirror itself was a parabola. You can say that the thin lens parabolizes the light falling on the spherical mirror. Such a Schmidt telescope can give good pictures of areas of the sky 25 times greater in area than obtainable with an ordinary telescope. Schmidt telescopes, which have a very short focal length, give a curved picture surface and cannot be used visually. This does not matter to professional astronomers who always take photographs and never observe by eye.

Large Schmidt telescopes have been set up among other places at the Hale Observatory at Palomar where there is one of 1.2 metre (48 inches) aperture and at the Anglo-Australian Observatory in Siding Springs where there is one of the same size. The amount of detailed information they produce on each photograph is astounding and astronomers are now fortunate that they no longer have to measure star positions, brightness and other factors slowly by hand using a special 'measuring microscope'. Now the details are obtained automatically on electronically controlled machines which can print out the results, feed them into a computer, and in one case, even draw up charts of specially selected objects. Moreover, these machines operate hundreds of times faster than is possible by hand, and only in this way is it possible to cope with the vast amount of information now being gathered.

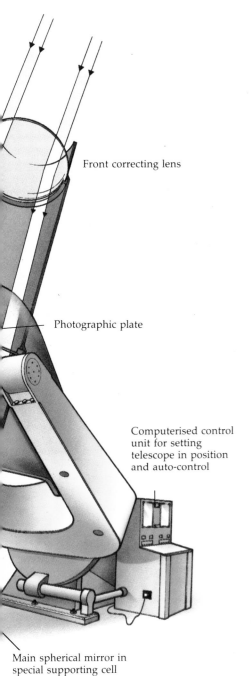

Front correcting lens

Photographic plate

Computerised control unit for setting telescope in position and auto-control

Main spherical mirror in special supporting cell

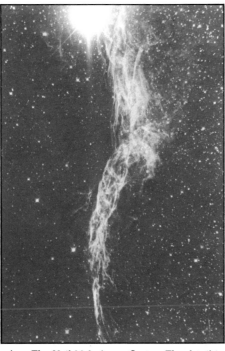

above The Veil Nebula in Cygnus viewed by a large modern reflector. The detail is excellent, but the field of view restricted.

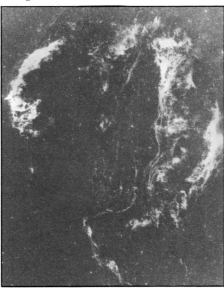

The Veil Nebula as seen through a Schmidt telescope. The nebula is now seen as part of a larger loop of gas.

A NEW GENERATION OF TELESCOPES

Astronomers now need telescopes which are many times larger than anything they have at the moment. Increasing the size of the type of telescopes we have now would be far too costly, so other answers are being sought.

The largest optical telescopes are the five-metre (200-inch) at Palomar and the Russian six-metre (236-inch) in the Caucasus Mountains, but astronomers are now wanting much larger instruments to help them probe far deeper into space. Yet to cast a very large mirror – not less than ten metres diameter – is difficult and may prove impossible; it will certainly be very expensive, at least ten times as much as a five-metre telescope. And a ten-metre aperture is not really large enough. Some astronomers are thinking of telescopes with apertures of 25 metres, and there is no way that engineers and optical manufacturers could build something similar to the Palomar 200-inch but five times larger. Even if they could, the cost would run into £5 million million (or ten million million dollars), which is far too much for a single instrument. What then can be done to make a very big telescope more economically?

One way is to make a series of smaller telescopes all linked together. Already American astronomers have built such a multi-mirror telescope (an MMT) at Mount Hopkins in Arizona. This consists of six 1.8-metre diameter mirrors mounted together, all of them aligned by a laser beam; in the centre of them all is a small 0.76-metre aperture guide telescope by means of which the six larger telescopes may be kept looking at a particular object in space. The whole telescope is equivalent in light-grasp or space penetrating power to an ordinary reflector with an aperture of 4.5 metres, but is some 47 percent cheaper, giving a saving of £3.8 million (seven million dollars). Such a telescope is no more difficult to make than a standard 4.5-metre reflector of ordinary design.

Another newly discovered way

to help in building really big telescopes is based on the fact that in any large telescope, the main mirror has to have special supports. These supports must be self-adjusting so that the mirror does not go out of shape when the telescope is swung in various positions to look at different parts of the sky.

Recently when the new United Kingdom 3.8-metre (150-inch) infrared telescope in Hawaii was built, it was decided that because infrared waves are longer than light waves, the mirror need not be as thick as usual; a little sagging would not matter as it would do with a telescope used at optical wavelengths. However the engineers

who designed the telescope used an electronically operated support system to detect not only when sagging occurred but also by how much, and then correct for it.

This system worked much better than expected with the result that the telescope performs twice as well as originally intended. As a thinner mirror weighs less, the mounting for this telescope did not have to be as hefty as one with a conventional (thick) mirror, so the instrument was less costly to build. Some astronomers believe that a large optical telescope could be built with a thin mirror; they think one with a seven-metre aperture is a practical possibility, both from an engineering

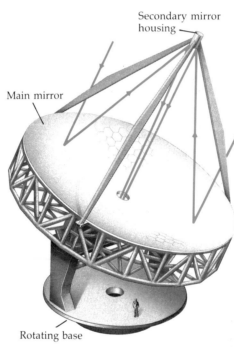

Secondary mirror housing

Main mirror

Rotating base

left An optical dish reflector using a tessellated main mirror and constructed along the lines of a large radio telescope dish. Observing equipment

– cameras, spectroscopes etc – is housed below the dish. The whole telescope rotates in azimuth, and swings up and down in altitude.

Alternative path for light from secondary mirror housing

Secondary mirror housing

Rotating base

Primary mirror

right
A proposed 'shoe' design. The main mirror is a tessellated strip of smaller hexagonal mirrors, and the entire structure rotates in

azimuth. The secondary mirror swings in altitude, and light from it can be directed to various observing positions in the telescope by other mirrors (not shown).

right
The proposed 'box' telescope. The entire instrument rotates in azimuth, light being directed to the main mirror (which is fixed) by a larger flat mirror which swings in altitude. Observing equipment lies behind the main mirror.

Main telescope mirror

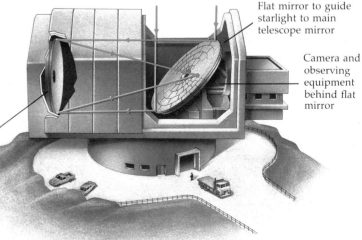

Flat mirror to guide starlight to main telescope mirror

Camera and observing equipment behind flat mirror

and a financial point of view.

There is another way of making large mirrors, especially those of unusual shape, that the new electronic self-correcting support system makes possible. This is the 'tessellated' mirror. A tessellated or mosaic mirror is one in which the surface is composed of a mosaic of small pieces of mirror (the word tesselated comes from the Latin for a mosaic surface). The pieces are hexagonal — shaped like the cells in a honeycomb — and this means that they fit closely together so that the gap between one piece and the next is minimal. One successful telescope using mirrors like this is the Narrabri Intensity Interferometer in New South Wales, Australia, designed by Hanbury Brown. This is a special telescope designed only to measure the diameters of stars, which it does by using the light received from two mirrors and mixing the light-waves from the stars electronically. For this, two large mirrors, each with a diameter of 6½ metres (255 inches), were mounted on a circular railway track. The crucial thing in this instrument was the separation between the two mirrors; it did not matter that both gave a poor optical picture of the sky. All they had to do was to collect light from each piece of the mirror-mosaic and reflect it to a light-sensitive surface at the mirror's focus. But in a telescope designed to give good optical images the mosaic pieces must be made more precisely and aligned more accurately than in the Intensity Interferometer. Making the mosaic more precise is not so difficult, and by using electronic correcting sensors – two on every edge where the hexagonal pieces of mirror meet one another – it is possible nowadays to have an optically satisfactory mosaic mirror.

The mosaic mirror makes it possible to consider all kinds of designs for a completely new generation of optical telescopes. Because such mirrors can be light in weight – any sagging is compensated for by the electronic sensors – even a very large altazimuth-mounted telescope can be considered, and a steerable dish design of 25-metre diameter is being studied in the United States. Another rather more conventional design, but with an altazimuth mounting and a 25-metre diameter mosaic mirror is being considered in Russia. Variations on the multi-mirror telescope are also being examined; one of these has six separately mounted ten-metre (400-inch) telescopes, each with a tesselated mirror. But more novel ideas still are being circulated.

First, there are variations using two large mosaic mirrors. In these, only one mirror is curved and the other is flat; the flat mirror alone is moveable in altitude, the azimuth mounting being given to the entire telescope. Both of these variations are thought to have great possibilities. However, more interest is being shown by some astronomers in what looks to be a most revolutionary design, although it is based on techniques now sufficiently well-known to make it an almost certain success. This is the 'shoe' telescope, so-called because the lower part is rather like a giant clog or wooden shoe. This part contains a vast curved, fixed, mosaic mirror, 25 metres wide and 75 metres long. Suspended from tall pillars and pivoting in altitude is a smaller mirror, equivalent to the smaller mirror of a conventional telescope. This picks up starlight reflected by the big mirror and passes it to a coudé focus in the shoe. The whole telescope rotates in azimuth, carrying both mirrors with it.

What designs will finally be made is at present uncertain; what is clear is that a new generation of very powerful optical telescopes will soon be with us, helping to probe deeper into space than was ever possible before.

below
A proposed layout for a very large multiple-mirror telescope (MMT).

Central observing point

Light from telescope in dome

The new but more conventional altazimuth mounted solid mirror 4.2-metre reflector on the island of La Palma in the Canary Islands. The huge platforms on each side of the telescope allow very large pieces of observing equipment to be mounted. This telescope, designed in the UK, is to be one of the instruments in an Inter-European Observatory.

The multiple-mirror telescope (MMT) at Mount Hopkins in Arizona.

PROBING BY HEAT AND RADIO

New methods have been devised for observing long wavelength radiation from space. Infrared and radio-telescopes now probe deep space, and are helping to revolutionize our picture of the universe.

When we go below the red end of the spectrum we come to still longer wavelengths. These are invisible though we can feel some as heat; these are the infrared rays with wavelengths ranging from just below a thousandth of a millimetre to about 1 mm. The shorter ones are those we feel as heat waves. Ever since infrared radiation was discovered by William Herschel in 1800, astronomers have tried to measure such radiation from celestial bodies, but only in recent years have very sensitive devices been available. What these do is to give out a voltage when they receive infrared radiation, but since infrared signals from space are very weak, they have to be used in a special way.

The detectors used in infrared astronomy work best at very cold temperatures; they are usually kept at the temperature of liquid nitrogen, which means they are at -196°C. Yet even this very low temperature is 'hot' to an infrared astronomer at a wavelength of one hundredth of a millimetre, a wavelength used for many observations because it is one to which the Earth's atmosphere is transparent. (The atmosphere absorbs some infrared radiation completely.) Although cold to the touch, the astronomer's telescope is hot and 'glowing' from an infrared point of view, and the surrounding cold night air is still at a temperature which is also bright in infrared.

One way to overcome these problems is for the telescope to have vibrating mirrors feeding the radiation to the detector. These mirrors give alternate pictures of the sky with the infrared source and then a patch of sky without it; the pictures follow one another about 20 times a second, giving a constantly changing electrical output from the detector. By subtracting one picture from the other, the radiation from the telescope and the surroundings – which is the same in both pictures – is cancelled out. All that remains is the infrared source being studied.

The world's largest infrared telescope is the United Kingdom's 3.8 metre reflector on Mauna Kea in Hawaii. Using the longer infrared wavelengths it gives detailed pictures of the sky down to 1 arc second (1/3600th part of a degree). This is not as good as a 3.8 metre optical telescope, which would detect details as small as 0.17 arc seconds, though it is still satisfactory. The problem of resolution (detecting detail) becomes a serious one, however, with the longer wavelengths used in radio astronomy. Here observations are being made between a few millimetres and a few metres. Yet even at a 'short' radio wavelength of 2 cm, for instance, a 3.8 metre telescope would only be able to resolve down to 3.4 degrees, and this would not be satisfactory. For longer radio wavelengths the situation would be far worse.

To obtain satisfactory resolution, radio-telescopes have to be very much larger than optical telescopes,

left
Sunlight shining on a thermometer causes the liquid in it to rise. However, if the sunlight first passes through a prism so that it spreads into its component colours, a thermometer will show no change when placed under any rays at the blue-violet end of the spectrum. Placed in the *deep* red, it will indicate a slight rise in temperature, and placed just below the red, it will rise noticeably. It does so because it is receiving invisible infrared rays which carry radiant heat from the Sun. By moving the thermometer still further along the invisible spectrum, you can find how far these rays extend below the visible end.

far left
An infrared map of Jupiter, observed by Voyager 2. Blue areas are cool; red areas are warmer.

left
The dome of the 3.8 metre infrared telescope – the world's largest – at Mauna Kea (4,267 metres high) in Hawaii.

opposite right
The world's largest steerable radio dish, at Effelsburg near Bonn, West Germany.

but because the signals they receive from space are processed electronically, it is possible to have great variety in design. Most radio-telescopes now being built, however, are basically the same; each has a large 'dish' to collect the radio waves, the dish normally being mounted so that it can be pointed in any direction of the sky. Such dishes are the equivalent of the large mirrors of optical reflecting telescopes. But because of the extraordinarily long wavelengths of radio waves compared with light, their surfaces do not have to be made with such precision. Unevenness up to a millimetre or so is satisfactory in most instruments. Yet the diameter must be very much greater than an optical telescope. The famous radio-telescope at Jodrell Bank near Manchester has a dish no less than

76 metres in diameter; yet at 2 cm its resolution is still only 1 arc minute (1/60th of a degree). The giant radio-telescope at Effelsburg in West Germany has a diameter of 100 metres giving a resolution at 2 cm no better than 50 arc seconds. Both these instruments can, however, be pointed anywhere in the sky.

The world's largest dish radio-telescope is at Arecibo in Puerto Rico. The dish itself is a giant natural dip in the ground which has been covered with a curved reflecting surface. It has a diameter of 305 metres but this cannot move, of course. However the receiving aerial or antenna which is suspended 145 metres above the bowl, can be moved and this allows astronomers to direct the beam up to 20° from the vertical. This giant radio dish has been used recently for radar mapping

of the surface of Venus – radar being a technique whereby pulses of radio waves are sent out and then reflected back, the time taken for the out-and-back journey giving the distance of the object. The Arecibo telescope is also used as a straightforward radio-telescope, receiving radio waves from space.

To overcome the problem of picking out detail, radio astronomers usually use, and even design, their telescopes to work as interferometers. In this case two (or more) dishes are used at once and the radio waves received in each are then mixed together. Such mixing improves the power of the instrument to resolve detail. For example, whereas two small dishes of 13 metres will have a resolution of only 1° at a radio wavelength of 2 cm, if two are spaced 1 kilometre apart, the resolution will be improved more than 70 times to 50 arc seconds. This is because together they are equivalent to a radio-telescope dish with a diameter of 1 km, not 13 metres. Within the last ten years or so, telescopes in different countries and even on different continents have been used as interferometers. With such very long separations or base-lines, radio astronomers can obtain better detail resolution than optical astronomers.

One specialized way to use the interferometer method is to mount a number of dishes on a railway track. These can be used as a multiple interferometer tracing out a large area of sky as they are carried round by the Earth's rotation. By moving the dishes and storing in a computer the results obtained at various positions, it becomes possible to build up detailed radio 'pictures' of the sky. Originally devised at Cambridge University, this technique has become widely used for mapping the positions of radio objects in deep space.

right
The principle of the radio interferometer telescope, of which the Very Large Array is a most sophisticated example. The radio signals received by each dish can come from a large area of sky (A). As the celestial radio source moves across the sky, the signals in each dish first become out of step and then in step with each other (B). By mixing these signals together electronically, they will interfere with one another, giving a result that is sharper and that covers a narrower area of sky.

below right
The Very Large Array radio interferometer telescope. It is a Y-shaped arrangement of 27 moveable dishes, each 25 metres in diameter.

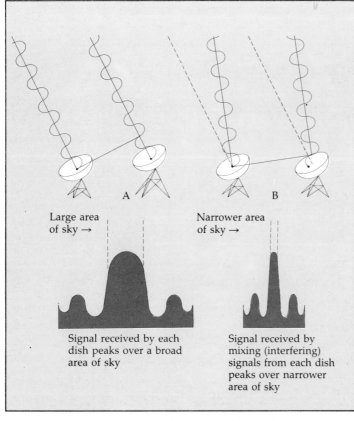

Large area of sky →

Narrower area of sky →

Signal received by each dish peaks over a broad area of sky

Signal received by mixing (interfering) signals from each dish peaks over narrower area of sky

OBSERVING WITH ELECTRONS

The use of electrons to create brighter images has had a profound effect on optical observing. Using sophisticated electronic methods, telescopes can now probe even deeper into space

Electrons are parts of atoms; they are the particles which orbit round the centre or nucleus of an atom. Electrons are used in many ways; in a television set their motions cause electric currents and in the cathode ray tube the pictures we see are built up by the movement of electrons. Here the electrons are shot from the back of the tube and make a picture by hitting a screen at the front. We can make the picture brighter by making the electrons travel faster and so hit the screen more fiercely. Using electrons in a somewhat similar way at the eyepiece end of a telescope, it is possible to get a bright electron picture in place of a dim one given by the light from the telescope itself.

This technique has now been applied to astronomy, using a device called an electronographic camera. The basic idea was developed in France by the astronomer André Lallemand, but the latest design is the result of work by James McGee and David McMullan of the Royal Greenwich Observatory. What happens is that the light from the telescope falls on to a 'photocathode' instead of on to the usual photographic plate. The photocathode is made of a substance which emits electrons when light strikes its surface, and its purpose here is to convert the light into an output of electrons. The electrons now have to be carried down the tube of the camera. They accelerate as they travel, so that they strike a special photographic film with sufficient energy to make a picture. This acceleration is achieved by metal plates (electrodes) which are fed with a high voltage. All this part of the camera – from the photocathode to the thin transparent window (made of the mineral mica) which lies just in front of the photographic film – is kept in a vacuum, because the electrons would soon be stopped by any air that was present. The electronographic camera can show up very dim objects and is extremely useful for some observations, such as making visible faint gaseous clouds in space.

In one sense, the electronographic camera is a mixture of old and new techniques. The old technique is the use of photographic plates; the new is the harnessing of electrons to make a stronger picture – one which can be photographed with a far shorter exposure than is possible using only a photographic plate. Another new observing method which produces a photograph at the end of an elaborate electronic technique is 'speckle interferometry'.

Speckle interferometry is based on the simple fact that the air around us is never still, even the air above a mountain-top observatory. You can see this for yourself by looking up at the sky at night; the stars twinkle because the air is continually in motion. When an astronomer takes a photograph of a star through a telescope, the result is not a perfect tiny disk of light (as it should be) but a blob of light. However, if the photograph is taken using a type of electronographic camera that enables a very short exposure of about two-hundredths of a second to be made

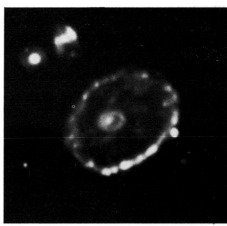

above The faint ring galaxy 7ZW466 photographed through a modern optical telescope. This picture was taken at the Cerro Tololo Inter-American Observatory, Chile.

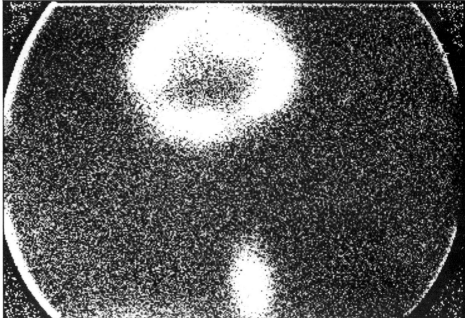

above The faint ring galaxy 7ZW466 photographed with a modern optical telescope using a photon counter. A series of such images are computer processed to give a complete picture.

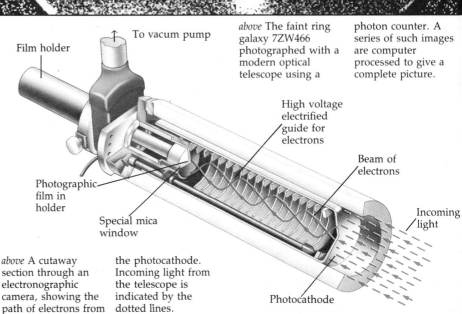

above A cutaway section through an electronographic camera, showing the path of electrons from the photocathode. Incoming light from the telescope is indicated by the dotted lines.

Film holder

To vacuum pump

Photographic film in holder

Special mica window

High voltage electrified guide for electrons

Beam of electrons

Incoming light

Photocathode

instead of the usual exposure of many seconds, the result is quite different. Instead of a small smudgy blob on the photographic plate, the star's image appears as a host of tiny points or speckles. Each speckle is a tiny star image formed by small

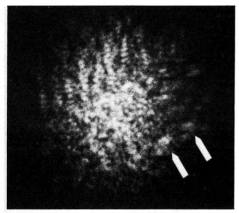

above Speckle image of the double star κ Ursae Majoris. The arrows indicate one pair of speckle images which give an image that can be measured when computer-processed with other speckle images.

'pockets' of air in the atmosphere. In some of these speckles the light-waves will be in step with one another; in the other speckles they will not.

By taking a large number of photographs in this way, the astronomer will end up with pictures of a lot of speckles of the star, each having some of the speckles – though not the same ones, probably – with their light-waves in step with one another. When all these photographs are combined together, the in-step light-wave speckles in one picture will interfere with those in another and an 'interference' picture will build up. This picture contains 'information' that is too muddled up in an ordinary photograph for it to be detected. However, to be of use, the information has to be extracted. There are two ways of doing this; first by building up a new picture by running a laser beam all over the interference picture; secondly by

feeding the results through a computer.

The results of speckle interferometry are spectacular. By observing stars which are binaries, with one orbiting about the other but too far away for a telescope to be able to see them as double, the speckle technique can show that the star really is a binary. This is because running a laser beam over the information gives an 'interference picture' of the star – a round disk crossed by dark lines. By measuring the distance between the lines and the angle at which they are tilted, it is possible to discover how far apart the two members of the binary are, and also the angle at which their paths are inclined to us. Another use of this technique is to apply it to observations of red supergiant stars that are not too far away. Betelgeuse is a good example. The speckle method allows astronomers to measure the diameters of such large stars and, with the aid of a computer, to build up a picture of the star itself.

Electronic methods of optical observing come into their own in a device developed in England by Alexander Boksenberg. Known as a 'photon counter', it can make use of every tiny amount of light coming into a telescope. Light travels as waves, but the waves themselves move along in little 'pockets' of radiation known as 'photons'. The smallest amount of light is one photon. What Boksenberg's photon counter does is to use an extremely sensitive photocathode to convert the arrival of light photons into an emission of electrons. These are multiplied electrically, rather as in an electronographic camera, and are then converted into special electronic counting pulses. They are examined 'digitally' and converted into a binary code such as is used in a computer or a pocket calculator. These results are then fed to a computer and the effects due to the equipment itself and any photons received from the night sky are removed. Finally a picture is gradually built up of the celestial object being studied.

The photon counter is very sensitive and semi-automatic, for it tells the operator when it has received sufficient photons to complete its picture. Since it increases the incoming light by something like seven hundred thousand times (7×10^5), which is far more than can be achieved by any other method, it noticeably improves the light-grasp of a telescope and so helps probe deeper into space.

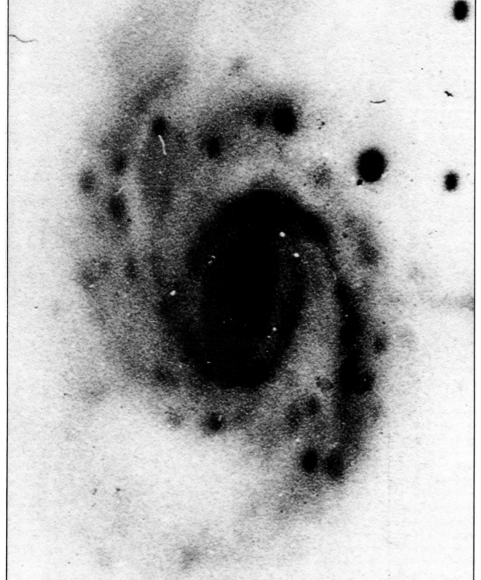

This photograph of the spiral galaxy M51 was taken with an electronographic camera. Note the detail in and around the spiral arms.

PROBING WITH X-RAYS AND GAMMA-RAYS

At the very short wavelength end of the spectrum, well below violet and ultraviolet light, lie the very penetrating X-rays and gamma-rays. It is important to observe these if we are to probe deep space properly.

The universe is a very much more exciting and explosive than astronomers once thought. They know this now because they can observe the very penetrating rays – X-rays and gamma-rays – which stars send out, rays which the Earth's atmosphere stop ever reaching the ground. To observe them we must send detectors and telescopes well above the ground to heights of at least 160 km, or better still, right out beyond the atmosphere into space.

The first X-ray pictures were taken over thirty years ago. In 1947, just after the end of the Second World War in Europe, the Americans launched a captured German V2 rocket to a height of 160 km. This contained an X-ray camera which took 'pictures' of the Sun. The first pictures were not spectactular, but they did show that the Sun does emit some X-rays. Later on, X-ray cameras were carried up in the British Skylark rocket, also to study the Sun. These cameras were very simple; they consisted of a piece of special photographic film in a metal box, in the front of which was a shutter and a filter. When the shutter opened the picture was taken, just as in an ordinary camera. The filter was a thin metal sheet through which X-rays could pass but not light. Later designs of camera also had a second

metal sheet that blocks out X-rays, only allowing them to pass through a tiny pinhole. Thus, early on, astronomers were able to get some pictures showing how the Sun was emitting X-rays. These pictures showed them that the X-rays were coming from the very thin and extremely hot outer atmosphere of the Sun known as the corona. Still later, in 1962, when an American Ranger spacecraft was on a mission to the Moon, it happened by chance to discover a very strong X-ray source in deep space. Known as Scorpius X-1 (because it lay in the direction of the constellation Scorpius) it was an indication that there were certainly distant and powerful X-ray sources as well. This observation was confirmed by astronauts on some of the Apollo missions to the Moon, who discovered that the well-known Crab nebula is also an X-ray source.

To probe deep space by examining it in the light of X-rays and gamma-rays is very important. If we do not do this we shall only ever know part of what is happening in the universe, and that part will not be quite correct because we are unaware of the short wavelength radiation. Such radiation is very powerful and it is evidence of very energetic and explosive events in space. To study these events, special orbiting satellites are needed, and a number have been launched by the Americans, Russians and British. The first pure X-ray satellites were launched in Kenya; one on Kenya's Independence Day in December 1970 and known as *Uhuru* (Swahili for 'freedom') and another in 1974 known as Ariel 5. More recently, in 1978, the Americans launched a much larger and more elaborate X-ray spacecraft known as 'Einstein'. As well as all kinds of other

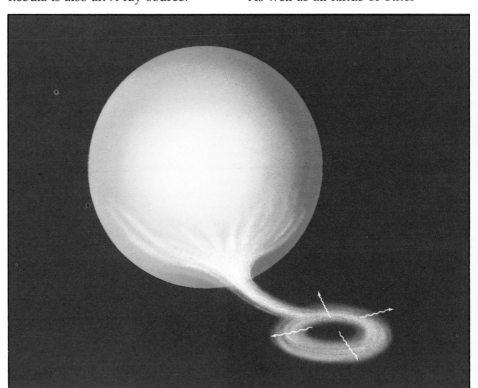

above A yellow star accompanied by a small compact star (possibly a black hole) on to which matter is streaming. This inrushing matter emits X-rays in certain directions.

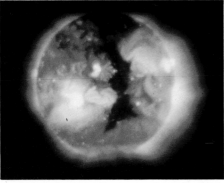

An X-ray photograph of the Sun made from Skylab. The X-rays are coming from the Sun's outer atmosphere and corona.

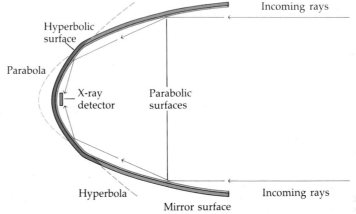

left
The optical layout of an X-ray telescope. The X-rays must meet the mirrors at very steep angles. Two types of curved mirror are shown – hyperbolic and parabolic – together with the X-ray detector, which works electronically. The mirrors are gold-plated, and thus present a very dense and highly reflective surface to the X-rays.

equipment, this carries an actual X-ray telescope with an aperture of no less than 0.6 metres and is still doing excellent work.

X-rays can be observed in various ways. One is to use simple X-ray cameras like those fitted to early rockets, but orbiting satellites use more elaborate devices. These are based on the fact that X-rays and gamma-rays are very energetic (even the longest wavelength X-rays carry 50 times more energy than light, while the shortest have 5,000 times) and gamma-rays are more energetic still. One result of this great energy is that these rays can electrify or 'ionize' a gas. They do this by knocking electrons off the gas atoms. So X-ray detectors in satellites carry gas in small sealed tubes. The tubes are sealed at one end by a very thin plastic sheet – only about one thousandth of a millimetre thick – and along the length of the tube, in

its centre, runs a wire. When X-rays enter through the plastic sheet, they ionize the gas. The ionized gas atoms move to the outside of the tube and cause a small electric current. This is what the device detects. Each time X-rays arrive, there is a tiny electric current, the strength of current depending on the quantity of X-rays received. The device is therefore called a 'proportional counter'. It consists of a collection of such tubes mounted together with other metal tubes in front to allow only X-rays from straight ahead to enter.

Because gamma-rays have more energy, they can be detected by letting the rays fall on a piece of germanium or silicon. The rays cause the material to conduct electricity and so allow their presence to be detected. Both devices can be made so that they only accept X-rays and gamma-rays from areas of sky about ½° by 5°, the direction being

determined by where the satellite is pointing. But still better results can be obtained using an X-ray telescope, like the one which is being carried in the Einstein satellite. This gives detailed pictures with a resolution of between three and four arc seconds, that is over 1200 times more precise than the proportional counter.

An X-ray telescope is a very special form of telescope. An ordinary optical telescope would be no use because the X-rays would just pass straight through the mirror. But if they just graze the mirror, then the X-rays will 'see' the atoms apparently closer together and this will be sufficient to reflect them. You can observe this principle for yourself, if you look at the page you are reading. Face on, the lines of letters appear separated by spaces. But if you tilt the book so that you are looking at a steep angle, the lines seem to close up. By making use of this principle of 'grazing incidence', and using a dense reflecting surface of gold-plating on the mirror, it is possible to build an efficient X-ray telescope.

The optics of such a telescope are strange because grazing incidence means that we are only using parts of the mirrors. In an optical telescope designed for ordinary light, the main mirror is shaped so that it follows a curve known as a parabola; its sides are steep compared with its centre. This is fine for the outer parts of a mirror for an X-ray telescope, but not for the inner parts. Here we need a different shape, a curve which is not so steep and which is known as an hyperbola. So the mirror of an X-ray telescope is a complex affair, composed of two different curves. These allow the incoming X-rays to be reflected to a detector in the centre of the mirror. Although such a telescope is difficult to make, an instrument like this is what is fitted into the Einstein satellite; the results, which are being radioed back to Earth, show that it is working very well indeed.

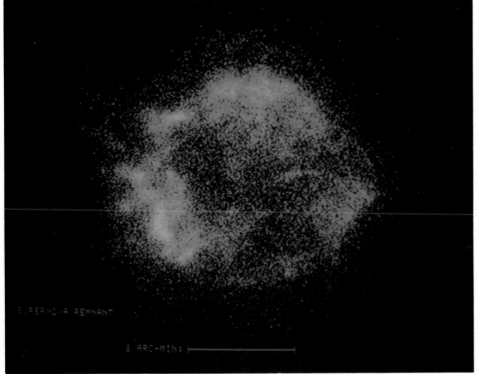

above The X-ray source Cassiopeia 'A', which is the remains of a supernova explosion. This source, which is about 300 years old, is a strong emitter of radio signals.

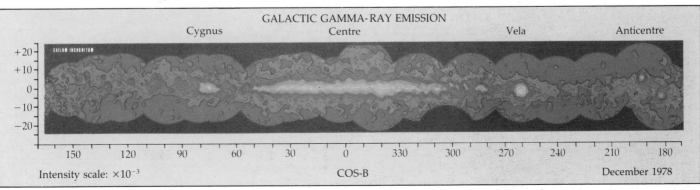

A gamma-ray profile of our Galaxy. The colours are false, but indicate gamma-ray intensity. The brighter the colours, the more intense the gamma-rays. This picture is not, of course, a photograph, but a drawing based on information gathered by specially equipped orbiting satellites.

PROBING WITH ATOMS AND GRAVITY WAVES

Atomic particles come rushing to the Earth from deep space. By detecting and examining these particles, we can discover new facts about stars and the way they shine. A further way of probing deep space lies in the detection of gravity waves.

Most people have fears of radioactivity. They know that radioactive substances like radium and uranium give off dangerous penetrating rays. Some 80 years ago, scientists began to show great interest in this subject, and found that radioactive substance emitted three different kinds of 'rays' — gamma-rays, β-rays and α-rays. Later they discovered that while gamma-rays were rays of very short wavelength, the α- and β-rays were not really rays at all, but atomic particles. In fact the β-rays were electrons, while α-rays turned out to be the central cores or nuclei of helium atoms.

What the scientists studying radioactivity and the nature of atoms also found was that, like X-rays and gamma-rays, these particles would ionize (pages 32–33) gas in a sealed tube. This happened because the particles had such energy, they knocked electrons off the gas atoms. However, there was a problem. Ionization of the gas in the sealed tube still occurred even if there was no radioactive material about, and there seemed no way to stop it. Only gradually did scientists realize that the answer must be that something was coming from outer space. To confirm this, sealed tubes of gas were carried up in high-flying balloons some 5,000 metres above the ground, and it was found that ionization increased as the balloons ascended. 'Cosmic rays' were coming from outer space, 'rays' which were later found really to be high-speed atomic particles.

What the cosmic ray particles do is to rush into the Earth's atmosphere and knock particles off the atoms in the air. The air particles are known as 'secondary particles' and they can be observed from the ground.

However, in order to observe the 'primary particles' – the ones that have actually come from space – high-altitude balloons and orbiting satellites are needed. The balloons usually carry packets of special photographic plates, which the cosmic rays strike, leaving a line on the plate to show where they have been. Should the particles break up, this will also be recorded on the photograph. But photographic plates can only be used because the balloons come back to Earth; in orbiting satellites astronomers need some observing device that makes the particles trigger off electric signals which can be radioed back to Earth.

There are three ways of doing this. One is to use a geiger counter. This has a sealed tube of gas, and when a cosmic ray particle enters, it makes the gas conduct electricity. However, most modern electric counters are of a different type, being either 'scintillation counters' or Cerenkov counters.

Scintillation counters depend on the fact that when atomic particles hit crystals of a substance like sodium iodide, electrons are emitted inside the crystals. If the crystals are not pure but contain a trace of some other material, the electrons will be captured by this material. At their capture, a flash of light is given off.

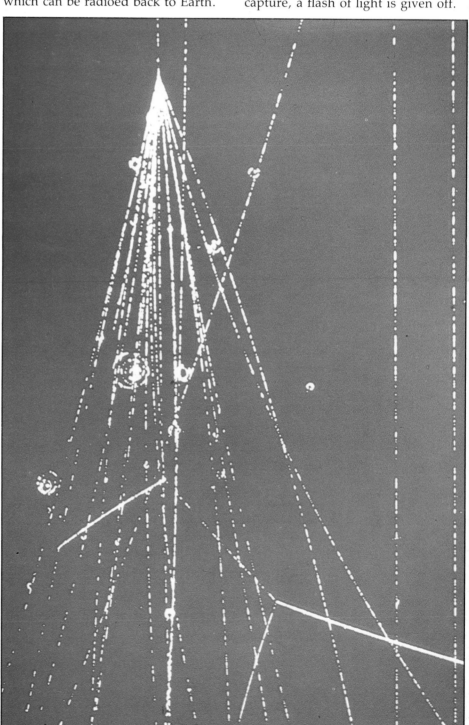

An incoming cosmic ray particle colliding with a proton, and causing the emission of other nuclear particles or 'secondary' cosmic rays.

This light is then detected by a 'photocathode' (page 30) which turns the flashes into electric currents.

A Cerenkov counter is a piece of transparent material that gives out light when a very high speed particle rushes through it. The light is emitted because the particle sends a shock through the material – a kind of optical sonic bang – and this light traces out the particle's path. The result is then viewed by a photocathode device. This detector can provide evidence of the direction from which the particle has arrived.

Cosmic ray particles are only one kind of atomic particle moving about in space. Astronomers also believe that deep inside the Sun and other stars neutrinos are emitted. Neutrinos weigh very little, if they weigh anything at all, and have no electric charge, so they readily pass through most materials. However, they do spin as they move and this means that now and again one will collide with the atoms through which it is travelling, provided these atoms are of the right kind. Chlorine atoms can sometimes capture neutrinos, and when they do so they are changed into atoms of the gas argon. The capture is not likely to happen very often, but if we have a good stream of neutrinos passing through a vast number of chlorine atoms, then we might expect to detect some.

An American scientist, Raymond Davis Jr, decided that the best way to capture them was to fill a vast tank with carbon tetrachloride, a liquid that is used for dry-cleaning clothes. In order to make sure that the chloride atoms were not affected by cosmic rays or any other atomic particles, the tank was placed 1.5 km underground, in an old gold mine in South Dakota in the United States. As a further protection the tank was submerged in water. This, then, is what has sometimes been called a 'neutrino telescope'.

Calculations led astronomers to expect a certain number of argon atoms after a given period of time but, in fact, four times fewer have been observed. Scientists are therefore having to think again about what is happening inside the Sun.

The detection of gravity waves is another way of probing space. Gravity makes itself felt throughout space, and the theory of relativity (page 132) tells us that this happens because space is bent round massive bodies (Chapter 3). Scientists have concluded that when massive bodies are in a state of motion or collapse, they send out gravity waves or make space itself ripple. However, to detect these ripples is very difficult because the effects are so very small. All the same, gravity wave 'telescopes' have been built. The most famous are those designed by Joseph Weber in the United States, though others are now being built elsewhere. They consist of a huge suspended lump of material, such as aluminium, fitted with detectors which can pick up any delicate vibration in the lump. (Weber uses a cylinder of aluminium weighing four tonnes.)

Such gravity wave telescopes are also sensitive to earthquake shocks and even passing traffic. More than one telescope is needed, so that vibrations can be compared and the unwanted results eliminated. Some results have been reported but additional observations are still needed to determine how much, if any, of the signals are from gravity waves. The first gravity wave telescopes were astonishing enough; they could detect movements of only one hundredth of the diameter of the nucleus of an atom. Now telescopes one hundred thousand times more sensitive are being developed. These could detect sources as far as the Virgo cluster of galaxies, which lie at almost 22 million parsecs (72 million light-years).

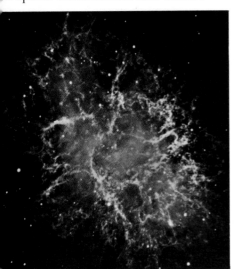

above The Crab Nebula supernova remnant may well be a source of gravity waves.

above Professor Joseph Weber adjusting the three tonne aluminium cylinder which is designed to vibrate minutely when a gravity wave is received.

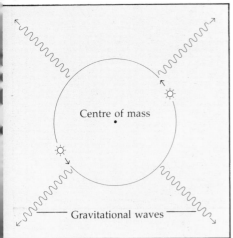

Centre of mass

Gravitational waves

above Changes in motion within a system where one body is orbiting another may give rise to gravity waves.

right Gravity waves have the effect of causing displacements in two directions at right angles to each other. This effect can be demonstrated by taking a rubber sheet marked with dots, and stretching it first in one direction and then in the other.

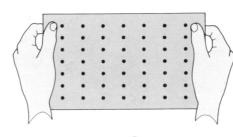

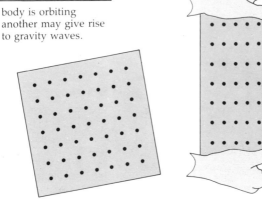

SPACE OBSERVATORIES

It is vital to get instruments up and away from Earth if we are going to observe all the radiation from space, because so much is captured by our atmosphere.

Observing from space is helpful to the astronomer in a number of ways. This is because there are all kinds of problems when we observe from the ground, most of them due to the fact that Earth-based observatories have to peer through a very thick and turbulent atmosphere. As we know, the atmosphere completely blankets out some radiation. We cannot see gamma-rays or X-rays, nor most of the ultraviolet, while some infrared and all long-wave radio waves are also blocked off. But even when radiation does get through (and light of all colours can pass quite freely unless there are clouds in the way) astronomers still have to put up with the fact that the air is turbulent. This turbulence makes the images we do observe dance about, so that they always give a slightly blurred picture. Something can be done using elaborate methods of observing like speckle interferometry, but it would be better if we could get away from the atmosphere altogether.

To see how true this is you have only to look at pictures of the Sun taken from out in space (page 34) though the most spectacular space pictures taken so far are those of the planets. Telescopes on Earth are very limited in what magnification they can use; even under the best conditions the planet Mercury is merely a bright disk with, perhaps, a vague dark marking or two. Yet the Mariner spacecraft have shown that the planet's surface is peppered with craters. Voyager spacecraft to Jupiter and Saturn have shown us details of these planets that were not visible in nearly such detail from Earth. New rings have been discovered round Saturn while the rings we already know are found to be more complex than previously thought.

Jupiter has also been found to possess a ring, and the moons or satellites of both planets have provided all kinds of surprises. Admittedly some of the discoveries were possible because the Voyager spacecraft could go close to these bodies. However, if we had our large observatory telescopes out in space, we could have seen at least some of this detail. So it is evident that the sooner we can start observing from space, the better.

One way of doing this besides launching spacecraft like the Voyagers, is to send up orbiting satellites. These have done wonders for high-energy astronomy by probing space with x-rays, gamma-rays and cosmic rays, yet each satellite can carry only a strictly limited number of experiments worked out in detail beforehand.

above Voyager 2 spacecraft picture of the rings of Saturn, showing far more detail than can be seen from the Earth.

above The mirror of the Space Telescope during manufacture. The honeycomb appearance is due to the fact that the reflective coating has not been applied.

A further way of tackling the problem is to send up an orbiting laboratory with a crew of scientists. The American Skylab project of 1973–74 was just such an adventurous project. Weighing some 90 tonnes, it provided ample accommodation of 292 cubic metres (the equivalent of six medium-sized living rooms). Skylab carried a three-man crew which was able to conduct experiments and observations for 12 weeks. Another project was the Russian *Salyut* 6 orbiting laboratory; this had less crew space, only 100

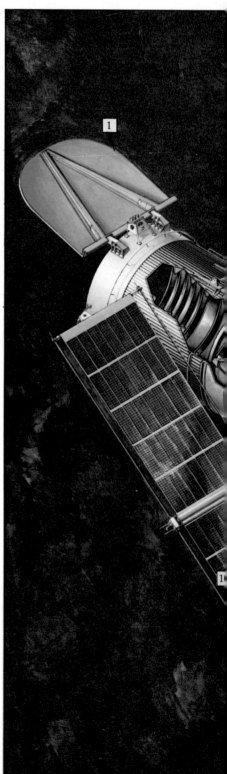

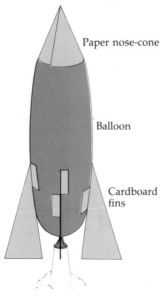

Paper nose-cone

Balloon

Cardboard fins

A rocket works by ejecting gases from its base. The principle is illustrated by fitting a paper nose-cone and cardboard fins to a long balloon. Let the air out, and watch the 'rocket' rise.

constantly changing programme of research on the Sun which, after all, is the nearest star to us. The Skylab crew took many excellent pictures of the Sun both in visual wavelengths and also in short ultraviolet wavelengths that never reach Earth-based observatories. Admittedly, special orbiting satellites such as the International Ultraviolet Explorer satellite can be used for this kind of ultraviolet observing, but what the Skylab crew showed was that the equipment on such a spacecraft could be turned to a wide variety of tasks. Indeed, they even turned their equipment on to a comet (comet Kohoutek) and made a discovery that could not have been made by Earth-based observers.

The most exciting project, now that Skylab has dropped back to Earth, is the large space telescope which is being built in Connecticut in the United States. This is a large instrument, with a main mirror, 2.4 metres (94½ inches) – almost the size of the famous '100-inch' (2.5 metre) telescope at Mount Wilson. But the space telescope will be more effective than the 100-inch. First of all, its light-gathering power will be greater. In theory this should not be so, because the 100-inch has a slightly larger aperture, but in practice the fact that there is no air to absorb any of the light entering the space telescope, makes all the difference. So the space telescope will be able to detect objects 100 times dimmer than the 100-inch can do.

The space telescope will also be able to detect more detail than the 100-inch. Again, this is simply because there will be no turbulent air to make the images fuzzy, and it is expected that the space telescope will be able to pick out details at least 100 times smaller. As a result, astronomers have the highest hopes of many new discoveries.

The space telescope is a pioneering project. It weighs 5.4 tonnes and the telescope itself is just over nine metres (29½ feet) long. Its supporting framework is made of new material – a cross between graphite (carbon) and a plastic epoxy resin – which changes its size hardly at all, even under the extreme conditions of heat and cold to be found in space. Attached to the telescope are sensors; the purpose of these is to keep the telescope pointing in the correct direction. What they do is to fix on a bright star near the celestial object being observed, and instruct the guiding mechanism. This consists of small gas jets for manoeuvering the whole telescope. The amount of gas the jets shoot out and the direction in which it goes has to be worked out by an on-board computer. This is a very sophisticated mechanism, and will allow the telescope to be pointed correctly and then hold a deep space image without moving more than seven thousandths of an arc second (two millionths of a degree). So although the space telescope has to be remote controlled from Earth, it has been designed to be a true orbiting space observatory.

The Space Telescope is scheduled for launch into Earth orbit by the Space Shuttle in the mid–1980's. This artist's impression shows a cutaway section of the Optical Telescope Assembly.

1 Protective cover against direct sunlight.

2 Framework of light but strong supports made of artificial graphite epoxy resin.

3 Ridged inside cover To prevent stray light reaching the telescope.

4 Central baffle against stray light.

5 Fine guiding sensors which observe a bright star and keep the telescope pointing in the correct direction.

6 Scientific instrument module

7 Focal plane of telescope

8 2.4m primary mirror

9 Radio antenna for communication with Earth.

10 Solar panel for feeding energy to telescope equipment.

11 Secondary mirror

Figure to scale

FUTURE PROBES

Observing from space, far from the Earth's atmosphere, is invaluable to astronomers. Exciting new methods of transport are now being planned.

Skylab, the Einstein satellite and the Mariner and Voyager spacecraft have all shown how important it is to observe from space. Only by being away from the Earth can astronomers receive all the incoming radiation of whatever wavelength and avoid the problems of air turbulence and cloud. Only in space can optical observations be made every night – and every day too – with images that provide more detail and show up dim objects much further out in space. Yet the drawback is that making spacecraft is costly, and launching them is very expensive indeed. If the cost of launching could be reduced, then the whole idea of permanent space observatories would become more practicable.

The cost of launching a satellite from Earth is high because the Earth's gravity has to be overcome and this means having a very large strong rocket to hold the immense amount of chemical fuel required. Such a rocket has three stages: the first carries the whole rocket up and then, when its fuel is all used, it drops away. The second stage then fires; this now has less weight to carry and reaches a higher speed. It too drops away when its fuel is consumed and the third stage puts the payload – observatory or spacecraft – into orbit, after which it drops off So at the end of the launch nothing is left. The three rocket stages have fallen back to Earth, burning up as they rush through the atmosphere, and there remain no pieces that can be used again. So much for the giant 110 metre rocket costing more than 100 million dollars (about £55 million). For regular launching something far less costly is vital, but fortunately the Americans seem to have found the answer; they have developed the Space Shuttle.

The Space Shuttle is a spacecraft which is built rather like a large airliner. It is launched using a large liquid fuel tank with two small solid fuel rockets strapped to its sides. Once used the large tank drops back to Earth, but as it does not go so very far into space, its fall back to the

ground is controlled by a parachute, so the tank can be used again. As to the Space Shuttle itself, this soars on into orbit at a height of some 800 kilometres above the Earth's surface. Then, when it finally returns to Earth, it comes down under gravity, starting off with a small

rocket thrust. It comes down into the atmosphere, floating on the air because of its large delta-shaped (triangular) wings. The Shuttle can be used again and again; indeed its designers believe that it can be used a hundred times before it will need a major overhaul. Its cost is much less

above
An artist's impression of a radio astronomical observatory on the Moon. Here, three lunar craters have been used to act as the giant dishes of an immense interferometer radio telescope. The Moon would be an ideal observatory for studies of the universe in all wavelengths, since it has no atmosphere whatever to blot out radiation.

left
An artist's impression of the Space Shuttle in orbit with its cargo compartment open.

than a large launching rocket, and many people believe that it will probably cut down the cost of space research by five to ten times.

But the Space Shuttle also has the advantage of greater reliability. Of all the satellites launched in the United States, problems with the rocket have accounted for six out of every ten failures; Space Shuttle should overcome this. And, of course, a vehicle like Space Shuttle can carry out all kinds of missions. Piloted by a crew of two, it can transport up to four mission specialists for as long as 30 days. It also contains an area for cargo that is equivalent to five ordinary sized living-rooms, and its load can weigh almost 30 tonnes. So it can be used to repair satellites already in orbit, or to launch new ones (thus saving on three-stage rockets which would otherwise be necessary); it can even have on board experiments that require to be done in space, or carry special astronomical telescopes for making specific space observations.

Space Shuttle seems to be the probe of the immediate future, but there are other projects which may be developed in the years ahead. The most ambitious of these is the Daedalus study, being carried out by the British Interplanetary Society. This is for a spacecraft driven by nuclear power instead of by power derived from burning chemical fuels. The scheme is to use nuclear fusion, that is making energy by fusing or welding together light-weight atoms. This is a process similar to that which goes on inside stars like our Sun. The fuel, a mixture of helium and deuterium (a special form of hydrogen), would be in the form of pellets. As each pellet is consumed, a pulse of energy is given off and the spacecraft is propelled by a series of pulses. It is calculated that such a spacecraft carrying a payload of 5,000 tonnes – this could include a number of planetary probes to examine any planets discovered on its journey – would be able to reach a speed of more than a tenth of the speed of light. It could be used to probe nearby planetary systems (page 184).

Other interstellar spacecraft have been designed using nuclear power for propulsion and one, the interstellar ramjet, is most ingenious. It is planned to scoop up its hydrogen and helium fuel from space, and then fuse this together to give energy. To obtain enough material the scoop would need to have an area of perhaps 300,000 square kilometres though being out in space, it could be of very light-weight construction. But such ideas lie far in the future. More immediate seems to be an observatory on the Moon. Such a project is not now as difficult as it once seemed. Space Shuttle could lift men and materials into orbit and an orbiting 'space tug' could carry them on to the Moon. As the Moon has no atmosphere to filter away radiation, it would make an ideal observatory for radiation in all wavelengths, from gamma-rays to radio waves; and it is near enough to turn this idea into reality within the next few decades.

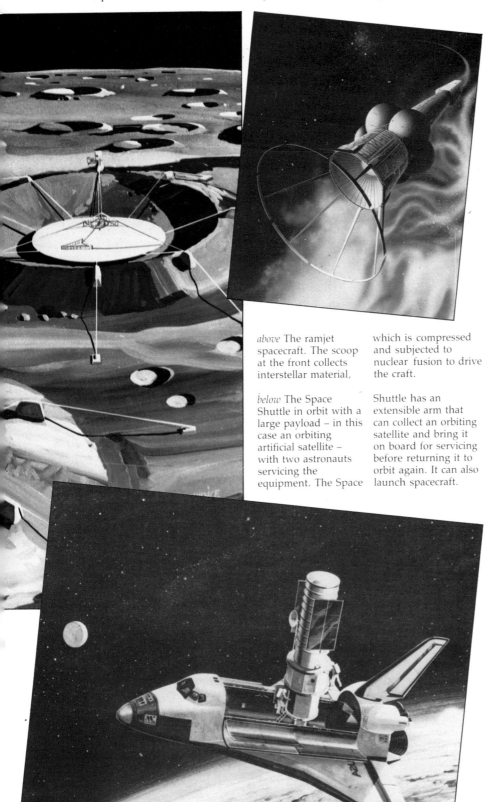

above The ramjet spacecraft. The scoop at the front collects interstellar material, which is compressed and subjected to nuclear fusion to drive the craft.

below The Space Shuttle in orbit with a large payload – in this case an orbiting artificial satellite – with two astronauts servicing the equipment. The Space Shuttle has an extensible arm that can collect an orbiting satellite and bring it on board for servicing before returning it to orbit again. It can also launch spacecraft.

CHAPTER 3
THE NATURE OF SPACE

Space is all around us, and stretches out far beyond the Earth. Various systems have been devised for plotting star positions, and all use co-ordinates. They are also used as a basis for describing space.

When we examine the night sky we are looking into space. But what is space really like? We know that though the stars all look as if they are fixed on the inside of a dome, they are not really like that at all. Some are comparatively near, others very far away.

Nevertheless, the idea of a dome with stars fixed to it is a useful one. It allows us to divide the stars into constellations and these are a useful way to start plotting star positions. This is important because for any detailed study of the stars in space we need to be able to refer to them unambiguously. You can do this in words – 'the middle star of the three stars in the tail of Ursa Major' – though it is easier to refer to it as ζ Ursa Majoris. But there are too many stars to be described by using the Greek or any other alphabet and the most certain and precise way is to use co-ordinates, so that each star may be referred to by a set of numbers. It is as if each star has its own telephone number, though the co-ordinates astronomers use also give an indication of where in the sky the star is to be found.

The co-ordinates we now use are similar to latitude and longitude on Earth, with celestial poles replacing the north and south poles of the Earth, and a celestial equator instead of a terrestrial one. This is logical and allows astronomers to refer to positions north or south of the celestial equator quite simply. Such positions or 'declinations' are taken as positive if north of the celestial equator and negative if south of it. Measurements are made in degrees and fractions of degrees.

The celestial equivalent to longitude is right ascension. Measured along the celestial equator in an eastwards direction, it starts at the point where the Sun's path in the sky – the ecliptic – crosses the celestial equator. This point moves westwards because the Earth's axis moves or 'precesses', like the axis of a slowly spinning top, in an anti-clockwise direction when viewed from above the celestial sphere. This motion is due to the gravitational effects of the Sun and Moon.

As a result of precession you will find that star charts and catalogues always give their co-ordinates for a particular date. Most now in use are dated 'epoch 1950.0' though at least

left
The colour photograph of the southern central region of Orion, taken by the amateur astronomer, Ron Arbour, shows the three stars of the belt and the stars of the sword. The famous Orion Nebula can also be clearly seen. Compare the positions of the belt and sword with those on the star map (*above*).

above
This star map, drawn by Will Tirion, has co-ordinates for the 'epoch 2000.0'. Although the map represents the curved dome of the sky on a flat chart, it gives co-ordinates correctly.

one modern chart has been drawn for the epoch 2000.0. The crossing point of ecliptic and celestial equator now lies in the constellation of Pisces (The Fishes) but in Greek and Roman times, when most of our constellation names were adopted, the point was in Aries (The Ram); it was then – and still often is – known as the 'First Point of Aries'. At this point the Sun, being on the celestial equator, gives equal periods of day and night, so it is also sometimes known as the Vernal (or Spring) Equinox.

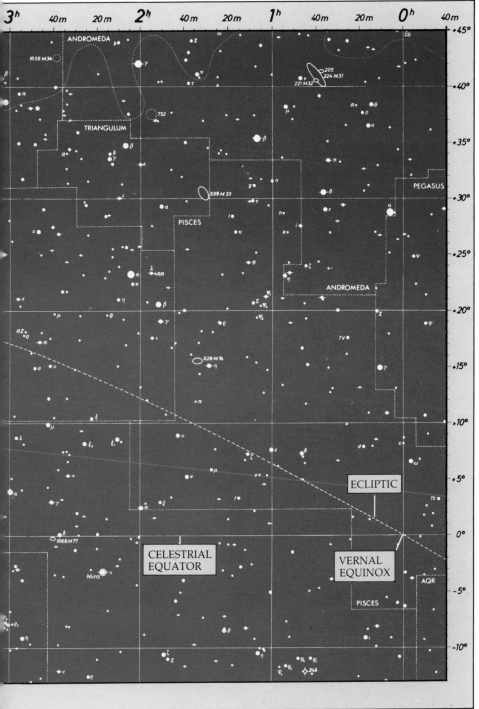

right
Co-ordinates and the measurement of distance. The use of Pythagoras' theorem to find the distance between two points from their rectangular co-ordinates is shown here, both in a general form (*Fig. 1*) and in a particular case (*Fig. 2*). See text (last column) for a full explanation.

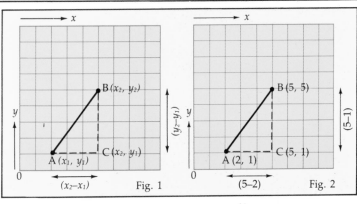

You may wonder why the term celestial latitude is not used instead of right ascension and declination. The reason is that they refer to an earlier system of co-ordinates, based not on the equator but on the ecliptic. Yet whatever system is adopted, all have one thing in common, they all make use of co-ordinates at right-angles to each other – rectangular co-ordinates – which are useful not only for defining precisely the positions of bodies on the celestial sphere or places on the Earth, but are also of use as a basis for using algebra to describe geometrical shapes and situations. This means that they can be used in studies of space.

The algebra and its associated mathematics can become very complicated, though a very simple example will show us the principle. Suppose we take two points on a sheet of paper, A and B, and want to find the distance between them. Then, as figure 1 shows, this distance AB can be thought of as one side of a right-angled triangle. To find its length we need to find the length of the other two sides. If the co-ordinates of A are x_1, y_1 and of B x_2, y_2, then the side AC of the triangle is $(x_2 - x_1)$; likewise the side BC is $(y_2 - y_1)$. Now we can make use of Pythagoras' theorem (in a right-angled triangle the longest side squared equals the sum of the squares of the other two sides). We know that $(side\ AB)^2 = (side\ AC)^2 + (side\ BC)^2$ or $(side\ AB)^2 = (x_2 - x_1)^2 + (y_2 - y_1)^2$. This gives us the distance AB because we know x_1, x_2, y_1 and y_2.

If you find using x_1, x_2, etc. difficult, just put in numbers. Use figure 2, where we have A's co-ordinates as 2, 1 and B's co-ordinates as 5,5. Then we have $(AB)^2 = (5 - 2)^2 + (5 - 1)^2 = 9 + 16 = 25$. So $AB = \sqrt{25} = 5$.

But whichever way you express it, the upshot is that mathematics allows us to calculate relationships in space; in this case the distance between two points. Here in two-dimensional space we have assumed Pythagoras' theorem can be applied, but all space may not be so simple. If it is not, then the distance between A and B would be different from what we have just calculated, though the principle of using co-ordinates and computing distances would be very similar. When they consider things on the largest scale, astronomers think that space is of such a kind that Pythagoras' theorem does not apply, for reasons which will become clear a little later.

THE SPACE OF EVERYDAY EXPERIENCE

From our everyday experience we feel that we understand space intuitively. But space is more varied than most people imagine, and can cause some strange effects.

What is space? One dictionary definition is 'the interval between two or more points or objects'. Another tells us that it is 'a boundless three-dimensional extent in which objects and events occur and have relative position and direction'.

We are familiar with three-dimensional space – the world around us lies in such a space – so what can we find out about the distance between two points? We calculated this distance on the previous page, but in that case our two points were restricted to a plane, which is a two-dimensional surface. What we now have to do is to extend our calculations to include a third dimension. This is not a difficult task.

In figure 2, the points A and B lie in a three-dimensional space, represented here by a cube. To calculate the distance between them, look first at the larger cube. Here the co-ordinates are given as numbers. A's co-ordinates are (2,1,0) and those of B (5,5,3). Considering first the distance between A and B' (which is the position of B projected down on to the base of the cube); this is 5 units. (We have already calculated this, see page 41). Now, using Pythagoras' theorem again, (the distance AB)^2 = (the distance AB')^2 + (the distance BB')^2 = $5^2 + 3^2 = 25 + 9 = 34$. Therefore the distance AB = $\sqrt{34}$ = 5.83

The smaller cube, figure 1, shows the same situation, but uses general terms instead of definite number values. Here the co-ordinates of A are (x_1, y_1, z_1) – the fact that $z_1 = 0$ does not affect the issue – and those of B are (x_2, y_2, z_2). So whereas on the plane the (distance AB)^2 = $(x_2 - x_1)^2 + (y_2 - y_1)^2$, now for three dimensions the (distance AB)^2 = $(x_2 - x_1)^2 + (y_2 - y_1)^2 + (z_2 - z_1)^2$. If we had four dimensions or even more, we could express them all quite simply by a similar technique, though we

could not draw a picture of the situation. If the surface were curved in some strange way we could still express the relationships, though we should have to multiply the terms in brackets – the $(x_2 - x_1)^2$, $(y_2 - y_1)^2$ etc. – by a number of some kind, known as a 'coefficient'. In general terms, then, we should have (AB)^2 = $a(x_2 - $

$x_1)^2 + b(y_2 - y_1)^2 + c(z_2 - z_1)^2$ where a, b and c are the coefficients.

The mathematicians' way of describing distances shows clearly the type of space in which bodies lie. Mathematicians can also help sort out all kinds of strange effects of which we must be aware if we are to interpret correctly our observations of

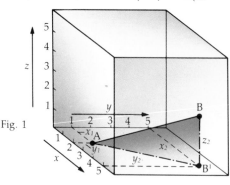

Fig. 1

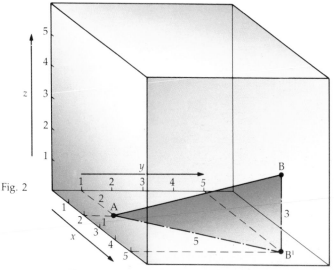

Fig. 2

above
Principles of perspective as depicted by the great German artist Albrecht Dürer (1471–1528).

left
The co-ordinates of a body in ordinary three-dimensional space. See text.

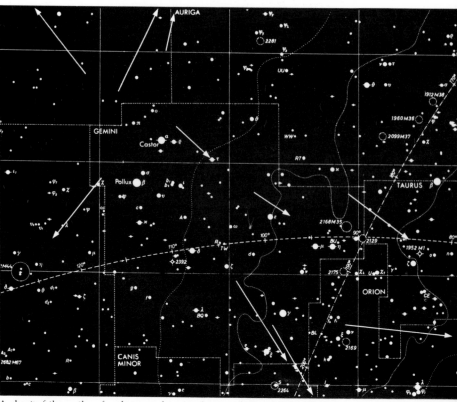

A chart of the paths of meteors during a shower, showing how they appear to radiate from a point. Key to chart on page 40.

the universe. Take the simple question of perspective, for instance. If we see a person in the distance we cannot tell how tall he is unless there is something nearby with which to compare him. We know a vehicle is far off if it appears small because we are familiar with its real size. But we cannot apply the same comparison to objects in space. This is where observers of UFOs have often come to grief. They observe a bright stationary light in the sky and think it is quite close to the Earth. Yet on a number of occasions it has proved to be the planet Venus which can, at times, be the brightest object in the night sky.

Perspective has another strange effect. If you stand on a bridge over a motorway the road dwindles to a point in the very far distance. Such an effect of a 'vanishing point' is visible at night during a meteor shower. Such showers occur when the Earth passes through a stream of meteors which are in orbit round the Sun. Then thousands of meteors stream through the atmosphere and become visible as bright streaks. We see them against the starry background and notice that they seem to be coming towards us, all originating from the same point or radiant. Yet they are not really radiating from a single point, but they are travelling along parallel lines like the edges of a road, and only appear to radiate outwards as they move closer to us before burning out some 80 km above the ground. If we were not aware of this effect of perspective it would be easy to be misled by meteor paths.

Another effect of perspective is one which has proved of great use to astronomers in determining the motion of the Sun in space. The principle involved is similar to that experienced when we travel along a straight road. As we drive, we see that distant objects straight ahead seem to be coming towards us before spreading out and passing by on our left or right. Looking round, we will see them receding into the background, moving towards one another until they meet at the vanishing point.

When we observe the stars over a period of years, we find that the nearer ones show a drift against the background of the more distant stars. The direction of such 'preferential motion' depends on where the stars are in the sky. We find that stars close to a point in the constellation Hercules appear to be moving towards us. Those to the left and right seem to move towards the side. In the opposite part of the sky, which lies in the southern hemisphere constellation Columba (The Dove), the stars appear to be moving towards a vanishing point. The explanation for all this is that the Sun and the whole Solar System is moving in space towards a point in Hercules called the Solar Apex (right ascension 18h, declination $+34°$) at a velocity of 19.5 km per second.

All these effects are obvious when we think about them, but there are other effects which are more subtle and which are concerned with the fact that the Earth's surface is curved and not flat.

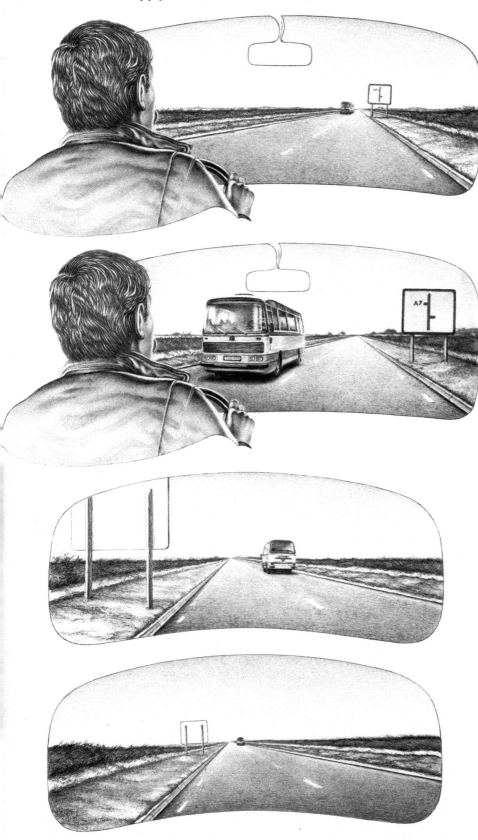

The apparent movement of approaching stars is similar to the situation experienced by a driver on the road. Oncoming traffic appears to originate from a point in front of him and to move to one side as it passes him by.

CURVED SURFACES

The curvature of the Earth's surface only becomes apparant over long distances. Over short distances, the curvature is not noticeable. The same principle applies to space.

Our intuitive ideas of space are that it is three-dimensional, just as a cube is. Its geometry is that of the Greek philosopher, Euclid (who lived in the third century BC); it is a geometry of flat surfaces. We are so accustomed to thinking in these terms that we can imagine what a shock it must have been to discover the Earth itself is not flat but a globe.

Yet space photographs show us the Earth is a globe, and we can see its curvature for ourselves. If we sit on a beach and look out to sea, the horizon looks completely flat; where sky meets sea the boundary is a straight line, or so it seems. Yet if you watch a ship sailing over the horizon it appears to sink into the sea. With a pair of binoculars you can watch first its hull, then its superstructure, sink below the horizon until only its funnels remain. This is caused by the fact that the Earth's surface is curved.

How flat the Earth seems to be is revealed by what happened when the first very long baseline radio interferometer telescope (5 km in length) was being built at the Mullard Radio Astronomy Observatory at Cambridge University. The telescope consisted of a number of dishes, all but one of which could move along a railway track. When the surveyors came to lay out the track, they did as they were accustomed to do for a level track, and laid it along the seemingly level ground. But the Earth's surface is curved, and for probing into space the radio astronomers wanted a truly straight track. So to achieve this the track had to slope and be lifted off the ground at the far end.

A curved surface is certainly

different from a flat one, as becomes very clear if we imagine the routes of two aircraft travelling in the same direction. Suppose they both set out from different airports on the equator, both travelling due north. Because the equator runs east-west and the aircraft are going due north, their courses both make an angle of 90° with the equator and should be parallel. However, if the aircraft follow their courses due north indefinitely, they will eventually arrive at the north pole; indeed, if they do not stop, they will end up crashing into one another! Yet their courses should never meet, and nor do they on a flat surface. The reason they do in this instance is because the Earth is curved and therefore the aircraft are travelling on

above A photograph taken from the orbiting spacecraft Gemini 7 showing that the Earth really is curved.

above
Flat and curved surfaces on the Earth. Tracks of a railway curve round the Earth; only those of a radio interferometer telescope are truly straight. (*Not* to scale).

left
Some of the moveable dishes of the 5-km radio interferometer telescope at Cambridge University.

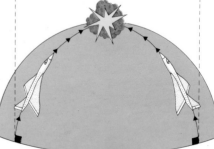

a curved surface. On the Earth, which seems so large to us, the curves appear very gentle. They seem to be straight when taken in small sections, but this straightness is in fact an illusion.

There is a sure way of deciding whether we live on a flat or a curved surface and that is to use geometry as our guide. Suppose we draw a triangle on a sheet of paper. Euclidean geometry tells us that the three inside angles, one at each corner, add up to 180°. But now draw a triangle on a curved surface like a ball. Draw an equator first, going right round the centre of the ball, dividing it in two. Now choose two points on this equator, some distance apart. Draw a line vertically upwards from the equator to the

'north pole' of the ball from one of these points; next draw a line vertically upwards to the 'pole' from the second point. You will now have a large triangle on the ball. The angles of this triangle will add up to more than 180°. They are certain to do so, because the two angles at the bottom – the ones at the equator – are each 90°.

There is another way of demonstrating this phenomenon. Suppose we found a steep rounded hill and drew a large triangle on it, using tape to mark out lines as straight as possible. (To make the demonstration work successfully we need a really large triangle.) Now if the angles at each of the corners of the triangle are measured with a pair of dividers, it becomes very obvious

that they add up to more than 180°. Clearly the 'straight' sides were really curves. But now add another piece of tape close to one of the angles, so that there is a smaller triangle at one corner. The sides of this triangle really are fairly straight and a measurement of its angles will show that these add up to 180° or very close to it. Although this demonstration may sound a little far-fetched, it has been done (and even filmed), showing how a small area may appear flat whereas a large area shows definite curvature.

The sides of a spherical triangle are curved; the sides of a Euclidean triangle are straight. The curved sides of the triangles we have been considering bulge outwards, giving us internal angles equal to more than 180°. But there are other curved triangles such as those drawn on a concave surface, where the sides curve inwards, and the internal angles add up to less than 180°.

As we have seen various curved surfaces can be recognized on the Earth by working out their geometry over a large area. However, in their exploration of deep space, mathematicians have to consider all kinds of curved surfaces and then extend these ideas to curved spaces. The mathematics used, which is known as tensor calculus, becomes rather complicated, but when it is applied to the universe as relativity theory (page 132) sees it, the whole picture appears much clearer.

above
The curvature of the Earth makes a ship appear to sink as it goes below the horizon.

right
A demonstration of the geometry of a curved surface and how a small part of it can appear flat.

left
'Great Circle' routes over the curved surface of the Earth.

below left
Two aircraft setting out due north from the equator on what appear to be, and are in two dimensions, parallel courses, will, because their flight-paths are curved, meet at the north pole. The two aircraft will collide at the Pole because they are travelling over a curved surface.

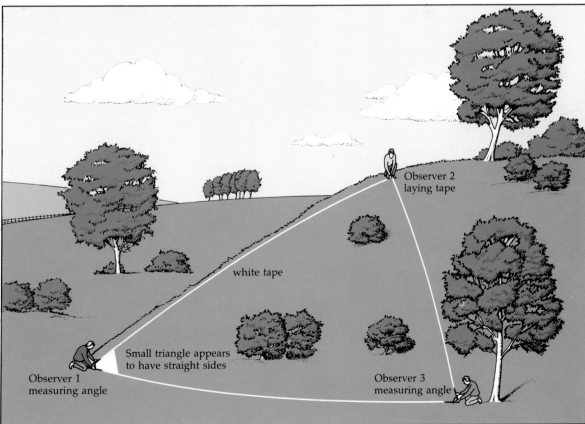

Observer 2 laying tape

white tape

Small triangle appears to have straight sides

Observer 1 measuring angle

Observer 3 measuring angle

THE CURVATURE OF SPACE

Some curved surfaces are very strange. By studying them, however, we can come close to discovering the true nature of curved space.

When you think of a curved surface you probably think of a ball or, more technically, of a sphere. This has certain properties. By measuring its diameter we can find its volume. For instance, the Sun has a volume great enough to contain 1.3 million Earths packed together. A sphere also has a definite surface area. The surface area of the Earth is 5×10^8 square kilometres, while that of the Sun is 6×10^{12} square kilometres. However, Betelgeuse has a surface area of some 8×10^{25} square kilometres, which is huge by any standards and is the reason it is so bright – there is so much of it to shine. Another property of a sphere is that its surface, though limited in area, has no edge. Mathematicians say that it is finite but unbounded.

Not all curved surfaces are like the sphere. Suppose, for instance, we take a cylinder, which can easily be made by wrapping a sheet of paper round a straight-sided bottle (figure 1). If you make a cylinder in this way, the first thing you can be sure of is that it has a definite surface area; this is equal to the area of the piece of paper used. But unlike a sphere, you cannot travel endlessly on it in every direction; at some time or another you are bound to come up against the upper or lower edge of the paper.

The cylinder and the sphere can be described in terms of Euclid's geometry but they can also be described by other geometries devised by mathematicians during the last 150 years. The problem for astronomers is to find which geometry really describes space. In order to get some kind of answer to this question, we shall first glance at three other surfaces. The first is a very simple one, the torus or ring doughnut (figure 2). This is made by taking a cylinder and bending it in a circle until the ends meet. This creates a surface which is finite but unbounded; in this it is more like the sphere than the cylinder from which it was made.

The next is a surface devised by the nineteenth-century astronomer and mathematician August Möbius. It seems very simple, for it is just a strip or band twisted over once before the ends are joined. (If it were not twisted over it would just form a rather short cylinder.) This 'Möbius strip' exists in three dimensions but, astonishingly, has only one surface. You can prove this for yourself by taking a strip of paper (½ metre long will do), twisting it over and joining the ends (figure 3). Now take a felt pen and trace a line on the strip without letting your pen leave the surface. When you are half way round you will find that you are writing on the back of the paper, though you are still on the same surface. If you continue you will find that you end up where you started.

The third surface is very strange and usually goes by the name of the Klein bottle (figure 4); its discoverer was another nineteenth century mathematician, Felix Klein. As you can see from the illustration, it also folds over on to itself. Like the

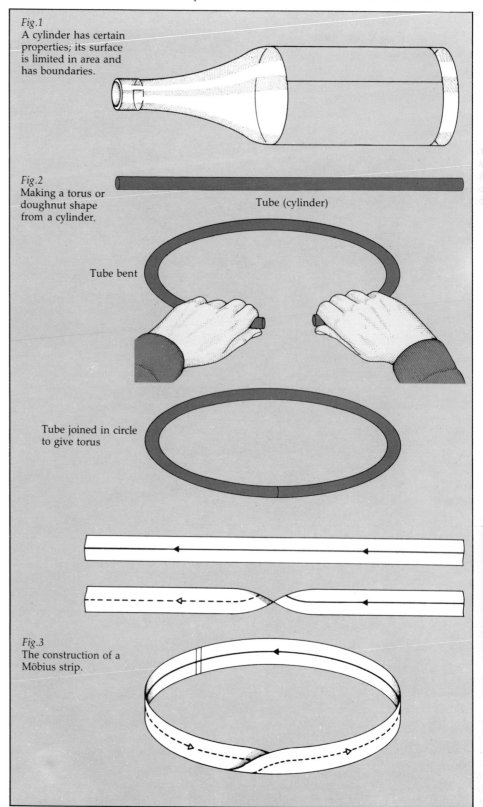

Fig.1
A cylinder has certain properties; its surface is limited in area and has boundaries.

Fig.2
Making a torus or doughnut shape from a cylinder.

Tube (cylinder)

Tube bent

Tube joined in circle to give torus

Fig.3
The construction of a Möbius strip.

Möbius strip, it has only one surface; the outside of the bottle is also the inside! Indeed, the Klein bottle has no separate inside as does the sphere or the torus, the two other figures we have met which have unbounded surfaces. Yet the Klein bottle is derived from a cylinder which is joined end to end but is partly turned inside out before the ends are allowed to meet.

The Klein bottle is something quite new in the way of surfaces, for while a Möbius strip, a torus, as well as a sphere and a cylinder can all be expressed mathematically in terms of Euclid's geometry, a Klein bottle cannot. The result of this is that you cannot actually make a Klein bottle from a cylinder because you would need to make twists in something more complex than three-dimensional Euclidean space. With a Klein bottle we enter the rich new field of what are called Riemannian spaces, because to describe them we must use a geometry devised by the mathematician Bernhard Riemann.

Riemannian geometry is too complex to describe here, but it gives a wider variety of spaces than Euclid's geometry can ever do. In fact we can look on Euclid's geometry as a special restricted case of Riemannian geometry. But Riemannian geometry is not just a mathematical fiction; it is used in relativity theory and helps to explain many things – gravitation is one – better than ever before. This is why astronomers use a curved Riemannian space because it allows them to have varying curvature and to increase the curvature close to a massive body. Thus they get the effect we call gravitation. We can see the kind of thing if we stretch a rubber sheet over a frame. If a weight is put in the centre, the sheet will sag, partly closing round the heavy body. Riemannian space curves round bodies in this way and gives rise to what we call gravity. Suppose you roll a ball along the sheet. If there was no weight in the middle, the ball would just run straight across the sheet. However, because of the distortion, the marble will veer towards the weight, and if it is not moving fast enough it will fall into the dip and end up next to the weight. This is just the effect we should expect from gravity. But, of course, this is only a simple demonstration of a more complex curvature – after all, we have only taken a two-dimensional sheet whereas we ought to have taken a three-dimensional space.

Incomplete though the demonstration may be, it nevertheless underlines the belief held by astronomers that the whole universe must be curved because of the vast amount of matter that it contains. They also believe that the amount of curvature varies from place to place, depending on where material is concentrated and in what amounts.

So the conclusion is that we live in a curved Riemannian space, which is finite but unbounded. This space is intimately linked with a fourth dimension – time. We must remember this as we continue our journey through deep space, though we shall not always have reason to refer to it, any more than we usually refer to the curvature of the Earth when we describe a journey we have taken. However there will be times when curved Riemannian space will be evident; we shall, for instance, see it in action in black holes (page 82) if not before, and making itself very evident in relativity (page 132).

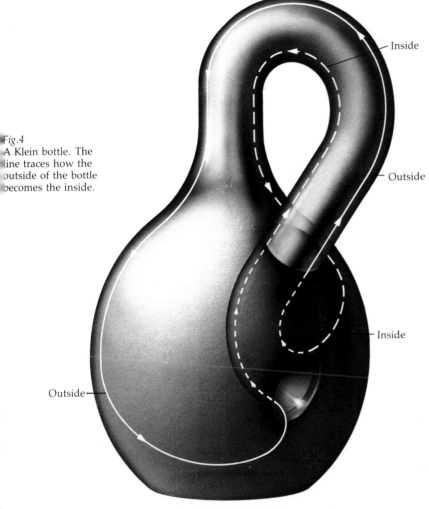

Fig.4
A Klein bottle. The line traces how the outside of the bottle becomes the inside.

Inside

Outside

Inside

Outside

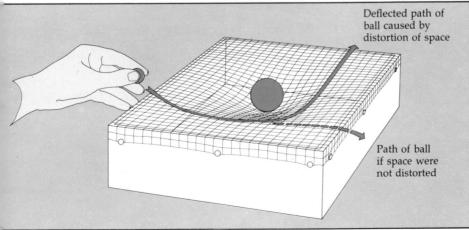

Deflected path of ball caused by distortion of space

Path of ball if space were not distorted

A stretched rubber sheet, which can be gently curved to represent curved space, becomes more curved by the presence of a weight. This is similar to the way a massive body is thought to distort space by its presence. This curvature affects other bodies nearby and gives rise to effects we say are due to gravity.

HOW FAR DOES THE SOLAR SYSTEM EXTEND?

Where are the outermost limits of the Solar System? The irregularity of the orbits of Uranus and Neptune suggests that there could be another massive planet beyond small, cold Pluto.

Space is curved when taken on the large scale. But to a traveller in a spacecraft any journey will seem to be in a straight line, just as a ship's navigator will set himself what appears to be a straight course. So for the present we shall not worry about curvature – though we shall come back to it later (page 82) – but see what a journey to the edge of the Solar System will reveal.

All but one of the outer planets of the Solar System are vast gaseous bodies. Each probably has a comparatively small core of icy rocks, which is surrounded by a shell of hydrogen so compressed that it behaves as if it were a metal. Outside this shell is a very thick atmosphere, rich in hydrogen and helium. This kind of composition covers Jupiter, Saturn, Uranus and Neptune, but Pluto, the outermost known planet, seems to be different. It is much smaller – not more than a thirty-seventh the size of Jupiter – and seems to be a small, cold, solid world. Indeed Pluto is something of a mystery.

In 1781 on March 13, the amateur astronomer William Herschel, observing from Bath in the West of England, discovered the planet Uranus. This was the first planet to be discovered in historical times because all the other known planets – Mercury, Venus, Mars, Jupiter and Saturn – had been recognized since before the dawn of history. It aroused great interest, but over the next fifty years it became evident that Uranus did not orbit the Sun in quite the way anticipated if Newton's theory of gravitation and planetary motion were correct. The only satisfactory explanation seemed to be that there was another planet, further away, that was pulling Uranus slightly out of its orbit. Two astronomers, John Couch Adams in England and Urbain John Joseph Leverrier in France made independent mathematical analyses which led them both to suggest the probable position of such a planet and in 1846 on September 23 Neptune was discovered. All this is well-known, but what is not so often realized is that while both men gave approximately correct positions, these were not exact. Their calculated orbits lay beyond the time orbit of Neptune. Moreover, they were both wrong in their calculations of the mass of the new planet.

As the years passed, Neptune too was found to have an irregular orbit and again attempts were made to find a planet which caused this effect. In the early 1900s the American astronomer, Percival Lowell, founder of the Lowell Observatory, Flagstaff, Arizona, made calculations to try to locate another more distant planet. His calculations were not as precise as those of Adams and Leverrier for Neptune, and he obtained two possible locations for his unknown planet. Then on February 18, 1930 Clyde Tombaugh, a young astronomer at the Lowell Observatory, discovered the image of a new planet on a pair of photographs taken a few weeks before, and many astronomers assumed that it was this body that was perturbing Neptune. It was given the name of Pluto. Yet it now

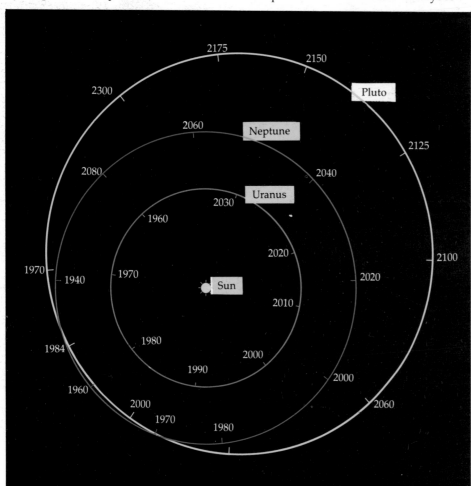

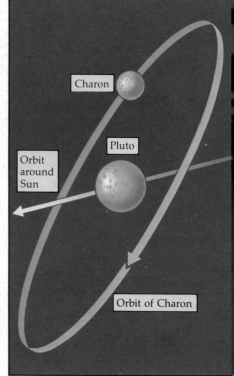

left
The orbits of the outer planets. The dates show their positions at different times. Pluto's orbit is so eccentric that, for a time, it lies inside that of Neptune.

above
A diagram of what seems to be the most likely orbit of Pluto's satellite Charon. This satellite orbit is almost at right angles to the orbit of Pluto itself.

seems that it is not the planet whose position had been calculated by Percival Lowell. Pluto is close to one of the possible locations at an average distance of 5,899 million km from the Sun, yet there are discrepancies. Pluto takes 247.7 years to orbit the Sun; Lowell's calculations gave 282 years. Again, Pluto is very small, and nowhere near massive enough to cause the perturbations or disturbances observed in the motions of Neptune and Uranus.

Recent studies of Pluto have revealed two facts. First, it has a satellite. The existence of this satellite was discovered in 1978 in America by James Christy; it has been named Charon and astronomers can now obtain a more precise value for Pluto's mass by examining Charon's orbit. It turns out that Pluto has a mass at least 7 times less than our Moon and this confirms that, even with Charon, it cannot be the disturbing force for which astronomers have hunted. Secondly, Pluto seems to be very like some of the larger satellites of Jupiter, Saturn or Neptune, and not very different either from some of those small planet-like fragments or 'asteroids' which mainly orbit the Sun between Mars and Jupiter. Indeed, one astronomer has recently suggested that Pluto is a misplaced asteroid,

quoting the fact that one such body (confusingly named Chiron) is already known to orbit between Saturn and Uranus.

As we travel out in space beyond Saturn and Uranus we shall come to Neptune and Pluto. Which we arrive at first will depend where the planets are in their orbits, for in part of its orbit round the Sun, Pluto comes closer in than Neptune. But we should have no difficulty in

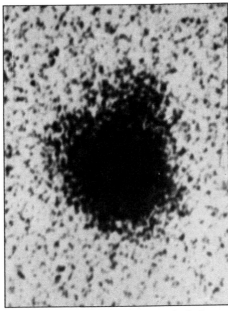

above A photograph of Pluto enlarged by more than 100 times.

Charon is the bulge on the top right-hand part of the white area.

recognizing which is which. Neptune is a large cloud-covered body, 48,400 km in diameter, and orbited by two satellites, one of which is at least as large as Pluto. When we have passed them, what should we find beyond? Many astronomers believe we might, after journeying for hundreds of millions more kilometres, come across another giant gaseous planet. Certainly some large body is needed to account for the perturbed orbits of Neptune and Uranus, for Pluto will not do. But the further out it lies, the larger it will have to be in order to cause those effects. Percival Lowell's calculations for his unknown planet gave an average distance of 6,450 million km from the Sun, while calculations by another American astronomer, William H. Pickering gave 8,250 million km. So if we watch out between these two distances we might come across it, provided, of course, that we are travelling in the direction where the unknown planet might be expected to be. (That direction could be determined from a study of the perturbations of Uranus and Neptune.) Yet although we should then be nearly twice as far off as Neptune from the Sun, we should still not have arrived at the edge of the Solar System. We should have to continue even further for that.

The discovery of Pluto. These two photographs, taken in 1930 – the first (*above left*) on January 23 and the second (*above right*) on January 29 – are sections of the plates taken by Clyde Tombaugh at the Lowell Observatory. The arrows indicate Pluto, recognized because it has moved against the background stars.

THE DISTANT PATHS OF COMETS

It is possible that there is a vast spherical shell of cold dust, ice and frozen gas surrounding the whole Solar System. This material could be the origin of all comets.

Comets which can be seen without a telescope are rare, and of these only a few appear really bright. But when such a comet does appear, it is an unforgettable sight. Its bright fuzzy head is remarkable enough, but it is the glowing tail stretching across the sky for many degrees that is astonishing. Little wonder that, in ancient times, the appearance of a comet alarmed people, for such a rare and spectacular visitor from space was often thought to be a portent of disaster.

We know that comets are probably collections of icy materials and dust orbiting round the Sun, and some at least contain enough material to hold these conglomerations together in the form of what has sometimes been called a 'dirty snowball'. When they come reasonably close to the Sun – a distance something like that of the planet Mars – some gases are driven off. These are mainly water vapour, carbon and cyanogen; they are set glowing and we see the fuzzy comet begin to take shape. Molecules of carbon dioxide and dust are also emitted as the comet moves closer to the Sun. These help form a halo of

ice and dust round the head, or coma, while the Sun's energy actually drives off dust back into space, forming the tail. Some gas molecules become electrified too; they also get carried away in the stream of atomic particles that are continually emitted by the Sun – the so-called 'solar wind' (page 70) – to form a second tail. Sometimes these tails can be seen separately.

Every time a comet comes close to the Sun, a little of its material is lost to form the tails, but this is not all that happens. Gravitational effects of the Sun and the planets cause some of the material to be distributed around the comet's orbit. We know this because when the Earth passes through such an orbit, we get a shower of meteors as the cometary

dust drops into the Earth's atmosphere.

Some comets return time and again. The most famous is Halley's Comet, recorded appearances of which date back certainly to the third century BC and possibly as early as the fifth. It reappears once every 76 years. But Halley's is only one of a host of what are called 'short-period' comets. These are comets whose periods of return are less than 200 years, and whose orbits are inclined at not too steep an angle to the orbits of the planets (which all lie in almost the same plane). Short-period comets move close to the Sun at one end of their elongated elliptical orbits, but at the other end, at aphelion (Greek for 'far from the Sun'), they mostly go out to distances beyond Jupiter's

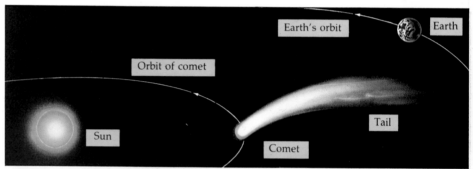

Earth's orbit | Earth | Orbit of comet | Sun | Tail | Comet

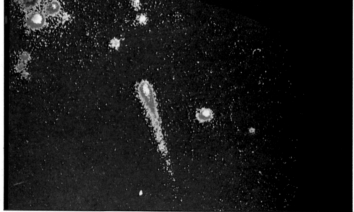

above
A cometary tail always points away from the Sun.

left
Comet Kohoutek photographed from Skylab. The false colour indicates intensity of radiation from gases associated with the comet.

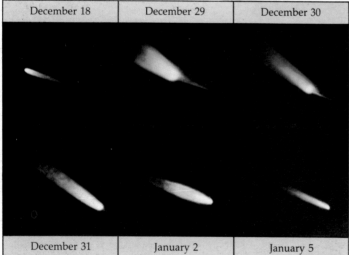

| December 18 | December 29 | December 30 |
| December 31 | January 2 | January 5 |

These drawings of comet Kohoutek were made by astronauts aboard Skylab in 1973/74. Some show a spike pointing towards the Sun; this is an optical illusion due to the position of the observer because both tail and spike are really pointing away from the Sun.

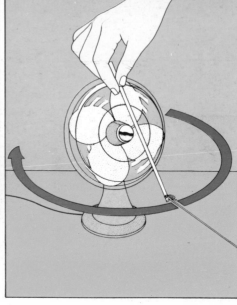

left
A diagram to show why a comet's tail always points away from the Sun irrespective of the direction in which the comet is moving. Here a piece of string tied to a stick represents the comet (the knot is the comet's head, the rest of the string is its tail). The electric fan represents the Sun. As the stick is moved round the fan, the string will always point away from the fan. Here the fan is blowing air but the solar wind (page 74) acts in the same way.

orbit. There are a few, however, whose aphelion points do not lie quite as far away as this; they are close to Jupiter's orbit.

The association of short-period comets with Jupiter is not really surprising. Jupiter is by far the most massive of the planets – it is almost 318 times more massive than the Earth and well over three times as massive as Saturn, the next largest planet – and its effects on any comet which comes close are immense. Indeed, astronomers now believe that all the short-period comets once had long periods and were pulled into short-period orbits by Jupiter.

Most comets have long periods and their aphelion points lie far out in space, well beyond the orbit of Pluto. Their orbits are often steeply inclined to the plane in which the planets orbit the Sun, but all the ones we know – and these amount to some 500 – have closed orbits; that is to say they will periodically return to pass close to the Sun, though their periods may exceed a thousand years or more. (The short-period comets only number some 100.) The trouble with long-period comets – and indeed with short-period ones as well – is that we cannot see them when they are more than a few 100 million kilometres away. The only observation astronomers can make is to use radio telescopes to detect cometary dust along a comet's orbit, but this cannot be followed all the way out to aphelion. The distant paths of comets have to be worked out mathematically from their infrequent close approaches to the Sun, when they glow and emit tails. Only then can they be observed in detail.

Where do comets come from? They are certainly very light-weight objects; the material of which even a large comet is composed only amounts to about one ten thousandth the mass of the Moon. Yet even so, how did this material come together? Most astronomers now think that they formed from some of the original material, some of the dust and gas, which formed the Sun and the rest of the Solar System. They are thus very old, since it is believed that the Solar System was formed four to five thousand million (10^9) years ago. Their material, and such meteoritic material as falls to Earth, is obviously of great interest to astronomers.

As we have seen (page 13), it has been suggested that the whole Solar System is still surrounded by a spherical shell of cometary material. When disturbed, perhaps by a passing star, some of this primeval material will fall into orbit around the Sun; in this way we get our long-period comets, some of which, if they come too close to Jupiter, will be transformed into short-period comets. So if we travelled out to the distant paths of comets, out beyond their aphelion points, we should come upon a vast shell of cold dust, ice and frozen gas. Dark, uninviting, yet the possible material of which spectacular comets are made. This shell would lie at a distance between $1^1/_2$ and 15 million million kilometres away, so far that travelling with the speed of light it would take up to $1^1/_2$ years to reach it. Here at the dark edge of deep space, we should at last have reached the boundary of the Solar System.

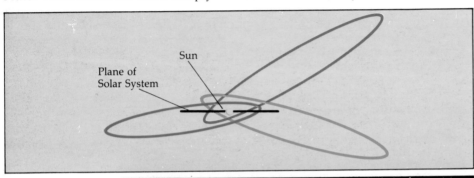

above
Some comets' orbits lie out of the plane of the Solar System, which is where the planetary orbits lie.

right
Comet Humason photographed in 1962 with the Schmidt telescope at Palomar in California. Note the unusual gaseous tail. This never developed to a large size because the comet never approached the Sun, even as close as the orbit of Mars.

above An impression of what a cometary nucleus might be like, when reasonably close to the Sun—a 'dirty snowball' of ice, frozen gases and other material. Some of the gas and other easily vaporizing material is shown being boiled away.

51

INTO INTERSTELLAR SPACE

Once outside the Solar System we find ourselves in interstellar space. The distances to even the nearest stars are vast, and the stars themselves are separated by great volumes of emptiness.

Once we have left the Solar System, and moved away from the aphelion points of the long-period comets and from the huge spherical shell of cometary material, we find ourselves in empty space. Between the Solar System and the nearest stars lies an immense void. Even at the speed of light three more years will pass before we reach the next nearest star to the Sun. This is α Centauri, a multiple system of three stars orbiting around each other. To Earth-bound observers this system lies at a declination of -61° or less than 40° from the south celestial pole. Centaurus A, the brightest of the three stars, has the same spectral class as our Sun, though it is 1½ times brighter – its absolute magnitude, M, is 4.35 compared with our Sun's 4.79. Of its two companions, Centaurus B is redder and almost 3½ times dimmer, while the other, Centaurus C, is much redder still and 1½ million times less bright than Centaurus A. Centaurus C is sometimes called Proxima Centauri because it comes the closest to us of the three. The distance for the α Centauri system is 1.34 parsecs, so light from it takes over four years to reach us.

The other stars of the Centaurus constellation are nowhere near the α Centauri system. For example, the next brightest star in the constellation, β Centauri (which we see in the sky only about half a degree further north in declination and about 36 minutes in time further west in right ascension) seems to be fairly close in the sky, but is in fact 149 parsecs further away. Thus, instead of its light taking a mere 4.3 years to reach us, it takes 490 years. Other bright stars in Centaurus are likewise very distant; γ Centauri lies at a distance of 49 parsecs and δ Centauri 113.5 parsecs. This emphasizes the fact that the stars in a constellation are a purely chance optical arrangement seen

from Earth. They are not physically connected in any way, thus removing any possible scientific basis for astrology which, of course, sets great store by the constellations.

Apart from the α Centauri system, the next nearest star lies some 45° eastwards, with a declination about 65° further north, thus putting it in the constellation of Ophiuchus, the Serpent Bearer. The star is generally known as Barnard's star because it was discovered in 1916 by the American astronomer Edward Emerson Barnard. A telescope is needed to see it from Earth, for although it is only 1.8 parsecs (5.9 light-years) away, its apparent magnitude is only 9.5, or 25 times less bright than the dimmest star detectable with the unaided eye. Though a single dim red star, with an absolute magnitude of 13.25, it is of interest because it may possess its own planetary system (see page 184).

Turning westwards a little more than 103° and moving north in declination 31½° we find ourselves moving outwards another 0.68 parsecs towards the star Lalande 21185 in the constellation of Ursa Major. Named after the eighteenth century French astronomer Joseph Lalande, this is another red star that can only be observed through a telescope, though it is some 12½ times brighter than Barnard's star. But of all the nearby stars by far and away the brightest is Sirius or α Canis Majoris. When observed from

above The star cluster Praesepe in Cancer can just be seen unaided as a hazy patch.

Proxima Centauri, (*left*) is the closest star to the four light-years away, Earth except for the Sun.

the Earth it outshines any other star, appearing as a brilliant object, magnitude – 1.5, down in a south eastern direction from the star κ Orionis which marks the 'left foot' of Orion.

Sirius is a hot blue-white star with an absolute magnitude of +1.4, making it more than 23 times brighter than the Sun. But Sirius is not a single star; it is part of a binary system. Its companion, Sirius B, is a dense white dwarf star, that is, a star which has collapsed and shrunk, and is approaching the very end of its life (page 78). As a result, it has an absolute magnitude of only 11.56. Sirius and its companion lie at a distance of 2.6 parsecs or half a light-year further away than Lalande 21185 (though in quite another direction). Sirius A and Sirius B are separated only by 11.5 arc seconds – and the star can only be seen as a binary through a telescope. Indeed, it is not easy to see the two objects separately even then, because Sirius A is more than 11,000 times brighter than Sirius B and its glare tends to swamp the dimmer star's light.

These stars are not the only ones near to us in space. If we travel within a radius of five parsecs (16 light-years) of the Sun we shall find there are 35 others. Of these nine are multiple star systems – one triple star (40 Eridani) and eight double or binary stars – and almost all of them are cool dim red stars. The exception is the yellow star τ Ceti, which is rather like our Sun in colour, though it only shines with about half the brightness. As it lies at a distance of 3.6 parsecs (11.7 light-years), it only appears in the sky as a star of magnitude of 3.5.

These remaining stars are not all scattered at random over the sky, however, for 13 of them, or over one third of the total, lie in or near the Milky Way. Perhaps we should expect this because, as even a small telescope shows, the Milky Way is made up of myriads of separate stars. The concentration of stars, even dim ones, in this direction indicates that there is one part of the sky in which more stars are likely to be found. The nearby stars clearly show this preference, for the remaining ones are spread over a very large area – the rest of the entire sky – whereas the Milky Way only occupies about one fiftieth of the visible area of the night sky.

What all this tells us is that there is an uneven distribution of stars, but as we shall now see this is because they are all part of our Galaxy.

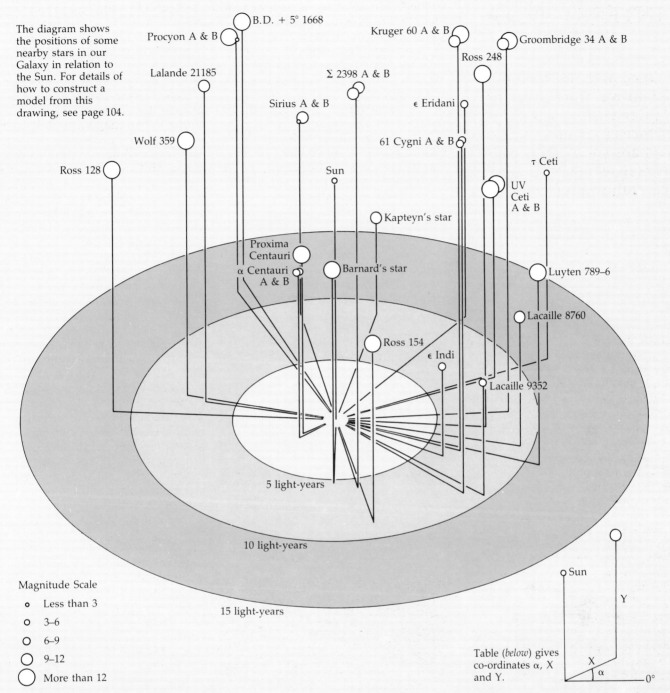

The diagram shows the positions of some nearby stars in our Galaxy in relation to the Sun. For details of how to construct a model from this drawing, see page 104.

Magnitude Scale
- Less than 3
- 3–6
- 6–9
- 9–12
- More than 12

Table (*below*) gives co-ordinates α, X and Y.

POSITIONS OF 24 NEARBY STARS

Name	α	X	Y	Magnitude	Name	α	X	Y	Magnitude
Sun	0	0	15	4.8	Proxima Centauri	216	2.0	11.2	15.1
Groombridge 34 A & B*	4	8.4	23	10.3 & 13.3	α Centauri A & B	219	2.1	11.3	4.4 & 5.8
UV Ceti A & B*	24	8.5	12	15.3 & 15.8	Barnard's star	269	5.2	15.4	13.2
τ Ceti	25	11.4	11.7	5.7	Σ 2398 A & B	281	5.8	24.9	11.1 & 11.9
ε Eridani	53	10.5	13.2	6.1	Ross 154	282	8.7	11.2	13.3
Kapteyn's star	77	9.0	6.0	10.8	61 Cygni A & B	316	8.8	22	7.5 & 8.4
Sirius A & B	101	8.3	12.5	1.4 & 11.6	Lacaille 8760	319	9.7	7.1	8.8
B.D. +5° 1668	111	12.2	16.2	13.0	ε Indi	330	6.1	5.6	7.0
Procyon A & B	114	11.4	16.1	2.6 & 13.1	Kruger 60 A & B	337	6.9	25.8	11.9 & 13.3
Wolf 359	164	7.5	16.0	16.7	Luyten 789–6	339	10.4	12.1	14.6
Lalande 21185	166	6.5	19.8	10.5	Lacaille 9352	346	9.4	8.1	9.6
Ross 128	176	10.8	15.2	13.5	Ross 248	355	7.4	22.1	14.7

*Pair

CHAPTER 4
EXPLORING OUR GALAXY

Looking at the night sky, we see that the stars are not evenly distributed. Most lie in the hazy area of the Milky Way. This is because our Sun and the other stars are part of a star island or galaxy.

The Milky Way is composed of myriads of stars, and the majority of them seem to lie in a plane, or at least a narrow band of the sky varying between 40° and 10° across. If you look at the sky for yourself, even without the benefit of a pair of binoculars, you will see that parts of the Milky Way seem to be missing; there is a great rift running across the northern constellations of Cygnus, Vulpecula, Serpens and Scorpius, and another in the southern hemisphere in Vela and Puppis. It appears as though great numbers of stars are missing. However recent research has shown otherwise.

Using up-to-date telescopes of large aperture and spectroscopes to analyse the starlight received, as well as gamma-ray, X-ray, infrared, and radio telescopes, a far more complete picture of the Milky Way has been built up. All the new techniques supplement the optical telescope; observations at X- and gamma-ray wavelengths make it possible to detect the high-energy events like the collapse of stars and other catastrophic phenomena in space. Infrared observations show up the actual birth of new stars, whilst radio waves can penetrate the dust and gas which blanket radiation at optical wavelengths. The result of all these observations over the entire wavelength range is that we are now quite sure that our Sun and almost all the stars we see when we glance up at the sky without a telescope are

above The star field in Sagittarius, seen here looking towards the centre of our Galaxy. The line is the path of an Earth satellite.

part of an immense island of dust, gas and stars – our Galaxy. Indeed, observations in the last few years have made it clear that it is even larger than previously thought.

Essentially our Galaxy is disc-shaped and contains well over 100,000 million stars. Our Sun is one of these, lying a good way from the centre of the Galaxy, present estimates giving the distance as 10,000 parsecs (about 33,000 light-years). Yet the Galaxy is not just a thin disc of stars with some dust and gas, it has a far more complex construction. The disc is simply what we see when we look at the Milky Way because the Earth itself lies within it (when we observe the other stars we are looking above or below the plane of the disc). In the central regions of the Galaxy – when observed from the Solar System, this lies in the constellation of Sagittarius – there is a large bulge of material, though parts of this are obscured by dust and gas.

Modern figures show that the Galaxy contains far more material than was once thought, much of this being dark gas which can only be detected by observing in radio and infrared wavelengths. There are other factors that have also influenced astronomers in coming to this conclusion; one of these is the velocity of the Sun as it orbits round

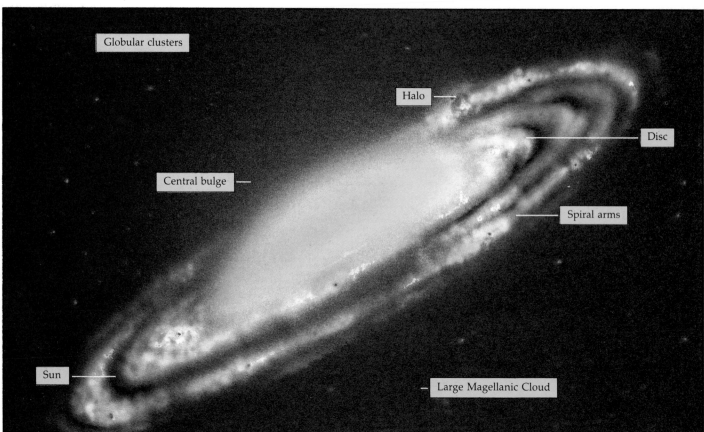

An artist's impression of what our Galaxy would look like if it were possible to observe it from far out in space. The evidence on which this picture is based is taken from observations not only of our own Galaxy but also of other galaxies of a similar type.

the centre of the Galaxy. Gravitation theory tells us that the velocity of any star in its orbit round the Galaxy's centre will depend both on its distance from that centre and on the Galaxy's total mass. The greater the mass, the faster a star at a given distance must move in order to avoid falling into the Galaxy's centre. More recent observations of and calculations about the motion of the Sun in space in relation to some of the more distant stars in its neighbourhood show that its velocity is 300 km per second and not about 250 km per second as previously thought. Astronomers think that a greater mass for the Galaxy is the most satisfactory explanation for this because it also fits in with very recent observations of hitherto unknown gas close to the Galaxy's centre.

To describe the Galaxy as astronomers now see it, using observations made at every available wavelength, it will be best if we start by considering the central bulge. This is shaped like a slightly squashed sphere. By measuring radiation intensity and the spectra from stars and other material, it is found to be very large, with a diameter of some 10,000 parsecs (about 33,000 light-years), while the boundary of this bulge is marked by some vast dark clouds of gas molecules, mainly of hydrogen. The bulge itself is

primarily made up of very old stars, fairly densely packed together inside it, and surrounded by dust and gas. This information has come mainly from infrared observations because old stars emit strongly in the infrared region of the spectrum.

Radio observations have made it clear that inside the bulge at a distance of 3,000 parsecs (10,000 light-years) from the centre, there is a ring of 'neutral' hydrogen (i.e. hydrogen which is not electrified or ionized and which only radio telescopes can detect). This ring is rotating and expanding, the gas moving outwards at a rate of between 50 and 150 km per second, thus pushing more gas into the Galaxy's disc (page 56).

From comparing radio observations made at various wavelengths, there would seem to be a small disc within the bulge itself, lying some 1,500 parsecs (4,900 light-years) from the centre. Composed of hydrogen atoms and hydrogen molecules, this is inclined to the plane of the Galaxy by between 15° and 20°, and is rotating. Further in still, at a distance of only 300 parsecs (about 980 light-years) from the centre, is a second rotating ring. It is composed of dust clouds, collections of molecules, and again plenty of hydrogen both as single atoms and as molecules. There is also some ionized hydrogen close

to some bright bluish-white supergiant stars. This is hot, with a temperature of about 10,000 degrees.

A third, cooler ring has been discovered only ten parsecs (approximately 33 light-years) from the centre. This ring has a temperature of about 5,000 degrees; it is also very dense and is rotating. But the most exciting region of the bulge lies between the centre and some three parsecs (about ten light-years) out. Here there are several million stars and some compact clouds of ionized gas, each about as massive as the Sun and with a diameter of a fraction of a parsec. These clouds are orbiting very fast around the centre, completing an orbit in only 10,000 years compared with our Sun which at its distance from the centre takes 200 million years.

Astronomers believe that these fast-moving clouds are orbiting some superdense massive object, whose mass may well be equal to 3 Suns. It is probably a large black hole (page 82) made up of hundreds of thousands of old stars which were not travelling fast enough to avoid falling into the Galaxy's centre and so were pulled there by gravitation. At least this seems to be the only explanation which fits the facts as we now know them. As one astronomer has put it, the centre of the Galaxy is a 'stellar graveyard'.

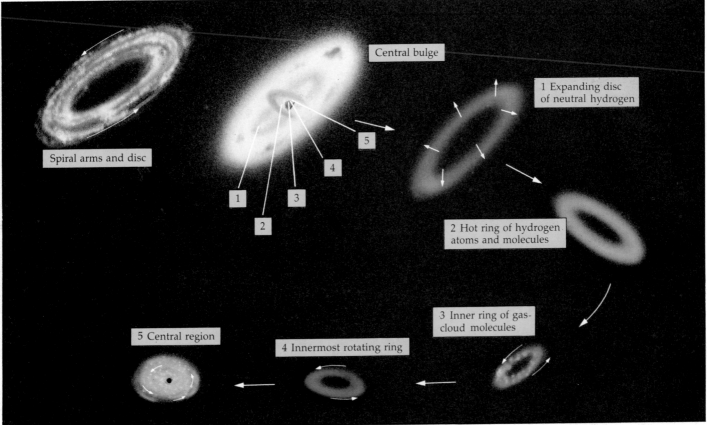

The constituent parts of the Galaxy and its central bulge, according to recent research. The illustration shows how active the bulge is and how much detail about it has been pieced together in recent years. Fuller details of the various parts are given in the text.

THE DISC OF THE GALAXY

The Sun and myriads of other stars lie in the thin disc of our Galaxy – in its spiral arms. Some of the stars in the spiral arms are loosely grouped in clusters.

The Milky Way shows us part of the disc of our Galaxy; the rest is hidden at the far side of the central bulge, in the direction of the Sagittarius region. What appear as empty gaps in the disc are in fact giant dark clouds – dark nebulae (see page 60) – which are blocking out the light from Milky Way stars which lie behind them. The Milky Way is therefore a continuous band of stars.

The Milky Way section of our Galaxy is not, however, one solid disc of stars packed closely together, but a series of spiral arms. These give it a roughly circular shape and, viewed from above, the disc of the Galaxy would show a bright central nucleus (the Galaxy's central bulge) with arms spiralling outwards. Its diameter is something like 30 thousand (3×10^4) parsecs.

The vast majority of stars in these arms are small dim red ones, with absolute magnitudes of about 15. (Stars which spend most of their lives in this form are known as red dwarfs.) By their very nature, such stars are difficult to detect, and can at present only be observed optically and then only out to a distance of something like 100 parsecs (326 light-years). The dimmest member of the α Centauri multiple star (Centaurus C) is an example of a star of this kind.

The spiral arms of the disc do however contain a proportion of bright young stars. These O- and B-type blue and blue-white stars are very bright in themselves, with absolute magnitudes of -8 or even -10; thus they are between 1.5 thousand million (1.5×10^9) and 10 thousand million (10^{10}) times brighter than the red dwarfs. As a result, they are bright enough to be seen over vast distances, and so they appear to be far more numerous than they really are compared with the red dwarfs.

The stars in the spiral arms are not evenly distributed throughout the thickness of the disc. The youngest ones and what we may call 'middle aged' – stars like our Sun – all lie within 40 parsecs (130 light-years) of the plane of the disc. This means that if you wanted to make a model of the Galaxy you could use one 30-cm long-playing record to represent it as far as diameter and thickness of the disc are concerned.

(This would not, of course, show the existence of the central bulge). On the other hand, the oldest stars would lie above and below your model disc; you would need a pile of six records to represent the boundaries in which they lie, because optical observations show them to extend up to 350 parsecs (1,100 light-years) above and below the central plane.

In the plane of the spiral arms some of the stars are gathered into loose associations or groupings, and there are also some 'open' clusters';

above An idea of how the photograph (*top*) relates to the Galaxy can be had by plotting the major features on a paper band and slotting it over a gramophone record.

right
Close-up of part of the disc of our Galaxy showing a section of the spiral arms. The evidence on which this is based has been obtained from radio and optical observations.

A Perseus Arm
B Orion Arm
C Sagittarius Arm

the famous Pleiades and Hyades clusters in Taurus, the Praesepe group of stars in Cancer and the southern hemisphere 'Jewel-box' centred on the star κ Crucis, are examples of such open clusters. Whilst 700 of these are known, it is thought that the total number is probably nearer 10,000 because astronomers can only recognize those within some 2½ thousand parsecs (8,000 light-years). The reason is that more distant clusters either merge into the background stars or are obscured by dust, gas and the Galaxy's central bulge. The open clusters are not big, astronomically speaking; most are only about two parsecs (seven light-years) in diameter and contain no more than 100 stars, though there are exceptions. The Praesepe cluster has a diameter of some 10–15 parsecs (approximately 33–50 light-years) and contains several hundred stars. Yet 'open' though these clusters are, they certainly represent far greater concentrations of stars than we find, for instance, close to the Sun.

It is the general view at the moment that the stars in each cluster were all formed at about the same time, but since not all clusters are of the same age, they provide ideal case studies of the ageing of groups of stars and are of great interest to astronomers. The youngest cluster known seems to be the Pleiades with an age of some 63 million years, the oldest known cluster being M67 in Cancer with an age of four thousand million years. Astronomers do not expect to find any much older than M67 because the motions of the stars in a cluster will have caused them to disperse if we go back much farther in time. Once dispersed, they would become lost among the evenly distributed stars in the disc.

Evidence that our Galaxy does possess spiral arms has come in part from studying large associations of stars because these give an indication of the way material is distributed, and display a common movement such as would be expected from stars in spiral arms. Further evidence comes from observations with radio telescopes of how neutral hydrogen gas is distributed. Detection of this neutral gas (which can never be observed visually) allows radio astronomers to penetrate much of the dust which hides the arms from visual observers. We now know that the three arms nearest to us are the Orion arm, which contains our Sun, the Sagittarius arm (which is closer to the Galaxy's centre) and the Perseus arm (which is further out than the Orion arm). Some astronomers believe that the Orion arm is not an arm on its own, but a bridge between the Perseus and Sagittarius arms.

The arms themselves are named after the constellations in which they seem to be embedded when viewed from Earth. But whatever we call them, it is generally agreed that they have formed because of density waves pushing out spirally in the plane of the Galaxy; astronomers think these waves are associated with outflows of gas from the Galaxy's centre. They have also concluded it is these density waves that trigger off star formation within the arms. That would explain why new stars in the Galaxy are found in the arms and not a long way above or below them.

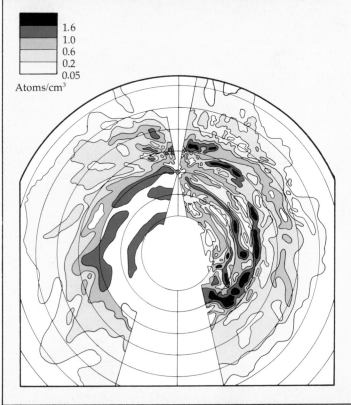

above
A composite photograph of the entire Milky Way. Taken from Earth-based optical observatories, this is not quite the same view as we would see from outside the Galaxy.

right
A map of the Galaxy's spiral arms derived from radio observations of interstellar gas. The gap indicates the area for which radio observations were not available.

below
The appearance of the Galaxy from outside, showing how thin it would appear if viewed edge-on.

1.6
1.0
0.6
0.2
0.05
Atoms/cm³

GLOBULAR CLUSTERS

Globular clusters of stars form a vast shell around our Galaxy. The fact that these clusters extend far out into space shows that the Galaxy is very much larger than was once thought.

The central bulge and the disc of the Galaxy are surrounded by a vast spherical shell of globular star clusters. Each cluster is shaped like a sphere and contains anything between some thousands and hundreds of thousands of stars. Their distances, measured from the Sun, range between three and 60 thousand parsecs (about 10,000 to 200,000 light-years). In these clusters the stars are packed more densely than they are outside them, and an average globular cluster of about 30 parsecs (some 100 light-years) in diameter contains tens or hundreds of thousands of stars. This gives an average distance between stars of about one light-year. It seems also, both from observations and from gravitation theory, that the stars in a cluster are not evenly distributed. The outer ones are probably a couple of light-years or so apart, whereas those near the centre are separated by only a fraction of a light-year. The general opinion is that the stars near the centre are so tightly packed that they are likely to be multiple star systems, and in some globular clusters, the centre may even be occupied by a black hole.

Of the roughly 200 globular clusters known, most are dim, telescopic objects. However there are four that are comparatively bright and can even be seen with the unaided eye, if you know precisely where to look. Two lie in the northern skies, M5 in Serpens and M13 in Hercules (apparent magnitudes 5.7), and the other two can be seen from the southern hemisphere, ω Centauri, with an apparent magnitude of 3.6, and 47 Tucanae, with an apparent magnitude of 4.0.

Observation shows that the stars in globular clusters are all old, probably thousands of millions of years old and older than the stars in our Galaxy. Presumably this is because the stars in the clusters condensed at a time when the gas in the Galaxy was still too turbulent to

do so. Most cluster stars are composed primarily of hydrogen and helium whereas more recently formed stars, such as our Sun, contain metals. The metallic elements only became available at a later date, after they had been manufactured in supernova explosions (page 76). However globular clusters, mainly those on the outside of our Galaxy, do contain stars with a metal content,

although their content is not as high proportionally as that of our Sun. This indicates that these stars were formed a little after some of the older ones had become novae or supernovae.

Globular clusters, like everything else in the Galaxy, are on the move. Observations over a number of years show that, as a general rule, they orbit the centre in highly elliptical paths, and once in a

above
An illustration of the Galaxy seen from outer space, showing some of the globular clusters which surround it.

left
The globular cluster M5 in Serpens Caput (The Serpent's Head) lies at distance of 8,300 parsecs (27,000 light-years) from us and has an apparent magnitude of 6.2.

while pass through the disc of the Galaxy. This happens only rarely – once every ten thousand million (10⁹) years for a cluster tens of thousands of parsecs from the Galaxy centre – but when it does, various things may happen. The cluster may be torn apart by the gravitational pull of other stars close by in the disc, or if its orbit brings it close to the Galactic centre, it will be distorted by gravity, bulging out on the side lying near the centre and possibly losing some of its stars. This is why the globular clusters in the central bulge are smaller than those out in the halo.

The suggestion that the stars in globular clusters were formed before those in the Galaxy would explain why the globular clusters lie scattered throughout the entire halo. They would have been in existence as compact collections of stars held together by their mutual gravitation before the Galaxy had contracted enough to draw them down either into its disc or into the central bulge.

Where are the limits of our Galaxy? How far does the halo of globular clusters and separate stars extend? Are there objects which ought to be included in the Galaxy that have hitherto been thought of as outside? The answers are provided by the globular clusters themselves. Some have been traced out to very great distances. Four have been found between 20,000 and 40,000 parsecs (65,000 to 130,000 light-years) away and two others have been discovered even further out than this, up to 60,000 parsecs (195,000 light-years) away. The Large Magellanic Cloud, a small separate galaxy (page 102), is also to be found at this distance. Another tiny, spherically shaped galaxy lies between 80,000 and 100,000 parsecs (260,000 to 326,000 light-years), and with it three more globular clusters. Although two other globulars have been found further out still astronomers look on them, and the four small spherical galaxies which lie up to 220,000 parsecs (720,000 light-years) away, as really being too far from our Galaxy to be considered part of it. However the other material, lying within 100,000 parsecs, is now thought of as forming a 'corona' (Latin, *crown*) to our Galaxy that is bound to it by gravity and is permeated by an extensive magnetic field. The existence of this field is known from two kinds of observation. Firstly it has been found that the starlight passing between dust grains in space is polarized – that is to say the light waves vibrate in only one direction instead of a variety of directions as is usual. This indicates that the dust grains are all turned in a particular direction, which is the effect a magnetic field would have upon them. Secondly radio observations show that the 21-cm wavelength of neutral hydrogen is split in two, just as it would be in a magnetic field.

The corona of globular clusters and small galaxies, together with our Galaxy, with its disc, central bulge and magnetic field, form a really immense system which is probably better thought of as a continent rather than an island in space. Certainly present views make it clear that our Galaxy itself is not one of normal size, as was once thought, but something very much larger than usual.

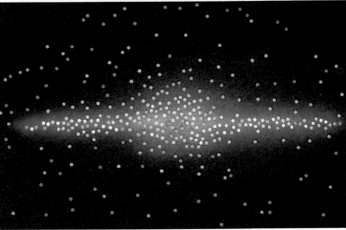

right
A chart of globular-cluster distribution around the Galaxy.

Population II
Old stars

Population II
'Middle-aged' stars

Population I
Young stars

59

GAS AND DUST IN THE GALAXY

The space between the stars in our Galaxy is not as empty as might appear. It contains much interstellar matter, such as dust and gas, but this is very thinly spread out.

Our Galaxy contains much interstellar matter in the form of dust and gas. Some of this can be observed optically, but much more can be detected by radio and, recently, by orbiting spacecraft, like the High-Energy Astronomical Observatory (HEAO) launched in 1977, which have shown evidence for more material still.

The gas is mainly, though not entirely, hydrogen. Much of it is dark, though some shines because it contains hot and bright young stars. It is widely spread throughout the Galaxy though, of course, there is a concentration in the central bulge and in the spiral arms that form the disc. It has been estimated that there is one gas atom per cubic centimetre of space, but this is only an average figure. In practice, the gas tends to be concentrated into clouds or thin wispy filaments.

The dark gas is invisible in optical telescopes unless it happens to lie in front of a patch of bright gas or a concentration of stars such as, for instance, in the dark rift you can see in the Milky Way in Cygnus. It is formed mostly of neutral hydrogen, which can be detected by radio telescopes, because of the way its atoms behave. Neutral hydrogen atoms consist of a nucleus composed of one proton and one orbiting electron. The proton spins and so does the orbiting electron. The direction of the electron's spin can be either in the same direction as the proton or in the opposite direction, and these directions can change. Such a change usually comes about when atoms collide, but since they are so widely spread out in interstellar space, this does not happen very frequently – about once every 400 years for any particular atom. Yet interstellar space is very large and there are trillions of millions of neutral hydrogen atoms out there, so collisions resulting in changes of spin are happening all the time. When a change of spin occurs, then some energy is given out. This

appears as a 'wave-packet' of energy called a photon; it has a wavelength of 21 cm, and it is to this that radio-telescopes are sensitive.

The neutral hydrogen lies in clouds as well as being spread along the spiral arms. Most of it is moving at only 20 km per second either towards us or away from us, though

some moves faster. It is also found at various temperatures. In the clouds it is no more than 100 degrees Kelvin (usually written 100K), but the gas that is spread out more thinly in space is at the much higher temperature of 1000K because it is heated by ultraviolet radiation and by X-ray energy, while some areas that

receive concentrations of cosmic rays may even reach 1,000,000K, because of the rays' immense energy.

Although the gas is at so high a temperature it is not hot; if you put your hand into it, you would not be burned. This is because its temperature is measured by the activity of the gas atoms (the more energetically they rush about, the higher the temperature); however, because there are so few atoms per cubic centimetre, there is little heat about. It is rather like the indoor firework called a sparkler which emits bright burning sparks that are so lightweight that they do not carry enough heat to cause noticeable burns.

The Kelvin temperature scale is a special one. As we shall be referring to it throughout the rest of this book, this is an appropriate place to explain how it differs from the usual temperature scales, which are connected with the behaviour of particular substances. For example, when Daniel Fahrenheit made his scale, he fixed its zero at the freezing point of an ice-salt mixture and took a value of 96° to be equal to the temperature of the human body; on this scale water boils at 212° and freezes at 32°. The centigrade or, more properly, Celsius scale takes its zero as the freezing point and 100° as the boiling point of water. But in the late nineteenth century, William Thomson (Lord Kelvin), wanted his scale to be independent of any particular substance. He managed to achieve this by basing it on the fundamental principles of heat exchange. The zero of the Kelvin scale is known as 'absolute zero' because at that point no heat energy whatsoever is available for exchange. A degree on Kelvin's scale is equal to a degree on the Celsius scale, and absolute zero is -273.15°C. The Kelvin scale is the natural and most convenient one to use for gases and for interstellar gas and stars.

Lit mainly by hot, bright young stars, interstellar gas glows in radio, infrared, visual and even ultraviolet wavelengths. But it also sometimes glows with X-rays. There is, for instance, a vast halo of hot gas in Cygnus which is emitting X-rays. Partly obscured by dust clouds, it looks like a ring; covering an area of 13° × 8° and lying at a distance of 1,840 parsecs (6,000 light-years), it is more than 40 times larger than even the giant Orion Nebula (page 62). Yet it is thought to be only one of many such 'superbubbles' in our Galaxy.

Also present in the Galaxy are dust grains, mainly concentrated in the disc. They can be detected because they absorb the starlight behind them, reducing it by six times for every thousand parsecs of space they cover. They absorb still more short wave and infrared radiation but are transparent to radio waves. By studying how much radiation they absorb it is possible to determine what kind of dust grains they are and it is found that some are of ice, others of the mineral silicon, and many are of graphite, which is one of the two naturally occurring crystalline forms of carbon. Unfortunately, the other form, diamonds, has not so far been discovered in space!

above
A radio map of our Galaxy derived from radio observations of the distribution of neutral hydrogen gas.

left
A photograph by the Anglo-Australian 1.2-m Schmidt telescope of the Horsehead Nebula. This picture makes clear that the nebula is obscuring bright material behind it and also how much gas and dust lie in this area of the sky. The distance of the Horsehead Nebula is 337 parsecs (1,100 light-years) and the bright stars are ζ Orionis (*top*) and σ Orionis (*right*).

right
Clouds of atoms in space make their presence known by absorbing starlight and so adding 'absorption' lines to the spectra of distant stars. The spectra shown here are calcium absorption in ε Orionis (A) and, also, more strongly, in HD 172987 (B). The lower three show sodium in ε Orionis (C), in 6 Cassiopeiae (D) and in HD 1413 (E). The last two are examples of double spectra and show the effect of two absorbing clouds moving at different velocities.

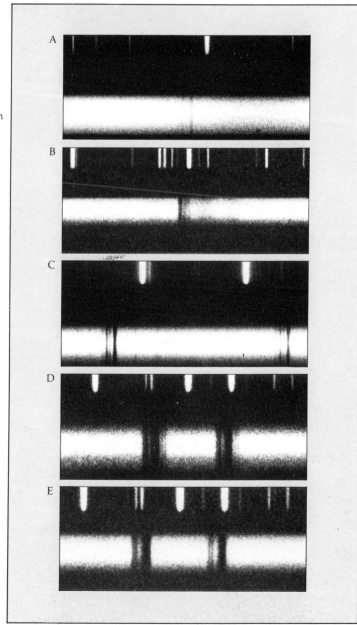

TRAVELLING THROUGH A BRIGHT NEBULA

What is a bright nebula really like? Here, in imagination, we travel through one. The description of what we might see is based on recent Earth-based observations.

There are a host of bright nebulae our side of the centre of the Galaxy, so there is a wide choice open to us if we want to travel through one. The photograph shows one example from the constellation of Monoceros, the Unicorn. This bright nebula surrounds the cluster of bright stars known as NGC 2264, which is partly hidden by the magnificent Cone Nebula.

Monoceros lies in the Milky Way just to the east of Orion, south of Canis Minor and north of Canis Major. It is certainly not a spectacular constellation for it has no star brighter than magnitude 3.7, but it does contain NGC 2264 and also the beautiful Rosette Nebula. Let us suppose, however, that we wish to visit NGC 2264. We should probably set our spaceship on a course which took us some 6° north of Sirius. We should pass Sirius after 8.6 years if we were travelling with the speed of light, but that would only be a very short step in our journey to the Cone Nebula region, because this lies at least some 1,500 parsecs (4,890 light-years) away. That means it is some 569 times as far off as Sirius, so that if astronauts had set off over 500 years before the time the Great Pyramid was built, they would only now be approaching the Cone. But supposing we could get there somehow, what should we find? We should immediately see that the bright cloud of the nebula is set glowing by the cluster of hot blue and blue-white stars which form NGC 2264 and are embedded in it. Our instruments would show us that the radiation from these stars is rich in ultraviolet and also contains a considerable amount of X-rays. This short wavelength radiation excites the gas atoms of the nebula so that they re-radiate it at their own observable wavelengths. If we brought samples of gas into our spacecraft and analysed them, we should find that hydrogen is by far

the main constituent; it makes the gas glow with a pinkish-red colour. Besides hydrogen, we should find neon and nitrogen, sulphur, argon and a very small quantity of chlorine. We should also discover oxygen, which shines with a greenish colour. For some time astronomers on Earth were puzzled by this, because in the laboratory ionized oxygen does not glow with a green light. However in 1928 the problem was solved by the American astronomer Ira S. Bowen, who discovered that because the gas in a nebula is spread out so thinly, the ionized oxygen atoms will recapture electrons in such a way as to cause them to emit radiation whose wavelength is green.

The behaviour of ionized oxygen in the nebula emphasizes how thinly all the gas atoms are spread throughout the cloud. Compared with the air we breathe on Earth, the gas in the nebula is really very rarified indeed. For instance the air at sea level contains some 5×10^{19} (50 million million million) atoms per cubic centimetre, whereas in NGC 2264 there will at most be only 500 per cubic centimetre; this is 10^{17} (100 thousand million million) times less. But if there is so little gas per cubic centimetre, how is it that we can see it at all? The answer is because it is so big—the bright central portion of the cloud probably contains 5.4×10^{51} cubic centimetres, or 2.7×10^{54} atoms, so there are plenty to observe.

The bright light we see as we travel through the nebula is not all the radiation our spacecraft is receiving. The nebula is also emitting infrared radiation, X-rays, gamma-rays and a vast quantity of ultraviolet radiation. The short wavelength radiation is strong enough to blind and kill us if we stepped outside the spacecraft with breathing apparatus but without proper protective clothing to keep out the X-rays and gamma-rays present. For this reason, our spacecraft would have no windows, because these would have to be very thick to protect us from all the very short wavelength radiation. Our views of the universe would be obtained using remote control colour television cameras mounted outside the spacecraft.

What all this makes evident is the very hostile nature of space. Astonishing though it proves to be, it is a totally inhospitable environment for human beings. It underlines the fact that even on Earth we exist only because conditions are not too extreme, and there is an atmosphere for protection.

TRAVELLING THROUGH A DARK NEBULA

A dark nebula contains dust and gas, but is not lit from inside by energetic stars. Sometimes this material reflects light from stars outside, but most remains dull and uninviting.

Gas in space is not always lit up by stars embedded in it. If it were, there would be no dark nebulae forming what appear to be gaps in the Milky Way. But on some occasions nebulae can be seen, even though they do not contain hot stars. We can find one in the Orion constellation—the bright nebula M78, which if we look at lies north of the three stars forming Orion's belt and something like a quarter of the way between the left-hand star of the three (ζ Orionis) and Betelgeuse. It appears fairly dim (magnitude 8.3), and so a telescope is needed to see it from Earth, but this is partly because it is 100 parsecs further away than the Great Nebula and partly because it is not lit up by any stars embedded in it. Instead, M78 is visible because it reflects starlight. If we travelled through it we should find that it was lit by hot bright blue-white stars. These stars lie outside the nebula, and their light is reflected, though they cannot be seen directly from Earth because they are hidden from us here by a dark patch in the nebula.

However, if we wanted to go through a dark nebula we might as well stay in Monoceros and travel from NGC 2264 to the Rosette Nebula. As this is only at a distance of 1,380 parsecs (4,500 light-years) we should have to re-trace our steps a little from the Cone Nebula, travelling in a north-eastern direction for some 120 parsecs (390 light-years). When we arrived, we should first of all see a bright nebula lit by the very young hot blue-white stars that surround it, and glowing with the pinkish red light of ionized

hydrogen. The cluster of young stars lies in a central empty region of the nebula because the radiation from its stars has pushed the gas away from the centre. This 'radiation pressure' is an effect which can happen whenever the wavelength of the radiation and the gas particles are of the right relative sizes. But as we can see from Earth, the whole nebula is not just a mass of bright gas. It contains many dark clouds. These lie between the Earth and the bright nebula and if we travelled into one, the Sun, the Earth and the whole of the Solar System would vanish; the dark clouds would blot them out completely. As we moved more deeply into the dark clouds, the bright gas forming so much of the

Rosette would vanish too, its radiation absorbed by the cold gas and dust in which we are now moving. But would our spacecraft be in complete darkness? Should we be able to see anything at all?

The answer is that we should not find ourselves utterly in the dark. When we observe from outside we see the nebula as a dark mass against the background of the bright gas, but then we are looking through the whole thickness of the dark nebula. When we are inside it, we do not have so great a thickness between us and the outside. Yet it would still be comparatively dark, optically, and also our instruments would register a far colder temperature than in the bright gas outside. In fact it is cold

enough inside a dark nebula for there to be complex molecules on the dust grains which are moving about in the cloud, some consequences of which we shall see later (page 172). But if we examine the inside of the dark nebula with an infrared telescope we shall soon see that it is far from being completely cold. Indeed there are patches which will seem quite warm. If we also make measurements of the density of gas molecules and dust particles, we shall find that they are not distributed evenly. In some places they are more concentrated than in others, and at some points in the dark nebula they are lumped together more densely still. These concentrations are the birthplaces of stars.

left
An impression of an interstellar spacecraft of advanced design travelling through a dark nebula.

right
The Rosette Nebula in Monoceros. When first studied visually it seemed to be an area of nebulous patches; they were catalogued as NGC numbers 2237, 2238, 2239 and 2246. The central cluster of stars is NGC 2244.

below.
Although the Coalsack in Crux (The Southern Cross), looks like a dark empty patch in the Milky Way, it is really a series of small dark nebulae, which absorb the light of stars lying both beyond and behind them.

PROTO-STARS

Astronomers now know that stars are born out of gas and dust, beginning as dark patches of concentrated material before condensing into stars of the kind with which we are familiar.

In our imaginary journey through a dark nebula, we came upon patches of gas that were more concentrated than the general background material of the nebula. Indeed, we know that there are density waves moving through the disc of our Galaxy (page 57) which cause gas in the patches to clump together ever more strongly. The density waves push the material into concentrations and gradually, over tens of thousand of years, cause enough to become amassed together for the concentration to begin to shrink. Such dark patches of concentrated material have been detected in photographs taken of bright nebulae. Some were seen by the American astronomer E. E. Barnard as early as the 1920s but it is only in recent years that another American astronomer, Bart Bok, has drawn attention to them and started a careful study of them as the places where proto-stars will form.

Such dark globules have been observed in many bright nebulae; in Orion, the Rosette, the beautiful Lagoon Nebula in Sagittarius and in the Cone Nebula in Monoceros. In fact, the globules seem to be present in every nebula lying in the plane of the Milky Way, but we should expect this, because such nebulae are all in the disc of the Galaxy. Recent research has however shown the existence of a proto-star in another galaxy.

The proto-stars themselves inside the globules are comparatively large; much larger than the stars into which they will finally shrink. In Orion some have been detected which appear to have diameters of about 0.2 parsecs, that is, they are about one thousand times larger in diameter than the distance from the Sun to Pluto. They are cool, with temperatures of only about 530K. (This is cool when you remember that absolute zero is –273.15° Celsius, so 530K is still only about 257°C, which is very cool as far as stars are concerned.) Such proto-stars cannot, of course, be seen because they emit no light, but they can be detected with infrared telescopes. You can observe something similar yourself if you go into a darkened room where a hot flat iron is standing on an ironing board. You will not be able to see it, but you will be able to detect its presence by the heat it gives out (though do not actually touch the iron!)

Before proto-stars were actually observed, the theory of how stars form had led astronomers to predict their existence. Such a theory states that these proto-stars will continue to shrink over a long period, though precisely how long depends on the kind of star which will form. If it is to be an extremely hot O-type star

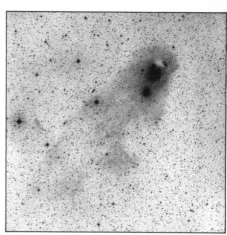

above A comet-shaped dark globule seen in this photograph may, perhaps, be a proto-star in the early stage of formation.

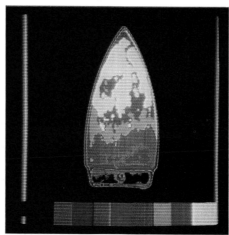

above A hot flat iron as seen by the light of its own infrared radiation. White is hottest and blue and black are coldest.

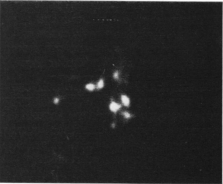

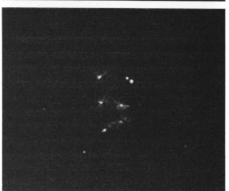

Two photographs of Herbig-Haro objects, observed separately by George Herbig and Guïllamero Haro. They have bright-line spectra showing that they are gas clouds. They are strong infrared emitters, and are believed either to be condensing into stars or to surround newly formed ones.

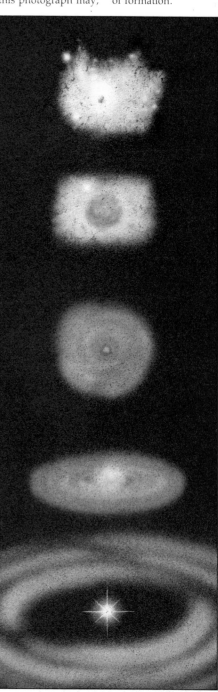

The stages in the formation of a proto-star are shown here, from a concentration of interstellar gas (*top*) to a primitive star (*bottom*). The whole mass will rotate as the gas condenses to form a more compact body.

above Buried in the dust clouds of the Orion Nebula lie several strongly emitting sources of infrared radiation. It is thought that these bodies are proto-stars – stars in the making. (Photographed with the UK 1.2-m Schmidt telescope.)

(one with a final surface temperature of something like 40,000K) then it will take a million years or thereabouts; if it should become a hot blue-white B-type star (surface temperature around 28,000K) the shrinkage will be about a hundred times faster. Of course, not all proto-stars will become O or B-type stars, some cooler stars will form. Whether a star will be hot and bright, or cooler and dimmer depends on the amount of material the proto-star possesses in the first place; the more massive a proto-star, the hotter the star that will eventually be formed.

As a proto-star shrinks, its central regions become denser, and as this happens, so gravitational energy – the energy that pulls the material together – is released and causes the gaseous material to become hot. In fact, the material in the centre of the star may heat up so quickly that nuclear reactions begin, and do this long before the outer material of the proto-star has all fallen in. The nuclear reactions which take place are similar to those in a hydrogen bomb (for a newly-formed star consists mainly, though not entirely, of hydrogen).

The main reaction that will occur in a new star is the proton-proton reaction, because this can occur as soon as the internal temperature at the centre of the proto-star reaches about 17 million K. The proton-proton reaction is an instance of nuclear fusion. Here two heavy electrically positive atomic particles or protons (each the nucleus of a hydrogen atom) collide to make a nucleus of heavy hydrogen (deuterium), which consists of a proton and an electrically neutral heavy particle known as a neutron. When this happens, two lighter atomic particles, a positron and a neutrino, are shot out. The next stage in the reaction is the collision of the deuterium nucleus with another hydrogen nucleus. This gives a nucleus of the next heavier type of atom, helium, and a gamma-ray is emitted. The helium nuclei next combine to give a heavier nucleus of helium (the one we usually find in space) and two hydrogen nuclei although, sometimes, the result is the formation instead of the nucleus of a still heavier atom (beryillium) and the emission of a gamma-ray. So what the whole reaction produces is the transformation of hydrogen into helium and the emission of energy, either as gamma-rays or as light (because the positron turns into a particle of light – a photon – when it meets one of the many electrons racing around in the gas.) There is also another more complex energy-emitting nuclear reaction which can occur if carbon and nitrogen atoms are present. The energy which these reactions generate is vast because while they are taking place, some matter is being completely annihiliated. For instance if enough reactions occurred to consume only one gram of hydrogen, enough energy would be emitted to keep over 35,000 million very large electricity-generating stations going for a year! So every time a proto-star condenses the energy released in the universe increases.

The photograph shows the gaseous nebula M 16 in Serpens. The dark areas are condensations where proto-stars are almost certainly forming.

PROTO-PLANETS

Theories to account for the formation of the planets have changed radically. Today, most astronomers believe that the Earth and the other planets originally formed as proto-planets out of a nebula.

We do not know for certain how planets are formed. For the last 230 years scientists have had various ideas, but astronomers now are mostly in agreement about the way they think planets began. The first theory to be put forward was known as the 'nebular hypothesis'. This idea has been revived in recent years to form today's favoured theory of planetary formation. To appreciate the theory properly we must first see why it was rejected, before once again becoming generally accepted, although in a modified form.

The nebular hypothesis, suggesting that the planets formed out of a nebula surrounding the Sun, was first put forward by the German philosopher Immanuel Kant. It was then developed by the French mathematical astronomer Pierre Laplace. In 1796 Laplace made out a very convincing case for the hypothesis but there was one problem he could not solve satisfactorily. This was the question of how the planets received enough angular momentum, that is, sufficient energy to set them orbiting round the Sun at the speeds they do.

The problem of angular momentum seemed to be a fatal objection to the nebular hypothesis, and after about 1900 astronomers began to consider alternatives, all of which go under the heading of 'catastrophe theories'. The first of these was proposed by the American scientists Thomas Chamberlin and Forest Ray Moulton and by the British astronomer James Jeans. They suggested that the planets had been formed from material pulled out of the Sun by a passing star. Their idea was that the passing star would cause great tides on the Sun, and that these would finally cause the Sun to eject material in large lumps. These lumps or 'planetesimals' would condense to form planets. But this theory also failed to explain angular momentum. To achieve such planetary speeds and masses as we observe, the passing star would have to pass dangerously close to the Sun.

Yet the 'planetesimal hypothesis' as it came to be called seemed attractive and other astronomers proposed variations. One of these was to have the second star graze the Sun and then move away very quickly, but mathematical analysis of this showed it still could not explain angular momentum. Then it was suggested that the Sun was once a binary star and that its companion was pulled away by the close approach of a third star, planetary material being ejected from both. Yet another theory was that the Sun's companion was itself a binary, the components of which joined one another when they and the Sun scooped up interstellar material as they orbited the Galaxy. This, then, would lead to the break-up of the now larger second star due to the gravitational pull between it and the Sun. Planets would then be formed from such material as did not escape into space.

One of the problems posed by every catastrophe theory was to account for the presence of many

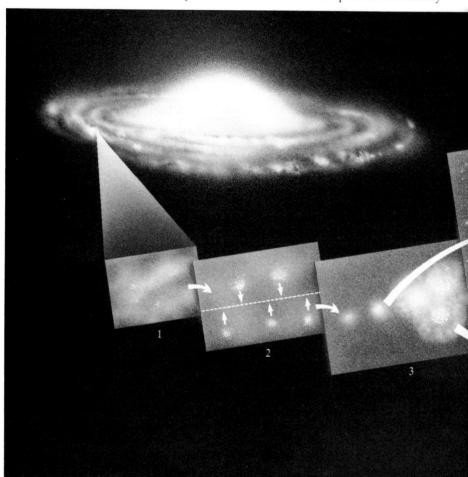

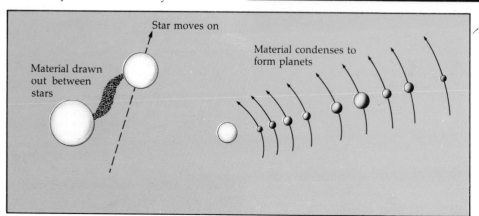

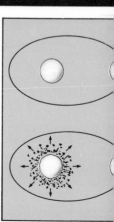

left
Diagram of the now obsolete theory that planets formed from material drawn out by the close passage of two stars.

right
Diagram of the now obsolete theory that planets form when one member of a binary system becomes a supernova and explodes.

heavy chemical elements on the Earth. Some could come from the Sun but not in the quantity or the proportions in which we find them in the Earth's crust. To overcome this difficulty, it was therefore suggested that the Sun's companion star might have become a supernova. This could account for the presence of such elements (page 76) as would be left behind after the companion star had been driven off by the explosion.

In the last decade or so, opinion has changed yet again; catastrophe theories have fallen out of fashion and a modified nebular hypothesis has now found favour. This seems to have come about because of increased understanding of the way in which stars form out of concentrations of dust and gas inside a dark nebula.

However, if planets did form from a nebula composed of the same gas and dust cloud that became the Sun, there are still some problems connected with angular momentum. Nevertheless, in the light of modern knowledge, they do not seem to present insuperable difficulties. Some astronomers, for instance, believe that strong magnetic pulls between the proto-Sun and the nebula, could solve any difficulties by causing an additional pull on the condensing planetary material. On the other hand, others think that the nebulous material was swept up later on by the Sun. In this case the motion of the Sun as it swept up the material could add momentum to the swirling nebula. In either case one point is clear. The Earth and the rest of the planets condensed out of a nebula

some five thousand million (5×10^9) years ago. Studies of radioactive material in the Earth show that it could not be much older than this – if it were, the material would all have decayed and turned into lead by now – while studies of the ages of rocks and rock materials show that this sort of figure seems to be about right.

The modern nebular hypothesis has to account not only for angular momentum but also for the basic differences between the gaseous outer planets and the rocky inner ones. Jupiter, Saturn, Uranus and Neptune are all giant gaseous planets which from mathematical studies of their masses, temperatures and gaseous composition (known from studies with the spectroscope), seem likely to have small rocky metallic cores at their centres. The main bulk of the planets is certainly made up of hydrogen and helium, and so it is thought that they probably formed directly from the gas which also made up our Sun. In brief, gas formed into a proto-star that shrank to form the Sun and then, later, some coalesced into proto-planets that shrank to become the gaseous bodies we now see.

Astronomers are not so certain about how the inner rocky planets – Mercury, Venus, Earth and Mars – were formed. They too could have been proto-planets, though smaller ones than those from which the larger planets formed. On the other hand, it has been suggested that some of the Sun's proto-star nebula condensed into small rocky metallic lumps – planetesmals – and that while some of these fell into the centre of the proto-Sun, others collided and coalesced into the inner planets. Certainly a computer analysis has shown that the planetesimal theory would work and, of course, it could also account for the presence of the minor planets or asteroids. But perhaps if the Space Telescope observes planets forming around another star, we might be able to decide with more certainty.

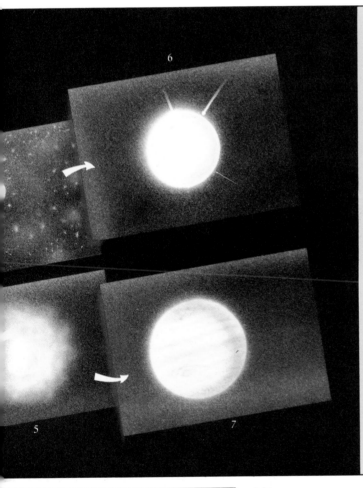

The formation of planets from gaseous material in the spiral arm of a galaxy is a possibility. Condensation of gas (1) is followed by clumping (2&3) to form either a hard lump of material from which most of the gases have been driven off (4&5) or a small hard core surrounded by a large gaseous atmosphere (6&7).

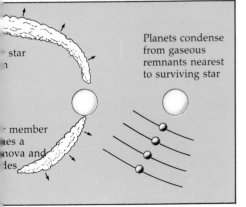

star

member
es a
nova and
les

Planets condense from gaseous remnants nearest to surviving star

right
The 'red rectangle', an area of intense infrared emission, thought to be the scene of the formation of a large planetary system. First observations showed that the radiation came from a rectangular patch, but it has now been found that the 'waist' of the 'hour-glass' nebula is the probable source.

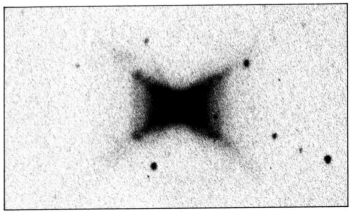

STELLAR WINDS

Planetary systems, orbiting stars, and their surrounding stellar neighbourhood are swept by winds of gas and nuclear particles, blown out by the stars into surrounding space.

Today astronomers believe that our Galaxy is more than 15,000 million years old, yet it still possesses a vast amount of free gas, creating a host of nebulae. Surely this should all have been consumed long ago in forming stars? Or is it, perhaps, being replenished in some way? Do fresh supplies of material make up for what is lost in star formation? This is, indeed, what seems to be happening; recent research has shown that new material is being poured into space by the stars themselves. This is most obvious in the case of the nearest star, our Sun. In 1957 the German astrophysicist Ludwig Biermann discovered the 'solar wind', a stream of electrified atomic particles – protons and electrons – constantly blown out by the Sun. The wind originates in the solar corona, the Sun's thin atmosphere which begins some 10,000 km above its disc, or photosphere, and extends several millions of kilometres out into space. Because it is so thin – about 100,000 million times less dense than the Earth's atmosphere, even at its closest to the Sun – the corona is impossible to observe from the Earth with the unaided eye, except during the few minutes of a total solar eclipse. Fifty years ago the French astronomer Bernard Lyot invented a special telescope, the coronagraph, an instrument which blocks out the photosphere and gives the effect of a total solar eclipse. When the coronagraph is used from a high-altitude mountain-top observatory it allows observations of the corona to be made at any time. The solar corona can also be observed whenever convenient by radio-telescope, and from out in space – indeed if you were on the Moon you would see the corona just before each sunrise and just after each sunset.

The solar wind is not constant. The hotter parts of the corona, which has an average temperature of one million degrees K, emit more material than the cooler parts and at greater speeds. Although the average speed of the particles is supersonic – some 400 km per second – variation in speed allows the faster particles to overtake the slower ones with the result that the wind travels in waves. Since the waves cause sudden changes in the pressure and speed as well as in the density of the gas, they are called shock waves. And because the Sun rotates, the solar wind is not blown out in straight lines, but in a spiral path. As the wind spreads out in space, the number of atomic particles becomes less so that near the Earth, for instance, there are on average some 10 million particles in every cubic kilometre of space, whereas out by Jupiter the figure has dropped to 40,000 and by the time the wind has reached Pluto the

above
A total eclipse of the Sun photographed by Dennis di Cicco. The Sun's faint but hot solar corona is clearly visible. Its shape depends on solar activity and the solar wind.

right
The material in a stellar wind, generated by a rotating star, spreads through the surrounding space in a spiral fashion, similar to water from a rotating sprinkler (*below*).

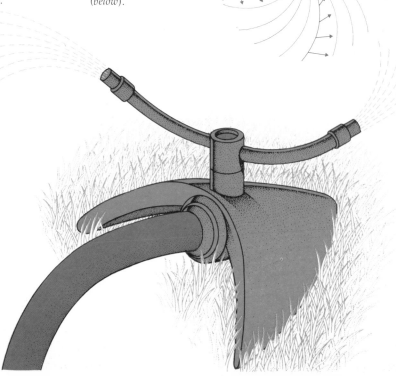

number is about 600. The solar wind blows all the time, most fiercely when sunspots are at a maximum, every eleven years or so; over the years the Sun adds tonnes of material to interstellar space.

Hot and very hot stars behave in the same way as the Sun. They also blow amounts of material into space. But what of the cooler stars, such as red giants and red supergiants. Do they also have a stellar wind? Observations made in recent years from spacecraft, and with the most modern telescopes, have made it clear that they do, but differ in certain respects. Some of the material they send into interstellar space contains both heavy atoms and light gas atoms as well as separate protons and electrons. It also seems that the atmospheres of these stars are very turbulent; the outer gases swirl about and experience what has been described as stellar hurricanes, which cause great masses of material to be ejected into space. Indeed the red supergiant Betelgeuse (α Orionis) has been observed to have a halo of gas surrrounding it.

Detailed studies of the two red-giant stars Rasalgethi (α Herculis) and 31 Cygni have revealed some interesting facts. Both are multiples; Rasalgethi is a red giant orbited by a much smaller yellow giant which in turn is orbited by an even smaller companion, while 31 Cygni is an eclipsing variable – a red giant orbited by a small, hot white star. Examinations of the hot companion stars' spectra has revealed evidence of moving gas clouds; as they orbit the red giant, they are seen to pass through changing thicknesses of gas. Both red giants therefore do produce stellar winds. But how they are formed is not understood.

Because both stars are very large, their outer atmospheres lie a long way from their centres and therefore the velocities their gas particles must reach to escape into space is not as great as it would be if the stars were smaller. On the other hand the stars are cool and the gas particles move so slowly that they do not even reach the low velocity required. However, recent observations show that the gas may nevertheless escape. It seems that particles of mineral substances such as magnesium silicate condense in the cool stellar atmospheres, close to the stars, and are driven out in two ways. Firstly, through the turbulent motion of the stellar atmospheres and secondly, by 'radiation pressure' from the red and infrared radiation produced by the star. The radiation can give enough push for the particle to escape provided the particles are neither too large nor too small, and it seems that these mineral particles are of just the right size. The particles then move outwards, bumping into the gas particles as they go, providing them with enough velocity to escape.

Stellar winds from cool red-giant and supergiant stars – binaries, multiples or even single stars – help to replenish the interstellar material used in building new stars. The release of the material reduces the mass of stars with the result that many, which would otherwise finish up as black holes, end their lives as neutron stars or even as white dwarfs (page 78).

right
A computer-generated colour picture made by Roger C. Lynds at Kitt Peak National Observatory showing the outflow of potassium gas from the red supergiant Betelgeuse (Orionis).

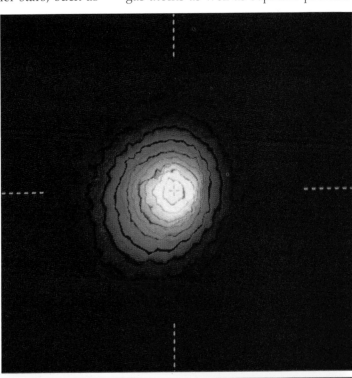

below
The steller wind from the red supergiant star 31 Cygni is thought to expand outwards in a spiral motion caused by the rotation of the star and the waves which travel outwards from it. The star has a small, hot companion, orbiting once every 10 years, and observations of it at different positions, A and B, have helped make this clear.

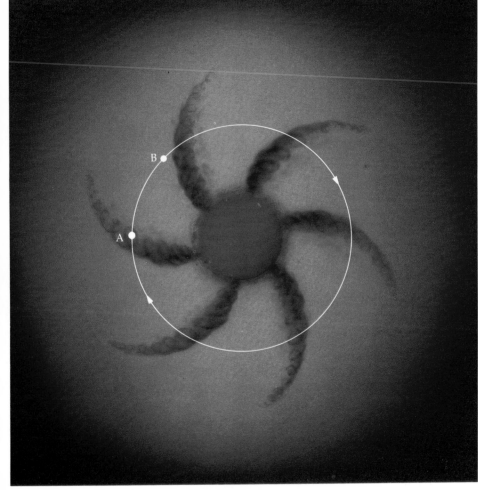

BINARY AND MULTIPLE STARS

Most of the stars in our Galaxy are not single, but are members of binary or multiple star systems. Studies of these systems have given astronomers greater insight into their formation and evolution.

If you look up at the handle of the Plough or Big Dipper and concentrate on the middle star ζ Ursae Majoris or Mizar you will notice that it is not one star but two. The name of its companion, 80 Ursae Majoris, is Alcor. The two stars differ by almost two magnitudes in brightness and are just over 14 arc minutes apart; the ability of anyone to see them as separate is a very ancient test of eyesight. If, however, you look at the pair through a telescope you will find

that there is a third star which is very much closer to Mizar. In fact Alcor and Mizar only appear close to one another because they are lying in nearly the same line of sight; they are in fact some four light-years apart. They are what is sometimes known as an 'optical double' to distinguish them from a true binary where the two stars actually orbit each other.

You can see the equivalent of an optical double whenever you go out at night into a road lit by street lamps. If you stand nearly in line with them you will see that the lights appear to be close though they are really quite a long way apart. Even if you did not already know how they were spaced, from your own experience, you could have deduced their positioning from the knowledge that the lights were all of equal brightness. But this is not true of stars; the two components of an optical double or a binary may well have different brightnesses. The only sure way to discover whether you are looking at a true binary is to watch for evidence that the stars are in

orbit. This will mean making observations over a period of time.

Although Alcor and Mizar do not seem to be physically connected, Mizar and its other companion do orbit round each other. They take almost 60 years to complete one revolution. But that is not the end of the story, for each of the components – Mizar and its companion – are spectroscopic binaries. That is to say, each of them has a second star in orbit around it and, in each case, the second star is too close to separate visually even in a telescope. However, if the spectrum of each star is studied, it will be found that the lines of the spectrum become alternately double and single in a regular way. This is because the dimmer companion star moves first towards us (blueshift) and then away from us (redshift) as it orbits the brighter. So Mizar turns out, in fact, to be a quadruple or multiple star system.

In recent years speckle interferometry (page 30) has also made it possible to detect binary

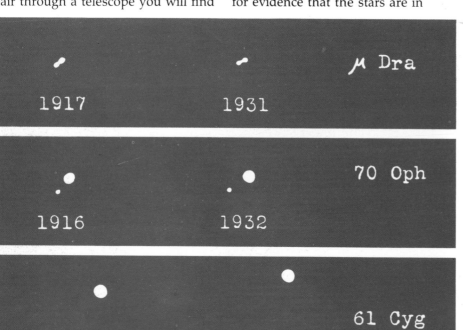

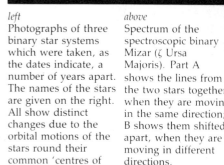

left
Photographs of three binary star systems which were taken, as the dates indicate, a number of years apart. The names of the stars are given on the right. All show distinct changes due to the orbital motions of the stars round their common 'centres of mass'.

above
Spectrum of the spectroscopic binary Mizar (ζ Ursa Majoris). Part A shows the lines from the two stars together, when they are moving in the same direction; B shows them shifted apart, when they are moving in different directions.

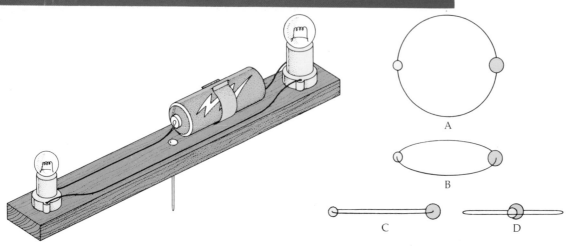

left
A binary star system can be demonstrated by using two torch bulbs, preferably of different brightnesses. The bulbs are rotated about the centre of the board and show orbits of different shape when viewed from directly above (A), from lower down (B) and from the side (C *and* D). In the case of D we see an eclipsing binary.

systems too close together to be seen visually as separate, but even this process does not exhaust the possibilities. There is yet another way of observing binary systems and that is by determining whether there are periodic changes of brightness of just the kind you would expect if the two components orbited round each other in such a way that eclipses were caused. A star of this kind is known as an 'eclipsing binary', but it is not essentially different from any other sort of binary; whether it is an eclipsing binary or not depends solely on the angle at which we are viewing it.

You can see the kind of thing if you make a model binary system by fixing two torch bulbs in holders, one at each end of a piece of wood, on which is also fixed a battery to light the lamps. If you first look down on the model from above and rotate it, you will see the lamps orbiting round each other (it is a good idea to do this in a darkened room). This is just the kind of effect you get with some visual binaries. Next look at it more

from the side. The two lamps now appear to be going round each other in much more elliptical orbits though, obviously, this is just an effect of perspective and depends on the angle from which we are looking at the lamps – the shallower the angle, the more elliptical the orbit will appear.

Finally, if you look at the rotation from an edge-on position, you will see the lamps moving in front of each other; this is the situation that gives us an eclipsing binary. The output of light we receive varies: there are periods of full light separated by dips in light output. When a light-curve of this kind is observed, astronomers know that the star is not a true variable (which displays a quite different type of variation and does not possess two evenly distributed troughs of lower brightness).

Observing binaries allows astronomers to determine the masses of the stars involved, since the distance between them and the time taken to complete an orbit depends on this; the greater the mass, the

shorter the period of rotation at a given distance. From observations of many optical, spectroscopic and eclipsing binaries, the masses of many stars have been found and from these together with the true brightness (absolute magnitudes) of the stars it has been possible to determine their actual sizes. This information is more precise than if it is determined in other ways (except for direct measurements of stellar diameters of very large nearby stars) and is of immense help in determining how stars evolve.

The reason why binary stars rather than single stars form from proto-stars (page 66) seems to be due to the rotation of the proto-star itself. As a proto-star shrinks then it must 'conserve its angular momentum', which means that as it shrinks it has to rotate faster and faster. If it was spinning comparatively quickly to begin with, the speed of rotation may become so large that the proto-star will split into two pieces and form a binary system, each part orbiting the other.

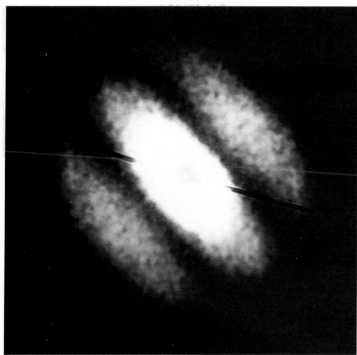

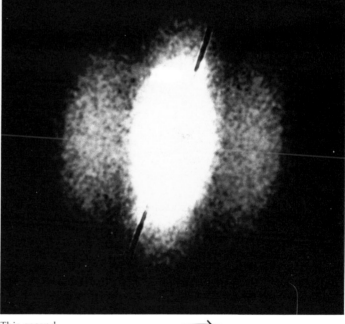

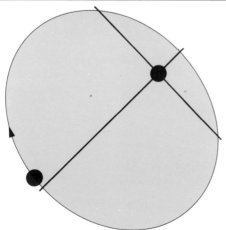

Observations of the star, 12 Persei, using speckle interferometry. The star is broken up into three images, indicating that it is a binary. The drawing (*right*) shows the position of the stars when the photograph (*above*) was taken.

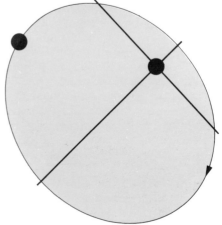

This second photograph (*above*) taken by speckle interferometry of the binary 12 Persei, shows the two components in different relative positions, as can be seen in the diagram (*right*).

THE AGEING OF STARS

Stars undergo a definite life cycle, though not all stars go through the same sequence. Some stars exist for a comparatively brief period; others live for thousands of millions of years.

As a proto-star shrinks (page 67) so its centre becomes hotter until its temperature becomes greater than seven million degrees K. Then thermonuclear reactions begin inside the centre of the star. If and when the temperature in the star's central regions reaches the astonishing figure of 18 million degrees, then a new reaction takes over and becomes the dominant factor. This is a very complex process, which is sometimes referred to as the CNO reaction because not only is carbon present but nitrogen and oxygen are formed during it, only to be used up again before the reaction is finished. The nitrogen is formed from a combination of carbon and hydrogen, while the oxygen is a product of the nitrogen and hydrogen. But the reaction begins with carbon and hydrogen and ends with carbon and helium, so the carbon finishes as it started; what is used up is the hydrogen.

Reactions like the CNO and the proton-proton one which occurs at lower temperatures emit vast amounts of energy and one may wonder why they do not blow the star to bits. After all, proton-proton reactions are what occur in a hydrogen bomb and this results in a colossal explosion. The reason why a star remains stable throughout its life – or at least for the greater part of it – is due to the way the electrified or ionized gases in the star react. They are, of course, pulled down to the star by gravity, but on the other hand the pressure of the radiation – i.e. of the photons (page 31) – from such reactions is very strong. This will press the gas outwards. But the most significant outward thrust is given by the great heat generated. This causes the pressure to rise so that the gases surrounding the central regions expand.

Fortunately the expansion of these gases does not go on for ever; if it did, every star would blow up soon after birth and we and our Sun would have ceased to exist ages ago. The expansion stops because the ionized gases cool as they expand, and thus they reach a point where the pressure between the gas atoms drops. Then gravitation takes over and the gases contract, their temperature and pressure rise and the cycle is repeated. Of course, during all this, the star is shining, radiating its energy out into space, and thus some of the heat is dissipated. The star reaches a balance, generation of energy inside is countered by radiation, by the emission of neutrinos (page 34), and by the cycle of expansion and contraction. Together these all act as natural regulators. The star stays stable and, if it is well-behaved like our Sun, the expansion and contraction remain small, at least for a great part of the star's life.

We can draw a diagram of a star's life, plotting absolute magnitude against spectral type, because spectral type is a direct indication of the surface temperature of a star. The basis of this is the famous HR diagram, the one drawn up first in 1914 by Ejnar Hertzsprung and Henry Norris Russell. You will see that the diagram (opposite page) has a line running from bottom right to top left. This represents the 'main sequence' – the period when a star is stable, when its energy output is in balance with the forces holding the star together. When a proto-star contracts, the star it produces can be plotted on this diagram: it appears somewhere along this main sequence. If it is large, young and very hot, it will appear as a B or A star, but if it is not so large and energetic, it will enter 'lower down', as an F or a G (like our Sun) or even as a red or deep red star, K or M.

What happens next depends on how luminous and how massive the star is. If it is hot, massive and luminous, then, though it begins with more hydrogen and thus more nuclear fuel to burn, it burns it so much more quickly that its lifetime on the main sequence is much shorter than that of a less massive star. For instance, whereas a star like the Sun will stay on the main sequence for something like 10,000 million (10^{10}) years, a star which begins life with, say, ten times the mass of the Sun will leave the main sequence after 10 million years and one of 20 times the Sun's mass after 1¼ million years.

In the CNO and in the proton-proton reactions, hydrogen is converted into helium, and the helium is not 'burnable'; we can think of it as a kind of nuclear 'ash' clogging up the central regions of a star where it has fallen because it is heavier than the surrounding hydrogen. In small or moderately sized stars, the hydrogen round this ashy core begins to burn in nuclear reactions, and as more helium ash forms, so the burning takes place nearer the star's surface. Meanwhile the core contracts, heats and as more ash forms, finally collapses. At this, the outer layers of gas expand and the star becomes a red giant.

If, on the other hand, the star is very large, the nuclear ash is replenished for a time with fresh hydrogen falling in towards the centre due to the bigger gravitational pull in a more massive star. But in the end the star leaves the main sequence; however, the helium is under such pressure that it fuses to carbon and a new stable period ensues. Yet this is short-lived, and again shrinkage of the core and burning lead to a red giant or supergiant phase. After this both massive and non-massive stars cease to be huge red stars and enter on the last phases of their lives. What then happens is very different and depends entirely on their mass.

above The planetary nebula NGC 7293 in Aquarius is not really a nebula, but a star which has released a spherical gas cloud.

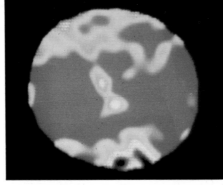

A computer-constructed picture produced at the Kitt Peak observatory of the red supergiant Betelgeuse (α Orionis).

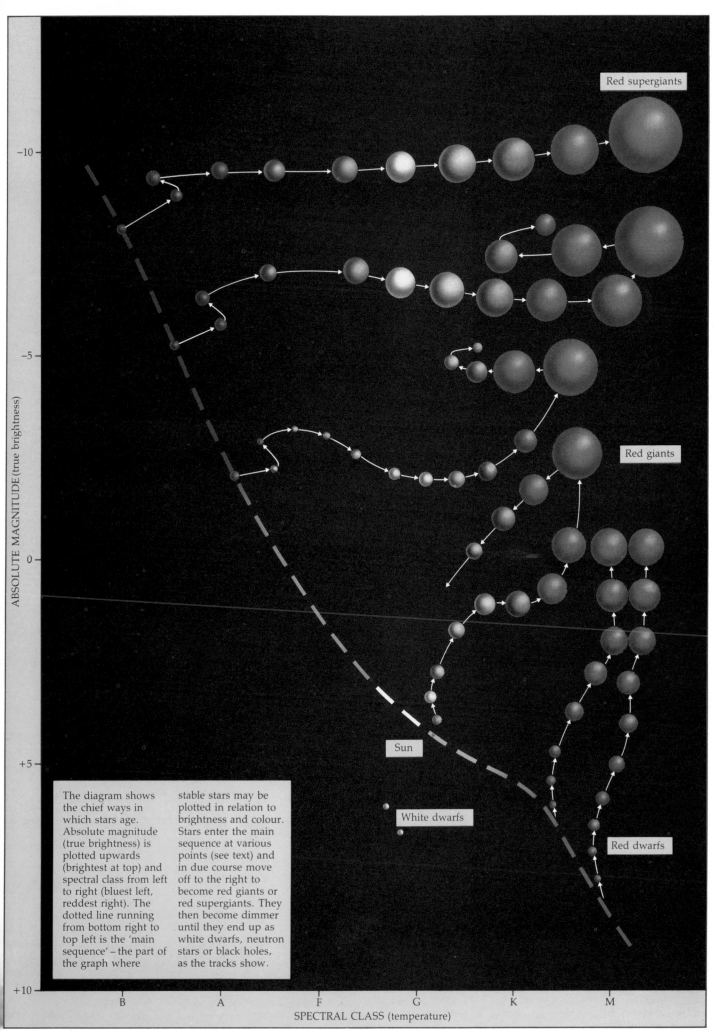

Red supergiants

Red giants

Sun

White dwarfs

Red dwarfs

ABSOLUTE MAGNITUDE (true brightness)

−10

−5

0

+5

+10

B   A   F   G   K   M

SPECTRAL CLASS (temperature)

The diagram shows the chief ways in which stars age. Absolute magnitude (true brightness) is plotted upwards (brightest at top) and spectral class from left to right (bluest left, reddest right). The dotted line running from bottom right to top left is the 'main sequence' – the part of the graph where stable stars may be plotted in relation to brightness and colour. Stars enter the main sequence at various points (see text) and in due course move off to the right to become red giants or red supergiants. They then become dimmer until they end up as white dwarfs, neutron stars or black holes, as the tracks show.

FLARE STARS, NOVAE AND SUPERNOVAE

Stars are not always stable throughout their lives. They may flare up suddenly and briefly, they may burst out as novae with a vast increase in brightness, or explode to extraordinary brilliance as supernovae.

Stars sometimes flare up. Our Sun does this, but not in a very spectacular way. Sudden brightenings occur in its outer atmosphere, especially in the corona. These are caused by a temporary heating due to increased radiation and atomic particles coming from below the surface gases. Flare stars are very dim red stars which, like the Sun, are still on the main sequence but which undergo similar eruptions though on a vastly larger scale. Sometimes known as UV Ceti stars because this was the first star of this type to be discovered, they are quite numerous; indeed one in 20 deep-red dwarf stars are flare stars. They display flares at both optical and radio wavelengths, but the flares are very short-lived. The stars brighten, anything up to two magnitudes or six times normal brightness in a matter of seconds, then fade back to normal brightness in a matter of minutes; perhaps 20 minutes at the most. The flaring up seems to be quite unpredictable and a star may even perform a number of times during an evening. Some like UV Ceti are excellent subjects for an amateur astronomer who possesses a telescope and a lot of patience.

Why do these stars emit flares? Why indeed does our Sun do so? In both cases the reason seems to be connected with a disturbance of the gases below the surface of the star, possibly due to a small extra amount of energy and atomic particles from the interior of the star. These disrupt the surface gases and the magnetism of the area, causing a shock-wave which travels through the star's upper atmosphere, ionizing the gases which then glow and emit radio waves. Of course, flare stars have much brighter flares than any that occur on the Sun, which never changes its brightness by one

magnitude let alone two (if it did, we would be fried alive). Indeed their spectra are very different from the Sun's, not only because they are much cooler and redder but also because they show bright lines of hydrogen. Presumably this hydrogen is in a cloud surrounding the star and it is this cloud which probably flares up.

Shock-waves travelling in a star

are not confined to flare stars. Such waves are thought to be the cause of variation in all Cepheid stars, both those which are massive young stars in the stage of their lives where they are steadily burning hydrogen, and those which are very old and burning helium in the last stages of their lives. But Cepheids, of course, have a periodic variation unlike flare stars or novae and supernovae.

above In May 1972 a supernova appeared in the spiral galaxy NGC 5253. In the photograph (*above right*) it can be seen below and slightly to the right of the central regions of the galaxy. The photograph (*above left*) taken in 1959 is for reference.

above The flare star that forms the fainter and more distant optical companion to 60 Krüger is shown in this multiple-exposure photograph. The last exposure shows the star flaring up to around four times its normal brightness.

Of these two photographs of Nova Aquilae, which appeared in 1918, the left-hand one shows the star in the nova phase (the larger of the two stars) and the right-hand picture shows it indicated by an arrow after it had faded back to normal.

In one sense novae are wrongly named. The word means 'new' but such stars are not new at all; they just flare up brightly, so they seem to appear where no star has been seen before. The amount by which a nova brightens may range from a couple of magnitudes (an increase of six times) to no less than 18 (an increase of 15 million times). Astronomers classify them into 'dwarf novae' (those which increase between two and five magnitudes); 'recurrent novae' which erupt regularly with periods ranging from 15 to 80 years and may change in brightness by six magnitudes (250 times); and 'ordinary' novae. Some astronomers believe that all novae are recurrent, with the periods of some extending into thousands of years. Some novae have been found to emit X-rays as well as visible radiation, and it may be that further observations will show that all novae do this.

Why does a nova shine so brightly? We can find the answer by examining what happens on such a star. Observation shows two things, first that the star suddenly increases in brightness and then tails off back to its original magnitude, either slowly over many months or, in some cases, a matter of weeks. Secondly, spectroscopic evidence shows a blueshift of bright spectral lines, which indicates that what we are looking at is a fast-expanding shell of gas racing outwards at 1,000 km per second or so.

We now have to ask ourselves why this happens. What triggers off the explosive emission of a gas shell? Further studies in recent years have made it clear that every nova is a binary system in which the stars are very close; one of them is a tiny, dense white-dwarf star (page 78), and the other a cool red star. The dense white dwarf pulls off material from the outer parts of the cool star. This material is hydrogen which, when added to the white dwarf, becomes unstable and may suddenly heat up explosively and be shot out into space. That is what causes the nova to flare so suddenly; it falls back to its original brightness as the hydrogen disperses.

A supernova, as its name tells us, is a much brighter occurrence. Typical supernova explosions give a brightness change of some 15 magnitudes (one million times) or even more. As such stars are red supergiants this means that they may shine for a time with a brilliance equal to 10,000 million (10^{10}) Suns. Their explosions also result in the ejection of a shell of gas and, like novae, they very quickly reach maximum brightness and then slowly fade. Unlike novae, they are not binary systems but single stars, and their explosions are due to catastrophic events inside the star itself. Such stars develop a heavy core which contains the element iron, and towards the end of the star's life, this core heats up, absorbing energy as it does so. It shrinks, the iron atoms are broken up and high energy photons (radiation) are emitted; then more energy is sucked in from the rest of the star. In the end this process gets out of control, the core suddenly collapses and emits vast amounts of energy as neutrinos. These rush out, hit the dense overlying gases of the star, and blow them away in a giant explosion.

Stages in the development of a nova from a binary star. *top* Material from the primary body is drawn off to the small, white-dwarf companion. *centre* The material accumulated by the white dwarf becomes unstable, heats, flares up, and explodes in a spectacular fashion. *bottom* After this phase the binary becomes quiet again, and the expelled gas cloud dissipates gradually into space.

THE DEATH OF STARS

No star lasts for ever. All stars die in the end, but the way in which they do depends on how massive they are; the larger die more dramatically than the smaller.

No star lives for ever. Gradually, over the ages, the helium ash inside builds up (page 74) and the star ages, but the nature of its final end depends on how large it is. If the star is not much more massive than our Sun – the critical figure is 1.44 times more massive – then it will end its life as a white dwarf. Such a star is extraordinarily dense, and shines with a white light.

About 150 years ago it was movements of Sirius which led astronomers to discover that Sirius was a binary with a very dim companion (page 52). This companion, called Sirius B, was later observed. Its magnitude was only 8.67, which meant that it was 11,000 times dimmer than Sirius itself (Sirius A). Studies of the spectrum of Sirius B showed that its light was white, but since it was so dim (its absolute magnitude was 11.5) it must have a small surface area otherwise it would be brighter. Calculation showed that it must be only about 1¾ times the size of the Earth. Yet a careful examination of its orbit as companion to Sirius A made it clear that its mass must be as great as that of our Sun. A teaspoonful of Sirius B would weigh not grams but tonnes!

Since the discovery of Sirius B, other white dwarfs have been found, and all the observations and calculations associated with them have made it clear to scientists that the material in a white dwarf is not material in its usual state at all. If a teaspoonful would really weigh tonnes, then obviously we have something far denser than anything we have ever met on Earth. Yet we know that there are only a certain number of chemical elements and only certain nuclear particles from which they can be built. So the only conclusion we can come to is that in a white dwarf, matter is in a 'superdense' state (sometimes called a 'degenerate' state because of the squashed-together arrangement of the nuclear particles and electrons).

Matter is composed of atoms, and every atom has a central core or nucleus which is orbited by one or more electrons. How many electrons depends on the electric charge of the nucleus – how many protons it has – and also on the state of the atom (whether it is ionized or not). What the discovery of white dwarfs has shown is that matter can, under special circumstances, exist in a different 'superdense' state. Here, instead of each atom occupying a relatively large space – the space needed for its nucleus and orbiting electrons – it is possible to pack the particles of the nuclei of many atoms close together with the electrons moving in between them like a gas. In other words, superdense matter consists of protons and neutrons

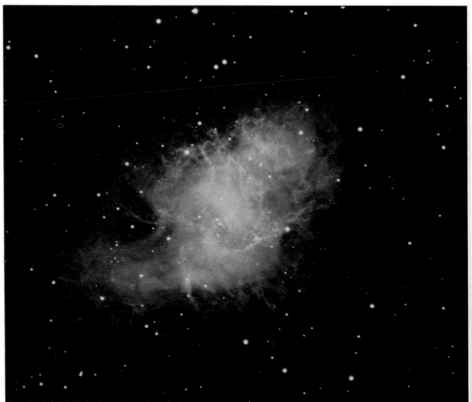

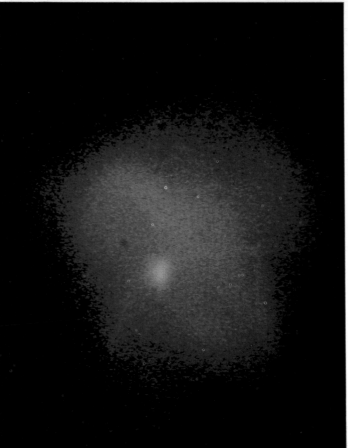

above
The Crab Nebula is the remnant of a supernova explosion. At its centre lies a neutron star that pulses at both radio and optical wavelengths.

left
A record of the X-ray emission from the hot gas of the Crab Nebula, made by the Einstein orbiting X-ray observatory.

packed far more closely than usual and surrounded by an 'electron gas'.

Calculations show that its nuclear particles cannot actually crush together – each one must remain separate – and that its electrons have to move with very high speeds that are well over half the speed of light. So this superdense matter does not behave like ordinary matter; if we increase the mass of a superdense body it gets smaller not larger, and the pressure the electron gas exerts on its surroundings does not depend on temperature at all as it would with an ordinary gas.

Not all of a white dwarf is composed of 'degenerate' matter. In the case of Sirius B, about three-quarters of its material is degenerate.

Most of its matter is in this state because the burning hydrogen has left helium ash and as this accumulated, the core containing it arrived at a stage when it collapsed in on itself. This process usually occurs after the star has become old enough to have reached and passed the red giant or red supergiant stage (page 75). (Our Sun will, it is thought, reach this stage in about 10,000 million (10^{10}) years.) However, some comparatively young white dwarfs are known, but these are previously unstable stars which have probably lost much of their material by throwing off a shell of gas; they are the kind of star which gives us a planetary nebula (page 74).

White dwarfs are found both as single stars and as members of a binary system, but in neither case can they be very large. This is because if a star has a mass of more than the critical value of 1.44 times the Sun's mass, then when its core collapses it will become not a white dwarf but a neutron star. This is a star in which the greater mass has caused the degenerate matter to pack even more closely together. The result is that the protons in the superdense core have been bonded to most of the electrons in the electron gas to give a solid core of neutrons surrounded by a 'fluid' of moving neutrons. Outside this there exists a crystalline crust of atoms about one km thick, and a gaseous atmosphere no thicker than a few centimetres. Such a star will have a diameter of only ten km or thereabouts, and a density a million times greater than a white dwarf.

Until 1967, neutron stars were only known as a theoretical possibility of what a very dense star could be like, but in that year Jocelyn Bell and Anthony Hewish at Cambridge University, England, discovered 'pulsars', stars which pulse or flash at radio wavelengths. The pulses are short (about 50 thousandths of a second) and are frequent, arriving every second or so – the first known pulsar had a period of 1.33730 seconds which it kept to exactly. Pulsars are interpreted as neutron stars because only stars as small as these could rotate so quickly. The stars are very strong magnets and the pulses come from ionized atomic particles rotating through this magnetic field.

It is thought that both white dwarfs and neutron stars will one day cease to shine altogether. Then, and only then, will the stars that made them be truly dead.

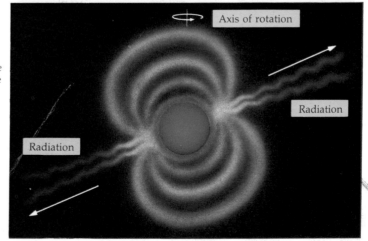

above
a wispy veil of gas is all that remains of the supernova explosion that took place some 10,000 years ago in the Vela constellation. The star that exploded is now a pulsar.

right
Pulsars rotate rapidly on an axis inclined to their magnetic axis. Radio radiation is emitted in the directions shown by the arrows.

Axis of rotation

Radiation

Radiation

X-RAY STARS

Some stars, such as our Sun, emit X-rays only weakly. Others are powerful X-ray sources. Recent research shows that those that emit strongly are the scenes of violent activity.

If a camera sensitive to X-rays, or an X-ray telescope, is sent more than 150 km above the ground and pointed towards the Sun, it will record the fact that the Sun does emit some X-rays. A careful examination of photographs has shown that the X-rays do not come from some source behind the Sun. We are *not* looking at an X-ray picture of the Sun similar to the kind of X-ray shadow picture we get of the human body in a hospital. What astronomers see is that the Sun's thin outer atmosphere

or corona is emitting X-rays. These rays come from patches in the corona which are extremely hot, reaching perhaps four million degrees K. Observations from Skylab, which took simultaneous pictures of the Sun at many wavelengths, show that these hot spots are associated with sunspots and solar flares.

These observations show us that some X-rays are emitted by the Sun and presumably, therefore, by other stars which have 'sunspots' and flares. However, these are the longer wavelength or 'soft' X-rays, which are not so energetic, and X-ray telescopes used in space at the present time are not likely to detect them. On the other hand, such telescopes have observed a considerable number of cosmic X-ray sources that are far more powerful. Some of these are stars, others are associated with clusters of galaxies. Such a source has been found in the Virgo cluster, another in the cluster known as Abell 1060.

The X-ray sources in distant clusters – the Virgo cluster is at about

21 million parsecs (68 million light-years), the Abell one at 46 million parsecs (150 million light-years) – do not seem to be collections of stars. They come from the central region of the cluster and seem to be generated by very hot, thin gas in which the whole cluster is embedded and which may well be at a temperature of ten million degrees. In one sense, then, the X-rays from the clusters of galaxies have one thing in common with those of the Sun, they both originate from hot gas, though the gas in the cluster is billions of times more extensive and far hotter; its X-rays are 'harder' (of much shorter wavelength). However, we can hardly call them X-ray stars, and astronomers usually refer to them by the vaguer term of 'X-ray sources'.

What of X-ray stars themselves? Many have been observed as intense sources in the harder X-ray region of the spectrum, yet from studies of the Sun, it is clear that such radiation is not from stellar coronas; it would be weaker and of different wavelength. The sources are in fact found to be of

The formation of an X-ray star takes place in a binary system (A) in which one star is much brighter than the other. Material is first transferred from the bright primary star to the secondary star (B). Eventually the primary star explodes (C). Material is then transferred back to whatever remains of the primary star and X-rays are emitted in the process (D).

two main kinds – the remnants of a supernova explosion or a binary star in which one of the components is either a white dwarf, a neutron star, or even a black hole (page 82).

That a supernova remnant can be an X-ray emitter is shown by the famous Crab Nebula in Taurus. In recent years observations in optical and radio wavelengths have shown that at the centre of the residue of a supernova explosion is a pulsar; the original star must therefore have collapsed down to a neutron star. However, it is also evident that there is a vast amount of swirling ionized gas and also an intense magnetic field which, of course, we should expect the neutron star to have.

What seems to be happening is that electrons from the ionized gas are moving in spiral paths through this magnetic field. Some are moving so very fast that they emit X-rays by the process known as 'synchrotron' radiation. Named after the synchrotron machine used by nuclear physicists for accelerating nuclear particles to high velocities, the

radiation was first discovered during experiments with it. Physicists found that when electrons were accelerated to high speeds in the magnetic field of the machine, they emitted radiation. The wavelength of this radiation depends on the speed of the electrons; the faster they move the shorter the wavelength becomes. The fact, then, that X-rays are received from the Crab Nebula means that astronomers have more details about what happens after a supernova explosion, namely that electrons are caused to move very fast through a strong magnetic field. This is important for developing further ideas about the way in which stars behave.

Binary stars act as X-ray sources when one of the pair is a white dwarf, neutron star or black hole, because of the transfer of material within the system. The small, very dense white dwarf or neutron star attracts material from its companion, provided the two components are close enough. When this gaseous material moves over to the very

dense star, it suddenly becomes heated strongly enough to emit X-rays. The heating will be sudden and intense, but will not last for long. As is the case with many novae it may shine brightly for longer at optical wavelengths. That is why many binary X-ray sources flare up in less than one second and then fade down in a matter of minutes. Such X-ray flashes or X-ray 'bursters' may occur a number of times within a few days. On some occasions, though, a binary develops less rapidly into an X-ray emitter, taking days to come up to full brilliance, and then may fade over a period of months. Then nothing else seems to happen. In such a case, it appears that the transfer of material is not regular: one large transfer may occur, to be followed by a long quiet period.

If one component of the binary is a black hole, then gas and electrons will stream into it from its companion star. In this case the material will swirl very fast round the hole before it falls in – another instance of the X-rays being synchrotron radiation.

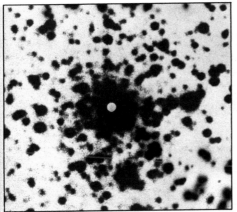

above The photograph shows an X-ray source and X-ray 'burster' – a sudden and intense emission of X-rays. The observations are of the globular cluster Terzan 2, made by the Einstein orbiting X-ray observatory.

Scorpius X-1 is the brightest of all steady X-ray sources and has been positively identified as the binary star V 818.

Abell 1060, a rich cluster of galaxies in Hydra, at some 46 million parsecs away, is an X-ray source. It is thought that the X-rays come from a gas at some 10 million degrees K, which lies in the inner regions of the cluster. The peculiar galaxy (*arrowed*) is really two galaxies. They only appear to be close together because of our line of sight and are in reality separated by millions of parsecs.

BLACK HOLES

Black holes result from the ultimate collapse of matter in the universe. Their nature is bizarre.

We have seen that when a star begins to die, gravity takes over and squashes nearly all its atoms into a superdense state. If the star is about 1½ times as massive as our Sun, then gravity is strong enough to crush the material so much that we end up with a neutron star. But what happens if the star is very massive indeed? What will happen to its matter then?

Theory tells us that if the core of a dying star is very massive, then a runaway situation will develop. Gravity will take over completely and the matter will be crushed down to nothing. The star will have turned into a black hole; 'black' because no light or any other radiation can escape from it, and 'hole' because Riemannian space (page 46) closes round it. It is just as if there were a hole in space, especially since any matter passing too close to it will fall in, never to be seen again.

The fact that so dense a body is black does not surprise astronomers because, almost 200 years ago, the French astronomer Pierre Laplace calculated that if a body were massive enough, it could stop light escaping. He based his ideas on the velocity of escape, in other words on the fact that to escape from any celestial body a certain velocity is needed. To escape from the Earth a spacecraft has to reach a velocity of over 11 km per second; to escape from the more massive Sun it would have to reach more than 617 km per second. Laplace calculated that if a body like the Earth were 250 times larger than the Sun, it would be so massive that nothing could escape, even if it were moving at 300,000 km per second – the speed of light. Light waves emitted from the surface of the body would turn round on themselves, and fall back to the ground.

In the case of a black hole, we are not of course considering material in the state we find it on Earth; we are considering completely degenerate matter. Furthermore, we are doing so in a situation where the theory of relativity (page 132) applies and in which we have every reason to believe that space will curve round the object. The situation is therefore

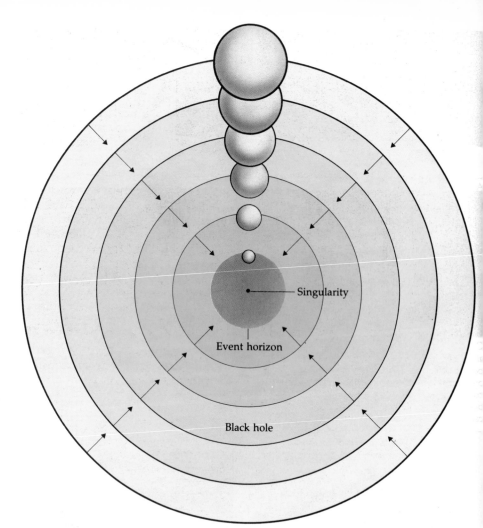

above Looking directly down into an area of distorted space (*see below*) caused by a collapsing body. As a star shrinks so the distortion of space around it becomes greater until, in the end, the collapsing body shrinks to a single point or singularity – a black hole. Space is then closed round it, forming an event horizon from within whose boundaries no radiation of any kind can escape.

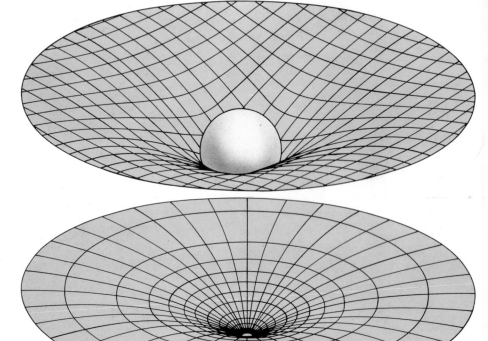

The distortion of space around a collapsing body. The upper picture shows the effect on space of a massive body, the lower one, the effect of shrinking to a singularity in a section of space (and time) cut off from the surrounding universe.

bove The behaviour of eams of light emitted y a massive ollapsing star. To egin with (A) light an escape from the

surface of the star but as collapse continues (B), the rays closest to the surface are pulled back by gravitation. At a still later stage (C)

most rays curve round to orbit the body; this bending takes place at the 'photon sphere' just before the star collapses to a

singularity, inside the event horizon. Only rays moving directly away from the body can escape (D).

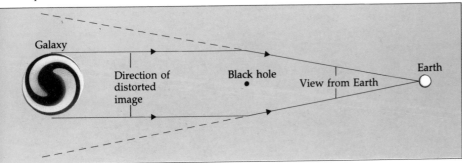

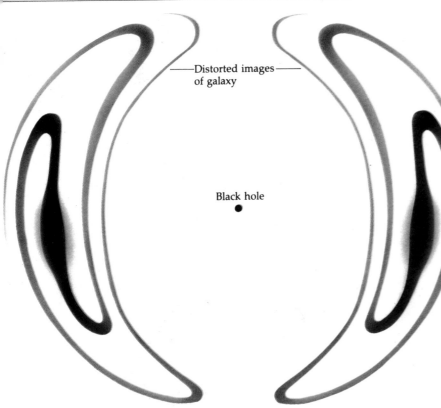

—Distorted images— of galaxy

Black hole •

The distortion of space caused by a black hole is responsible for the

gravitational lens effect (*top*). Light travelling past a black

hole is bent so that the observer sees two distorted images (*above*).

a little different from that envisaged by Laplace, and theory tells us that although the star would shrink to nothing, there would be a space around it within which light could not escape. The size of this space, which is spherical in shape, is known as the 'Schwarzschild radius' after the German astronomer Karl Schwarzschild who first discovered it in 1916.

Interestingly, the mathematical equation he calculated for this space is the same as that calculated by Laplace, although the other equations associated with black holes are entirely new. If we took the Earth and could in some way squash down its material into a black hole, then the equation shows us that the Schwarzschild radius would be only three km. For a star of three solar masses the radius would still be no more than nine km and for a supergiant like Betelgeuse it would only reach 30 km. So where gravity has taken over and a black hole results, even the Schwarzschild radius, the 'no-go' area around the hole, is very small; in the case of Betelgeuse it would have shrunk 6½ thousand million million million (6.5 x 10^{21}) times, and still not be at the black hole stage. That is so tiny we can think of it as no larger than a point; even a dot on this page is larger than the centre of the black hole into which the star's material has gone.

So massive an object as a black hole in so small a volume as even the Schwarzschild radius means a terrific distortion of space. Light rays passing near the no-go Schwarzschild sphere would be bent, in a somewhat similar way to their bending by a lens. Indeed, astronomers refer to the 'gravitational lens' effect (illustrated left). It can, in theory, give rise to two images of the same object which may, as here, be a galaxy. In practice, astronomers believe they have at last observed such an effect (page 97). The distorting body is a galaxy and the two images are those of a quasar (page 94).

The distortion of space around a black hole is immense, but what would happen if we crossed over the boundary given by the Schwarzschild radius? It is not, of course, a solid boundary, but it has a very real existence nonetheless. In general terms what would happen is that as we reached the boundary and moved over it we should notice nothing very different. We should rush into the black hole, to vanish for ever, though on the way any astronaut would be stretched out like a piece of elastic because, in so intense a gravitational field, the pull on an astronaut's feet would far exceed the pull on his head – the 'gravity gradient' from one point to another would be immense. From outside the Schwarzschild sphere, a strange series of events would occur. An observer would see the spacecraft plunge towards the boundary and appear to hover there. No one could see it inside the Schwarzschild sphere because no radiation can escape from within it. What goes on in there is a closed book to anyone outside, so that scientists sometimes refer to a black hole as exercising 'cosmic censorship'. The peculiar effect of the spacecraft hovering at the boundary instead of plunging in is due not only to the distortion of space at the boundary but also to the stretching of time. (This is one of the many effects of relativity theory, as we shall see later – page 138). As no event that happens inside the Schwarzschild sphere can be seen from outside, it has generally become known as the 'event horizon'.

So far we have a very simple picture, because we have imagined a stationary star just collapsing in on itself. But in reality we know of no star likely to be standing still. Like our Sun, all stars rotate, and even the core of a supernova remnant that is massive enough to form a black hole will not be stationary. What is more, evidence from neutron stars shows that a superdense body of degenerate material will rotate very fast, and we need not expect the collapsing core that forms a black hole to be different.

When a black hole rotates it drags space round with it in a kind of whirlpool action so that any body falling into it and any light or other radiation is dragged around with it. The space that is being dragged round extends beyond the event horizon (further out than the Schwarzschild radius) and the region is called the 'ergosphere'. It is here that a distant observer would perceive a moving body as stationary due to its motion and the drag of space around it. A peculiar result of this phenomenon has been pointed out by Roger Penrose of Oxford University, England. Ordinarily, the event horizon of a black hole increases as more material falls into the hole, but it is possible in some circumstances to reduce the event horizon of a rotating black hole by reducing its rotation. If this happened, then energy could be extracted from the hole.

Suppose, as Roger Penrose has suggested, that a spaceship enters the ergosphere in an orbit which would take it out again; and imagine that while inside the ergosphere, a container of waste material is thrown out of the spacecraft. If the material is thrown in the right direction it will slow down the rotation of the hole as it falls into it. This will allow the spacecraft to escape from the ergosphere. What is peculiar about all this is that detailed calculations show that the spacecraft will leave with more energy than it possessed when it entered the ergosphere. The end result is that it would extract energy from the black hole. Of course, we do not ourselves have the technology to do this, but the example is not just an idle dream. There may be natural processes occurring in space whereby it could happen.

Of course, it seems impossible that a black hole could radiate any energy at all because nothing – no energy – can escape from inside the event

Gravitation increases so rapidly close to a black hole that an astronaut falling feet first would have his legs stretched out more than his chest and head.

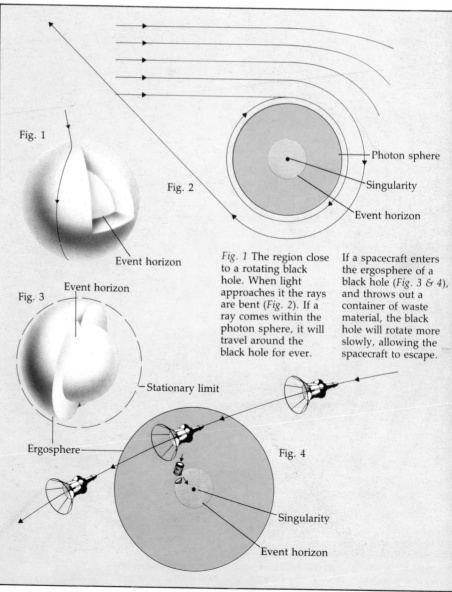

Fig. 1

Fig. 2

Fig. 3

Event horizon

Event horizon

Stationary limit

Ergosphere

Event horizon

Photon sphere

Singularity

Event horizon

Fig. 4

Singularity

Event horizon

Fig. 1 The region close to a rotating black hole. When light approaches it the rays are bent (*Fig. 2*). If a ray comes within the photon sphere, it will travel around the black hole for ever.

If a spacecraft enters the ergosphere of a black hole (*Fig. 3 & 4*), and throws out a container of waste material, the black hole will rotate more slowly, allowing the spacecraft to escape.

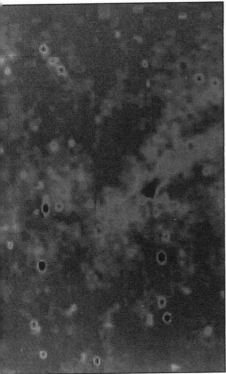

horizon. Yet the fact that something could escape quite naturally is due to an unexpected discovery about black holes: they are not completely cold. At the centre of a black hole, space forms a point, a 'nothingness' or, in more technical language, part of a singularity (the other part is time – page 138); the nuclear particles of the collapsed star which formed the hole are no more. Yet, astoundingly enough, the hole behaves like a generator of fresh nuclear particles, which are moving about inside the event horizon, thus giving all the effects we usually associate with temperature. In brief, black holes have a temperature which depends on their size; the smaller they are, the greater the temperature. A black hole formed by a collapsing star would only be one ten millionth of a degree K, but if microscopic sized black holes were formed at the time of the big bang creation of the universe (page 156), their temperature would be enough for them to be evaporating at about the present time.

above A view looking towards the central regions of our Galaxy. Although it cannot be directly confirmed by observation, it seems likely that a black hole lies in its vicinity.

But if nothing can escape from a black hole, how can it lose energy? How can it radiate? The answer comes from the very studies that have proved that black holes are not cold. Among the nuclear particles that are generated inside the event horizon will be particle pairs – one ordinary particle coupled with its antiparticle. (An antiparticle is one which has the same mass as an ordinary particle but an opposite electrical charge.) For instance electron/positron pairs will be generated. One of these will slip back into the black hole but the other will move through the event horizon and then speed away through the ergosphere, just as a spacecraft would do after dumping its waste (which is equivalent to one of the members of the particle pair slipping back into the hole).

Have any black holes been observed? Mini black holes should be hot enough to detect, or at least their final evaporation, which is explosive, should be. Yet so far none have been found and some astronomers doubt their existence. The case is quite different, however, when it comes to large black holes of the kind left by a collapsing star, or something even larger. Although, of course, one cannot observe such objects directly because they do not shine at any wavelength, their presence can be deduced by their gravitational effects. At least three galaxies come into this category. The galaxy M87 has a jet of material connected to its central regions and this, together with the movement of stars within the galaxy and the emission of X-rays, makes it clear that there is something very massive at the centre. A vast black hole would meet the case admirably. Again our own Galaxy may well contain a large black hole at its centre (page 54), while X-rays from another galaxy, Centaurus A, make it seem likely that these are due to material streaming into a central black hole. In all cases, the X-rays would be emitted due to synchrotron radiation (page 81), as they would be by material streaming from one component of a binary star system to the other, which seems to be the explanation for the X-ray source Cygnus X-1. Here one companion is totally invisible and it could well be the remains of a large star that exploded and left only a black hole. Indeed, astronomers think that many black holes of this kind may exist, for there are many X-ray stars and, as so many stars are binaries, the astronomers may well be right.

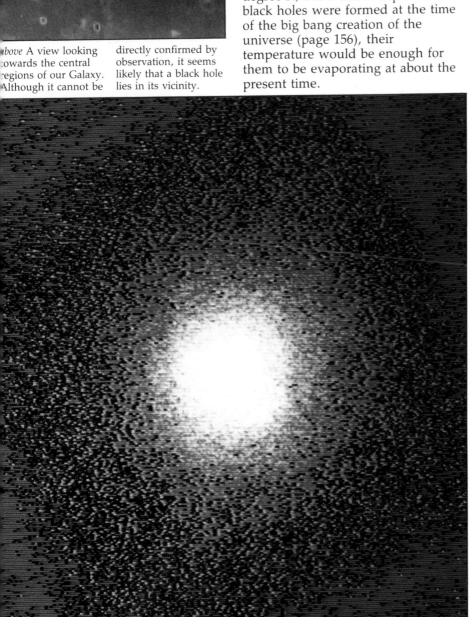

An X-ray picture of the elliptical galaxy M87 in Virgo. The galaxy is extremely active and it is thought that it might have a black hole at its centre.

CHAPTER 5
GALAXIES AND
INTERGALACTIC
SPACE

With a powerful telescope, we can discern hundreds and thousands of galaxies. In recent years, studies have shown that galaxies are surrounded by intergalactic gas and dust.

It was almost 200 years ago that astronomers first began to detect and catalogue galaxies, but without at the time knowing what they were. Only within the last 60 years have astronomers known that we and our Sun were part of one galaxy among millions, and only since then have they discovered that galaxies come in a vast variety of sizes and shapes. Galaxies, large and small, are found in every direction in which we can observe, some gathered together in groups and clusters, others seemingly existing on their own.

To begin with, astronomers had only one band of radiation to bring them such information as they could obtain about galaxies. This was light. Only by photographing these distant objects – for even the nearest are further than 50,000 parsecs (160,000 light-years) away – was it possible to study them. But now there are a host of other wave-lengths in which they can be examined, and of these X-rays and radio waves are the most important. Indeed, radio observations of galaxies have proved of immense significance and there are even 'radio galaxies' (page 92), the study of which has given us a clue as to the explosive, energetic nature of these objects.

When photographs were first taken of galaxies, most seemed to be separate objects, just as the first photographs of stars made it look as though most stars were separate, whereas we now know that many are really binary or multiple systems. We now recognize that some – probably the majority – of galaxies are connected together in some way. As we have already seen (pages 54–57) our Galaxy extends much further into space than was once believed. Whether our Galaxy incorporates smaller nearby galaxies like the

Magellanic Clouds (page 102) or not, it is certain that they interact with our Galaxy. Evidence of this interaction is to be seen in what is now called the Magellanic Stream – a stream of neutral hydrogen gas which passes near the south pole of our Galaxy and envelops the Magellanic Clouds. Being neutral (i.e. not ionized), hydrogen does

not show up visually, though it can be readily detected by radio-telescope.

We are not sure how the Magellanic Stream came about, although astronomers at the present time think there are two possibilities. One is that the hydrogen was pulled out of the Clouds by their close approach to our Galaxy some time in the not too distant past. The other is

The spiral galaxy M31, photographed with the four-metre telescope at Kitt Peak. A companion elliptical galaxy can also be seen.

that the gas stream, which is moving very fast – around 200 km per second in the neighbourhood of the Sun – was never part of the Clouds, or of any other galaxy for that matter. It is suggested instead that the Stream is part of an intergalactic gas cloud which envelops not only our own Galaxy and the Magellanic Clouds, but also the other galaxies which form what astronomers call the Local Group (page 104).

Whatever the true explanation of the Magellanic Stream may be, its existence underlines the important fact that gas not only surrounds galaxies but often forms 'lanes' between one galaxy and another. Moreover, new telescopes with superior optics, using more sensitive photographic plates, as well as electronographic cameras and even photon counters, have detected such gas connections in other galaxies. Perhaps some of this is not unexpected. Galaxies are collections – islands, if you like – of dust, gas and stars, and are still the scenes of star formation. We might therefore expect them to be enveloped in gas far beyond the boundaries which appear so clear in earlier photographs. What is more surprising, though, are the lanes of intergalactic matter. These show clearly that interactions are taking place between galaxies, especially those in groups or clusters, even though such reactions stretch over tens of thousands and even millions of parsecs.

Detecting and studying such intergalactic material is important because at the present time astronomers are trying to work out how much material – stars, dust and gas – the universe contains. The answer to this crucial question will tell them whether the universe will continue to expand for ever or not (page 160). Each new observation of material has, therefore, considerable significance.

Galaxies are always on the move. Observations with the spectroscope show that they all have redshifts and an analysis of this movement is evidence that every galaxy is moving away from every other galaxy. It means, of course, that galaxies were closer together in the past than they are now, and we may wonder whether they ever collided when they were closer together. Is there any chance of galaxies, such as those in a group or cluster, colliding? The answer is that collisions were and are possible, and are not as unlikely as one might imagine.

There is a class of galaxy – a 'ring' galaxy – each one of which is thought to be the remains of a collision. One such example is NGC 1510, the 'Cartwheel' galaxy. A computer study indicates that it seems to have been caused by a collision about 300 million years ago between a large flat galaxy with spiral arms and a smaller galaxy without spiral arms which penetrated the central regions of the larger galaxy. The collision caused a ripple, or density-wave, to pass through the larger galaxy, the passage of this wave setting off the birth of what are now young blue stars. Hot glowing gas also marks the passage of the wave. Clearly, a study of galaxies like these provides additional evidence of the way in which stars are born.

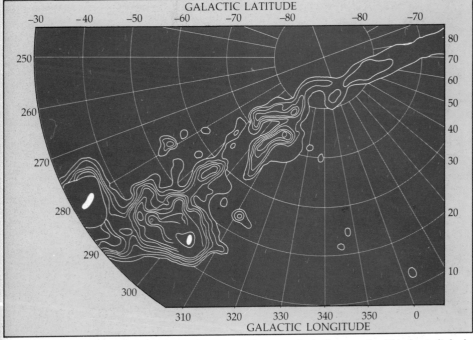

above A chart showing the strength of radio waves received from the Magellanic Stream. These results indicate that our Galaxy and the Clouds are linked by gas.

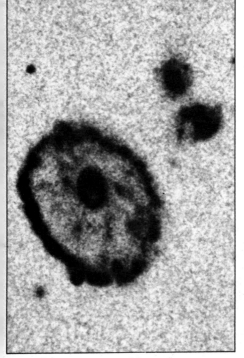

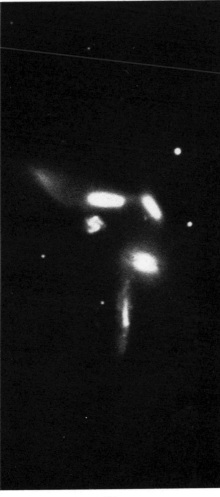

above
The Cartwheel ring galaxy was formed by collision between two older galaxies; one now forms the ring and the other the right-hand of its two companions.

right
A group of five galaxies, NGC 6027, in Hercules. The photograph shows the unusual connecting clouds between them.

OPTICAL GALAXIES

Optical galaxies are those which can be photographed in ordinary light. They were the first to be detected by astronomers and form the basis for the classification of all other types of galaxy.

Although there are three galaxies that can be seen with the unaided eye – the Andromeda galaxy M31 in northern hemisphere skies, and the two Magellanic Clouds for observers of the southern skies – most galaxies need to be observed by photography with large telescopes. Some advanced amateurs have, it is true, taken astonishingly good pictures of a few nearer ones, but only because they use specialized photographic techniques; most galaxies need telescopes of 1½ metres aperture or more if their detail is to be shown up sufficiently well for study.

If astronomers are going to understand the nature of galaxies and sort out the multiplicity of types which even the earliest photographs showed to exist, they have to devise means of classification. One possible means would be brightness, though, unless one could measure distances accurately, this would not be very satisfactory. Spectroscopic studies show that galaxies are collections of stars, but this again does not provide a sound basis for distinguishing one kind of galaxy from another. The most useful way to classify them for future research is to do so according to shape. This was the method used by the American astronomer Edwin Hubble in the 1920s and it forms the basis of the classification used today.

Hubble noticed that there were primarily two kinds of galaxies, spiral and elliptical. Spirals, as their name implies, have a bright centre from which spiral arms radiate. Our own Galaxy is just such a spiral, though Hubble did not know this when he made his classification. Elliptical galaxies are quite different. They show no spiral structure at all and seem to have a rather hazier edge than many spirals. Some ellipticals also display a conspicuous lack of bright gaseous material and seem to be composed almost entirely of stars alone.

A more detailed examination shows that elliptical galaxies come in all kinds of shapes from almost

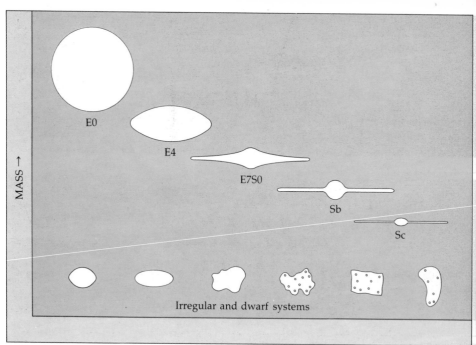

above A new classification system of galaxies, running from elliptical E0 to spirals Sc, has been suggested. Irregular and dwarf systems and objects like the Magellanic Clouds are classified separately. The classification assumes a relationship between mass and angular momentum. The spiral galaxies possess more rotational energy than the massive elliptical ones and are therefore flatter.

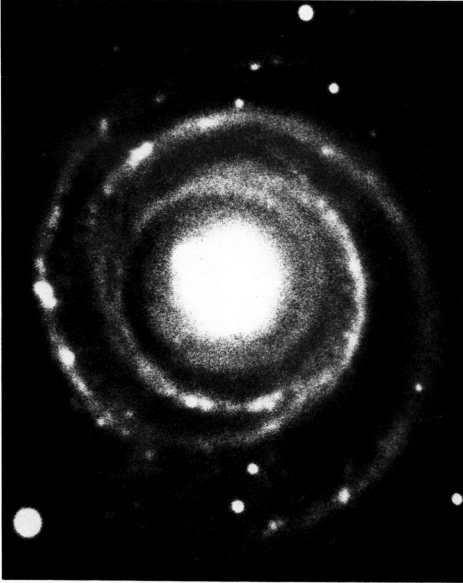

In the spiral galaxy NGC 4622, the shape of the arms is somewhere between that of an open and a closed spiral galaxy. It is classed as an Sb, as is our own Galaxy.

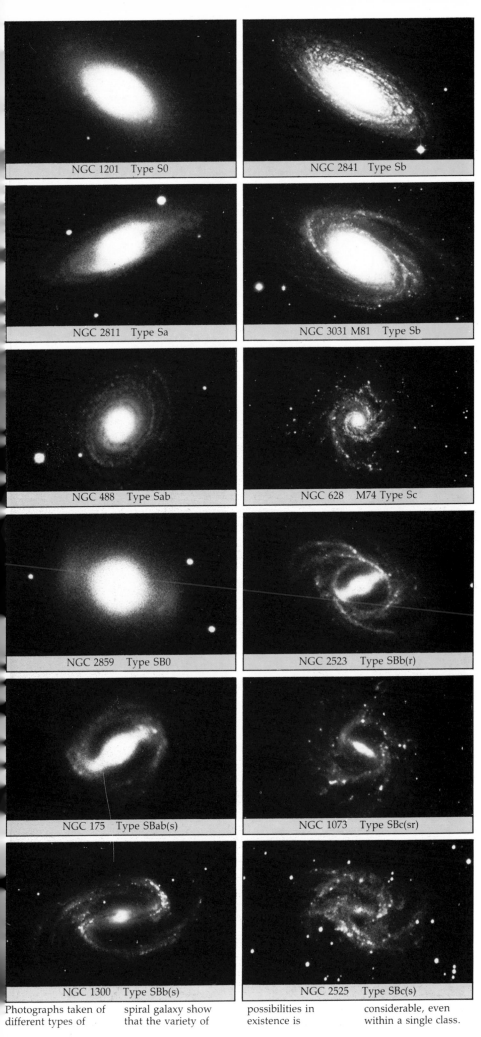

NGC 1201   Type S0

NGC 2841   Type Sb

NGC 2811   Type Sa

NGC 3031 M81   Type Sb

NGC 488   Type Sab

NGC 628   M74 Type Sc

NGC 2859   Type SB0

NGC 2523   Type SBb(r)

NGC 175   Type SBab(s)

NGC 1073   Type SBc(sr)

NGC 1300   Type SBb(s)

NGC 2525   Type SBc(s)

Photographs taken of different types of spiral galaxy show that the variety of possibilities in existence is considerable, even within a single class.

spherical to very elongated, like a magnifying lens seen edge-on. One of the problems of classifying them is that how elliptical they appear to be depends partly on the length of the photographic exposure, since dimmer outlying stars do not show up unless the exposure is long enough. The shape also depends to some extent on our viewpoint. Nevertheless a general scheme has been worked out, and ellipticals are classified according to their shape as seen in photographs on which they are not over-exposed. An elliptical is given a letter 'E', followed by a number denoting ellipticity. E0 is a spherically shaped elliptical galaxy while E7 denotes a very elliptical one; none are found to be more elliptical than E7.

For those who like mathematics, the way the number is assigned to an elliptical may be of interest. An ellipse has two axes or 'diameters', a long one a and a shorter one b. If we take the ratio of the difference between these and divide by the longer axis – i.e. if we take $(a - b)/a$ then we get a series of numbers. If $a = b$, as it does for a circle, then the ratio is zero; that gives us E0 for a spherically shaped elliptical galaxy. If the system is very flat then b will be very small compared with a, and the ratio becomes almost equal to a/a or 1. So the number range runs in theory from E0 to E1, with E0.1, E0.2 etc. in between. For convenience, astronomers omit the '0' part of the number and classify ellipticals from 0 to as high as their observations take them, which turns out to be an ellipticity of 0.7 or E7.

Elliptical galaxies closely resemble one another, whatever their E number may be. Their colours are all similar and the stars which compose them are all yellow and red, with K-type yellow-orange stars and M-type red ones predominating. Towards the centre, ellipticals are redder than towards the outside, and this is probably so for two reasons. First, it is possible that the stars at the centre were the first to form and so are now the oldest, having reached the red giant stage of their life cycle. Alternatively the colour may be due partly to differences in composition, for studies with the spectroscope show that the amount of elements heavier than helium is concentrated in the central regions, and diminishes as we go away from them.

Because the stars in an elliptical galaxy are all moving about, its most likely shape is a 'solid oval' or, to be more precise, an 'oblate spheroid' – an elliptical shape with its longer axis sideways (bun-shaped rather than egg-shaped). Taken together with the fact that photographs do not show up the whole faint edge of an elliptical, it seems that this means elliptical galaxy classes such as E0 and E1 are really more flattened than they seem. And there is another factor too; we may well be viewing some from their ends, in which case they would appear rounder than they really are, due to their position relative to us. The conclusion is, then, that ellipticals really are elliptical, even though some look spherical.

Though elliptical galaxies appear to be similar in composition, they certainly vary widely in size. The smallest are the dwarf ellipticals, which probably have a mass equivalent to no more than 100,000 (10^5) Suns, whereas the large ellipticals are a million times more massive. The most massive galaxy known, M87 (a photograph of it appears on page 168), is equivalent to 10 million million (10^{13}) Suns. A count of ellipticals shows that dwarfs are the most numerous, with very large giant ones well in the minority. Recent studies have also shown that much of their matter is not in a

particularly luminous form, so the old idea that they were composed only of stars is misleading. On the other hand, what precisely this material may be is uncertain. Stars, we know, shed material in the form of stellar 'winds' (page 70) and sometimes more violently in nova and supernova outbursts; some of this material turns to dust, at least that material shed by cooler stars, such as those predominating in elliptical galaxies. However, the problem is still not completely solved, for observation makes it clear that ellipticals do not have the vast amounts of gas, spiral galaxies have.

Spiral galaxies, the other main type of optical galaxy, are clearly recognizable because they have a bright central core with spiral arms wrapped round it. A study of the many spirals that have been observed shows that the spiral arms lie in a very thin plane. This is true in the case of our own Galaxy (page 56).

Spirals are divided into two main classes, those in which the central condensation is roughly circular, and those which have a bar of material that appears to pass through the central nucleus. The second type are known as 'barred spirals'. Both

ordinary spirals as well as the barred ones vary in the way the arms are wrapped. They may be wrapped closely round the bright central nucleus or they may present various degrees of 'unwrapping'. Edwin Hubble therefore classified spirals into S (ordinary spirals) and SB (barred spirals), and in each class he began with a zero – S0 and SB0 – to denote those which have a disc only and no spiral arms. Then for those which do have arms, he added the letters 'a', 'b' and 'c' to denote how tightly the arms are wound. Sa and SBa are tightly wound, Sb and SBb are more open, while Sc and SBc refer to the most open-armed types. If you want to add numbers to describe the degree of unwinding, you can do so by taking the angle between the bright nucleus and the arm as 10° for 'a', about 15° for 'b' and something like 20° for 'c', but obviously some judgement must be exercised; this classification is not exact and the borderline between one class and the next is vague. Hubble looked on the S0 and SB0 type galaxies as a kind of transition between ellipticals and spirals, a point to which we shall come back later (page 98).

The irregular galaxy NGC 3077 in Ursa Major is a type II irregular and is therefore composed of older (Population II) stars. The bright object at the top right of the photograph is the over-exposed image of a star in our own Galaxy.

Examples of 'peculiar' galaxies which defy classification. *Fig. 1* is a spiral with additional material, *Fig. 2* is either an irregular, or two interacting galaxies.

Since Hubble's original classification, far more observations have been made, and astronomers have subdivided the classes, so that spirals poor in glowing gas ('anaemic' spirals) are differentiated from those with the usual amount. The 'transition' S0 and SB0 galaxies between E7 ellipticals and Sa and SBa have also been subdivided in a way which depends, firstly, on the size of the central nucleus and, secondly, on the size of the whole disc.

The main difference between spirals and ellipticals is, of course, the presence of plenty of dust and gas in spirals as well as the appearance of spiral arms. What does this signify? Why are ellipticals so different? The answer to these questions seems to lie in the kinds of stars the galaxies contain. As we have seen, elliptical galaxies have predominantly old stars, but not so spirals. In the Sa types we find two star populations: Population II are old stars and are to be found mainly in the central regions – as we saw with our own Galaxy (page 54) – and Population I, which are young stars. These, as we know (page 66), form from gas and dust in the spiral arms, and as we go from Sa through to Sc,

we find them in increasing numbers. What is more, the amount of neutral hydrogen in spirals increases as we move from Sa to Sc, and in Sc types we find many patches of ionized hydrogen; in Sa types such patches are far fewer.

Spirals are bluer in colour than ellipticals because of the presence of so many young Population I stars. In ellipticals this number is very small. So we must conclude that the real birthplace of stars at the present time, whatever happened in the past, is in the arms of spiral galaxies. And since the number of stars being born is related to the degree in which the arms are wrapped round the central nucleus (with the less wrapped (Sc) producing more stars) it becomes evident that there really is a link between spiral form and the processes in the galaxy itself.

In barred spiral galaxies, the arms spiral inwards until they meet the bar of material stretching out each side of the nucleus. The distance from the centre of the galaxy to which the bar stretches varies from one barred spiral to another, but only over a comparatively small range. Examination of photographs shows that this distance varies between

5–10,000 parsecs (between 16,000 and 33,000 light-years). In other respects barred spirals are like the unbarred type; SBc galaxies contain more young stars and more neutral and ionized hydrogen than SBa ones.

Not every galaxy in the sky is covered by the classification into ellipticals and spirals. There are some which almost defy classification; some are just called lenticular galaxies because they are shaped very like lenses, sometimes displaying a dark curved patch or two of obscuring matter. They are, in fact, virtually the same as Hubble's S0 galaxies. As far as other irregular galaxies are concerned, some (type I) are very blue, which means they contain many young stars, and others (type II) are yellowish in colour. Most irregulars are less massive than spirals; their masses are equivalent to rather less than 10,000 million (10^{10} Suns), whereas spirals all have at least this mass and may reach the equivalent of 100,000 million (10^{11}) Suns.

By and large, elliptical, spiral and even irregular galaxies may seem to be unexciting bodies, at least from an optical point of view. But as we shall soon see, this is an illusion.

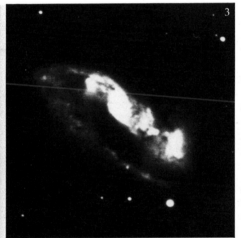

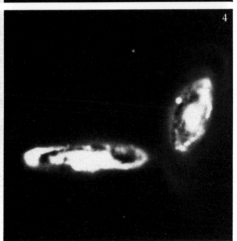

These two further peculiar examples (*Figs. 3 and 4*) are both interacting pairs. The upper shows a galaxy associated with a vast amount of intergalactic material.

The dwarf elliptical galaxy, M32 (NGC 221), is one of two companion galaxies to the Great Galaxy, M31, in Andromeda.

RADIO GALAXIES

Some galaxies are strong emitters of radio waves. Studies at certain wavelengths confirm that explosive events are responsible.

Do galaxies emit radio waves? As we detect radio emission in our own Galaxy, particularly from neutral hydrogen gas at a wavelength of 21 cm, we might expect other spiral galaxies to emit some radio radiation.

From 1951 onwards studies were made of nearer galaxies, such as the great spiral in Andromeda. As radio-telescopes improved and radio interferometer telescopes (page 28) were developed which could provide more detailed information, it became evident that these other spirals also emitted radio radiation at the 21-cm wavelength, in a similar way to our own Galaxy. Radio waves it seemed were just one of many wavelengths coming from normal spiral systems and did not indicate anything out of the ordinary.

However, during the early cataloguing of radio sources, radio astronomers also noticed several other very strong sources, some of which did not seem to have optical counterparts. It later turned out that these were galaxies in which particularly energetic events were occurring, with the result that radio waves were being emitted in great profusion. They had not been noticed before, either because they did not strike optical astronomers as being unusual or because they were dim and inconspicuous.

Some of these 'active galaxies' are very rich in both ionized and neutral hydrogen and, as can be seen when examined by modern optical telescopes, though they are small and compact, they are highly luminous for their size. A probable explanation is that such galaxies are at an early stage of development and are producing numerous new stars.

Other galaxies do not emit much thermal energy – they do not shine brightly at any wavelengths, either optical or radio, generated by heated gas – but nevertheless emit strongly at some other radio wavelengths. These 'active galaxies' are undergoing some kind of upheaval with the result that electrons are spiralling very fast in a strong magnetic field, giving rise to synchrotron radiation (page 76).

Galaxies which are strong emitters of radio waves are called 'radio galaxies' and many thousands are known. Of those that can be linked with optical counterparts, only a minority are probably producing large numbers of new stars at present.

Most radio galaxies display two separate components – two radio bright 'lobes' separated by an arc minute or thereabout. When the first pair of lobes, known as Cygnus 'A', was detected in 1950, they formed the brightest known radio source in the sky. Their nature remained a mystery, however, until in 1954 when, using the 5-m Palomar telescope, they were found to be

above
The galaxy NGC 2623 is a strong radio source and seems possibly to be undergoing an eruption.

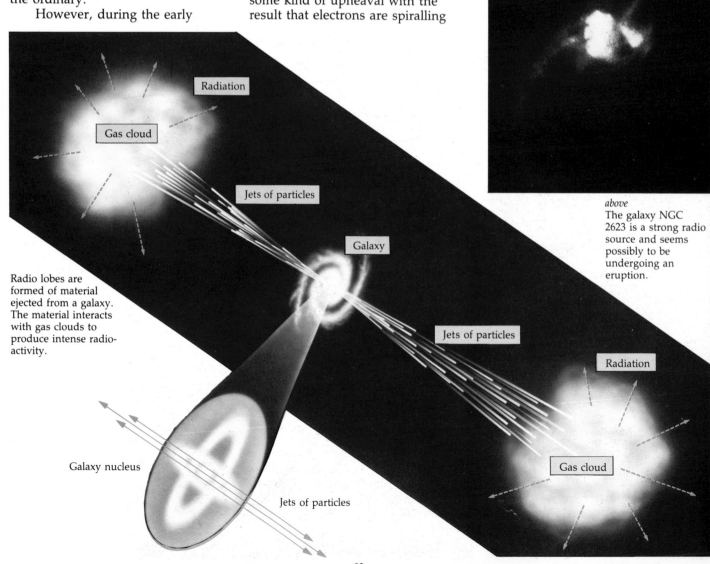

Radio lobes are formed of material ejected from a galaxy. The material interacts with gas clouds to produce intense radio-activity.

Radiation

Gas cloud

Jets of particles

Galaxy

Jets of particles

Radiation

Galaxy nucleus

Gas cloud

Jets of particles

situated on either side of what seemed to be a dim optical galaxy with a magnitude of only 16, that is more than 30,000 times dimmer than the great Andromeda Galaxy. A spectrum taken with the telescope showed that as well as the usual dark-line spectrum the galaxy also displayed bright emission lines, a sure sign of hot gas and eruptive conditions.

But as the radio lobes were situated on either side of the optical galaxy, separated by 1½ arc minutes, an estimated distance of something like 70,000 parsecs (240,000 light-years) apart, the immediate question was whether they really were associated with the galaxy. However as time went on, other similar objects were observed. Pairs of lobes were discovered lying from anything

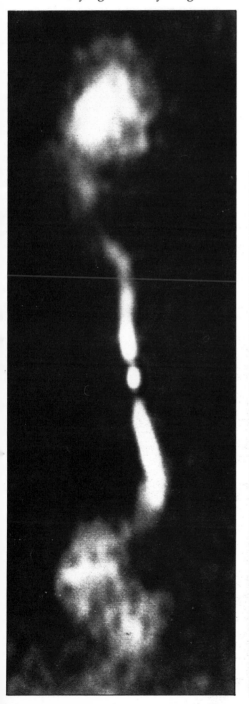

between ten thousand and a million parsecs from an optical component. The lobes themselves, it was found, ranged between one and 50 thousand parsecs across.

What does the presence of these lobes indicates? Are they really part of a ring of gas around the galaxy, ejected by some gigantic explosion? This could certainly explain some isolated cases, but does not seem to fit all the evidence. If they were ring-shaped gas clouds, (rather like ring doughnuts), then we would expect to see them from a variety of angles, so that some at least would appear to encircle galaxies. Yet in every case all we observe are separate patches of gas. It seems instead that some gigantic explosion has occurred in these galaxies, shooting out two jets of gas and nuclear particles. We would expect this gas to be highly magnetized because of the ionized particles within it and to react in some way with the gas found in intergalactic space. Detailed studies in recent years have confirmed this idea. The clouds often contain regions where radiation is being emitted very strongly, especially at their edges, and is just the sort of thing we should expect where the

clouds meet the intergalactic gas. It should also be expected that the electrons from the ionized gas in the clouds could be forced to move at very high speeds inside the magnetic field. This would cause the synchrotron radiation and give just the kind of radio picture we receive. The radiograph of the radio galaxy 3C449 shows it all very clearly.

Radio galaxies with gas clouds may be either ellipticals or spirals. But whichever they are, they must be in rotation to prevent them from collapsing in on themselves. And yet the strange thing is that the direction of the clouds and any jets associated with them seem always to remain the same in space relative to one another. The only answer seems to be that the material forming the clouds is always ejected from the north and south poles of the galaxy; in other words along the axis of rotation. Certainly, observation shows that this is true of the giant elliptical radio galaxy Centaurus 'A'.

Radio galaxies, then, are certainly regions where immense upheavals are taking place on a galactic scale. But they are not the only sources of prodigious radio radiation in deep space.

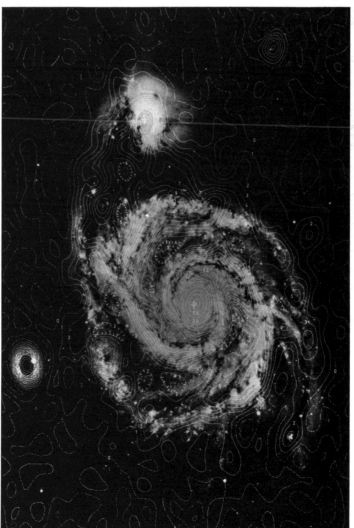

left
From this radio map of the spiral galaxy M51, which has been superimposed on the galaxy's optical image, it can be seen that most radio emission comes from the centre of the galaxy and from the two companion galaxies to the left of it. The galaxy at the top is also a radio source.

far left
The radiograph of 3C 449 – a picture prepared from radio observations – shows clearly the lobes of radio-bright material ejected by the galaxy.

QUASARS

Quasars are blue star-like objects, but they are certainly not stars. Modern research shows that they may be the compact central regions of very distant galaxies

The discovery of quasars was quite unexpected. In 1960 the position of a radio source, 3C48, was found precisely enough for it to be identified optically. It appeared to be an insignificant blue star, yet it gave a spectrum which no astronomer could recognize, and emitted radio waves which were far too strong for an ordinary star, even a hot blue one.

Two years later, in 1962, the position of another strong radio source, 3C273, was precisely determined. It was found to comprise two sources, one coinciding again with a dim blue star, and the other, with a star which had a faint jet associated with it. The spectrum of this source also could not be identified. It was only later realized that the spectral lines of these two sources had not been recognized because they had shifted from the ultra-violet into the visible range, far greater redshifts than had been previously observed. Both radio sources looked like stars, but in reality they were something else and became known as 'quasi-stellar radio sources' or quasars for short.

Since those discoveries a host of other quasars have been found and now more than 1,500 are known. With their appearance another peculiar fact has come to light; the majority of quasars are not strong radio emitters. It was radio emission from objects in the 3C catalogue of radio sources that drew attention to them in the first place, but it has now turned out that the emitters are in a minority. Indeed, astronomers now tend to refer to them as QSOs, omitting the 'r' for radio.

QSOs are distributed all over the sky; they do not show a preference for any particular area, and in this respect are just like galaxies. In appearance, those that are near enough to be seen in some kind of detail, look rather like Seyfert galaxies – spiral galaxies with bright central regions and dim arms, such as those catalogued by the American astronomer Carl Seyfert in the early 1940s. But how do their spectra compare? Are they of the type

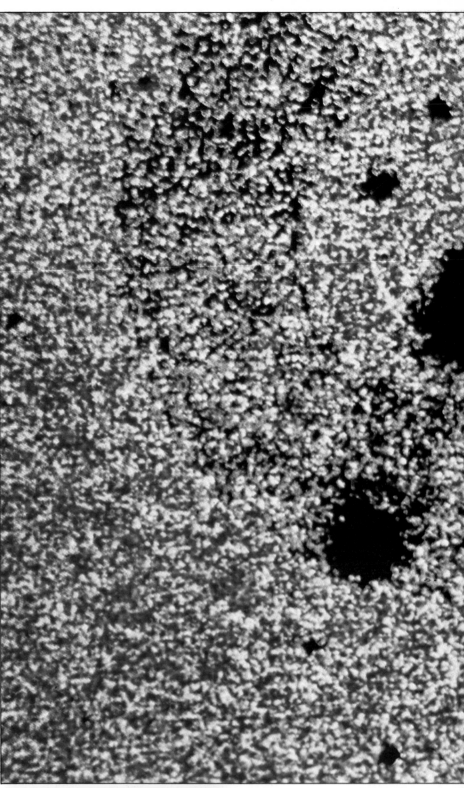

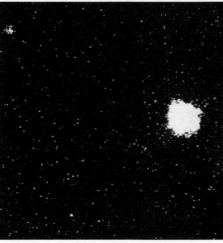

left
The photograph of X-ray emission from the Quasar 3C 273, and also from a new and yet uncatalogued quasar, was taken by the Einstein orbiting X-ray observatory.

above
In this negative picture of quasar 3C 273, the contrast has been enhanced by computer. The broad ring has nothing to do with the quasar but is a feature which has been introduced by the telescope, the 2.2-m at the University of Hawaii. The quasar's irregular appearance, however, is due to gaseous material around it.

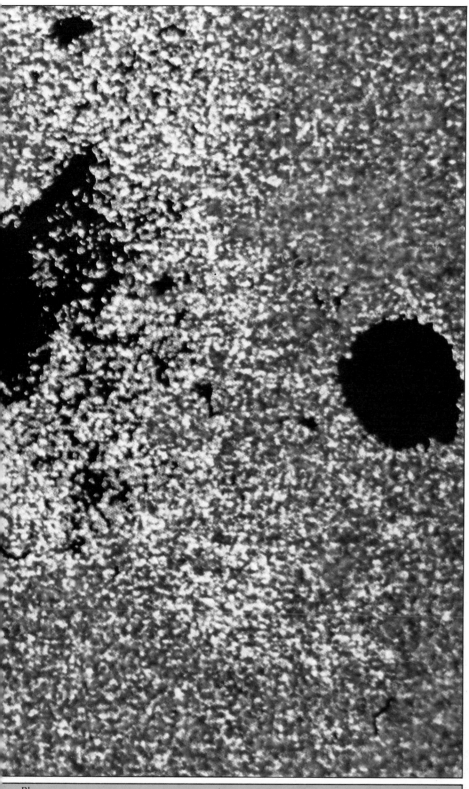

Blue   Red

Quasar Spectrum

Hβ   Hγ   Hδ

Reference Spectrum

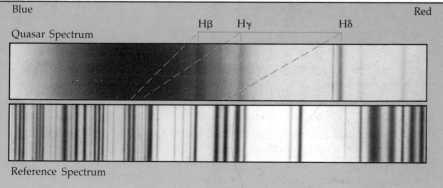

associated with galaxies? The answer is both 'yes and no'; they do show dark lines in the same way as galaxy spectra, but they also exhibit bright lines, which, of course, we should expect with a radio source.

One puzzle, however, is that a single QSO spectrum can show a series of different redshifts. One QSO in particular, QSO PHL 957, shows the highest possible redshift for its bright line spectrum and exhibits five other different, slightly smaller, redshifts for the ordinary dark line (galactic type) spectrum. What this means is not certain, but it may indicate that the object has shed a number of envelopes of gas, each with a different velocity.

Another characteristic of QSOs is that their radiation does not remain constant. Neither does that of a Seyfert galaxy, but the distinction is that QSOs often have a very much shorter period of variation, ranging from a few days to ten years and more. The range of brightness is not great – it is never more than 3 magnitudes – but what is important is that the region from which the variable radiation comes is very small. We know this to be so because the faster a body's radiation-output varies, the smaller it must be. This is true for the simple reason that radiation takes time to travel. If, for instance, a body's output varies over a period of weeks, then it must be small enough for radiation in all parts to be in step and therefore its diameter must be comparatively small. Calculation shows that the diameter must be not larger than 3 million million (3×10^{12}) kilometres. If the body were larger, then some regions would be dim while others would be bright, and overall no variation would be observed. So QSOs must be small. However this raises another serious problem; how does such a small object radiate so much energy, for QSOs can emit a hundred times more radiation than a normal galaxy.

If QSOs were not as far away as most astronomers think, the problem would not arise, because the energy source would not have to be so intense. Why are they, therefore, generally thought to be so very distant? The answer is in the way the distances of remote galaxies are measured. Galaxies close to us (whose distances have been measured by other means) are known to show increasing redshift velocity (page 20) the further away they are, and this fact has led astronomers to use velocity as a

The lines of the spectrum of quasar 3C 73 are extremely redshifted. A comparison between lines Hβ, Hγ and Hδ, which relate to hydrogen, on the quasar spectrum and on the reference spectrum shows the redshift to be 16%.

measure of remoteness. The very large redshifts of QSOs, in some cases reaching 80% the speed of light, imply that QSOs, are very distant objects indeed. Some are believed to lie further away than even the remotest galaxies.

Is there some other explanation for the vast redshifts of QSOs? We know that they are very compact bodies – some of them have diameters less than one thousandth of an arc second – and relativity theory (page 136) tells us that the more massive a body is, the more energy radiation has to use to escape. Consequently the lines in a QSO spectrum are redshifted. Unfortunately, this relativistic redshift will not account for the kind of shifts that are observed, nor for even a substantial number of them. The answer therefore seems to be quite definite: the redshift of QSOs is due to their motion away from us.

A simple way to explain this would be to assume that QSOs are the remains of some explosion, perhaps within our own Galaxy, which has shot out material far and wide. This does not seem very likely.

Radio galaxies show us that material emitted tends to be shot out in only two directions, and to release intense amounts of radio radiation. But could QSOs be the remains of some gigantic explosion or series of explosions in intergalactic space? After all, we have seen galaxies which seem possibly to be breaking up. The radio source Centaurus 'A' (photograph on page 162) is a case in point. However, again we come up against the problem that the majority of QSOs are not radio sources at all, or not strong ones anyway. And if QSOs were due to explosions in intergalactic space, we should expect to see some coming towards us as well as some moving away; in other words we should expect to observe high blueshifts as well as redshifts.

It is, of course, possible that what are called QSOs are two different kinds of object: those which are strong radio emitters, and those that are radio quiet. The radio emitters certainly do display all the characteristics we would expect of explosive galaxies such as M87 (photograph page 168). But what of the radio quiet QSOs? Might they be

something quite different? This is an attractive idea but the evidence does not seem to bear it out; both types of QSO may be associated with galaxies though there are certainly some observations that need explanation.

Some QSOs seem to lie very close to galaxies, for instance the radio-emitting QSO 3C275.1 and the galaxy NGC 4651, and if photograph of QSOs are examined five other pairs like this one can be found. However as the QSOs and galaxies have quite different redshifts, perhaps their apparent nearness is just an effect of perspective. However the odds against this are high; one astronomer calculated that they are as much as 25,000 to one. What is more, some pairs of QSOs have been observed in association with galaxies with much smaller redshifts than their own, inferring that the galaxies and the QSOs must be travelling at quite different speeds. Could it be that QSOs are composed of material emitted from galaxies after all.

In support of the view that QSOs cannot be as distant as they are generally supposed is yet another

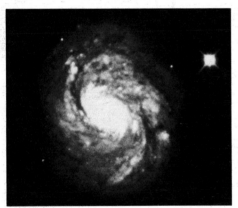

above The Sb spiral M77 (NGC 1068) in Serpens is a Seyfert galaxy. It is thought that its bright central region may contain a QSO.

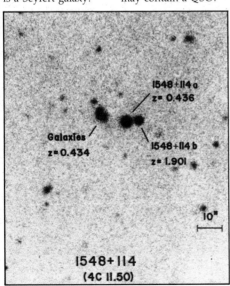

1548+114a
z= 0.436

Galaxies
z= 0.434

1548+114b
z= 1.901

10"

1548+114
(4C 11.50)

The galaxies and QSOs, seen here in the same field of view, appear to form a group. But they have different redshifts.

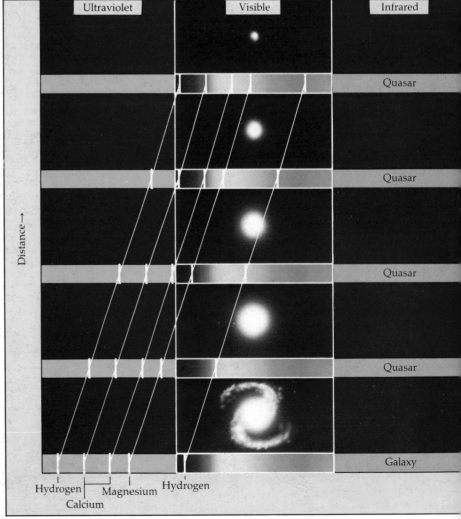

Ultraviolet	Visible	Infrared
		Quasar
		Quasar
		Quasar
		Quasar
		Galaxy

Distance →

Hydrogen | Magnesium | Hydrogen
Calcium

As the spectra of quasars become more redshifted with distance, there comes a point where the entire visible part of the spectrum moves into the infrared and the part normally occupied by it is take up by the ultraviolet range.

rgument. It runs like this. 'If the QSOs are distant they must be radiating so intensely that the radiation they emit would disrupt any fast moving electrons or other electrified atomic particles which would normally give rise to synchrotron radiation'. But as synchrotron radiation is just what we observe, the intensity at QSO sources cannot be as great as would be necessary to disrupt it.

We seem now to have arrived at an impasse. Some evidence seems to point to QSOs being very distant objects, while other evidence is uncertain and can even be taken to support the view that QSOs are associated with not too distant galaxies. There is also the serious theoretical question of how QSOs, if they are really immensely distant, could generate the vast output of energy observed. What we need are some crucial observations, particularly of the association between galaxies and QSOs, if such an association exists. Fortunately some very recent studies seem to give us a clue.

First of all, thirty QSOs with comparatively small redshifts amounting to no more than one third of the speed of light have been examined optically in great detail. A significant number appear fuzzy, which may indicate that they are rather like distant Seyfert galaxies with faint arms which cannot be seen clearly and appear merely as a haze. More significant, however, are the discoveries that QSO 4C37.43 appears to be seated within a galaxy, and QSO 3C48 is actually the nucleus of a galaxy. Some other QSOs also appear to be centred in galaxies, and it may therefore be that they are all galactic nuclei, in which case, their redshifts may well imply vast distances.

The final answer to the question has come a stage nearer with detailed observations of three other quasars, one of which appears in some way to be related to the spiral galaxy NGC 4319. This QSO, known as Markarian 205, has a redshift of 0.07 times the speed of light, and is travelling at more than ten times the speed of the galaxy NGC 4319. As the galaxy appears distorted in the region of the QSO, it was originally suggested that they were associated and therefore their difference in redshift could not be due to distance. More recent observations have, however, shown QSO Markarian 205 to have fuzzy edges like a galaxy nucleus and to possess a companion, a dim galaxy whose redshift is the same as its own. So it would appear that the relationship between the QSO Markarian 205 and the galaxy NGC 4319 is not real but entirely due to perspective.

Another QSO, catalogued as 3C 206, has now been re-examined. It is ringed by faint galaxies and appears to be distorted. However, new observations with the most modern telescopes have shown no distortion in the QSO itself (although it has in one of the galaxies ringing it). Using a photon-counter it has proved possible to determine that the redshift of one of the faint surrounding galaxies is the same as the QSO. Thus providing additional evidence that a QSO is a peculiar galaxy or a galactic nucleus. And recent observations of the QSO 3C273 indicate that it, too, is the nucleus of a galaxy.

Some recent observations seem to support the view that QSOs may lie at the centre of many galaxies. This artist's impression is of one such QSO at close range. The gas jets indicate a strong magnetic field.

HOW GALAXIES HAVE EVOLVED

Did elliptical and spiral galaxies each condense separately at about the same time, or did one kind evolve into the other? Recent research shows that galaxies owe their shape to conditions at their formation.

When Edwin Hubble drew up his classification of galaxies in the 1920s he wondered whether his diagram of galactic types (page 88) was more than just a way of arranging observations. Could it be that it gave a clue to their evolution as well. Might they, as the diagram suggested, have begun as spherically shaped ellipses and then, because of rotation, have become increasingly elongated until they formed into flattened discs, giving the S0 types of normal and barred spirals? Then, perhaps the spirals grew arms which spread out ever wider until the galaxy lost shape and became an irregularly shaped collection of dust, stars and gas?

We now know that Hubble was mistaken. In the intervening half century astronomers have learned enough about stellar evolution to tell that the sequence Hubble proposed could not have occurred; the picture has also become far more complicated with the discovery of variations within each class of galaxy. We now know that ellipticals can be large or, as in the majority of cases, small (dwarf ellipticals), with masses no greater than a few hundred

thousand Suns. As for spirals, there are not only large formations similar to our own and the Andromeda Galaxy, but also small spirals and Seyfert galaxies, which have bright central regions and dim arms, and which radiate strongly in ultraviolet, and infrared.

In recent years other galaxies with bright central regions have been discovered. There are the 'N'-type galaxies, first identified as a separate class in 1958 by the American astronomer William Morgan and later proved to be strong radio emitters. There are also the Markarian galaxies. These last came out of a study by the Russian astronomer B. E. Markarian of spiral galaxies that were strong emitters of ultraviolet. Of the galaxies in his grouping, about 10% were normal Seyferts, but many of the remainder, now referred

to as Markarian galaxies, seemed to have a high proportion of hot blue and blue-white stars in their nuclei. The classification also includes a number of dwarf spirals that are strong ultraviolet emitters. Similar galaxies visible to southern-hemisphere observers have been catalogued by Guillermo Haro in South America.

There are also what are known as BL Lacertae objects. Originally the star BL Lacertae was thought to be a variable, but in 1968 it was discovered to be a radio source and since then about 40 objects of a similar kind have been discovered. Careful optical studies have shown them to be similar to Seyferts or 'N'-type galaxies; their main radiation output is in the infrared and all suffer rapid variation in energy emission over a matter of weeks at

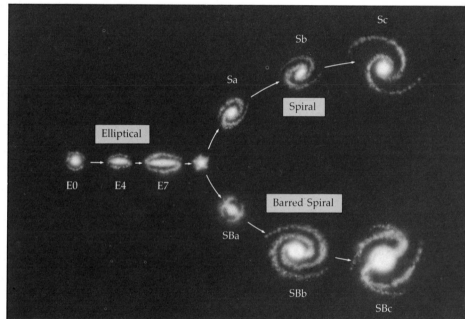

above According to Hubble, shape was a feature of galaxies that evolved over a period of time. He believed that everything went through an elliptical phase before evolving further. The sequences of spirals and barred spirals shown here are only two of a total of five branches that made up Hubble's complete system.

The Sa-type spiral galaxy NGC 7331 in Pegasus may be linked with a group of five other galaxies known as Stephan's quintet.

all wavelengths. And, of course, there are the mysterious QSOs which, as we have just seen (page 97), now appear likely to be the cores of very distant galaxies. For this reason QSOs have become very important to the question of galaxy evolution. Because the more distant of these objects are at least some 5,000 million (5×10^9) parsecs (16×10^9 light-years) away, light from them has taken 16,000 million years to reach us. We therefore observe the galaxies as they were 16,000 million years ago.

As a first step in attempting to answer the question of the evolution of galaxies, it would be best if we were to look at our own Galaxy to see what evidence there is of gradual change with time. First of all most astronomers are agreed that our Galaxy formed about 10,000 million (10^{10}) years ago. It condensed from a diffuse mass of gas which would have been mainly hydrogen but may also have contained some helium and a few other light elements as well. The size of this mass of gas is, of course, uncertain but it may well have spread over at least a million parsecs (3×10^6 light-years) and have been rotating, very slowly, taking a couple of thousand million years to complete a revolution.

Over the ages since the Galaxy formed, the gas has gradually been converted into stars until now only a few per cent remains uncondensed. Calculations based on the way stars form lead to a figure of 10,000 million years for the Galaxy's age, an estimate supported by studies of the ages of stars which are burning steadily and are still on the main sequence (page 74). Such calculations also show that at least half the stars in the Galaxy were formed in the first couple of thousand million years, and around three-quarters had formed after 4,000 million years. The figures are not certain, but at least they give a possible picture of the way things went.

As well as being carried round by the rotation of the Galaxy, the stars in the spiral arms are moving almost directly outwards from the centre, indicating that the gas from which they were formed was not itself moving very fast. Star formation, as we have seen (page 66), may have been caused by density-waves passing through the disc of the Galaxy. Again, we know that the Galaxy does not rotate uniformly but that the outer parts move more slowly than the inner regions. This fact, together with the change from gas into stars, gives a clue to the formation of the Galaxy's spiral arms.

As the Galactic disc rotated, it would have become thinner. Stars already formed outside would be able to pass through it easily but uncondensed gas would not and would tend to clump together in certain places. Studies of the distribution of the stars in the disc would have given a clue to where these clumps would have formed. In recent years all the various factors involved have been analysed by computer and two general ideas or 'models' have resulted. In one, the spiral arms are shown to form as a result of clumping, and are kept together by the effects of density-waves. In the other the arms are seen to be a product of clumping and rotational motion and are not permanent, though this model indicates that bars could readily form, giving the pattern we see in

above The spiral galaxy in the constellation Pegasus is an Sb spiral, similar in form to our own galaxy.

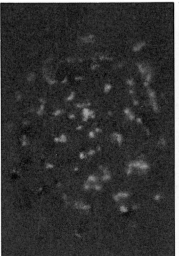 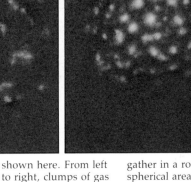 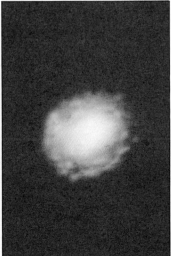 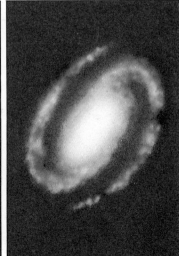

Galaxies may have formed in the way shown here. From left to right, clumps of gas gather in a roughly spherical area of space. They then condense to form either an elliptical or spiral galaxy.

some spiral galaxies. As far as our own Galaxy is concerned, the spiral arms seem to have been in existence for a very long time and the first model – maintenance by density-waves – is to be preferred. There is therefore no real evidence that our Galaxy is changing from a spiral into an elliptical.

Not all the gas used in star formation is lost for ever. Some stars blow off envelopes of gas, and others explode violently (page 76), returning gaseous material to interstellar space to be used again. This is an important process as far as supernovae are concerned, because they throw out material containing heavy atoms, such as those of iron, which were synthesized in the intense heat that ultimately caused the explosion. The presence of these heavier chemical elements does not affect change within, or the evolution of the Galaxy, but does provide a clue, when other galaxies are examined, to stellar age and the rate at which stars have been forming. The movement of stars also provides evidence about the evolution of particular galaxies, including our own. Old stars – those formed when a galaxy was comparatively young – will have rather elliptical orbits around the galactic centre, while those formed more recently will have more circular orbits. This difference is due to the way the interstellar gas was moving when the stars were formed, and clearly has a bearing on the type of galaxy which finally appears.

With all this evidence to hand, what, then, can be said about galaxy evolution in general? Firstly, there are basic differences between ellipticals, irregulars and spirals in the amount of interstellar gas they contain. Radio telescopes allow us to detect the presence of neutral hydrogen, and have shown us that irregular galaxies contain the most interstellar gas. In some, about half the total mass is still gaseous, though usually gas amounts to only about one fifth of the total. Spiral galaxies come next. Their gas content is not as high, and seems as a general rule to be about 7%. Ellipticals have less still; some may have about 4% while others appear to have hardly any at all.

If we read Hubble's classification in the opposite way from which he intended, we see a progression from irregular galaxies, where star formation has not progressed very far, through spirals to ellipticals where, in some cases, the entire gaseous content seems to have

above The cluster of galaxies in Pavo lies at a distance of about 100 million parsecs and is centred on a giant elliptical galaxy. The cluster contains every known galactic type; in the outer parts spirals are more common than ellipticals.

The S0-type galaxy M84 (NGC 4374) in Virgo looks like a cross between an elliptical and a spiral system.

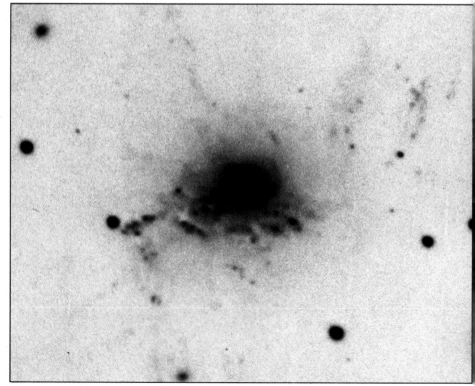

The Seyfert galaxy NGC 1275 is optically the brightest galaxy in the Perseus cluster and is associated with the radio source 3C 84. Because it emits radio waves further out on one side than on the other, the galaxy has a tadpole appearance.

condensed into stars. Is this evidence that the types of galaxy are all linked in one evolutionary sequence?

Recent observations make it clear that the answer is no; the situation is more complex. In our own Galaxy two things are becoming evident: the globular clusters seem definitely to have formed first and, as we have already seen (page 54), the Galaxy's halo is much more extensive than was originally believed, suggesting that huge haloes may also exist around other galaxies. Using X-ray and other observational techniques, gas containing heavy chemical elements has been detected outside galaxies. This discovery implies that supernova explosions have been occurring for a very long time indeed and therefore star formation in some places probably took place at a much faster rate than in others.

Two other significant points in the latest research have also affected the way astronomers view the evolution of galaxies. Firstly, recent detailed examination of elliptical galaxies and the motions of the stars within them has led to the conclusion that ellipticals are not simple bodies – not ordinary 'ellipsoids of revolution' – but complex systems with three unequal axes, which makes it seem less likely that they evolved from spirals. Secondly, it is becoming clear that many ordinary galaxies actually display the kind of behaviour observed in active galaxies like Seyferts, N and Markarian galaxies, and from QSOs, but on a much smaller scale.

What does all this mean? Is the idea of an evolutionary sequence still tenable? Ten years ago it did seem that there was such a sequence. But in the light of the latest observational evidence, including QSOs, astronomers now think that most, if not all galaxies, condensed at the same time, and which kind of galaxy they turned out to be depended solely on the rate of star formation. Elliptical galaxies are believed to be those proto-galaxies in which star formation occurred very fast indeed. Spirals are thought to be galaxies in which formation was slower, at least after an initial burst of activity, and irregular galaxies are thought to have formed where, for some reason or other, connected with the nature and movement of the gas, star formation was very slow indeed. This is the view that has now overtaken the earlier idea of transformation from irregular to spiral and on to elliptical, and is the scheme that seems to fit in best with all the latest data.

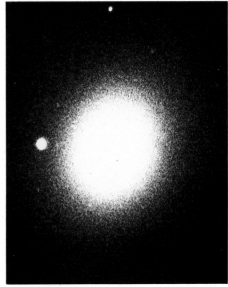

An edge-on view of the Sb-type spiral NGC 4565 in Coma Berenices shows a thick band of obscuring matter in the plane of the spiral arms. Our own Galaxy may look like this viewed from deep space.

The E1 elliptical galaxy NGC 4472 in the constellation Virgo displays the typical spherical shape of the E1-type.

THE MAGELLANIC CLOUDS

The Magellanic Clouds are galaxies of stars, not just clouds of gas. They are the companions in intergalactic space of our own Galaxy

The Magellanic Clouds, areas of the night sky that look like pieces broken off from the Milky Way, are not visible to most northern-hemisphere observers. No one living north of a latitude of 30° (north of New Orleans or Cairo, for example) can ever observe them, although they are a familiar enough sight to anyone living in the southern hemisphere. They were first described for northern-hemisphere observers by Antonia Pigafetta who accompanied the Portuguese navigator Ferdinand Magellan on his voyage round the world between 1505 and 1516.

The two Clouds are galaxies in their own right, but there is some difference of opinion about whether they should be described as outside our own Galaxy or as a part of it. As we have seen (page 54) new research has shown that our Galaxy is larger than was once thought and, therefore, in a sense the Clouds can be thought of as outlying components. However, most astronomers would probably still think of them as satellite galaxies.

There is no doubt about the fact that both Clouds are in orbit around the centre of our Galaxy. The Large Magellanic Cloud takes something like 37,000 million (37 × 10⁹) years to complete one orbit and the Small Magellanic Cloud takes even longer, orbiting in 65 thousand million years. These times are very long – our Sun completes one circuit every 220 million years – and since astronomers think the age of the Galaxy is no more than about 12,000 million (12 × 10⁹) years, this means that neither cloud has even completed half an orbit.

Interestingly, there are other links between the Clouds and our Galaxy. The Magellanic Stream – the gas flow between the Galaxy and the Clouds – has already been mentioned (page 70), but there is also a strong gravitational effect. Some of the stars in both Clouds are being pulled to one side by a tidal effect due to the Galaxy, in the same way as tides on Earth are caused by the gravitational pulls of the Moon and Sun.

The Clouds vary in size; the large Magellanic Cloud has a mass equal to 10,000 million (10¹⁰) Suns and has a diameter of some 12,000 parsecs (39,000 light-years). The Small Cloud is about three-quarters this size and has a diameter of 9,000 parsecs (29,000 light-years) and a mass equivalent to 2,000 million (2 × 10⁹) Suns. As they are classified as irregular galaxies it may seem strange to give their diameters. However, they are of Irregular I type, a step

'beyond' the Sc or SBc class of galaxy, and are not particularly misshapen. It is the Irregular II type of galaxy which has the less definite outline. Some astronomers even think that the Large Magellanic Cloud might be better classed as a barred spiral of type SBc.

The classification of galaxies as Irregular I or Irregular II is based essentially on the stars they contain rather than on their shape. However, the shape of the galaxy does vary with the type of star it contains. Irregular I galaxies have mainly young, hot blue and blue-white stars – stars of Population I (page 59) – while Irregular II type have primarily older (Population II) stars. Although the Magellanic Clouds have a small proportion of old (Population II) stars in a halo around them, they are both rich in Population I stars and contain a greater proportion of gas than our own Galaxy, indicating that they are both places where new stars are being born.

A study of the chemical composition of the Clouds gives us a clue to their age. As a galaxy grows older, so the chemicals present change. To begin with hydrogen predominates but as time passes and stars condense, heavy chemical elements like iron are formed and injected into the interstellar gas. When the spectra of the Magellanic Clouds are examined, we find that few heavy elements are present. The Clouds are thus comparatively young and certainly younger than our Galaxy.

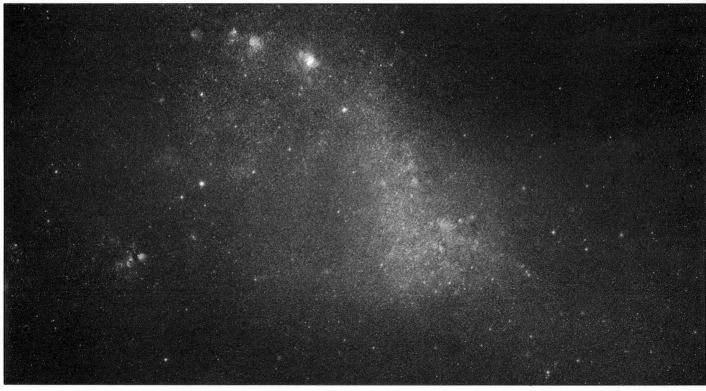

The Small Magellanic Cloud lies at a distance of some 60,000 parsecs from our own Galaxy. The Clouds can be seen with the naked eye, but are only visible from the southern hemisphere. They are named after Ferdinand Magellan.

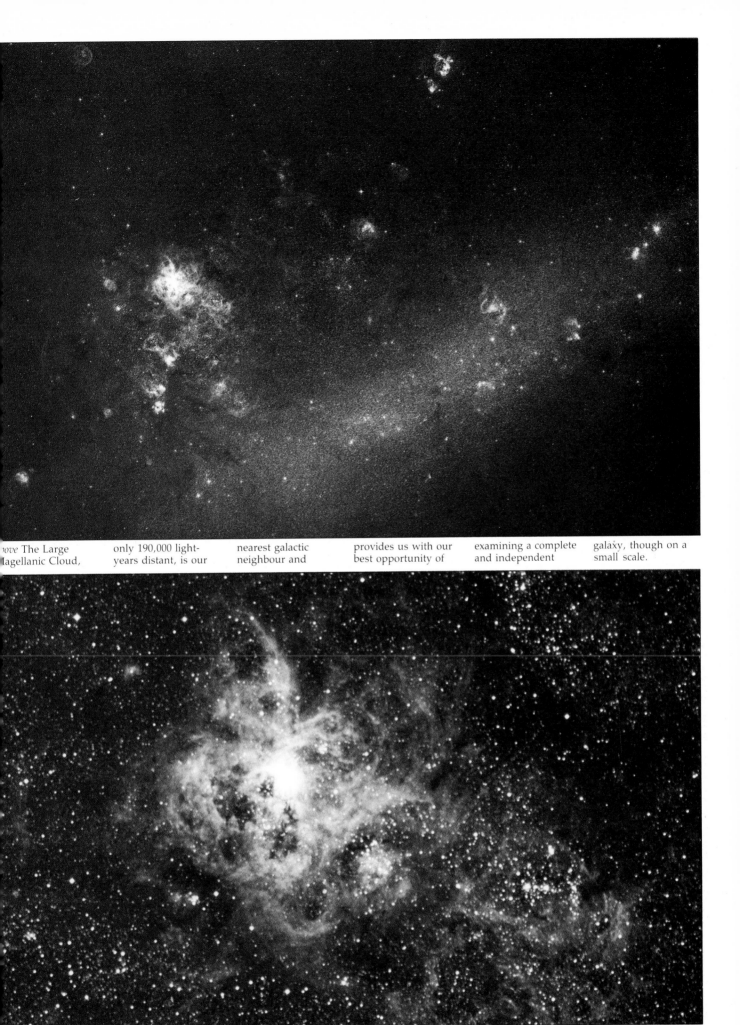

ove The Large Magellanic Cloud, only 190,000 light-years distant, is our nearest galactic neighbour and provides us with our best opportunity of examining a complete and independent galaxy, though on a small scale.

The huge Tarantula Nebula in the Large Magellanic Cloud. It is a very active and explosive region of gas at the centre of which is a cluster of young sisters. In its dark regions, new stars are being born.

OUR OTHER GALACTIC NEIGHBOURS

Our Galaxy and the Magellanic Clouds are not isolated in space. They are members of a small cluster of galaxies known as the Local Group.

The number of galaxies we place in the Local Group depends on the limit we put on its size. For instance, of the two strongly infrared emitting galaxies, Maffei I and Maffei II, which lie in the direction of Cassiopeia when viewed from the Earth, only Maffei I is considered to belong to the Local Group. Maffei I lies at 1.2 million parsecs (about four million light-years) or about twice as far as the Andromeda Galaxy, and Maffei II is situated at a considerably larger but, at the moment, uncertain distance from us.

With this example as an indication of scale, present counts give the Group a total of 30 members, of which 18 are notable objects, though some, as we shall see, are rather small by galactic standards.

The largest galaxy in the Local Group besides our own is M31, the famous galaxy in Andromeda (photograph, page 86). It is an Sb spiral and is seen from Earth at a fairly steep angle, within only 15° o[f] the 'edge-on' position. Just as our Galaxy is accompanied by the two Magellanic Clouds, Andromeda has its own companions, the dwarf elliptical galaxies, NGC 205, a class E5 elliptical, and M32, which is an E[

The other large galaxy in the Group is the Sc-type spiral in Triangulum M33. It is only 800,000 parsecs from us, half a million light-years further away than Andromeda (M31). These two galaxies are comparatively close, as are all the members of the Local Group, compared with the distances from them to more distant systems like th[e] Virgo cluster which, though it is the next nearest system, lies more than

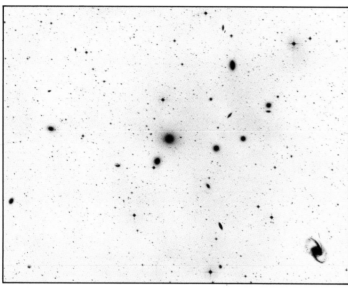

above The Fornax cluster of galaxies is one of the groups in our Local Group.

above The elliptical galaxy NGC 185 is a distant companion of the great Andromeda Galaxy, M31.

Of the two Maffei galaxies, probably only Maffei 1 can be considered to be a member of the Local Group. Maffei 2 is thought to be much further away.

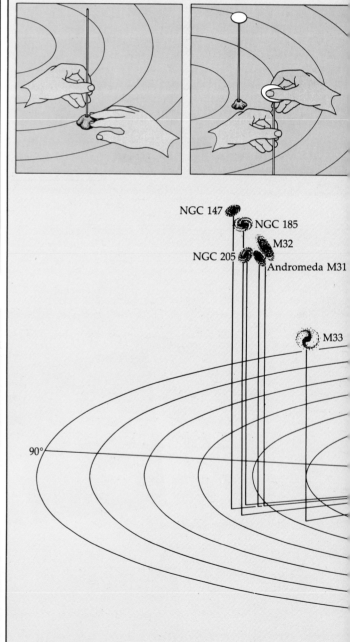

NGC 147
NGC 185
M32
NGC 205
Andromeda M31
M33
90°

This diagram, showing the relative positions of the brightest members of the Local Group, can form the basis of a model. Take a large board, some 1½-m square. Cover the board with paper and plot the positions of the galaxies with a ten times further off at almost 30 million parsecs (98 million light-years) away.

Apart from the main irregular galaxies of the Local Group, which are, of course, the Magellanic Clouds, there are two others, catalogued as NGC 6822 and IC 1613. They are both smaller than the Clouds – one, NGC 6822, is less than a sixth as massive as the Small Magellanic Cloud, and the other is only a tenth the size – yet in spite of these differences, they are very similar to the Clouds.

The elliptical galaxies of the Group show a wide variety. The largest, Maffei I, is probably as massive as our own Galaxy; the smallest, the Draco and Ursa Minor

systems, are two million times less massive than Maffei I. The two elliptical systems Leo I and Leo II are no more than ten times larger than Draco and Ursa Minor, and it is clear that dwarf galaxies predominate. Among them, though, are two unusual objects, known as the Fornax and Sculptor systems. Both are centred on elliptical galaxies and situated at distances of 85,000 parsecs (277,000 light-years) for the Sculptor system and more than double that – 190,000 parsecs (619,000 light years) – for the Fornax system. In each of them there is a main elliptical galaxy surrounded by a swarm of star collections, which are larger than the usual globular clusters we find in our own Galaxy, and larger than any of

the 200 clusters that surround Andromeda, but smaller than true elliptical galaxies. They are composed mainly of stars similar to our Sun.

In spite of the number of galaxies and stars contained in the Local Group, if the total amount of constituent material were spread out over the space occupied by it, the distribution would be very sparse, compared with the average for the interstellar space inside a galaxy like our own. Whereas interstellar space would have ten million atomic particles per cubic centimetre, the Local Group would have almost 700 thousand times less. This, then, is a measure of the vastness of space between galaxies compared with the space between the stars.

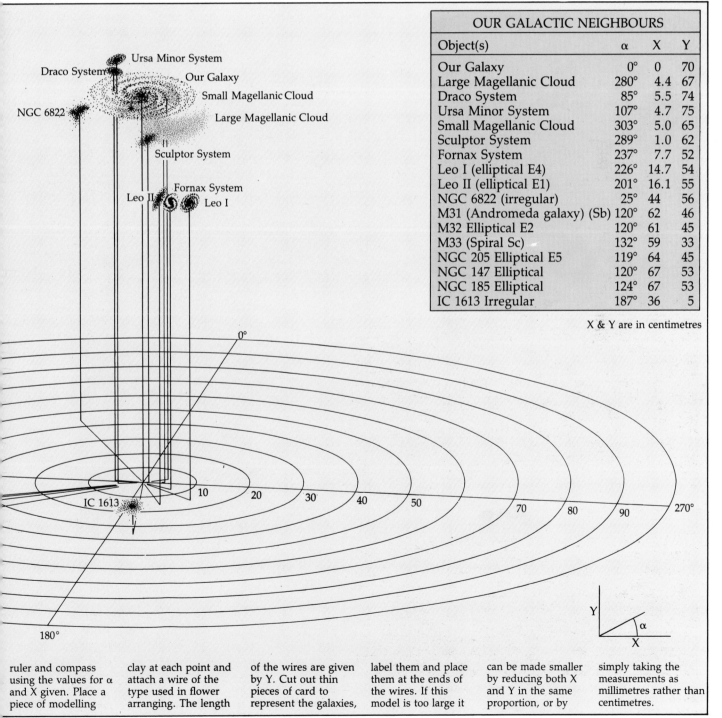

OUR GALACTIC NEIGHBOURS			
Object(s)	α	X	Y
Our Galaxy	0°	0	70
Large Magellanic Cloud	280°	4.4	67
Draco System	85°	5.5	74
Ursa Minor System	107°	4.7	75
Small Magellanic Cloud	303°	5.0	65
Sculptor System	289°	1.0	62
Fornax System	237°	7.7	52
Leo I (elliptical E4)	226°	14.7	54
Leo II (elliptical E1)	201°	16.1	55
NGC 6822 (irregular)	25°	44	56
M31 (Andromeda galaxy) (Sb)	120°	62	46
M32 Elliptical E2	120°	61	45
M33 (Spiral Sc)	132°	59	33
NGC 205 Elliptical E5	119°	64	45
NGC 147 Elliptical	120°	67	53
NGC 185 Elliptical	124°	67	53
IC 1613 Irregular	187°	36	5

X & Y are in centimetres

ruler and compass using the values for α and X given. Place a piece of modelling clay at each point and attach a wire of the type used in flower arranging. The length of the wires are given by Y. Cut out thin pieces of card to represent the galaxies, label them and place them at the ends of the wires. If this model is too large it can be made smaller by reducing both X and Y in the same proportion, or by simply taking the measurements as millimetres rather than centimetres.

CLUSTERS OF GALAXIES

More galaxies exist as members of a group or cluster than are found separately. In some cases a cluster may contain several thousand galaxies all gathered together.

As telescopes, cameras and other equipment for probing deep space improve, and as new surveys of the sky are made, it is becoming clear to astronomers that isolated galaxies are unusual. They more commonly occur in pairs or in groups of three or more; our Local Group is no rarity but a typical example. As well as in small groups, galaxies are to be found in clusters, from a hundred or so up to thousands.

Clusters vary in shape. Some seem to have no definite form at all and are just irregular collections of galaxies united by gravitation between the different members; others have a great number of galaxies and are more densely packed together, and have a spherical shape. Just as the shapes differ, so do the galaxies which compose a cluster. The spherically shaped ones contain either ellipticals or S0-type spirals for the most part, whereas the irregular clusters, which tend to be either small or very large, are composed of galaxies of every kind.

Radio galaxies are also found in clusters. Of the nearby, rich, regularly shaped clusters, half contain radio galaxies, whereas only a quarter of the irregularly shaped ones do. Indeed, it has been found that about one-fifth of all known radio galaxies are inside rich clusters. However it would not do to set too much reliance on this figure because distant radio galaxies may only appear to be alone because the rest of the galaxies in the cluster are too dim for our present equipment to detect; only the radio galaxies show up.

The nearest cluster to the Local Group is the one in Virgo. Irregular in shape, it is a vast collection of some 2,500 galaxies of every conceivable type. Three-quarters of the brightest members are spirals but as the irregular galaxies in the cluster are rather dim, it may well be that many are as yet unobserved, and the proportion of spirals has been over-estimated. The cluster lies at a distance of almost 22 million parsecs (almost 72 million light-years), so its brightest members show up only as eighth magnitude or even a little dimmer. Although invisible to the unaided eye, some of the galaxies can be seen with a 15-cm aperture reflector. To find them you should look towards the boundary of Virgo with Coma Berenices, and many members can be seen if you look a little west of α Virginis; they form an equilateral triangle with the stars

The Virgo cluster is the nearest cluster of galaxies to the Local Group. It lies at a distance of around 72 million light-years and contains some 2,500 individual galaxies. Only a proportion of the total number can be seen in this photograph.

Arcturus (α Boötis) and Cor Caroli (α Canis Venaticorum).

The whole Virgo cluster is moving away from us at a velocity of some 1,100 km per second, and certain individual galaxies are also moving even faster than that at velocities of more than 2,000 km per second. Such speeds indicate that either the galaxies in the cluster are very massive or that there is a lot of invisible gas about; if this were not so the members of the cluster would have dispersed long ago. Most astronomers think that the presence of invisible gas is the more likely explanation because the grouping of so many massive galaxies seems unlikely. However, our own Galaxy has recently been found to be larger than was once thought (page 54) and so it is difficult to be certain.

The next nearest galactic cluster is the one which lies in Coma Berenices, at a distance of some 120 million parsecs (about 390 million light-years). It is 5½ times further off than the Virgo cluster and is therefore unfortunately unsuitable for observation with a small telescope. It is a spherically shaped cluster with at least 1,000 members which are either ellipticals or S0 spirals. At its centre are two radio galaxies. One of these, Abell 85, is known as a 'tadpole' galaxy because its radio emission spreads out like a tail in one particular direction. A number of these galaxies are known, and are thought to behave this way because of a strong intergalactic 'wind' of electrified nuclear particles streaming past them.

Observations with orbiting X-ray telescopes have shown that many clusters of galaxies emit X-rays. The Virgo cluster, for example, has an X-ray source near its centre. Such emissions are thought to indicate the presence of hot electrified gas at a temperature of some 100 million degrees. The gas generates X-rays by the slowing down of very high-speed electrons as they come close to protons and are pulled into a new path, an effect usually known by the German word *bremsstrahlung*, 'braking radiation'. Such X-rays are, therefore, further evidence of the presence of intergalactic gas within clusters of galaxies.

Although there are so many galactic clusters in space, they are not equally distributed, and astronomers believe that many if not all are grouped into larger arrangements, or superclusters. For instance, it is thought that our Local Group is part of a supercluster with a diameter of something like 75 million parsecs (244 million light-years), centred on the Virgo cluster. What is more, comprehensive surveys of the sky seem to suggest that there are even clusters of superclusters. Be that as it may it is clear that the existence, at least of superclusters, provides us with a clue to the way gas was distributed and galaxies formed after the big bang that began the universe (page 156).

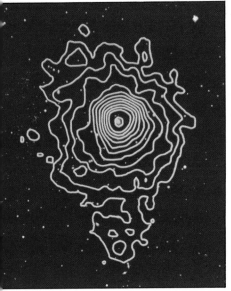

above In this computer-generated picture of the northern-hemisphere sky, clustering can be seen in the vast number of galaxies shown.

A plot of the cluster of galaxies Abell 85, surrounded by gas. Such gas often connects galaxies in a cluster.

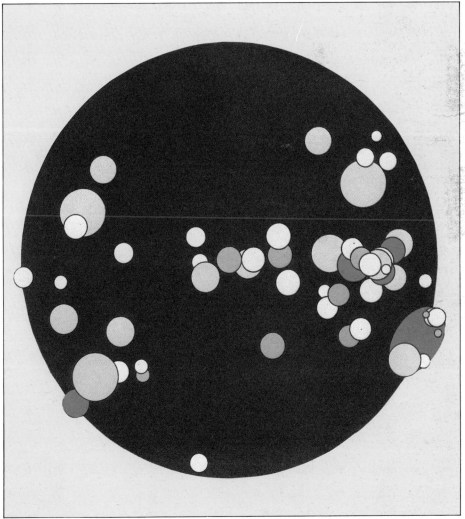

The neighbouring clusters of galaxies to our own can all be shown to lie within a sphere, 100 million parsecs (326 million light-years) in radius, and thus to form a supercluster. By constructing similar diagrams, to the one above, for other groups of galaxy clusters, superclusters can be shown to exist in other parts of the universe. It is the existence of these large groupings that has led astronomers to believe that gas was not evenly distributed immediately after the big bang (page 156) and there must have been some 'clumping' quite early on. Clusters of galaxies certainly do not seem to be evenly distributed throughout space.

FAR DISTANT GALAXIES

Galaxies are visible as far into space as we can probe. As we probe, so we travel back in time. Our limit is the beginning of the universe.

In whatever direction we point our telescopes there are galaxies. Only in the plane of the Milky Way do we see none because of the dust, gas and stars of our own Galaxy that lie in the way. Galaxies exist nearly as far as the telescope can reach; only QSOs are more distant and, as we have seen (page 96), it seems that even these are the bright central regions of galaxies.

The most distant galaxy that has so far been detected is the galaxy 3C184 which has a redshift (z) of 1, that is to say the wavelengths of the lines in its spectrum are doubled. This does not mean that the galaxy is moving as fast as the speed of light, but at three-fifths the speed – for large redshifts, z has to be worked out in accordance with the theory of relativity (page 132), which takes account of the fact that nothing can travel faster than the speed of light. (For readers who enjoy mathematics, the redshift (z) and the velocity of the source (v) are related by the equation $1 + z = \sqrt{(c + v)/(c - v)}$, where c represents the velocity of light). Therefore 3C184 is moving away at the immense velocity of 180,000 km per second.

As we have already seen (page 20), the distances of remote galaxies are calculated from the size of their redshifts, the larger the shift the more distant the object. But what was not said was that astronomers have difficulty at present in deciding precisely how great a distance is indicated by a particular redshift. If we wish to determine precisely how distant 3C184 is or how remote the furthest QSOs are, then we are doomed to disappointment; we can at present only get a general idea from this method.

The difficulty lies in fixing what is known as the 'Hubble constant'. In 1929 the American astronomer, Edwin Hubble, discovered that distant galaxies had larger redshifts than near ones. By 1935 he thought the evidence showed that for every million parsecs, the velocity of galaxies increased by 530 km per second, but this figure is now known to be inaccurate. Astronomers have discovered that the stars in galaxies are divided into two stellar populations, allowing them to estimate true brightness and therefore distance more accurately. Also they have found out far more about gas and dust in interstellar space and so are now better able to assess by how much apparent brightness is reduced by interstellar material. Moreover, new facts have been learned about the absolute magnitude of Cepheids and Cepheid-like stars such as the W Virginis variables (page 18). All this new evidence has reduced the value of the Hubble constant from 530 to between 55 and 100 km per second. Some astronomers think that 77 km

per second is the most likely value, but the majority favour 55.

These figures indicate that the universe is far larger than was thought in Hubble's day. For example, if we work out the distance of the galaxy 3C184, using Hubble's original value of 530, we get a distance of 180,000 ÷ 530 or about 340 million parsecs. However, if we adopt the modern value of 55 for Hubble's constant, the distance of 3C184 works out as 180,000 ÷ 55 or 3,273 million parsecs, that is more than 9½ times further off. When we take the most distant quasars, which have velocities of some 240,000 km per second, we arrive at the gigantic distance of 4,364 million parsecs.

When we look into the depths of space, we are actually looking back far into the past. For instance, because 3C184 is 3,273 parsecs or 10,670 (3,273 × 3.26) million light years away, we see it not as it is now but as it was 10,670 million (10.67 × 10^9) years ago, and when we observe the most distant QSOs we are seeing light emitted almost 14 thousand million (14 × 10^9) years ago.

The modern view is that the universe is about 18 thousand million (18 × 10^9) years, or perhaps a little older. So in observing the most distant objects we are really going back to the early years of the universe. If we could be transported 'in the twinkling of an eye' to those distant regions as we see them now, we should expect to find them somewhat different from our own. We should find galaxies in an earlier stage of evolution, and we might even see ellipticals and spirals condensing into stars.

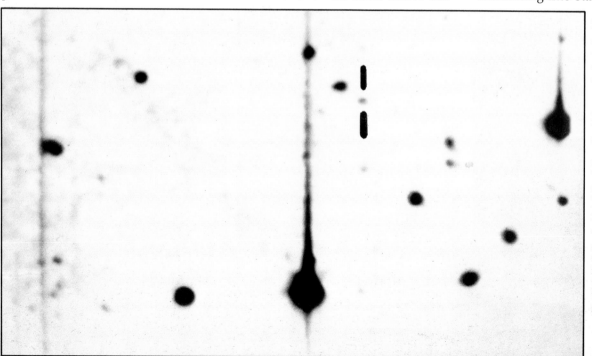

left
The light captured in this photograph of the distant galaxy, originally catalogued as the radio source 3C 184, set off more than 10 thousand million years ago, long before the Earth itself was formed.

right
The 64-m diameter, fully steerable dish-type telescope at Parkes in New South Wales, Australia. Telescopes like this, often coupled together to form interferometers, can probe deep into space to detect very distant galaxies.

CHAPTER 6 MOVEMENT IN SPACE

Nothing is fixed in space; every celestial body is in motion.

Nothing remains motionless in space. Even stars which seem to keep fixed positions in their constellations are moving, though because they are so far away, we can only detect their motion by precise measurement with a telescope. The stars in our Galaxy together with the Sun, orbit round the centre of the Galaxy and also possess individual motions.

The Earth is also continually in motion, though it took many thousands of years before everyone accepted this. The Earth rotates on its axis once a day carrying us round with it. It is also in orbit round the Sun, so we take part in this motion too. But the Sun is not still; it is in orbit round the centre of the Galaxy and also has an individual motion of its own. And, of course, our Galaxy, like every other galaxy in space, is moving. Nothing, but nothing, is fixed in space.

These facts make it difficult to decide what we should take as a fixed reference point. Should we take the Earth itself, or the Sun, or our Galaxy, and if none of these, what should it be? The answer is that it all depends on what it is we want to measure. For instance, suppose we are concerned with calculating the times of sunrise and sunset. Then we assume the Earth to be immobile and instead we imagine that the Sun is moving in orbit around the Earth, rising in the east and setting in the west. This deception makes it easier to compute sunrise and sunset. Similarly, if we wish to calculate the future positions of the planets, then we assume that the Sun is standing still and consider the orbits of the planets as they move round it.

All this was completely understood by the astronomer Galileo. In his famous book, *Dialogue on The Great World Systems*, published in 1630 in which he discussed the then new idea that the Earth orbits the Sun. He wrote that if people were shut up in a large cabin aboard a ship, they would be unable to tell whether they were moving across the ocean or remaining in one place. Even if they had a tub of water with fish swimming in it and allowed birds to fly about in the cabin, everything would appear just the same whether the ship was sailing along or anchored. Of course, any sudden change in motion on the Earth can be detected. If you are having a drink on a train, you will see that the liquid slops about when the train starts suddenly. This is because the glass starts moving with the train but the liquid, because it

left
Galileo described this experiment by way of an analogy to demonstrate that it is impossible, without reference to the rest of the universe, to tell whether or not the Earth is in motion. He suggested that the ship's cabin should be filled with birds and fitted with a fish tank to make the comparison with the real world as strong as possible.

flows easily, tends to remain where it is. However as the Earth's motion is steady and regular and is not subject to sudden jerks, it seems quite still and we can hardly believe that it is both moving through space and revolving on its axis. How then can we tell that the Earth really is moving through space?

If a pendulum (for this experiment, a very heavy weight on the end of a long steel wire) is fixed to a high ceiling and set in motion, it will appear that the direction of swing changes as the day goes on. However, in reality the pendulum continues to swing in the same direction in which it was started and it is the room that is moving round with the rotation of the Earth. As far as the orbital motion of the Earth is concerned, there are also observations that can prove this too. The observations are delicate, and concern tiny apparent shifts in a star's position. Apart from angular shifts due to trigonometrical parallax

(page 16), tiny changes in a star's position in a telescope eyepiece are also observed throughout the year. Because the telescope is moving with the Earth, light entering when the telescope is pointing at an angle to the Earth's direction of movement will end up at a point on the eyepiece that does not correspond with the point at which it entered the telescope. The telescope has moved forward during the time that the light has taken to travel down it, causing the apparent shift.

Our descriptions of the orbits of all bodies in space depend on the place from which we view them, on what we take as our fixed point. The motion of the Moon is a simple example. Viewed from the Earth, the Moon appears to pursue an elliptical orbit round the Earth, but viewed from the Sun, it seems to move in an elliptical orbit round the Sun. From the Sun, the Moon's orbit seems to have a wavy edge due to the Moon weaving in and out of the Earth's

orbit. Such a motion is important when we come to try to answer the question of whether other stars have planetary systems (page 184).

A binary star system is yet another example of relative orbits. If we return to our model, using two torch bulbs for a binary system (page 72), we can soon see how they orbit round their centre of mass. From this it is easy to plot how the stars actually move. But, of course, the observer cannot make his original measurements in this way because he cannot see the centre of the star's mass; indeed until the orbits and masses of the stars are known, the centre of mass cannot be determined. So observations are made taking the brighter component as fixed and noting the orbit of the dimmer component round it. This gives a different orbit but one from which the true orbit can be constructed.

Thus, the motions of celestial objects, are always relative to some chosen fixed point.

above Although uniform motion cannot be detected without reference to something unaffected by it, sudden changes in motion can be felt without outside reference. When a train starts moving anything such as a liquid which is not firmly fixed to it is pushed back in a direction opposite that of the train's motion, as is shown in the right-hand illustration.

right Viewed from the Sun the Moon appears to weave in and out of the Earth's orbit. How a body appears to move depends where we are in space.

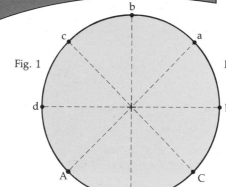

Fig. 1

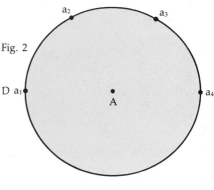

Fig. 2

bottom The actual motions of the stars in a binary-star system (*Fig. 1*) differ from how their motions would appear if one were situated on one of the stars (*Fig. 2*). The positions of the stars are indicated by capital and small letters – when one star is at A, the other is at a and so on.

THE MOTIONS OF THE PLANETS

The motions of the planets present astronomers with two important questions. The mathematical question of their apparent motion, and the physical question of what makes them orbit in space.

The problem posed by the motions of the planets against the background of the stars has presented a challenge to astronomers for more than 2,500 years. Do they move as they seem to do? If not, what kind of motion do they perform? Do they really travel in a series of loops, as it would seem from the Earth?

The actual motion we say the planets have depends both on our viewpoint and on the place in space we consider to be fixed. If we take the centre of our Galaxy as the fixed point, we would find that each planet would move on a most complicated path. Its track would be a combination of the motion of the planet round the Sun; the Sun's own individual motion and the Sun's orbital motion round the centre of the Galaxy. This fixed point would put all kinds of difficulties in our way and make the prediction of the future positions of the planets very complicated to calculate.

Much of this complexity, however, can be eliminated. For instance, we need not take the motion of the Galaxy into account. Nor do we need to take account of the Sun's motion through space, because it carries the Solar System with it. All we need to consider is the motion of the planets round the Sun and we can, in fact, think of the Sun as fixed, which simplifies things enormously.

In ancient times, when astronomers first began to study the mathematics of planetary motions, they believed the Earth to be fixed at the centre of the universe and therefore, to explain what they observed, they had to transfer the motion of the Earth to the motion of every planet, making the problem far more complicated mathematically than it actually was. For the loops which the planets Mars, Jupiter and Saturn appear to move through are mere illusion and are a result of the Earth moving faster round the Sun than they do.

The Greek astronomers used some most ingenious mathematics to solve the problem of planetary motion – including the loops of the three outer planets. Their solution was described with great clarity and elegance by the astronomer Ptolemy, a little over 1,850 years ago.

When, in 1543, the Polish astronomer Nicolaus Copernicus placed the Sun at the centre of the universe instead of the Earth, not all the mathematical complications disappeared; there was still one legacy of ancient thinking – the

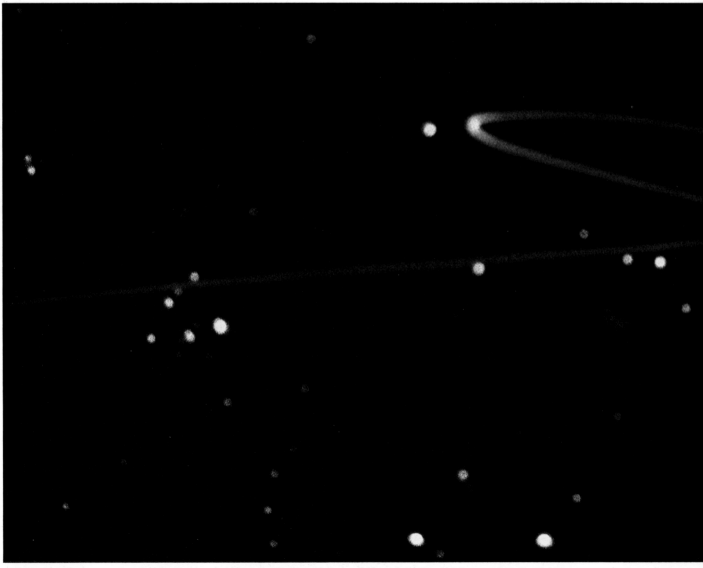

A long-exposure photograph shows the path of Mars as observed from Earth. The loops occur because the photograph records the planet's motion as if the Earth were fixed. The existence of epicycles was invoked by the Greeks to account for the loops in their Earth-centred view of the universe.

112

Greek belief that all the planets moved round the Sun in circles and at unchanging speeds. It was not until 1609 that there were enough observations of sufficient accuracy for the German astronomer Johannes Kepler to show that the planets did not move in circles but in ellipses. Kepler also showed that the size of the orbit was related to the speed of the planet and that instead of orbiting at a regular speed, the planets moved fastest when closest to the Sun and most slowly when they were furthest away.

The discovery of elliptical orbits gave astronomers a much simpler picture of the Solar System; gone were the large and small circles, the 'deferents' and 'epicycles' of the Greeks, which had been needed previously to explain the loops. But this simplicity brought with it a new mathematical problem: how to deal with the ever changing velocities of the planets. The problem first arose when Kepler began to consider what caused the planets to move in

elliptical paths. He believed it was due to a force emanating from the Sun that acted according to the inverse square law (the strength of the force falling by one quarter when the distance is doubled and so on) and suggested that it might be magnetism. A number of astronomers believed that while Kepler was correct in thinking that the Sun kept the planets in their orbits and that the force exerted acted according to an inverse square law, it was not magnetism. However, the scientists of the time could not even prove the mathemathical relationship, never mind whether it was magnetism or not.

The problem was that, because the planets were moving in elliptical orbits, the distance between them and the Sun was constantly changing and the mathematics to deal with such a circumstance did not exist.

It was Isaac Newton who finally solved the problem. He invented a new mathematics – what we today call calculus – which could deal with

continually changing forces and then applied it to planetary motions. His book *The Mathematical Principles of Natural Philosophy* (now known as the *Principia*), which appeared in 1687, contained the key to the age-old mystery of planetary motion around the Sun.

Newton showed by careful mathematical reasoning that if the planets are held by some force – he used the word 'gravitation' – which comes from the Sun and diminishes with distance according to an inverse square relationship, then the planets are bound to move in elliptical orbits.

What gravitation might be was not explained; Newton was content to show that whatever it was, it worked. He did not commit himself by saying it was possessed by every body; all he would say was that the gravitational pull of a body depended on how massive it was and not, as with a magnet, on what it was made. This view completely altered our outlook on space and in particular our understanding of the Solar System.

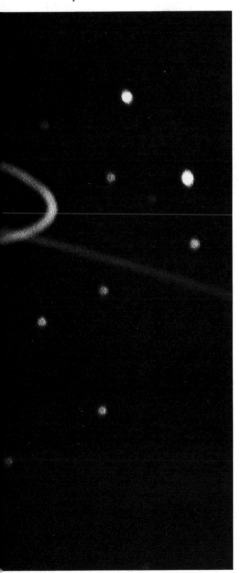

right. In Kepler's earliest plan of the planets, he showed that a regular solid could be placed between each orbit.

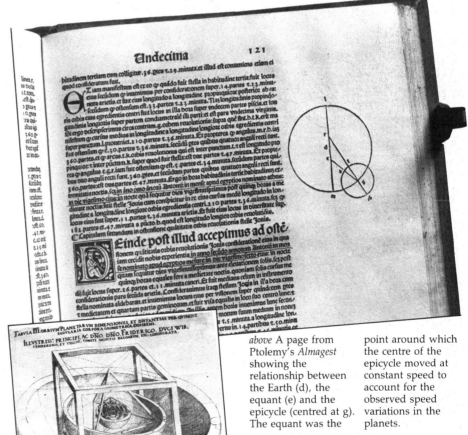

above A page from Ptolemy's *Almagest* showing the relationship between the Earth (d), the equant (e) and the epicycle (centred at g). The equant was the point around which the centre of the epicycle moved at constant speed to account for the observed speed variations in the planets.

above Kepler's discovery that the planets orbited in ellipses accounted for their variation in speed. He also showed that the areas swept out in a given interval of time were equal: i.e. ABS = DCS

COMETS AND METEORS

The orbits of comets and meteors are different from those of planets. They are, however, centred on the Sun and obey the same laws of motion under the influence of gravity.

Comets and meteors long presented a problem to astronomers. Comets, because they appeared unexpectedly, shone for a time, and then vanished again. Meteors, too, were unexpected visitors, arriving in the sky for a few moments and then disappearing without trace; they looked for all the world like stars dropping out of the heavens, and thus got the quite inaccurate name of 'shooting stars'. Yet both comets and meteors obey the laws of motion drawn up by Isaac Newton, though it took some time before this was realized. Cometary motions were the first to be understood.

The reason comets were such a mystery for so long is that, as we have seen (page 50), it is only when they are near to the Sun that they can be detected by Earth-based observers. Back in the seventeenth century comets were only picked up when they were bright enough to be seen with the unaided eye, which meant when they were very near to perihelion (their closest approach to the Sun). But this part of their orbit is very similar to any of a whole range of paths possible under gravity – the ellipse, the parabola and the hyperbola – and it proved impossible to decide which was the correct one.

Indeed some comets appeared to travel in straight lines, though this later proved to be a misunderstanding due to too few observations having been available to plot comet positions accurately. In 1705 Edmond Halley, who had helped Newton publish his *Principia*, recognized that three comets – those of 1531, 1607 and 1682 – were really reappearances of the same object, and was able to show by a detailed mathematical analysis, that the comet moved in an ellipse. What is more, his calculations enabled him to predict correctly its next appearance in Christmas 1758.

Halley's research and subsequent work on other comets showed that comets followed the same pattern of behaviour as planets – they orbited the Sun at a constantly changing velocity. The main difference in their paths was that comets' ellipses were much more elongated. Astronomers express such elongation in numbers by referring to the 'eccentricity' of the orbit. Their definition of eccentricity is based on the fact that an ellipse has two points, or 'foci', about which the curve is drawn, and that the further apart these points are, the

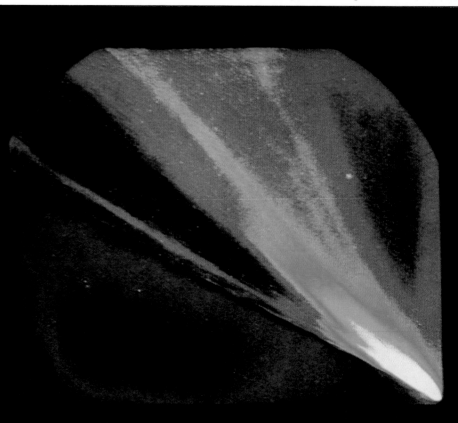

above This photograph of Comet West was taken in false colour by the UK-Schmidt telescope and computer enhanced at Kitt Peak. From the pattern of colours it is possible to pick out certain details of the comet's tail.

The Giotto spacecraft is being planned by the European Space Agency to meet up with Halley's Comet in 1986. It will be equipped to take photographs at a variety of wavelengths, and will examine the tail and nucleus of the comet. The spacecraft is named after the painter Giotto di Bondone who incorporated the comet in his Adoration of the Magi of 1304.

Comet West was discovered in the southern hemisphere in late 1975. It reached perihelion in early 1976 and was visible in pre-dawn skies to northern-hemisphere observers.

ore elongated the ellipse proves to
e. Conversely, the nearer they are
gether, the more closely the ellipse
mes to resemble a circle; indeed in
circle the foci coincide to give one
oint, the centre of the circle. So if
e take the distance between the foci
nd divide this by the longer axis,
e. the longer 'diameter', of the
lipse we obtain the eccentricity. In a
ometary or planetary orbit, the
nger axis is the distance between
erihelion and aphelion (the most
istant point from the Sun). The
ccentricity of ellipses may vary
etween zero and one. A circle has

an eccentricity of zero and an ellipse
with an eccentricity of one would be
a straight line. For most planets the
eccentricity is much less than 0.1 –
the Earth's orbit has an eccentricity of
0.0167 – whereas the eccentricity of
comet orbits is of the order of 0.6, for
those with a short period of return of
something like 5 or 6 years, and up
to 0.9 for those with far longer
periods of 70 years and more.

Current ideas of comet formation
run something like this. It is thought
there is a cloud of cometary material
surrounding the Solar System (page
13) and that material from it may be

pulled out of orbit by a passing star
and fall into a highly elliptical orbit
round the Sun. Such a comet might
well come close enough to Saturn or
Jupiter to be deflected into a different
elliptical orbit. After all, these planets
are very massive; Saturn is 64 million
times more massive than the largest
comet, and Jupiter is 260 million
times greater. Distortions or
'perturbations' of original orbits are to
be found throughout the Solar
System and are one of the
consequences of Newton's gravitation
theory, which states that every body
pulls every other body with a force
that depends on the masses involved
and the distances between them. As
Jupiter is the most massive of all the
planets its power to perturb other
bodies is immense, and it has
captured permanently a group of
more than 1,000 minor planets – the
Trojan group – which are made to
orbit the Sun at the same distance
and in the same orbit as Jupiter itself.

Meteors, on the other hand, are
pieces of interplanetary or cometary
rocky material perturbed from their
orbits round the Sun by the Earth.
The Earth captures them and
sometimes they fall to the ground,
though most burn up as they race
through the atmosphere. The mass of
the Earth is even great enough to
perturb a comet if one comes near
enough. Some astronomers think this
is what happened in 1908 when a
body from deep space exploded
violently near the River
Podkamennaya Tunguska in Siberia.
And, of course, if a comet passed for
any reason too close to the Sun,
perturbations would cause it to fall
into the Sun itself. Such an event
occurred in August 1979 when the
comet Howard-Koomen-Michels
plunged out of its orbit into the Sun.

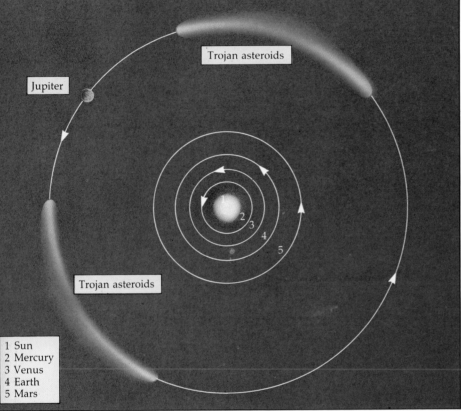

1 Sun
2 Mercury
3 Venus
4 Earth
5 Mars

ove The Trojan
teroids orbit the Sun
almost the same

path as Jupiter. The
asteroids, named after
the heroes of the

Trojan wars, lie in two
main groups, one well
ahead of the planet

and the other some
way behind.

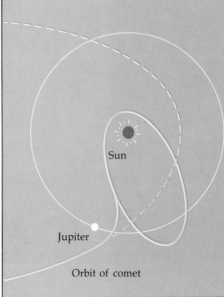

left
Jupiter's mass is so
great that it can
change a long-period
comet into a short-
period one. If a comet
comes too near the
planet, the comet's
orbit may be bent
round, greatly
shortening its orbital
path around the Sun.

Sun

Jupiter

Orbit of comet

far left
Thin rock sections are
an important aid to
the identification of
minerals and have
helped in the analysis
of meteorites, such as
the one seen here. It
is thought that
meteorites and
asteroids may have
similar compositions.

THE MOTIONS OF STARS

The stars were once thought of as fixed in space, but we now know that they move. Their motions are not random but follow the law of 'universal gravitation'.

For most of the time astronomers have been studying the skies, they have believed the stars to be fixed. This was because the stars always appeared in the same groupings. From the times of the ancient Greeks and early Chinese to our present age, more than 2,000 years later, the constellations appear to have remained unchanged. But this is only because the stars are too far away for any motions to be detected by the unaided eye. Accurate observations using telescopes tell a quite different story.

Precise observations of the stars made over a period of years show that besides having a shift due to parallax (page 16) the nearer stars also display a true movement or 'proper motion' of their own. This motion shows itself in two ways; one is in a movement across the celestial sphere with respect to more-distant stars – this is known as 'tangential' motion because the star appears to be moving in a tangent to the celestial sphere. The other is a movement towards or away from us along the line of sight from the Earth to the star; this 'radial' motion shows up as a blueshift or a redshift in the lines of the star's spectrum.

To measure tangential motion precisely, astronomers take photographs of a star some six months apart and then measure the star's position on the photographs they have taken. The measurements are made along the two coordinates, right ascension and declination. By simple trigonometry it is easy to find in which direction the star's actual tangential motion lies and how great it is. The photograph showing such observations for Barnard's star will make this clear. The picture is a multiple exposure, each exposure being separated by six months and taken at times that show the greatest shift due to parallax. Being very close – only 1.81 parsecs (5.9-light years) away – its parallax is comparatively large, 0.53 arc seconds. Barnard's star is also notable in having a very large proper motion – 10.31 arc seconds per year – compared with other nearby stars whose proper motion is only four or five arc seconds or even less. Three actual photographs have been used; the images on the left have been shifted vertically and those on the right have been superimposed over each other. On the right-hand photograph, the north-south differences between the images show the proper motion and the east-west ones the shift due to parallax.

The measurement of radial velocity is by comparison rather more complicated, though the observation is easier to make. A photograph of the star's spectrum is taken and

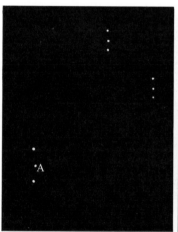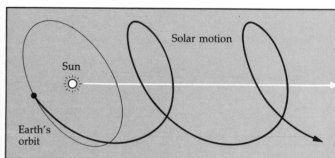

left Three photographs of Barnard's star (A) and two distant stars are shown vertically shifted (*far left*). When the photographs are moved so that the distant stars are superimposed (*left*), the proper motion and parallax of Barnard's star can be determined.

above Measured from the centre of the Galaxy, the Earth's path would appear to be a spiral because of the Sun's motion.

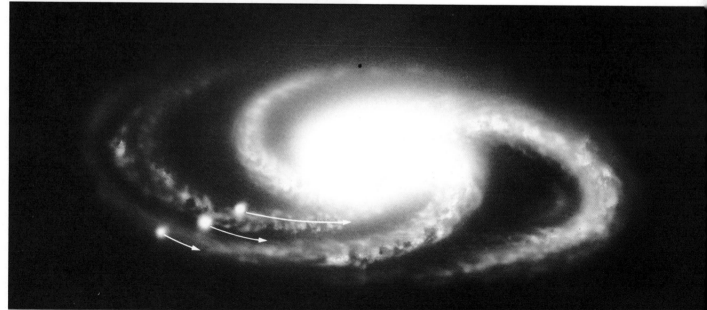

By measuring tangential motion away from and towards the Galactic centre it has been found that stars move faster the closer they are to the centre of the Galaxy. (The length of the arrow is proportional to speed.)

116

eside it is placed the spectrum of a
laboratory source of light such as the
spectrum produced by a spark
generated between two iron rods fed
with a high voltage. Iron is used
because it displays a lot of lines
throughout the entire spectrum, and
as the wavelengths of all the lines
have been measured in laboratories
with great precision, it is an ideal
standard for measuring the lines in a
stellar spectrum. To counteract any
changes in the spectroscope during
the time of an exposure, two
companion spectra are taken, one at
the beginning of the observation and
the other at the end. The process has
now been greatly speeded up and
made more accurate using electronics,
but the basic principle is the same.

The shift of the lines in the star's
spectrum does not depend only on
the star's true radial velocity but also
on three other factors. One of these,
the Earth's rotation on its axis, gives
a small blueshift or redshift
depending on how the observer is
positioned relative to the star;
however, this is a very small effect

all motions of stars,
no matter how
complex they might
be, can be sorted into
two movements at
right angles to one
another: tangential
motion – across the
sphere of the sky, and
radial motion – along
the line of sight.
You can demonstrate
this principle for
yourself by moving a
model figure in front
of a grid and
observing the effect
through a cardboard
sighting tube.

amounting to no more than half a
kilometre per second. More
significant, though, is the Earth's
orbital motion at 30 km per second.
Whether it gives a redshift or a
blueshift depends on the season of
the year and the position of the star
in the sky relative to the observer.
The third factor, the Sun's motion
with respect to the more distant stars
in the sky, is also important because
the Sun carries the whole Solar
System with it. This motion can
amount to 19.5 km per second,
though the actual figure, and
whether it is a redshift or a blueshift,
depends on the position of the star
being measured in comparison
with the position of the solar apex
(i.e. the point in the constellation of
Hercules to which the Sun seems to
be moving).

The Sun's motion is referred to
the more distant stars, which are
taken as fixed, and is measured from
effects of perspective (page 42); it is
therefore the Sun's 'proper motion'
in space, yet it is not the only motion
the Sun has. As we have seen (page

54) our Galaxy is rotating and the
Sun is also taking part in this motion;
because of the distance it lies from
the centre, its rotational speed is
some 300 km per second. Further out
from the centre of the Galaxy the
stars are moving more slowly and,
when observed from the Solar
System, appear to lag behind.
Conversely, stars closer in to the
Galactic centre appear to be moving
more quickly and to be overtaking
us. Both effects are rather similar to
the impressions we receive inside a
moving vehicle at night. If we pass
another vehicle, we see it moving
ahead if it is overtaking us, and
apparently moving backwards if we
are overtaking it.

It is, of course, detailed
observations of the movements of
stars at varying distances from the
Galactic centre that have provided
the evidence from which astronomers
have been able to measure the rate of
rotation of our Galaxy. Because
differential rotation is known to exist
in our Galaxy, we are led to expect it
in others.

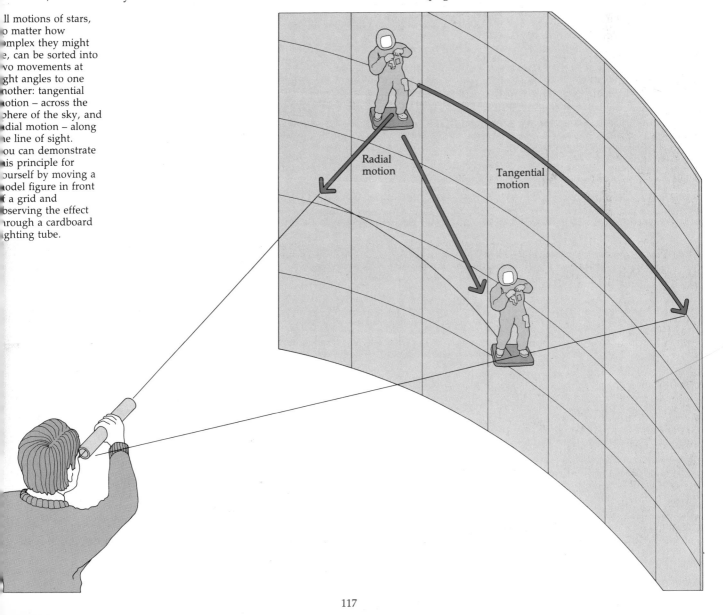

Radial
motion

Tangential
motion

THE MOTIONS OF GALAXIES

The motions of galaxies pose many problems for the astronomer because of the difficulty of determining distances with accuracy. They are, however, most important in developing theories about the nature of the universe.

When astronomers wish to look at the universe on the largest scale and formulate theories about its nature, they turn to the galaxies, because these are to be found throughout all space. On the largest scale they are the building bricks of the universe. Their behaviour gives us clues both to the past history of the cosmos and also to its present state. Yet, as we shall see, there are difficulties when we come to consider the motions of galaxies, because there is some doubt about how far some of them are away; just as there is about many QSOs (page 94).

One of the problems in determining the motions of galaxies is, of course, that we have no fixed base from which all measurements can be made. We have already seen (page 112) the way that the choice of a fixed point alters how we describe the orbit of the Earth and planets, or even something as straightforward as the calculation of sunrise and sunset. Without a fixed point in space how should the motions of galaxies be described? The most practical way is to consider our Sun as fixed in space.

With the Sun as base, we might expect to find distant galaxies moving at a tangent across the celestial sphere, but in fact we observe nothing of the kind – perhaps because the galaxies are so far off that any such motion is too small to detect. Galaxies have only been photographed over the last ninety years and therefore the amount of change we should expect to detect will be small; however, nothing of any real significance has been observed, so we cannot say anything about the 'proper' motion of galaxies.

Immediately astronomers turn to radial velocities, however, they find that the situation is very different. As early as 1912 – some 20 years before it was proved that galaxies are islands of stars, dust and gas, separated by great distances from our

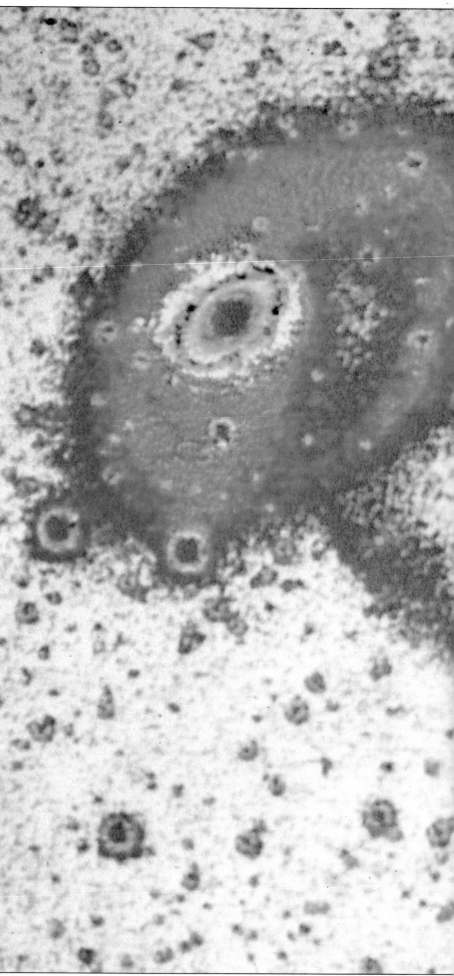

This colour photograph of the two interacting galaxies ESO B 138,29 and 30 has been computer-enhanced to bring out differences in composition. It is possible that the left-hand galaxy has passed through the right-hand one; a

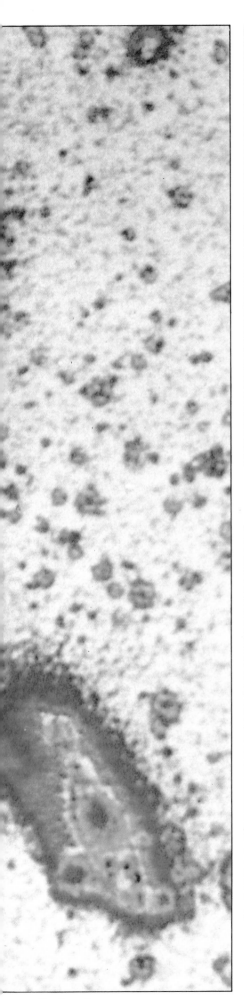

connecting bar of
material can be seen
lying between the two.

above The companion
galaxies NGC 205
(*bottom*) and M32 (*top
right*) can be seen in
this photograph of
Andromeda which
was taken at the Hale
Observatories, USA.

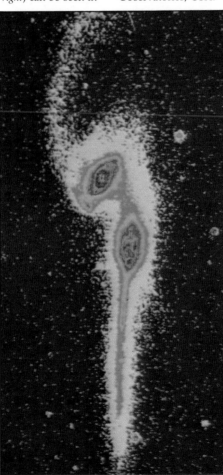

A computer-enhanced
photograph brings out
details of structure in
two colliding galaxies.
The galaxies are
nicknamed 'The Mice'.

own Galaxy – the American astronomer Vesto Slipher managed to obtain a spectrum of M31 (the Andromeda 'Nebula' as it was then called), which allowed him to measure the galaxy's radial velocity. The result surprised him, and every other astronomer as well. His measurements showed a large redshift indicating that the nebula was moving away at a velocity of 200 km per second. Considering that star velocities had never been discovered exceeding 50 km per second, the figure was astonishing. The spectra of other nebulae also indicated red not blueshifts almost without exception. This was puzzling because galaxies were still then believed to be nebulae within our own Galaxy. Admittedly Slipher's sample was small, yet when two years later a total of thirteen galaxies had been measured only two showed blueshifts, while the maximum velocity had gone up to 300 km per second. By 1917 a redshift indicating a motion of 600 km per second had been found. But it was not until 1924 that Edwin Hubble proved that the nebulae were galaxies, outside and far beyond our own.

After Hubble's discovery, a host of other measurements were made, from which it became clear that our own Galaxy was rotating and that our Sun took part in this rotation. This made it clear that although we might consider our Galaxy to be stationary in space, it and our Sun were in motion and we were therefore observing from a moving platform. When a correction for this movement was applied to previous measurements, the velocity of recession given by the redshift of the Andromeda galaxy was reduced by half to only 100 km per second, which is still a very large figure all the same.

The other factor that came out of these observations was that in galactic spectra, redshifts were in the majority. Indeed we now know of only three blueshifts for certain; these are for the two Magellanic Clouds **and the Fornax System – galaxies** which are all members of our own Local Group. All other galaxies show redshifts. What Hubble then discovered was that the redshifts increased with the distance of the galaxy, and ever since 1929, when the 'Hubble Law' was established, other observations have confirmed this strange fact. The universe of galaxies is spreading ever further out into space as time passes. What is more, there seems to be no centre from which the galaxies began to move outwards; in other words neither our Galaxy nor any other is at the centre of the expansion. It is just that space is expanding, carrying the galaxies with it, so that the distance between them all is steadily increasing. We are, therefore, part of an expanding universe. The redshifts we measure are relative to our Sun, though, because the velocities of galaxies increase rapidly as we observe further and further out into space, the Sun's own velocity as it orbits the Galaxy becomes less significant.

In looking at the motions of galaxies in general we can take our own Galaxy as the fixed point, because in a large-scale picture of the universe galaxies, not stars, become our units. The universe is composed of galaxies and their motions tell us about its behaviour.

The expansion of the universe which we see when we look at galaxies must be due to some particular past event, for otherwise we would expect that, under gravitation, galaxies would move closer together and finally collapse in on one another to form, presumably, a gigantic black hole. The possible cause of this expansion we shall discuss later, particularly when we come to the big bang theory (page 156).

The fact that the universe is expanding does not mean that gravity does not operate out in intergalactic space. It most certainly does, as the galaxies in our Local Group show. Here the various members are not moving about at random, but are actually all moving in orbit around a common 'centre of gravity'. This point is the centre of mass of the system – if you add up all the masses of the members of the Group and take into account their distances from each other, you will find a place about which the gravitational pull on the system is concentrated. Of course there are perturbations because each galaxy affects every other galaxy as it orbits, and detailed observations indicate that the Local Group is not stable. Gradually, over millions of years, the mutual gravitational pulls between the members of the Group will cause velocities to increase until its members disperse.

Galaxies in other groups and clusters both large and small, all take part in orbital motion around the centre of mass of each group or cluster. But the redshifts observed for every galaxy still occur because every

group and cluster is taking part in the expansion of space, and of course that is in addition to their motions within the group or cluster of which they are part.

Since the galaxies in our Local Group look as though they will disperse in time, what about the galaxies in other groups and clusters? Will they also disperse in due course, or are there some so closely bound and stable that they will always remain together no matter what happens?

To answer this question astronomers have devised what they call the 'virial theorem'. This theorem deals with the two forces that are in operation in a cluster: the force of gravitation, pulling the members of

the cluster together, and their motions which tend to separate them. The theorem states that twice the energy contained in the motion of the members added to the energy stored up by the gravitational potential of the system must equal zero. The gravitational potential is the energy stored in the gravitational field. When you lift something off the ground gravitational energy is stored in it. This energy is released when you let it fall. So what the theorem does is to let astronomers equate one form of energy with another. When applied to a cluster of galaxies, the equation can either give an answer of less than zero – in other words, a negative quantity – or one of more than zero. Should the result

above
The Sc-type galaxies, NGC 4038 and NGC 4039, in the constellation Corvus are sources of radio waves and are clearly interacting with one another.

left
The galaxies NGC 5426 and NGC 5427 are both spirals and lie in planes that are tilted at slightly different angles to each other. The faint stream of material between them indicates that the galaxies are interacting with one another.

be negative, then gravity is pulling the members together more strongly than the force due to kinetic energy is pulling them apart. In that case, the cluster will remain as a close knit collection. If the equation comes out positive, then the kinetic energy is the stronger and is greater than the gravitational potential, with the result that the galaxies in the group or cluster will disperse. This, of course, is the state of affairs in our Local Group.

The situation may not always remain the same because some galaxies undergo vast explosions, as we have seen (page 92), which may affect their motion and therefore their kinetic energy. Again, some galaxies collide or come so close to one

another that their motion may be altered. It would seem that ring galaxies (page 118) are the result of such close encounters. We must remember that galaxies are not solid bodies and when they collide the stars, dust and gas of which they are composed pass through each other. There may, however, be some interchange of material, even, perhaps, of stars, and doubtless alterations to the kinetic energies of the galaxies involved. However, the motions of some other galaxies, in strange or unusual situations, are more difficult to fathom. For instance, some galaxies seem to be paired, with streams of intergalactic material stretching out between them. Presumably they are orbiting

round each other though no actual observations proving this have yet been made. Stranger still are chains of galaxies, such as the one in the Perseus cluster, where a whole series of 24 galaxies appear strung across a distance of half-a-million parsecs (1½ million light-years) or more.

There are other instances where it is difficult to be sure of the way in which galaxies are actually interacting. For example, in cataloguing interacting galaxies the Russian astronomer Vorontsov-Velyaminov noted a group of three galaxies, VV159, two of which had a velocity of recession of 10,500 km per second while the other, which looks just like them, was receding at 13,500 km per second. However, astronomers are not sure whether this third galaxy is rushing past the other two or whether, it is perhaps a larger but more distant galaxy. Then there is the group of six galaxies known as 'Seyfert's sextet' after their discoverer Carl Seyfert. They comprise one irregular and five spirals. It is thought that the irregulars may be composed of material detached from one of the spirals by one of the others, for all are close; their average separation is only 17,000 parsecs (55,420 light-years). Also, this group contains one spiral receding with a velocity 4½ times larger than the others; is this one therefore further away than the rest?

One of the most intriguing groups as far as motions are concerned is 'Stephan's quintet', a group of five galaxies discovered in 1877 by the French astronomer E. M. Stephan, who of course thought they were nebulae. The redshifts of four of the members vary between 5,700 and 6,700 km per second and so, clearly, the group is unstable and will disperse. The main interest lies in the fifth member, which has a velocity of recession of only 800 km per second. It is most likely that this galaxy is much nearer to us than the other four, which now seem to be merely a compact group at the centre of a scattered cluster, some 70 million parsecs (230 million light-years) away. It has been suggested that the galaxy was ejected towards us from one of the other galaxies, or that all five galaxies were ejected from another nearer galaxy. Certainly radio observations seem to confirm that there was some explosive activity in the region. But whatever the final answer may be, it is obvious that their individual motions are very varied and need much further investigation.

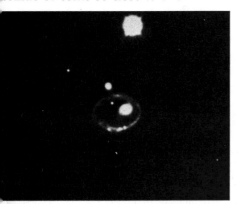

bove Two ring galaxies photographed at the Kitt Peak National Observatory. Both galaxies probably began life as spirals and have been penetrated by a second galaxy, which can be seen lying at their centres.

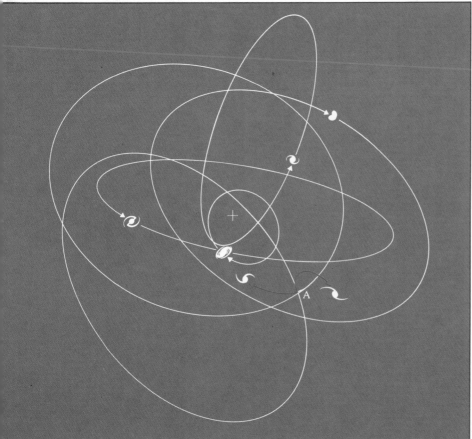

The galaxies within a cluster orbit the centre of mass. The path of any galaxy may, however, be altered at any time by a close encounter with another (A).

INTERPRETING THE REDSHIFT

A redshift signifies motion directly away from us. But are there other factors which could also give rise to an increasing redshift with distance?

There is a vast body of evidence to show that when a body, which emits radiation, moves away from us the lines in its spectrum are redshifted. We have seen this to be true in the case of a rotating body like the Sun; it is also detected in the spectra of binary stars, and in the motions of galaxies in our Local Group, nearly all of which can have their changing distances checked by other means. The Hubble law, that the redshift of galaxies increases with distance, seems certainly to be correct for nearer galaxies, but is it really true right out in the furthest depths of space? Is it safe to apply it to galaxies and QSOs whose distances we cannot measure in any other way? Is there, perhaps, some other redshift effect which is so small that it does not show up over comparatively short distances and only becomes important when distances become extremely great?

These are not idle questions; they are of the utmost importance, especially in view of the fact that QSOs seem, on the basis of Hubble's law, to be immensely distant, and yet are very small and astoundingly powerful. QSOs still present us with problems as far as the generation of their energy is concerned and a few astronomers have considered other explanations for at least a proportion of their redshifts, though not the whole of them – the connection between redshift and radial motion away from us seems too well established for that. If an alternative explanation exists, it would bring the QSOs nearer and so get over the problem posed by the generation of so much energy from so small a space. It would also mean that the universe is not as large as it is at present thought to be.

One explanation along these lines which has been suggested is that light loses energy as it travels. The effect would be too small to be noticeable as far as distances on Earth are concerned, or even distances within the Solar System, and would really only become significant over intergalactic distances. However, if the energy loss was sufficiently great to produce a change to longer wavelengths, large enough to play a significant part in replacing the redshift due to motion, other effects besides a redshift would also be expected. In particular, distant observers would see a noticeable loss of sharpness in the appearance of very distant galaxies, yet no such deterioration in image quality has been observed. Photographs of distant galaxies seem to be as well defined as those taken of nearer ones.

On the other hand, relativity theory tells us that light loses energy when escaping from a massive body. This causes a small redshift which becomes larger the more massive the object from which the light is escaping. However, although galaxies are certainly massive objects, the amount of 'relativistic' redshift would be small, and QSOs are not massive enough to make a really substantial change to the way distance and redshift are connected.

Still yet another possibility has been suggested in connection with a theory known as 'kinematic relativity', proposed by the British astronomer and mathematician Edward Milne. He suggested that atomic behaviour ran on a different time-scale from the one we now experience at this period of development of the universe. Originally, when the universe began, the two scales were in step but have now become progressively different. The effect of running on a different

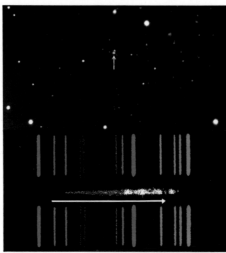

Beneath this photograph of the Hydra cluster, taken with the 5-m telescope at Palomar, a spectrum is given for the galaxy indicated by an arrow. The Galaxy's spectrum is shown between a spectrum produced at the observatory for reference purposes. The length of the arrow indicates the amount of redshift in the galaxy spectrum. It represents a velocity of recession of 56,000 km per second.

time-scale would result in the frequency of radiation emitted in the past being lower than the frequency we measure for the same kind of atoms now; we should therefore observe a lengthening of wavelength. This would give us a redshift which increases with distance, because the more distant a body is the longer ago its light set out on its journey to us. This certainly sounds like a possible alternative to the simple Hubble explanation, until one begins to calculate how much of a redshift there would be on Milne's theory. It turns out that the shift would be only small. For this reason and also because it has proved to be a more restricted kind of relativity theory than the one proposed by Einstein (page 132), kinematic relativity has lost favour among astronomers. So this explanation, which in the event could not present a useful alternative for the redshifts, has been discarded.

This account of the alternatives to the normal interpretation of the redshift seems to show that there is no satisfactory substitute. It seems therefore that QSOs are indeed very distant, and the problem of the huge amounts of radiation they generate is therefore still with us. However, the British astronomer Geoffrey Burbidge, who now works wholly in the United States, has pointed out an interesting fact about QSOs concerning the dark absorption lines observed in their spectra. As we have seen (page 94), QSOs do present a number of different redshifts from each component part, and it is generally agreed by astronomers that the separate redshifts come from a number of shells of gas shot out from the QSO and which move away at different speeds. We should, of course, expect the velocities of the shells to vary from one QSO to another, and so they do except for one thing. An unusually high number of shells show a redshift of 1.95. Certainly, with the large number of redshifts observed, the value of 1.95 might well appear more than once, but what Geoffrey Burbidge claims is that it occurs far more often than chance would lead anyone to expect. It is as if there is some unknown factor operating in these cases. So while there is at present no satisfactory alternative to the normal interpretation of redshifts as being due to the recession of galaxies and QSOs away from us in every direction, there may be another factor which might prove to be important and could conceivably modify the interpretation.

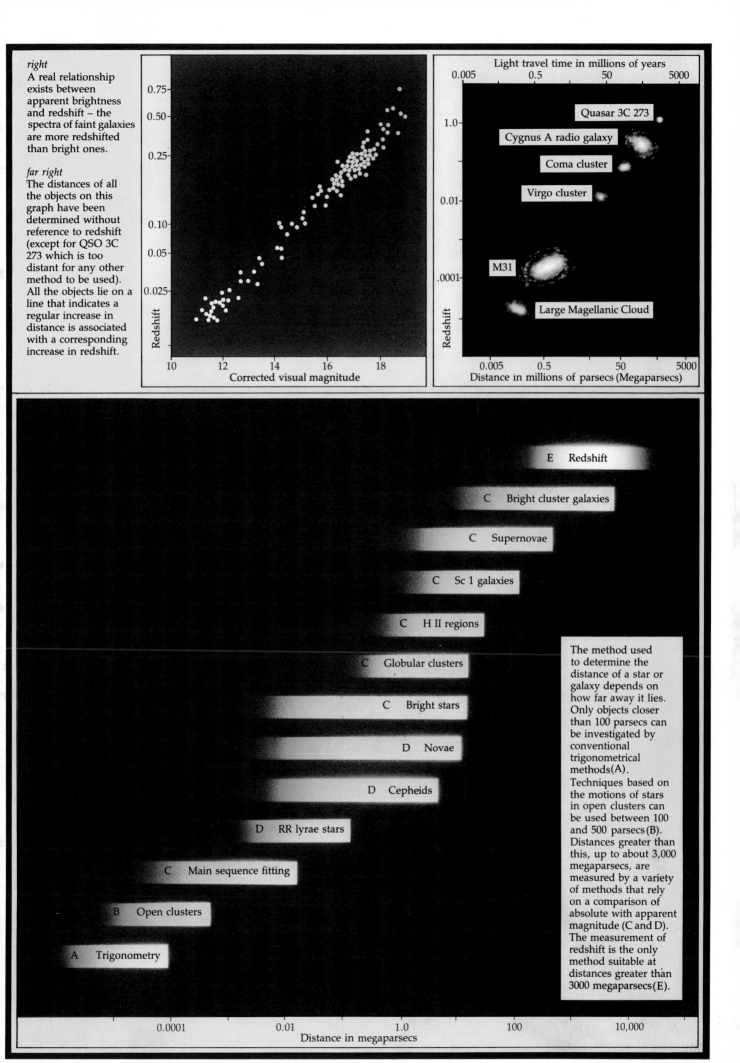

right
A real relationship exists between apparent brightness and redshift – the spectra of faint galaxies are more redshifted than bright ones.

far right
The distances of all the objects on this graph have been determined without reference to redshift (except for QSO 3C 273 which is too distant for any other method to be used). All the objects lie on a line that indicates a regular increase in distance is associated with a corresponding increase in redshift.

Redshift
Corrected visual magnitude

Light travel time in millions of years

Quasar 3C 273
Cygnus A radio galaxy
Coma cluster
Virgo cluster
M31
Large Magellanic Cloud

Redshift
Distance in millions of parsecs (Megaparsecs)

E   Redshift
C   Bright cluster galaxies
C   Supernovae
C   Sc 1 galaxies
C   H II regions
C   Globular clusters
C   Bright stars
D   Novae
D   Cepheids
D   RR lyrae stars
C   Main sequence fitting
B   Open clusters
A   Trigonometry

The method used to determine the distance of a star or galaxy depends on how far away it lies. Only objects closer than 100 parsecs can be investigated by conventional trigonometrical methods(A). Techniques based on the motions of stars in open clusters can be used between 100 and 500 parsecs (B). Distances greater than this, up to about 3,000 megaparsecs, are measured by a variety of methods that rely on a comparison of absolute with apparent magnitude (C and D). The measurement of redshift is the only method suitable at distances greater than 3000 megaparsecs(E).

Distance in megaparsecs

MOVEMENT AND TIME

We observe increasingly large velocities the deeper we go into space, which also means the further back we go in time. Evidence from such observations indicates that the universe was different in the past.

Seeing things not as they are but as they used to be applies not only to the most distant objects but also to those that are comparatively close at hand. The Moon, for instance, is not observed as it is now, but as it was 1.31 seconds ago; the Sun we see is the Sun as it was 8.3 minutes ago, and the most distant objects known, the QSOs, take us back thousands of millions of years to the universe as it was, not so very long after the big bang (page 156), if that indeed is how it all began.

What this movement back in time means is that we can never see the universe as it is at the present time, but as it was at different times. When looking into space we should therefore expect to observe differences between galaxies that are comparatively near and those which are very far off. Of course we should not, in general, expect to notice any great differences from the point of view of the evolution of galaxies. As we have seen in our own Local Group, the Magellanic Clouds (page 102), give every indication of being younger than our own Galaxy. Looked at by astronomers on some far distant galaxy, the Clouds and our Galaxy would also seem to be of different ages (though of course younger because of the distance from which they were being observed). So observing remote galaxies will not, as far as we can tell, provide us with direct information about their ages. It is their distance in light-years that gives us a direct measure of the age at which their light was emitted.

There is, however, another aspect of age of which observations at great distances ought to provide evidence, one that has to do with the theory that we live in an expanding universe. If the Hubble law – that the velocity with which galaxies move away increases with distance – is applied in the reverse sense, then the further back we go in time, the closer the galaxies should be together. Using a value for the Hubble constant for expansion of 55 km per second per million parsecs of distance, calculations show that the universe must have begun expanding something like 20 or more thousand million years ago (20×10^9 years). However, astronomers do not think that the universe is quite as old as that, because immediately after the big bang, the velocities of recession of the galaxies would have been greater than now and the galaxies would have therefore travelled further in a shorter time. So the actual age of the universe must be somewhat less; a figure of 18 thousand million years is the value accepted by most astronomers at the present time.

What this means is that when we observe galaxies and QSOs in the more distant regions of the universe, we are looking at them when they were not so far apart as they are now; in consequence we ought to see more in any given volume of space compared with regions close to us. But making observations to detect a closer spacing between galaxies is not easy, because there are always the

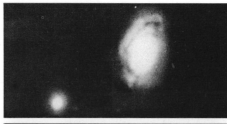

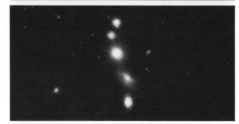

These three photographs represent something of a problem; they all show objects which seem to be related but have different redshifts.

top The active galaxy NGC 7603 seems to be connected to a small galaxy which has twice the redshift and is therefore older.

centre The active galaxy NGC 1073 seems to have a redshift that differs from material (indicated by numbers) which it has ejected.

bottom Here a stream of five galaxies appear to be connected, but their individual motions make it doubtful that they are all of the same age.

effects of local clusterings and groupings to be taken into account. The question is being tackled by radio astronomers because they can more readily detect more-distant objects than optical astronomers. Their investigation consists of counting the numbers of radio sources brighter than a particular radio intensity in certain regions of the sky, and then doing the same again for other particular brightnesses. Their results are most revealing and have shown that the dimmer the radio brightness, the greater the number of sources. Of course this is to some extent what one would expect if galaxies were equally distributed all over space, because the dimmer the sources, the further away one would be looking and the greater the volume of space one would cover and the more galaxies one would see. Also, the larger the redshift, the dimmer the sources would appear both at optical and radio wavelengths, because longer wavelengths of radiation are less energetic than those of shorter wavelength. Yet even when allowance is made for the redshift effect, the radio astronomers' source counts show that there are more 'dim' galaxies than one would expect, even on the basis of an equal distribution.

There are two possible explanations for this result, either the sources were all brighter in the distant past than they are now or the galaxies really were closer together at one time. In view of the evidence already available from the nearer parts of space in support of an expanding universe, the second explanation seems by far the more likely.

Studies of QSOs confirm the findings for galaxies. Counting both radio QSO sources and optical ones, and taking into account that in each case there is a danger of getting counts that are affected by the way the evidence is taken, astronomers find that there are more QSOs with large redshifts than one would expect if they were distributed evenly throughout space. Certainly observations show that there seem to be clusters of QSOs, just as there are clusters of galaxies, and that they are about as common. But this does not affect the result of the QSO source counts any more than it does the count for galaxies. In conclusion, observation back in time, by going deep into space, does indeed show us that we seem to live in a universe that was different in the past.

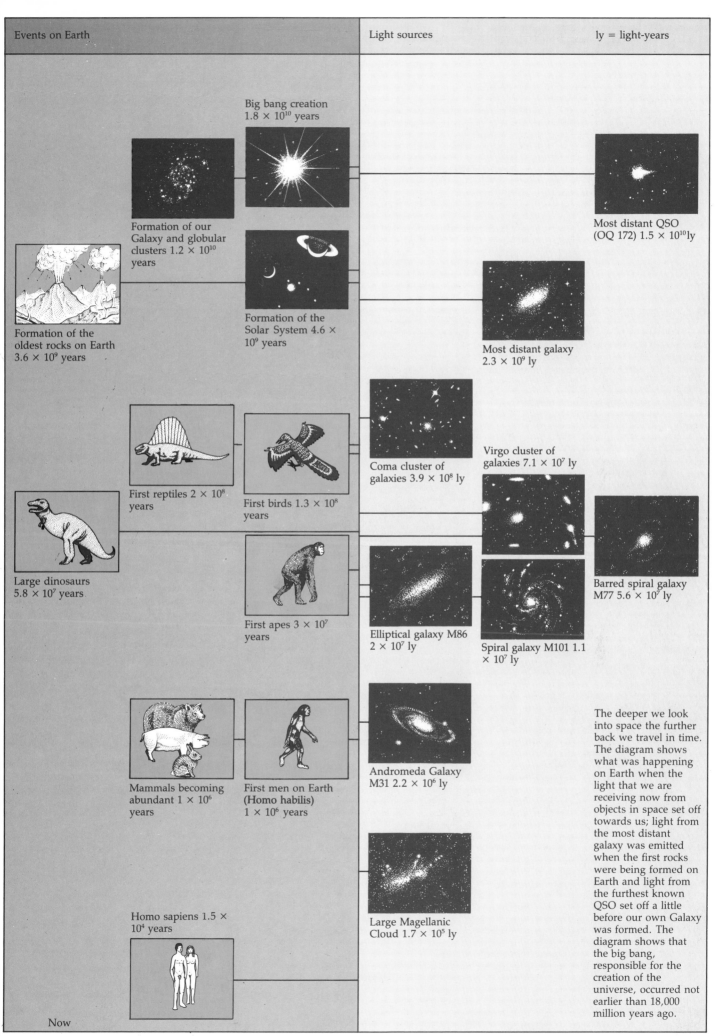

Events on Earth	Light sources	ly = light-years

Big bang creation 1.8×10^{10} years

Formation of our Galaxy and globular clusters 1.2×10^{10} years

Formation of the oldest rocks on Earth 3.6×10^9 years

Formation of the Solar System 4.6×10^9 years

Most distant QSO (OQ 172) 1.5×10^{10} ly

Most distant galaxy 2.3×10^9 ly

First reptiles 2×10^8 years

First birds 1.3×10^8 years

Coma cluster of galaxies 3.9×10^8 ly

Virgo cluster of galaxies 7.1×10^7 ly

Large dinosaurs 5.8×10^7 years

First apes 3×10^7 years

Barred spiral galaxy M77 5.6×10^7 ly

Elliptical galaxy M86 2×10^7 ly

Spiral galaxy M101 1.1×10^7 ly

Mammals becoming abundant 1×10^6 years

First men on Earth (Homo habilis) 1×10^6 years

Andromeda Galaxy M31 2.2×10^6 ly

Homo sapiens 1.5×10^4 years

Large Magellanic Cloud 1.7×10^5 ly

The deeper we look into space the further back we travel in time. The diagram shows what was happening on Earth when the light that we are receiving now from objects in space set off towards us; light from the most distant galaxy was emitted when the first rocks were being formed on Earth and light from the furthest known QSO set off a little before our own Galaxy was formed. The diagram shows that the big bang, responsible for the creation of the universe, occurred not earlier than 18,000 million years ago.

Now

THE EDGE OF SPACE

The most distant objects we can observe take us to great distances and astronomers confidently expect to observe others still further away. Will they ever reach a limit and come to the end of space?

How far we see into space when we observe distant objects depends on what value we accept for Hubble's constant, because the only way we have at the present time of determining really great distances is by measuring redshifts and using the constant to convert them into distances. We can in this way calculate at what point redshift velocities would reach the speed of light. For reasons already mentioned (page 108) the most favoured value for the constant is 55 km per second per million parsecs. If we therefore divide 300,000 km per second (the speed of light) by 55 km per second we find this distance to be 5454.5454 (etc) megaparsecs (million-parsec units) or 17,781.818 million light-years. But, of course, this is only a very rough figure, because we are here assuming the Hubble constant remains the same as far out as we can observe. Though this may well be incorrect. When we observe we go back in time and, as we have just seen (page 125), the constant of expansion may have been rather different around the time of the big bang.

If we set observation aside and ask whether the constant is the same far out in the depths of space as it is nearer to our Galaxy, again there is

no certain answer. In an expanding universe the pieces (which in our universe are galaxies) are separating from one another and the density of the material in every region of space is becoming less. As the force of gravity depends not only on the masses of objects but also on the distance they are apart, so as expansion continues the increase in redshift for a given distance may become even greater. In short, the Hubble constant may increase. So there is bound to be more than a little uncertainty in quoting a value for the limits of the universe we can observe – though, of course, this is limited to objects travelling at less than the speed of light.

Astronomers now accept the view of the theory of relativity (page 132) that states that nothing at all can travel faster than the speed of light. So any very distant galaxies or QSOs we observe (which, of course, must be travelling at less than the speed of light otherwise we could not see them), cannot according to this theory ever reach the speed of light whatever they do. The redshift equation (page 108) makes this clear. However big the redshift z in the equation $1+z = \sqrt{(c+v)/(c-v)}$ may become, the velocity v can never reach the velocity of light. (You can prove this for yourself by giving different values to z. For example if z equals 10 then v becomes 98.36% the

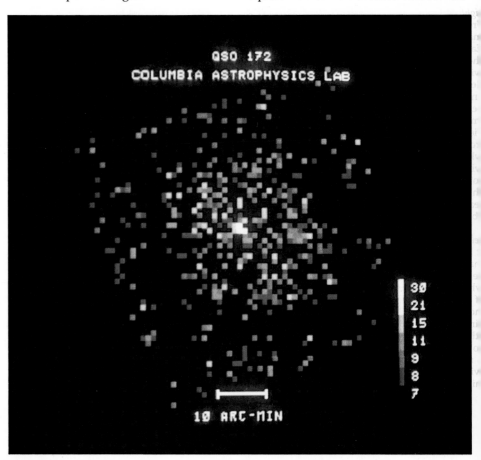

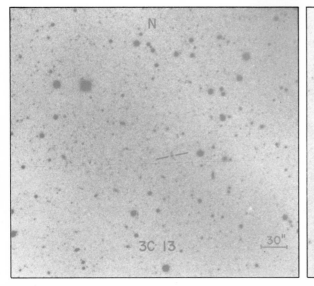

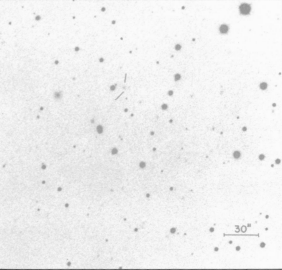

above
At some 15,000 million light-years, QSO OQ 172 is one of the most distant known objects in space. The colour intensity in this X-ray image indicates the strength of the X-rays received.

left
Photographs taken at Kitt Peak National Observatory of the distant QSO 3C 13 (*far left*) and the even more distant QSO 3C 427.1 (*left*). These objects, pinpointed on each photograph by a pair of straight lines, lie at the 'edge' of space.

speed of light, if it is 100 then v reaches only 99.98%, and if $z = 1,000$ v still only becomes 99.998% the velocity of light.)

At the time of writing the most distant galaxy detected lies at a distance of 700 megaparsecs or 2,300 million (2.3×10^9) light-years and the furthest QSO at 4,600 megaparsecs or 15 thousand million (1.5×10^{10}) light-years. But if experience is anything to go by they will not be the most distant objects for long. Future observations with new equipment may be expected to bring into view galaxies and QSOs that are still further away; indeed the Space Telescope alone ought to extend our boundaries much further. And the

right
Freed from the masking effect of the Earth's atmosphere, the Space Telescope will be able to probe deeper into space than any optical telescope before it. This artist's impression gives a view of the telescope from the back end, where the main mirror will be housed. The cover at the front is shown open in readiness for observation.

below
It has been suggested that our universe may be within another in which the total mass of our own makes no more than a small dimple or well in the other, as shown here. So far, however, there is no observational evidence to support this notion.

strange thing is that however powerful our telescopes, however sensitive our recording equipment, we shall always find more galaxies and QSOs to observe. Even if we could go out to the most distant objects known, taking no time to reach them, we should still see galaxies and QSOs. We should observe no boundary to space. Even so astronomers do not believe that space is infinite.

The reason for this strange state of affairs is the nature of space itself (page 46). Space is finite but unbounded; at least this is the kind of space that fits in best with the universe as we now understand it. The universe, as described by

Reimann's geometry, is spherical, though not shaped exactly like the sphere we are most familiar with from Euclid's geometry. The Reimannian type of spherical space is folded over on itself; distances are measured not in straight lines but in curves, and beams of light travel in curved paths called 'geodesics'. Over short distances these geodesics look just like straight lines, and the difference only shows up over long distances. Light curves round so that we can never observe a boundary, but always more space, and more galaxies and QSOs. We can never reach the edge because there is none.

To picture all this look at a ball. It has a curved surface. You can move something about on this surface as much as you like but it will never come to a boundary. The ball, however, does have a boundary of its own, but only in terms of three-dimensional space; the surface is unbounded only for two-dimensional movement (i.e. left or right, or forward or backward, but not up and down).

In Reimannian space we have a 'sphere' with a three-dimensional surface and it is this three-dimensional curvature that we have to imagine. This is not easy, and it is not the same as having a thick shell all round the ball; it is far more complicated. Perhaps it is best to explain it by saying that a Klein bottle (page 47) bears as much resemblance to an ordinary bottle as a Riemannian sphere does to an ordinary everyday sphere. This complex folding over is something we cannot draw, though its properties can be specified in full mathematical detail. The mathematics show that we can never get to the edge of Riemannian space any more than we can to the edge of a Klein bottle.

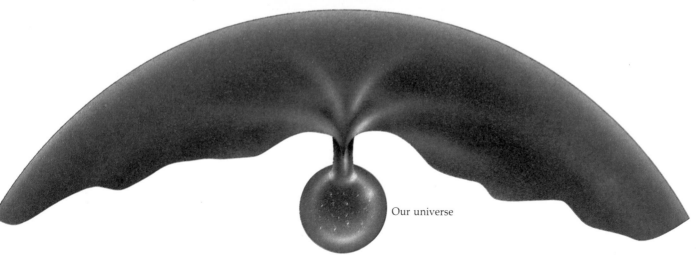

Our universe

CHAPTER 7 GRAVITY AND DEEP SPACE

Why do things fall to the ground? What keeps the Moon in its orbit and prevents it from falling down on top of us? The idea of gravity was developed to explain both.

When you pick up something, and then let it go, it falls straight towards the ground. It does not matter where you are on the Earth's surface, things always drop vertically. With a globe for the Earth – a view held even by the ancient Greeks at least 2,600 years ago – this means that everything falls towards the centre (even though the Earth is not a true sphere but bulges at the equator, and also slightly at the north pole). But why do things fall as they do?

The ancient Greeks devised a simple but ingenious answer which tied in with their ideas of planetary motion and, indeed, with their concept of the whole universe. Things fell towards the centre of the Earth because it was the centre of the universe. It was, they claimed, therefore natural for heavy 'earthy' substances to fall towards the centre of the Earth. Water spread out over the surface of the Earth because that was its natural place. The natural place for air was around the Earth's surface, and for fire, above the sphere of air, this being the reason why flames always travel upwards. In other words, what we call gravity was due to things seeking their natural place in space, and for 'earthy' bodies this meant the centre of the universe.

Why then did the planets move in space round the Earth? Why did the Moon, the Sun and the five planets known in the ancient world not fall to the ground? Again, the answer the early Greek scientists provided was that motion in a circle around the centre of the universe was the natural motion for a celestial body. Circular motion had neither a beginning nor an end, which fitted in admirably with bodies that seemed never to undergo any ageing but always remained the same; clearly, celestial bodies were essentially different from terrestrial ones.

The scheme of the ancient Greeks seemed an excellent explanation, and for well over two thousand years it satisfied the most acute-minded scientists and astronomers. But there were found to be difficulties on two counts. On the one hand, explanations of the motion of bodies on Earth posed problems which could not be solved, and on the other, more observations of the planets showed the old Earth-centred explanation to be too cumbersome. By 1609 Kepler had clear evidence that the planets orbit the Sun not the Earth, and they did so in ellipses not circles (page 112). All this made it necessary to formulate new laws of motion that would explain why things fell to the ground and why planets orbited in ellipses.

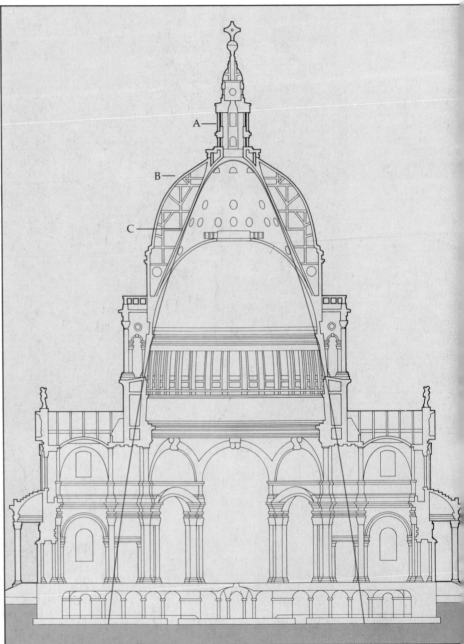

The dome of St Pauls survived the Second World War whereas most of the surrounding buildings were destroyed by heavy bombing. The dome's stability depends on the materials used in its construction and their proper application in relation to gravity. A brick cone (C) supports the outer dome (B) and heavy lantern (A). When extended down to the ground the cone can be seen to form the upper part of an inverted catenary. (A catenary is the shape that a chain makes hanging under gravity.) This shape directs the entire weight of the dome and lantern downwards and prevents the forces involved from thrusting outwards, bulging the walls and causing the cathedral's collapse.

The Greek laws of motion failed on Earth because they claimed that a moving body needed something to push it all the time it was in motion. This brought difficulties when, for instance, one considered an arrow shot from a bow. What kept pushing the arrow after it had left the bow? The usual answer was 'the air', but it was eventually felt that this explanation was unsatisfactory. So too was the Greek belief that the Sun, Moon and planets orbited in circles because it was the natural motion of celestial bodies, which were essentially different from terrestrial ones. Kepler suggested a magnetic force emanating from a rotating Sun gave the planets the necessary continual push to keep them in orbit. He had still not got away from the old Greek idea that a body needed a continual force to keep it in motion, even though he had rejected the idea that the planets remained in orbit around the Sun, just because it was their nature to do so.

Although it was Galileo who began to work out new basic ideas about motion (page 130), it was Isaac Newton who in 1687 finally resolved the matter and, in his *Principia* of 1687 (page 112), published a theory that both explained the behaviour of the planets and the motion of bodies on Earth. Newton was able to prove that if a 'force of gravity' acted between the Sun and every planet then the planets would orbit around the Sun. He expressed the force (F) mathematically by saying that it was proportional to $(m_1 \times m_2)/d^2$, in other words it attracted according to the masses of the bodies concerned, multiplied by each other and divided by the distance between them squared. It acted according to an inverse square law.

As far as the Moon was concerned it was pulled downwards by the Earth and, for its part, it tried to pull the Earth towards it. But, because the Moon was in motion in space, its momentum carried it forward; this forward motion and the pull towards the Earth balanced each other, so that the Moon was kept in orbit around the Earth. The Moon's pull, and that of the Sun, can be seen in the tides, which Newton's theory of gravitation also explained. And because his theory was universal and operated between all bodies all the time wherever they might be, it could be applied to all motions on Earth; it could also be applied to the beams and structures of bridges and buildings. In fact, its applications seemed endless both on Earth and in space.

However, Newton could not say what gravity was. When the third edition of his *Principia* was being prepared in 1728, the editor Roger Coates suggested that gravity was something inherent in bodies – it was something like mass, on which it depended and which was part of the nature of a body itself. When he was told of this, Newton commented "Pray, do not ascribe that notion to me, for the cause of gravity is what I do not pretend [i.e. claim] to know." Newton's refusal to commit himself was taken by some of his critics as an excuse to doubt the very existence of gravity, but as will become clear later, events were to show how wise he was to remain undecided.

A geophysical research satellite being prepared for launch at NASA in 1976. It was designed to provide a point in the sky from which laser light could be reflected to provide information that would give evidence of gravity variations over the Earth's surface.

The Greeks thought that flames always burned upwards because they were seeking their natural place in the sphere above the air. We now know they rise because their hot gases are lighter than the surrounding air, which is more strongly attracted by gravity.

GRAVITY OBSERVED

Gravity can be observed on Earth causing all kinds of effects. From these some idea of its nature may be determined.

Once the idea of bodies having their natural place had been discarded, a whole series of questions presented themselves, the most obvious being why did 'earthy' bodies fall to the ground. The Greeks had said this was a natural motion, a reasoning which led them to consider any other motion as unnatural and due to the application of a continual force.

One of the most important investigators who attacked these ideas was Galileo, and the story of how he dropped bodies of different masses from the top of the Leaning Tower of Pisa is well known. Historians have some doubts about whether the story is indeed true, but no matter, one thing is certain: Galileo established the important fact that all bodies fall at the same speed, whether they are heavy or light. Of course in the everyday world light bodies actually fall more slowly because they are buoyed up by the air. Watch a leaf falling to the ground and you will see it float on the air as it drops, whereas a twig or branch falls much more quickly. But if a feather and a coin are placed in a glass tube, from which the air has been pumped, you will see that they both fall at the same speed. (This is not an easy experiment to prepare, but many museums which deal with physical science have a standing demonstration of it.) In contrast, according to Greek ideas, the speed at which bodies dropped to the ground depended on their weight, and how massive they were. Galileo proved that this was wrong and opened up the way to new laws of motion.

Galileo came very close to stating what has since become known as Newton's first law of motion: that any body will continue in a state of rest, or of motion at an unchanging speed and in a straight line, unless acted on by some other force or forces. In other words, if you set an object moving in a straight line, it should go one for ever. Yet this is not what we observe. If you lay a coin flat on the surface of a smooth table near one edge and give it a

shove, it will slide along the table and so long as you have not pushed it so hard that it lands on the floor, it will eventually come to a stop. This is where the notion of gravity comes into play. Gravity pulls the coin downwards causing it to rub against the table and this rubbing or 'friction' slows the coin down until it stops.

Gravity can also explain the Moon's motion, which, according to Newton's first law, should be a straight line. The Earth's gravity and the Moon's gravity together pull them towards each other but, because the Earth is 81 times more massive than the Moon, the Moon is pulled more strongly towards the

A small charge of explosive is all that is needed to demolish a factory chimney – gravity does the rest.

Earth than the Earth is towards the Moon. The result is that, although the Moon tries to continue to move in a straight line it falls towards the Earth and enters an elliptical orbit around it. The point around which the Moon actually orbits is not, however, the centre of the Earth but the 'centre of mass' of the two bodies; this point lies inside the Earth at a depth of some 1,600 km below the surface.

The Moon's pull on the Earth not only helps to cause tides, both in the sea and to a much smaller degree in the Earth's crust, but it also affects the Earth's axis. This axis, about which the Earth rotates once every day, makes a turning motion, completing one revolution every 25,800 years. This is why the First Point of Aries moves westwards along the celestial equator (page 40). The movement of the axis is caused by the more powerful gravitational pull exerted by the Sun and Moon on the bulging surface of the Earth around the equator.

The Earth's axis also makes a nodding motion. This 'nutation' has a rather complicated cause and depends on a number of separate factors. First there are the continually changing distances between the Earth and Sun (because the Earth orbits the Sun in an ellipse) and between the Earth and Moon (because the Moon's orbit is an ellipse); there are also the changing relative positions of the Moon and the Earth due to the tilt of the Moon's orbit to that of the Earth's. Taken together these factors cause the Earth's axis to wobble as it precesses westwards. This nutation is small; it amounts to only a total movement of 9 arc seconds on either side of the average position, the Earth going through a complete cycle every 18.6 years. Even so it is large enough to be observed.

The Earth's gravity pulls everything down to the planet's surface with a force that depends on the distance from its centre. Because the Earth is not a true sphere but bulges at the equator and at the north pole, gravity varies slightly over the Earth's surface. Gravity is also affected by local geographical features. For instance, the presence, nearby, of a mountain will exert a detectable gravitational pull on a plumb-line (a steel wire with a heavy lead weight at the lower end used for determining the true vertical at any place). The plumbline indicates the zenith, the point vertically above the observatory, a necessity if astronomers are to measure the positions of stars accurately.

Today local changes in gravity are determined by specially designed instruments – gravimeters – and detailed surveys of the shape of the Earth are obtained from careful studies of orbital variations of artificial satellites.

Gravity is obvious to us on Earth because of its local effects, but its influence throughout space is also there for us to see. We are made aware of it whenever we see a meteor falling towards the Earth or look at the Moon in its monthly orbit around us. It is the controlling force in the annual pageant of the seasons, as the Earth orbits the Sun.

above The disturbance caused by a water droplet falling into a tank will be smoothed out by gravity in a very short space of time.

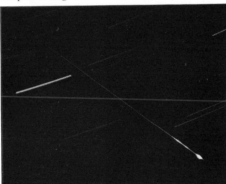

above Fireballs and meteors often collide with the Earth's atmosphere and are drawn down to the ground by gravity. The photograph shows a Perseid fireball.

above The force of gravity acting on the river water will eventually remove this waterfall in Watkins Glen, New York State, eroding the cliff to a smooth slope.

RELATIVITY AND PLANETARY MOTIONS

Although Newton's laws of motion and gravitation largely explain planetary orbits around the Sun, there are some slight anomalies. The theory of relativity can account for these.

As we have already discovered (page 110) nothing is fixed in space, a fact which poses problems for Newton's laws. For example, if we apply a force (F) to a moving body at a fixed speed, we shall cause it to accelerate. How much of an acceleration depends on the strength of the force and the mass of the body. (The equation which expresses this relationship is $a = F/m$, where a is the acceleration and m the mass.) However to discover the new speed at which an accelerated body is travelling, we must know what its original velocity was and that in turn depends on which point in space we choose to call fixed. For motions in the Solar System, for instance, it is convenient to choose the Sun. Using the Sun as a reference point we get a particular set of results when we calculate planetary speeds; if we chose some other point, however, the answers would be quite different. So Newton's laws are really not as universal as they seem, and when we apply them we must always be aware of their limitations and specify the frame of reference within which they are being used.

A new way of expressing the laws of motion, and indeed all the basic laws of physics, which took account of the fact that nothing in the universe is fixed, was formulated by Albert Einstein between the years 1905 and 1915. It regarded the speed of light as the limiting velocity in the universe; nothing could travel faster than that. The theory also took the speed of light and of all electromagnetic radiation to be constant, unaffected by the movement of its source and independent of all observers. (Thus the theory was able to explain the strange results of the Michelson-Morley experiment, page 140.) But in making these radical assumptions Einstein dismissed many basic ideas. He showed that what we measure as the dimensions and masses of bodies

were variable, as we shall see (page 136), and that even the rate at which time passes is not fixed (page 138). Indeed Einstein, and others who also worked on the theory, showed that we cannot really consider space alone but must consider a four-dimensional universe of space-time. It is a universe of Riemannian construction (page 46), in which gravity is seen as a distortion of space-time rather than as a property of matter.

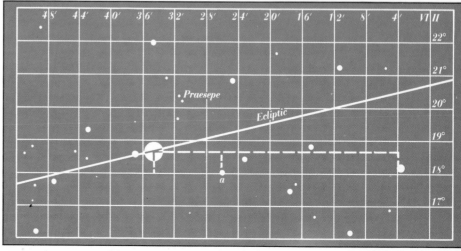

Newton never committed himself to defining gravity, though he did, at one point, go so far as to say that it 'must proceed from a cause that penetrates to the very centres of the Sun and planets . . . that operates . . . according to the quantity of solid matter which they contain, and propagates its virtue on all sides to immense distances . . .'. In other words gravity operates as if all of a body's mass is concentrated at its centre. With Einstein's idea that gravity is a result of the bending of space-time round a massive body, this seems now to be quite obvious.

The laws of gravity in relativity space-time are very like those of Newton, though not exactly the same. Which is the more correct? The answer for the Solar System certainly favours Einstein, and the motion of the orbit of Mercury is a case in point.

Mercury, is the ideal planet for showing up the difference between the two theories; its orbit is highly elliptical, more so than any other of the nearer planets, and it takes only some 115 days to complete a circuit of the Sun. Therefore changes in its orbit are easy to detect. The pull of the other members of the Solar System on Mercury causes it to behave just as if its orbit were rotating very slowly. According to Newton's theory of gravitation this apparent rotation should amount to 531 arc seconds per century; the observed rotation is, however, 574 arc seconds.

When the difference was first discovered, the important nineteenth-century French astronomer and mathematician Joseph Leverrier calculated that it could be accounted for by the presence of another planet of about the same size as Mercury, orbiting the Sun at half Mercury's distance. No sooner had Leverrier made his announcement in September 1859, than a Dr Lescarbault, a physician and amateur astronomer who lived at Orgères near Paris, said he had observed such a planet six months earlier. Leverrier visited him at once and was convinced by the observations; they were, he said the proof he needed. Leverrier named the planet Vulcan and some subsequent observations were reported. But when professional astronomers watched for the planet in 1877 and 1882, when it should have been visible passing across the disc of the Sun, no trace could be seen. What is more, no successful observations of the planet have ever been made since, and astronomers have now abandoned any belief in the planet's existence. The non-existence of Vulcan really meant that a new theory of gravitation was needed to account for Mercury's orbit, and Einstein's theory does give a very much better answer than Newton's. Relativity predicts that the perihelion of Mercury will move 573 arc seconds per century which is within one arc second of the observed figure.

left
This star chart, which appeared in *Nature* in 1878, shows the supposed location of the planet Vulcan. The chart was made following observations of the solar eclipse of that year in North America. During the eclipse a Professor Watson saw a hitherto uncharted object (a) which he took to be the elusive planet.

above
Within the framework of Newtonian physics, calculations of how Mercury's orbit should behave differed from the observed facts. The photograph shows the planet's surface.

right
The movement of the perihelion of Mercury's orbit was the particular orbital characteristic predicted better by Einstein's theory. The perihelion (A) moves slowly round the Sun.

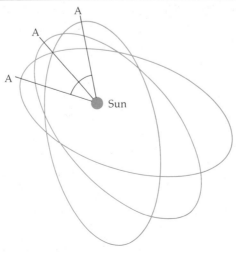

RELATIVITY AND ECLIPSES OF THE SUN

Relativity theory tells us that space becomes more deeply curved near a massive body. Studies of total eclipses of the Sun and other observations show this to be so.

Relativity theory tells us that gravitation is a curvature of space-time. But is this really so? Does space curve; do we live in a Riemannian universe and, if we do, is there some observation we can make that will prove it to us?

Rays of light are everywhere in space and it is due to them that we have gained our picture of the universe. (At least this was certainly so when Einstein formulated his theory almost half a century before radio-telescopes.) Perhaps light can

therefore give us a clue?

If you look at sunlight shining through the clouds, you can see great shafts of light coming through. You will notice that they are straight shafts, not curved in any way. But this straightness is an illusion. As we have seen (page 44), curves that are very gentle often seem to us to be straight lines. If this can be seen on Earth it must of course, be even more marked when we consider distances in space because they are so much greater. Light beams will appear to travel straight in space and astronomers make all their measurements as if light does travel in straight lines. Yet if space is curved, the light beams must be curved as well.

Because curved space-time varies in curvature, being greater where there is a massive body, perhaps we might be able to detect the curvature where light beams pass close to one. The most obvious massive body near to us is the Sun, for although the Moon is nearer, its mass is too small to distort space-time sufficiently for us to observe any deflection. This is

also true of the other planets; none of them, not even Jupiter, is massive enough to cause any noticeable deflection of starlight. Only the Sun is large enough to make a sufficiently large distortion of space-time for us to observe the bending of beams of light for sure.

The trouble in trying to use the Sun is that when it is shining, no stars are visible. If it is bending starlight passing close to it, then it is not observable from Earth. However, things are quite different at the time of a total solar eclipse; the Moon gets between us and the Sun's disc, blotting out the light and allowing the stars to be seen and photographed. Einstein realized this and, when he put forward his relativity theory, suggested that observations made during a total solar eclipse ought to be able to detect the bending. The observations would, he also pointed out, appear to an observer on Earth as a shift in the apparent positions of stars away from the Sun. The shift would be small – less than 2 arc seconds – but observable nonetheless.

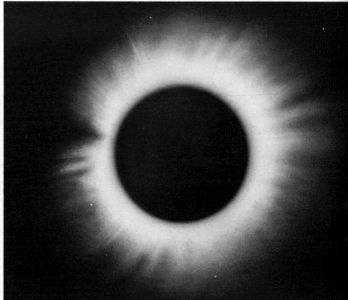

above The positions of the stars on the original photograph of the Sobral eclipse showed evidence of the Einstein shift.

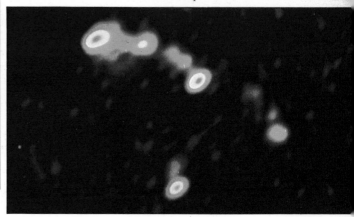

The 1919 solar eclipse, which provided evidence to support the theory of relativity was photographed at Sobral, Brazil with the equipment shown here. Sunlight was fed from the mirror through a fixed telescope to the camera.

The gravitational lens effect is responsible for the double images of the QSOs shown here.

Einstein's full theory was published in 1915, and in 1919 a total solar eclipse was due. British astronomers at the Greenwich Observatory decided to make observations to see whether the 'Einstein shift' really did happen. Two expeditions set out, one to Sobral in Brazil and the other to the Island of Principe in the Gulf of Guinea. Photographs of the area of the sky in which the eclipse would occur were taken. It was calculated that during the eclipse the Sun would be in the region of the Hyades in Taurus, an area rich in bright stars which would show up close to the brightish inner part of the corona. The photographs were taken at the appropriate time of year, when the stars appeared in the night sky, for comparison with the photographs to be taken later, at the eclipse in September. When the eclipse was over, measurements from the photographs obtained by both expeditions showed a detectable shift in star images as the theory predicted.

Three years later, another test was carried out when two American observers photogaphed the 1922 total solar eclipse in Australia; their observations and others since, have confirmed the original results. In every case, the same amount of shift has been detected, and there is now no room for any doubt about the gravitational bending of starlight – an effect predicted by relativity but not by Newton's theory of gravitation.

Although they were not the only demonstrations of the correctness of Einstein's theory, the 1919 and 1922 eclipses were particularly important because they brought a clear and quite independent proof of Einstein's theory at a time when such proofs were needed for the theory to become accepted. Even so, it still took a long time before all astronomers and physicists were convinced that relativity really was more correct than Newton's theories of gravitation and motion.

The 'gravitational lens' effect, which we came across when discussing black holes and that affects some QSOs, is another example of the distortion of light waves by gravity. When a light beam from a distant source passes close to a very massive body, such as a galaxy or a large black hole, the beam is split into two or more parts, the precise path of each depending on the relative positions of the massive body and the source. The light beams are deflected out of their gently curved paths in Riemannian space-time and bent so that an observer sees a double image. Sources providing such double images have been observed; the QSOs 0957 and 561 A and B are typical examples and give further confirmation of relativity theory.

With Einstein's theory established, does it mean that Newton was entirely wrong? After all, his theory was used most successfully for many years, and did give not an unreasonable estimate of the motion of the perihelion of Mercury (page 132). The answer is that while Newton's theory is excellent for many applications over small regions of space, relativity theory is necessary when we consider space in its widest aspects.

Near a massive body light is bent by the gravitational field so that what appears to us as a straight line of sight will be curved.

RELATIVITY AND MASS

Relativity theory tells us important things about mass. It explains how stars shine and predicts a gravitational redshift for starlight as it escapes into space.

Apart from the bending of starlight, one of the most obvious demonstrations of the theory of relativity as it applies to mass is the gravitational or Einstein redshift. We came across this before, when we considered how the redshifts of distant galaxies should be interpreted (page 122). The effect is due to the energy expended by photons of radiation – the 'wave packets' in which radiation travels (page 142) – in climbing out of a dip in space-time caused by the presence of a massive body. It is a very small effect and needs the most delicate observations to detect it, observations which are, however, necessary if relativity theory is to be confirmed.

In the case of the Sun although the gravitational redshift amounts to no more than two parts in a million, observations made of spectra, formed by heating substances in the laboratory and comparing them direct with the Sun's spectrum, do indeed show a tiny redshift of precisely the amount relativity predicts. Of course, if the Sun were a much denser body, a white dwarf, say, then the effect would be even more noticeable. The compaion to Sirius, for instance, is a white dwarf and in recent years a detailed examination of its spectrum has shown that the lines have a redshift that is thirty times greater than that of the Sun, which is just what relativity theory predicts for so massive a body.

Another proof of what relativity theory predicts about mass can be seen by merely looking up at the Sun and the stars, because the way they shine depends on the conversion of mass into energy. As we discovered earlier (page 74), the stars shine because nuclear reactions occur deep inside them. Hydrogen is converted either straightforwardly into helium in the proton-proton reaction, or in a more involved process where carbon plays a part. But in either reaction, when energy is given off the mass of the remaining material becomes less than it was before the reaction began.

What has happened is that mass in the form of nuclear particles has been converted into energy, and a vast amount of energy at that. It is because the quantity is so enormous (the hydrogen bomb is a very small scale example) that the stars keep shining for so many millions of years. The vast scale of energy production in these reactions is due to the relationship between energy and mass given in relativity theory.

This relationship is expressed in the famous equation $E = mc^2$, where E is the energy generated, m is the mass converted and c is the speed of light. c^2 is therefore a very large number and makes E immense.

The theory of relativity has much to say about mass itself, and in particular tells us that what we measure as the mass of a body depends on how fast it is moving relative to us. The relativity principle

above Electrons accelerated down the linear accelerator at the Harwell Atomic Energy Research Establishment in England show an increase in mass as predicted by relativity.

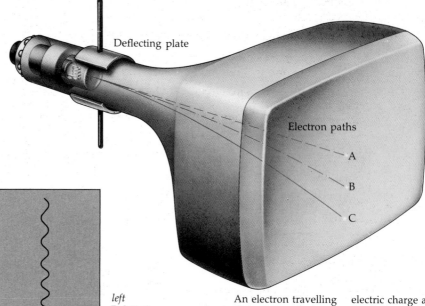

Deflecting plate

Electron paths

A

B

C

left Relativity predicts that the wavelength of light emitted from a massive body will be lengthened by gravity to give a redshift effect.

An electron travelling through a cathode-ray tube will be pulled downwards by gravity. A slow-moving electron ending up at B can be brought back along a straight path to A by placing a certain electric charge across the deflecting plates. A fast-moving electron is more massive and therefore curves further down to C. It needs a stronger charge across the plates to bring it back to A.

dictates that the measurements of all physical qualities (except the speed of light) are relative to the motion of the measured body with respect to the observer. This is true for length as well as mass, measured lengths becoming shorter the faster a body moves relative to us. As far as mass is concerned we find that a body increases in mass the faster it moves in relation to us, and at the speed of light its mass becomes infinite, which is another way of saying that nothing can travel as fast as light. The equation which expresses this relationship is $m = m_o \div \sqrt{(1 - v^2/c^2)}$. You can see from this that as v, the velocity of the body, increases so v^2/c^2 becomes closer and closer to 1, and the expression $\sqrt{(1 - v^2/c^2)}$ becomes smaller and smaller. It can therefore be divided into m_o (the mass of the body at rest) more and more times, and so m increases as v gets larger.

Is this really so? Does mass increase the faster a body moves relative to us? And if so, how can it be checked? We can weigh an object at rest using a sensitive laboratory balance, but how can we measure the mass of a moving body, and do so with great precision? The answers to these questions have been found by nuclear physicists working with huge 'linear accelerators', in which atomic particles such as electrons and nuclear particles such as protons are made to travel at very high speeds indeed. The velocities they reach are so high that they are an appreciable fraction of the speed of light – 80% is not uncommon – and so their change in mass is certainly noticeable; a speed of 80% that of light gives a mass of almost 1.7 times the mass at rest. We have then a means of accelerating particles, but how can their mass be measured?

As the particles travel along the accelerator they pass at certain points between deflecting plates that carry an electric charge. The plates deflect the particles according to their masses; the greater the mass the less the deflection will be. If the particles are allowed to strike a screen after they have passed between the deflecting plates, then the actual deviation can be measured. Using equipment like this it has been found that as particles are speeded up, they are seen to become more massive by precisely the amount that relativity theory leads us to expect.

Another aspect of relativity that bears directly on astronomy is the generation of gravity waves. According to the theory, a massive body which is accelerating should radiate energy in the form of gravity waves which move through space at the speed of light, like other forms of radiation. The waves predicted are very weak and detection by instruments is uncertain (page 34). But there is another way of observing them. If one observes a binary system, one member of which is a pulsar, then by studying the very precise pulses emitted by the pulsar itself, it is possible to map its orbit and to detect any slight changes in gravitational energy. Joel Weisberg and his colleagues in the United States have done this for the pulsar PSR 1913 + 16 and have found it to be losing gravitational energy at a rate very close to what would be expected if gravity waves were being emitted as relativity predicts. So it seems that not only have the illusive waves been detected but relativity is now even more secure than before.

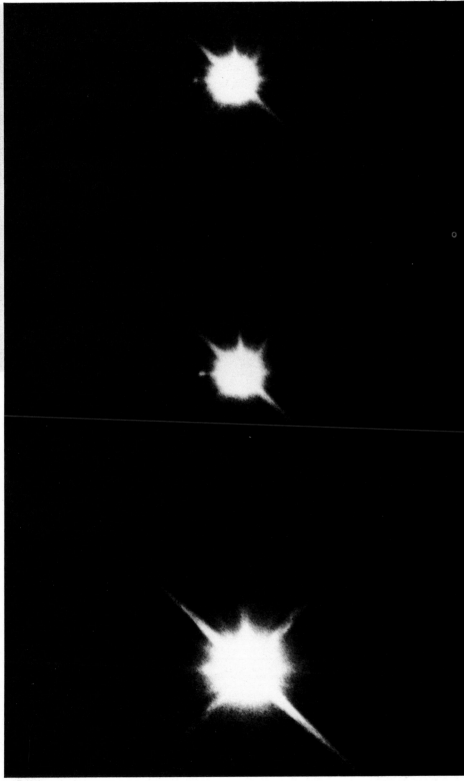

Binary star systems such as Sirius and its white dwarf companion Sirius B, seen on these three photographs (to the left of the main image), undergo changes with time that give rise to gravity waves. These changes can be observed on Earth if one member of the binary is a pulsar.

THE QUESTION OF TIME

One of the strangest results of relativity theory is that time is not constant. Time measured for a system moving relative to us runs at a different rate from time in our own system.

Time seems to be something quite unalterable. Clocks run at a definite rate, and in Newton's laws of motion and gravitation theory, time is taken as passing at a regular unvarying rate. Of course, as humans we experience time passing at different rates; if we are enjoying ourselves time passes quickly if, on the other hand, we are doing something boring time seems to pass very slowly indeed. But when it comes to making measurements in physics or in astronomy, we take time to be regular.

Time, as we use it in studies of the physical world, is based on measurements made originally of the rotation of the Earth. Indeed until half-way through this century time was still regulated by observing selected stars to keep a check on the speed of the Earth's rotation, for it is not regular and undergoes slight variations. Now, however, time is measured using vibrations of hydrogen atoms as the basic standard. Such atomic maser clocks – so-called because *m*icrowaves are *a*mplified by *s*timulating the *e*mission of *r*adiation – are extraordinarily precise and keep time correctly to one part in 30 million million (3×10^{13}), which means that they will not be out of step by more than one second in 100,000 years!

However, what relativity theory tells us is that time, measured in our frame of reference, runs at a different speed from time in another frame of reference, which is moving relative to ours. The equation expressing this is precisely similar in form to the one used to express increase in mass (page 136), with t for time replacing m for mass. So when a body is moving relative to us at a velocity v, its clocks will appear to us to go slower because its intervals of time become longer. There is 'time dilation'. The equation which predicts this stretching out of time is $t = t_0 \div \sqrt{(1 - v^2/c^2)}$ where t_0 is the length of a time interval for us in our frame of reference, and c is, as usual,

the speed of light. So if a body is travelling away from us at a velocity of 80% the speed of light one second in our time lasts almost 1.7 seconds on the moving body. On the other hand an observer on that body, watching our clocks would see ours going slow compared with his. How can that be? Surely one is correct and the other wrong?

The answer to the question is emphatically 'no'. There is no 'correct' time from which other times can be measured or with which they can be compared to give an absolute value. When bodies are in relative motion, the picture gained by observers of each other's world is distorted. It is distorted both in space *and* in time, because we live in a space-time universe. We shall see this kind of distortion in evidence again when we discuss the speed of light itself (page 140).

The fact of time dilation brings us to the astounding realization that

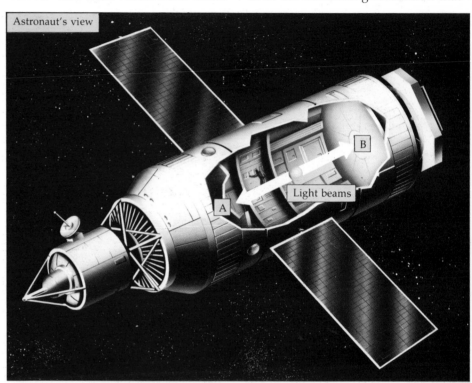

Astronaut's view

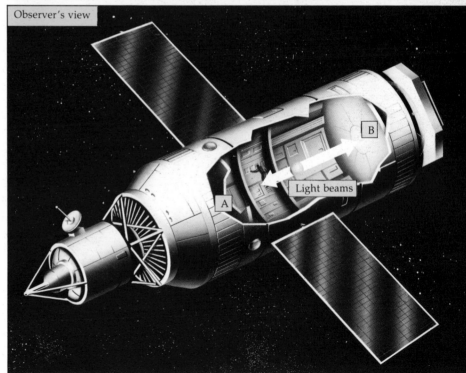

Observer's view

Light from the centre of a spacecraft will appear to an astronaut on board to reach both ends simultaneously.

To an observer on the ground it will appear to reach wall B, which is moving towards it, before it reaches wall

A, which is receding from it. The difference between these experiences is predicted by relativity

which says that we can never be sure two events are simultaneous.

there is no such thing as absolute simultaneity. We cannot say that any two separate events in the universe occurred at exactly the same time. They may, of course, appear simultaneous to us, but that is no guarantee that they really happened at the same instant. This has nothing to do with the fact that light takes time to travel, but is an effect of the relativity of time. For instance, suppose we see two supernova explosions at the same instant, one in our Galaxy and another in a galaxy 10 million light-years away. We can readily appreciate that the supernova explosion in the distant galaxy happened 10 million years ago and therefore they cannot be said to be simultaneous. But if there had been a supernova explosion 10 million years ago in our own Galaxy, could we say that that was simultaneous with the distant explosion? Again, the answer is 'no', and the following simplified example will make this clear.

Suppose a spacecraft, made so that we can look inside it, is passing us at a high speed. Let us imagine that there is an electric lamp in the middle of the spacecraft and that it is suddenly switched on. Using the most accurate apparatus, an observer on what, to him, is a stationary spacecraft will find that the light from the lamp reaches each end of the spacecraft simultaneously. But we on Earth will observe something quite different. Because the speed of light is constant, regardless of the movement of its source relative to an observer, the light from the lamp appears, as we see it, to be unaffected by the spacecraft's motion, as if in fact the lamp were stationary. But as the spacecraft is actually moving relative to us we see one light-beam moving towards a wall in the spacecraft that is receding from it and the other beam moving towards a wall which is approaching it. Therefore we do *not* see the light-beams strike the walls simultaneously. Our picture of the events will therefore be fundamentally different from that of an observer on board the spacecraft.

All this may sound amazing and even artificial, because we have the idea of a basic even flowing time ingrained in our minds. Yet time does dilate and experiments prove it. When two identical maser clocks are placed, one in an aircraft and the other on the ground, little difference in their rates is observed when the aircraft is travelling slowly. But at high speeds it has been shown that the clock in the aircraft does run slow, although only a maser is accurate enough to show the difference.

An even more dramatic example is given by cosmic rays. When a high-speed cosmic-ray particle hits a particle of air, a new particle, a π-meson (pi-meson), is produced. We know from theory and also from nuclear experiments that this particle has a very short lifetime and lasts for only about 100 millionth (10^{-8}) of a second before it decays. When they are generated by cosmic rays, such particles are moving very fast and so time goes more slowly for them relative to us. As a result they are observed by stationary observers on the ground to have a much longer lifetime than normally expected.

So, time dilation really does occur. It is the reason why something falling into a black hole appears to hover for ever at the event horizon. Time dilation there is so great that even a tiny fraction of a second is extended almost indefinitely.

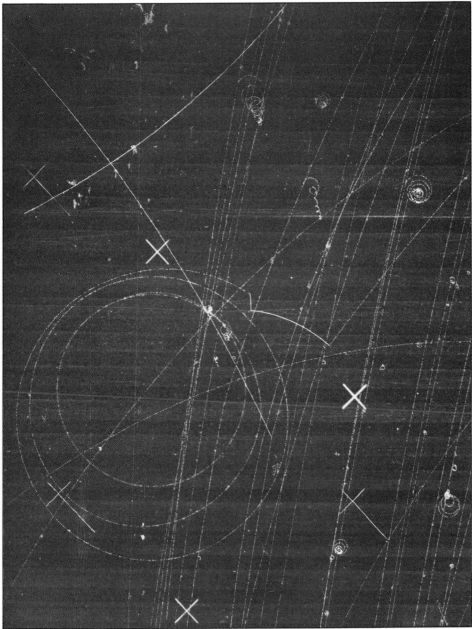

above
From traces such as these, made inside a hydrogen bubble chamber, measurements can be made of the lifetimes of subatomic particles. It has been found that, in accordance with relativity theory, fast-moving particles live longer than slow-moving ones of the same type.

right
Time dilation can scarcely be noticed below speeds of ¼ the speed of light. At velocities higher than ¾ the speed of light the effect is dramatic, eventually almost halting the passage of time completely.

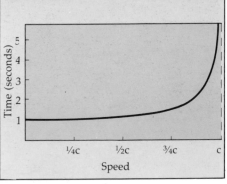

THE SPEED OF LIGHT

The speed of light can be measured with great accuracy and is a constant, whatever the velocity of the source emitting it may be. Yet some 'faster-than-light' particles could, perhaps, exist.

When, in the early nineteenth century, light was shown to travel like a wave, scientists began to wonder in what substance or 'medium' it travelled. They reasoned that because you cannot have waves by themselves, they must always be in something. We know from experience that we cannot get hold of a disembodied wave. This is because a wave is really a disturbance, not a thing in its own right.

You can see this for yourself if you drop a cork into a bath of water or into a pond, and then let a coin or a small pebble drop in afterwards. The coin or pebble sets up waves, radiating outwards from the place where it entered the water; you can see them moving outwards in rings. But now look at the cork. When the waves pass it they do not carry it along, they only make it bob up and down. This happens because the wave is a disturbance, an up-and-down motion of the water molecules, caused by the original disturbance which the coin or pebble made as it dropped in.

Scientists know that light waves can travel in a vacuum and in this respect are quite different from sound waves which can only travel in air, in a liquid or in a solid. (That is why there can be no sound on the Moon, or on Mercury; there is no atmosphere through which it can travel.) Some museums have an exhibit to demonstrate this fact. An electric bell is fixed in a large glass jar and by pressing a button you can see and hear it ringing. Yet by switching on a vacuum pump to remove the air from the jar, the sound fades away – because there is no air to carry it – even though you can still see the device is working, with its clapper striking the bell. And here is the problem. If light travels through a vacuum, what is the medium in which the disturbances act?

In the nineteenth century scientists invented the aether to act as the medium in which light waves could travel. This aether weighed nothing and was perfectly elastic, responding precisely to the motions of light waves and taking no energy from them. The Earth in its orbit round the Sun was thought to move through the aether and in 1880/81 Albert Michelson conducted an experiment which it was hoped would detect this movement. He designed a special 'interferential refractomer' in which light from a lamp was split into two paths at right-angles to each other and then sent out to two mirrors. The light was reflected back and the two beams made to interfere. Because the Earth is orbiting in space, the speed of light in the direction of the Earth's motion relative to the aether should be different from its speed at right-angles. Michelson's apparatus was

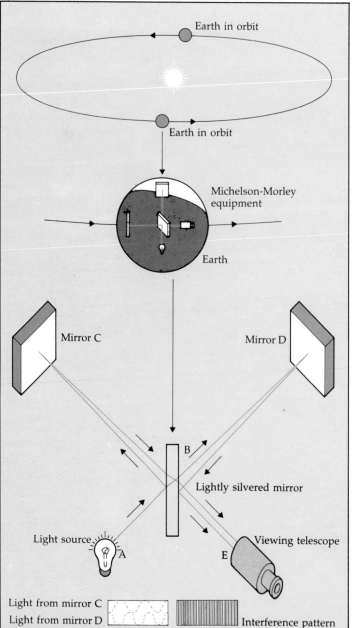

Earth in orbit

Earth in orbit

Michelson-Morley equipment

Earth

Mirror C

Mirror D

B

Lightly silvered mirror

Light source A

E

Viewing telescope

Light from mirror C
Light from mirror D

Interference pattern

left
In Michelson's interferential refractometer (interferometer), light was emitted from a source (A) towards a half-silvered mirror (B) and transmitted to mirrors at C and D. The light reflected back from C and D was partially reflected again at B to an observer at E who could observe the interference pattern produced by the beams. The whole apparatus was then rotated. Any change in the interference pattern would have indicated that the speed of light between B and C, and between B and D had been different and therefore the Earth's passage through space (top) was relative to some medium (the aether) through which light waves travelled.

below
If two people roller-skate towards each other at 10 km per hour and one throws a ball to the other at 5 km per hour, the speed of the ball relative to the other will be 15 km per hour. However, light always travels at 300,000 km per second regardless of the speed of its source.

sensitive enough to detect the expected result, yet when he first tried the experiment in Germany no difference was detected. Michelson returned to the United States and with another scientist, Edward Morley, tried repeatedly to obtain the result that was expected. Yet, in spite of using more delicate apparatus and sending the light beam back and forth many times in each direction to magnify the difference between the two paths, Michelson and Morley always obtained a zero result.

The fact that the speed of light was the same in both directions seemed to make nonsense of everything known about the way in which one adds and subtracts velocities. For example, if two railway trains are approaching one another at 100 km per hour and if you were sitting in one train, you would see the other approaching at 100 + 100 or 200 km per hour. Yet although the Earth moves in its orbit at a speed of 29½ km per second, this is not added to the speed of light; its total velocity does not change, it is always 299,792.46 km per second. It turns out that you cannot add or subtract velocities to the velocity of light, strange though this may appear to be.

Relativity theory, which was developed quite independently of the Michelson-Morley experiment, makes sense of this apparently crazy result. By proposing that length, mass and time are not fixed but depend on the relative motion of bodies, and by using a Riemannian space-time universe, the Michelson-Morely result becomes expected. No longer is it something peculiar, though it does turn out that the speed of light is the limiting speed in the universe. This means that we can plot events in space-time by using a diagram of a 'light-cone' (*below left*) with two dimensions of space and one of time. Drawing a light-cone shows how a signal of light, or any other radiation, will spread out in space-time and depicts the history of the signal's progress. Of course, if we just wanted to depict the signal's motion in space, we should draw a sphere centred on the point from which the light was emitted because light spreads out in every direction, but in many cases – black holes are examples – astronomers find light-cones can help them gain a picture of what is happening. At the event horizon of a black hole, a light-cone tips over so that one side is vertical, indicating that the light in that direction is hovering in one spot, which is just what astronomers believe happens.

Can anything travel faster than light? The equations used in relativity say 'no' because a body's mass would become infinitely great and its length zero. Yet in some nuclear reactions events occur which, at the present time, can best be explained by assuming the creation of new particles called 'tachyons' which travel faster than light. Nuclear physicists find that the tachyons' mass becomes less the faster they go and, as they lose energy, so they travel more quickly. They can never travel *at* the speed of light, only faster. In short, tachyons behave in just the opposite way from matter, but nevertheless fit in with relativity theory. No one, however, has actually observed a tachyon.

Light source — Adjustable mirror — Unsilvered glass plate
Mirrors — Silvered glass plate — Mirrors — Brass holders — Mirrors
Telescope
Mirrors
Sandstone slab
Mercury
Iron container
Brick

above
The apparatus used by Michelson and Morely in the United States to try to detect the Earth's motion through the aether was much more sensitive than Michelson's original equipment (*opposite*) and sent the light back and forth between the mirrors many times to magnify any effect. But still no change in the interference pattern was observed when the apparatus was rotated.

right
Light cones show how radiation travels through space and time.

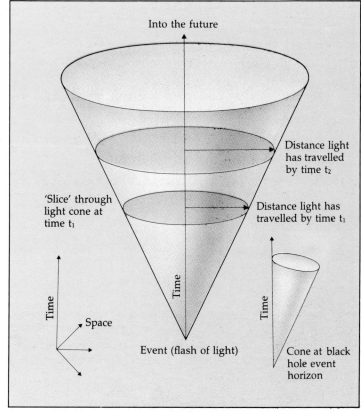

Into the future

Distance light has travelled by time t₂

'Slice' through light cone at time t₁

Distance light has travelled by time t₁

Time

Space

Time

Event (flash of light)

Time

Cone at black hole event horizon

CHANCE IN THE UNIVERSE

Though radiation travels as waves, it also acts as if it were made of separate particles. This shows that there is an element of chance in the way the universe behaves, and that even gravity and space may be in separate 'pieces'.

In 1905, when Albert Einstein announced the first stage of his theory of relativity, he also wrote about the photoelectric effect. This effect concerns certain metals which are good conductors of electricity and are found to emit electrons when light or other radiation shines on them. In Einstein's day there was a problem, for contrary to what was expected, the energy of electrons emitted did not depend on how bright the light was, but on its wavelength. The shorter the wavelength, the greater the quantity of electrons that were given off. Einstein was able to show that the effect could be explained if one assumed that radiation travelled in discrete or separate units, called 'quanta'. Eleven years later, the American physicist Robert Millikan proved by experiment that Einstein was correct.

Einstein's suggestion that radiation is emitted as quanta seemed to be very strange to some physicists, because they knew that light behaved like waves and therefore could not at the same time be composed of particles. There was no doubt about the existence of light waves, for when two beams of light from the same source are mixed together, they interfere. The ups and downs or crests and troughs of the waves either strengthen each other, or weaken, or even cancel one another. We have already seen how this is made use of in astronomy with radio interferometer telescopes (page 28) and speckle interferometry (page 30), and there really is no doubt about it. Yet there was no doubt about the photoelectric effect either, and the existence of light quanta seemed equally strongly confirmed.

The contradiction stems from the fact that, as we shall see, the tiny world of the atom and of particles smaller than atoms such as light quanta is rather different in some

details from the larger world of everyday experience.

As far as light and other radiation is concerned, the quanta or 'photons' as they are sometimes called, are best thought of as little packets of waves. They have no mass when at rest, they possess no electric charge and they do not spin. But when they move they do have some momentum or impetus, as we can see from the effect of radiation pressure from the Sun, which helps to keep the tails of comets pointing directly away from the light source (the Sun) and out into space (page 50). And, of course, they travel with the speed of light.

The idea that radiation is emitted

in quanta had all kinds of important effects on physics and astronomy and, not least, on the development of a new theory about the nature of the atom and why radiation from it is emitted only at certain specific wavelengths.

The old theory, developed primarily by the Danish physicist Neils Bohr, had run into difficulties. Bohr imagined that each atom had a central core or nucleus around which one or more electrons moved in orbit. He stated that when energy was put into the atom by heating it, for example, the orbiting electron jumped outwards to a new orbit. Afterwards, the electron dropped back to its original orbit or, perhaps,

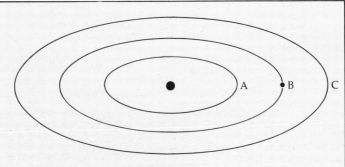

left
In Bohr's model of the hydrogen atom, the orbiting electron may occupy any of several orbits of which three are shown here.

below
A photograph of a crystal lattice taken by the 600-kilovolt electron microscope at Cambridge.

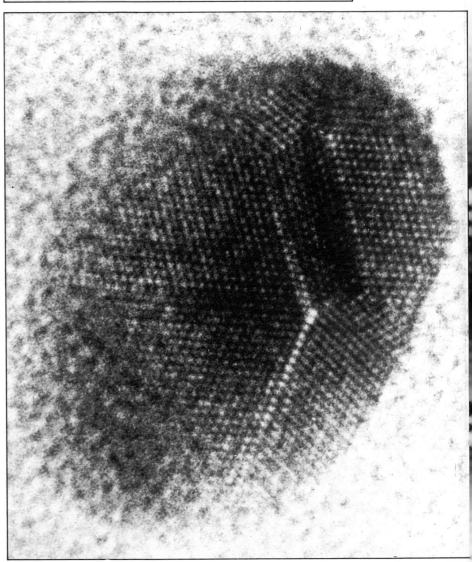

142

to one nearer the nucleus, emitting energy as it did so. One puzzle was why, when it had given out energy, did the electron not fall right back into the nucleus. Why did it always remain in some orbit whatever happened?

Once the idea of quanta was accepted, Bohr saw that the truth of the matter was that electrons could only orbit a nucleus in certain fixed orbits, and in no others. When an atom received energy, an orbiting electron would move from orbit B out to orbit C, say, but not to any orbit in between them because none existed. Then, when it dropped back, it would go from C to B, and again not stop anywhere in between. The drop between these specific orbits would cause the atom to emit a specific quantum of energy at a specific wavelength. If the electron fell back from orbit C beyond B to a specific orbit which we may call A, the quantum of energy emitted would be even greater and the wavelength therefore shorter (the shorter the wavelength of a photon, the more energy it possesses).

What is more, Bohr realized that there was a lowest orbit beyond which an electron could not fall. Once it had reached that position it was in what was called the 'ground state', and remained there. It could not drop further and fall into the nucleus because of the specific nature of the quantum orbits characteristic of every atom. The behaviour of an electron as it orbited the atomic nucleus was therefore not quite the same as a planet round the Sun.

Inside the atom there is a nucleus composed of protons, which have a positive electric charge, and sometimes also neutrons, whose charge is zero. Both are more massive than electrons. Since like charges repel each other we might expect the nucleus to split apart, every proton trying to get away from every other proton. What is it then that holds them together? Gravity due to the mass of the protons and neutrons (if present), is certainly not sufficient. It is believed that there is a strong 'binding force', a thousand times a million multiplied by itself six times (10^{39}) stronger than gravity, and that the force is due to exchanges of particles known as mesons, which have very short lifetimes (never more than one hundredth of a millionth of a second).

All this makes it clear that the world of the atom is different in some basic ways from the world we ordinarily observe. New forces operate, strange short-lived particles come into existence and then vanish away. Yet although we talk about nuclear particles, name them, measure their masses and the electric charges they carry, none has ever been seen. All that nuclear physicists can observe are either the areas where they operate – the atoms which they form by interacting together – or the other interactions which they undergo. Thus, it is known that mesons are short-lived because the interactions involving them happen in a tiny fraction of a second. But no one has ever seen a meson directly, or an electron for that matter, or will they ever be able to do so.

Suppose we wish to discover where an electron will be at a particular instant. It should be possible to determine its position by bouncing a photon of light off the particle. However an electron is so very small that if we used an ordinary beam of light, each photon would be so large by comparison that the light would merely flow round it. We must instead use extremely shortwave radiation. Gamma-rays, which are the shortest possible, and therefore the most energetic and penetrating, would appear to be ideal. If we bombarded the electrons with gamma-rays, we would discover that when a photon struck an

The 600-kilovolt high-resolution microscope is the most powerful instrument of its kind in the world. It is an example of how electrons can be used to show things the size of atoms, even though the electrons cannot be shown themselves.

electron, the electron would be pushed out of its original position, and at the same time the photon would recoil from the collision. If we could measure the angle of recoil precisely, we would be able to calculate where the electron would be at the instant the photon hit it. Unfortunately, very short-wavelength photons, such as gamma-rays, spread out after impact and it is therefore impossible to make accurate measurements of the angle. We are now in something of a dilemma; we need short wavelengths to detect an electron's position and long ones to determine the motions of recoil.

It is therefore impossible to determine precisely where an electron will be at a given instant. We can only say that it will lie within a certain area at a certain time, for we can fix a place and say that it will be there within some interval of time but we cannot specify place and time precisely for the same electron. This result is due, not to any faults in us or in our apparatus, but to the nature of things themselves. When we examine the smallest components of matter, we find there is a certain amount of indeterminacy or vagueness about what we can specify. This property of nature was first discovered in 1927 by the physicist Werner Heisenberg and it is sometimes known as 'Heisenberg's principle of indeterminacy'.

Perhaps this is not all as strange as it sounds, because it has been found that electrons behave not only as particles but as waves. If a beam of electrons is shot through a tiny

hole in a metal sheet, the electrons will spread out on the other side just as waves would do. So electrons are to some extent like photons; they are packets of waves. On the other hand they differ because they do have a mass when at rest and possess an electric charge. They also can and do spin. To express their behaviour precisely, scientists use a special mathematical expression that is

essentially a 'wave equation', and which demonstrates the fact that an electron has wave-like aspects. However, the equation is very similar to that expressing the probability, or likelihood, of certain classes of event and this ties in nicely with the Heinsenberg indeterminancy principle. In other words, the electron and other fundamental atomic particles have a certain

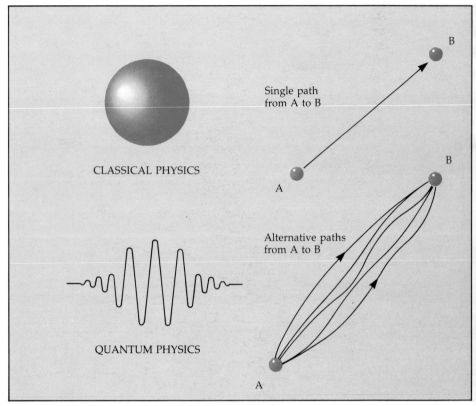

CLASSICAL PHYSICS

QUANTUM PHYSICS

Single path from A to B

Alternative paths from A to B

above In classical physics electrons were assumed to take fixed paths and therefore their routes could be described precisely – there was only one path an electron could take between A and B. In quantum physics the positions of electrons can only be given precisely in time or space, not both together. Their behaviour is described in terms of waves – there are several probable paths that an electron might take.

Fig. 1
Events that we think of as being subject to chance are not all of the same type. Some, such as throwing dice. (*Fig. 1*), are pure chance and the probability of a particular number

Fig. 2
occurring is 1:6. Athletics (*Fig. 2*), however, is more predictable. In a race not every runner has an equal chance of winning; some may be stronger or fitter than the others. The chance

element of chance built into them.

We should therefore not be too surprised when we come down to atomic and nuclear particles and find ourselves in a world of chance. This chance is not capricious; it works within certain closely specified limits. When we come to the universe at large we can, of course, quite properly talk of planets being in certain places at specific times for

then we are dealing with millions upon millions of atoms and even more nuclear particles, the effect of chance is averaged out and can be neglected without bringing in any noticeable error.

Yet the fact that electrons and nuclear particles are wave-packets behaving like 'lumps' of material, has prompted scientists to consider whether gravity also has a quantum

nature. Since all radiation behaves not only as waves but also as quanta, and as there seems to be evidence that there are such things as gravity waves (page 34), could it be that there are quanta of gravity? Such 'gravitons' would, it is thought, travel with the same velocity as all other radiation, that is at the speed of light. If gravitons do exist, then it is thought they too will be affected by the Heisenberg indeterminacy principle. It will not be possible to be certain about any particular graviton, whether it has been absorbed or transmitted at any particular instant, and we will be able only to express the probability that it has.

The existence of gravitons with a built-in indeterminacy would produce tiny ripples in space-time which of course could not be determined precisely in both space and time simultaneously. Space-time would therefore be full of pockets of uncertainty. Calculations show that these pockets will be extremely small, one hundred million million million times (10^{20}) smaller even than the nucleus of an atom, so minute that light would take only one thousand million million million million millionth ($1 \div 10^{33}$) of a second to travel across one of them. Nevertheless, the possibility of their existence opens up a completely new basic approach to the universe and although the consequences have yet to be worked out in detail, a preliminary study shows that it is possible that there are an infinite number of space-times, of which ours is only one.

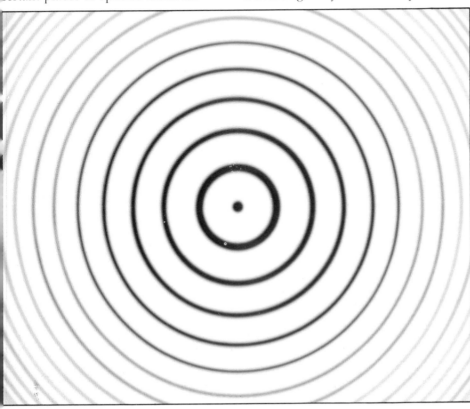

above When electrons are shot through a microscopically small hole in metal foil, they spread out on the other side to produce a wave pattern. This wave aspect of the electron's nature is the reason why we can never tell exactly where a particular electron will be at a given time.

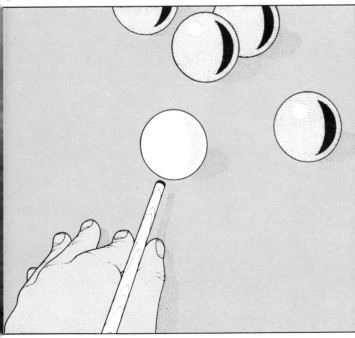

Fig. 3
of a snooker ball (*Fig. 3*) being knocked into a pocket is more predictable still. The angle at which it should be struck to be pocketed successfully can be calculated from classical physics.

Fig. 4
Chance enters astronomy in the study of large star fields. (*Fig. 4*). By analysing the motions of the stars statistically, the future configuration of the field can be predicted.

CHAPTER 8
THE EVOLUTION
OF THE UNIVERSE

**One of the oldest
questions to be
asked about the universe
was 'how did it begin?'
Throughout the ages
civilizations have held
different views.**

The question of how the universe began has always puzzled mankind. The way the question is answered depends both on the basic beliefs of the civilization to which an astronomer belongs, and to an even greater extent on his knowledge of the universe.

In the earliest times the universe was closely linked with the actions of gods and goddesses, who were believed to rule the world and could be persuaded to help man by prayers and sacrifices. It seemed natural to claim that the Earth and the heavens were formed by one of these gods whose special responsibility they were. But how he actually performed the act of creation they did not inquire. Such actions were divine and lay outside the everyday behaviour of ordinary things. They were beyond man's comprehension. It was enough to describe the universe as a dome or a sphere and say that its creation was due to a god who, having made the universe, had some permanent connection with it afterwards. Indeed the ancient Greek philosophers managed to incorporate these views into their marvellous scientific picture of the universe, for while they described the motions of the planets with mathematical precision, they believed them to be, like the stars, made of some special celestial material that never aged or decayed. Thus the formation of the planets was something removed from the ordinary world of which the philosopher and astronomer tried to make sense. In consequence the question of the creation of the heavens, of the universe, did not seem to be a scientific one.

Nevertheless, the Greeks did suggest that the universe had originally been a motionless uniform mixture, which later became a whirling mass in which cold matter fell to the centre and formed the Earth; the Sun, Moon and planets were thought of as having been torn out of the Earth.

In other civilizations the problem did not appear answerable either, though the reasons given were sometimes different. In ancient India it was believed that the universe was cyclic, undergoing periodic destruction and rebirth, each cycle taking millions of years. This view has been revived in recent years, though for quite different reasons; the Indian belief was a religious one but the modern notion is based on recent observations using the latest observing techniques (page 160).

In ancient China, the whole universe, everything on Earth and in the sky, was considered part of a giant organism, and its ultimate origin was not something which it was considered possible to discuss fruitfully. The Chinese, however, envisaged a universe that was many millions of years old, and in this

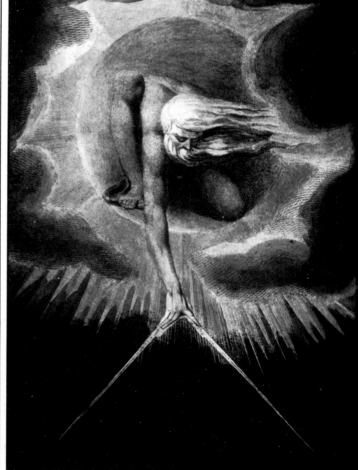

The Hindu god Shiva symbolizes the ancient Indian belief in a cyclic universe. The surrounding halo of fire represents the god's dominion over the cycle of creation, destruction and rebirth.

The Scientific Revolution did little to shake people's belief in a God-created universe. God, however, was thought of being mathematically minded, as Blake's painting shows.

146

respect took a view not so very different from our own.

Our western civilization has grown up in the knowledge of Greek ideas and has also been greatly influenced by Christian teachings, which insist on a single God who is creator and sustainer of the universe, a God who is, incidentally, also the God of the Moslem faith. Here again we have a divine cause to which the universe is due. The universe is spoken of as being without form in the beginning and then being ordered into existence, a belief that has something in common with the views of the ancient Mesopotamian civilization and of the Greeks. In some traditions, a detail of a later stage is given; the creation of woman out of the body of man, for example.

Even after the beginning of the modern scientific period, when Newton had discovered the way to explain the motions of the planets in mathematical detail and had invented the idea of universal gravitation, people still thought of the creation of the universe as a divine act. It was a mathematically precise universe, certainly, but it was now thought that God was a mathematically minded creator, as William Blake's painting of God creating the universe shows. Yet gradually, over the years, astronomers and other scientists moved further away from any form of divine creation. Galileo used to be fond of saying that the Bible teaches the way to go to heaven, not the way the heavens go. Increasingly men began to look at the universe as a machine and its beginning as something which could be explained by means of the laws of physics.

With the vast amount of information collected by observation of deep space in the last sixty years, as well as the development of relativity and quantum theory, scientists are at last in a position to work out how the universe began, using only the forces of the natural world to help them. The modern scientist never invokes deities to explain the facts of the physical universe. However, with all modern observations to hand, there are a number of alternative explanations which a twentieth-century cosmologist can give to account for the way in which the universe began.

He can place its origins at infinity, saying that the universe had no beginning, but has always been in existence, and has and will be, generally speaking, always the same (page 152). However, such a view has still to explain a number of observations that seem to show that the universe is changing with time. Alternatively, while putting its origin back to infinity, he may state that the universe is constantly changing – continually expanding, contracting and expanding again ever more into the future. If this is so, certain evidence should be available from observations (page 160).

If we do not push the beginning of the universe back indefinitely we have to consider a beginning. The universe would then start with space-time filled with material. What this material could be is not as difficult to imagine as we might suppose, because only a limited number of chemical elements or types of atom could have been available. In fact it seems that hydrogen would have been the basic component and, with this in mind, it is possible to work out the very earliest stages in detail.

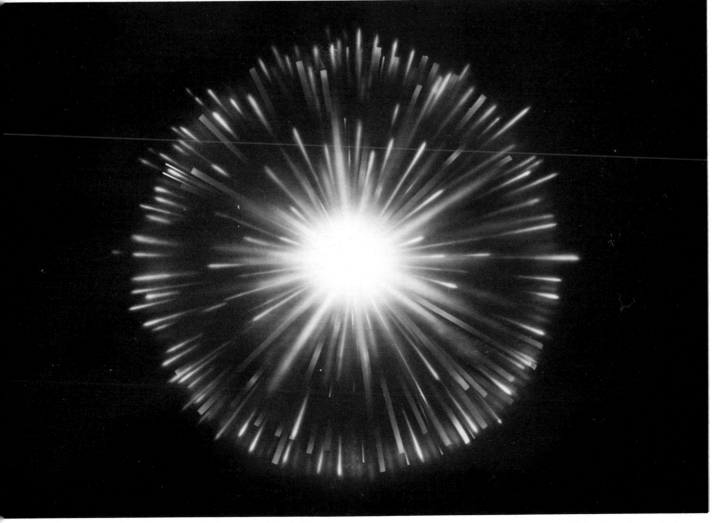

The explosion of a superatom in what is known as the big bang is at present the leading scientific explanation of the creation of the universe.

147

THE CLOCKWORK UNIVERSE

When we examine the ever-changing pageant of the skies, we find events occur in a regular way. It appears as if the universe behaves like a giant piece of mechanical clockwork.

If we are to consider the beginning of the universe from a scientific point of view, we must base our ideas on our observations. Theories about the nature of space-time are, of course, important, but we must also take into account certain basic observational facts. Perhaps the most obvious of these is that everything seems to follow a regular pattern of behaviour. The planets may not orbit the Sun tidily in circles at unchanging speeds, as the ancient Greek astronomers once believed, but they do move all in the same direction, in virtually the same plane and in regular elliptical paths, governed by laws based on the universal nature of gravitation. It is an apparently well ordered system that allows us to plot the future positions of all the planets.

Yet not everything in space is as predictable; there are some phenomena, some events, that we cannot foresee because we do not possess enough information. The most obvious of these are the appearances of bright comets. Although we know the orbits of a great number of comets and can compute their next appearance, we cannot be certain how bright they will be when they return. They may have lost so much material at their last appearance that they will be unable to emit enough gas to make them notable objects in the sky. And this is also true of the dimmer periodic comets which are only ever visible with a telescope. Yet these facts are unknown only because we do not possess enough information about the physical behaviour of comets and what happens to them when they move out to aphelion, to the distant parts of their orbits.

The existence of a comet cloud (page 114) around the Solar System has been suggested to account for both those comets which have been observed and those which will appear in the future, but we know so little about the cloud that we cannot even predict when the next bright comet will arrive. Yet we do not doubt that comets, just as much as planets, obey the laws of behaviour we have derived using the idea of gravitation. In brief, despite our ignorance in certain areas, we look on the Solar System as if it were a giant piece of clockwork, set going when it condensed from the solar nebula (page 68), and running ever since in the way our laws of physics lead us to expect.

When we look at the large-scale

The Alfonsine tables were a detailed record of astronomical information from which it was possible to predict the movements of the planets. The tables were compiled in the mid-thirteenth century under the patronage of Alfonso X of Castile.

The astronomical clock at Wells Cathedral, England depicts the movement of the celestial sphere as well as the passage of time. It seems to indicate that the universe does act like clockwork.

spects of the universe and move from the confines of our Solar System out into the Galaxy and then into the depths of intergalactic space, we still see a universe governed by the same laws. It still appears to be like a vast system of clockwork, every part affecting every other part. The galaxies rotate according to the laws of gravitation and they move away from each other at a speed that depends on distance. These points must be taken into account when we consider the origin of the universe, for we need an origin which fits in with the universe we observe.

However, we still do not know all the facts. Our inability to predict the return of bright comets, or the brightness of periodic ones, is only a simple example. There are also other areas of uncertainty. Eclipses of the Sun, for instance, are believed to occur at regular intervals and can be predicted in advance by working out the future positions of the Sun and Moon in the sky. They are such

astounding events that total solar eclipses have often been recorded far back in historical times; indeed Chinese eclipse records go back to 1217 BC. The Chinese also recorded eclipses of the Moon more than a century before this. These ancient records naturally do not compare in accuracy with modern determinations, but not all the errors they contain can be put down to a lack of precision or to errors in timing, many are too great for that. It seems as if these eclipses happened at slightly the 'wrong time' according to modern calculations, as if indeed another timescale was in operation. One explanation for this is that the 'constant of gravitation' is not in fact constant at all, but changes slowly with time (page 156). Perhaps the curvature of space-time alters as the galaxies move further apart, but whatever the reason, there is some evidence – uncertain at the moment – that gravity is not constant in the Solar System and is therefore

presumably not constant in the universe at large. If this is so, then it is obviously going to have some bearing on its history.

There is also the additional fact that an element of chance or indeterminacy exists in the universe (page 142), something that the old clockwork view of the universe, as Newton thought of it, could never have possessed. This must be taken into consideration when discussing the actual atomic and nuclear processes at work at the time of the creation of the universe. And, of course, there is the additional question of whether gravity and space-time are really separate packets or quanta because, if so, it may be that 'other universes' may not only exist but also interact with our own. However, we must be careful not to introduce imaginary forces or other universes at this stage. Our theory must accommodate what we observe, and work for a universe that is self-contained.

Comets, such as the one of 1577 shown in this woodblock by Peter Codicillus, were, as the original caption says, 'fearful and wonderful' sights. They were, nevertheless, shown to behave the same laws as planets and would therefore fit into a clockwork view of the universe.

MODELS OF THE EVOLVING UNIVERSE

We now have evidence that the universe changes with time. We must therefore choose a theory of the universe which takes this into account.

Does the universe change with time, or is it generally speaking one which always presents the same picture, as the Greeks believed? Are such changes as we see only minor ones or are they part of a universal evolution?

To begin with let us look at evidence from fairly close at hand, from the constellation of Canis Major. Here studies of the very bright and easily visible star Sirius have shown (page 72) that it is part of a binary system and has a small, white and very massive white-dwarf companion. An examination of other white dwarfs have made it clear that these are stars which are nearing the end of their lives. Yet the same research has also made it clear that Sirius itself has still a long way to go before it reaches this stage or becomes a neutron star or, at any rate, until it has burned its nuclear fuel and begun to shrink, and its core becomes degenerate (page 78). So Sirius, the brightest star in the sky, gives us clear evidence that change goes on as far as stars are concerned; they age and die. Recent research, especially that making use of infrared observations, makes it evident that new stars are at this moment being born in dark nebulous clouds of dust and gas. There is, then, no doubt at all about stellar evolution; observations show us that it is happening everywhere in our Galaxy. Photographs of supernova explosions in other galaxies and studies of the types of stars in different kinds of galaxy make it clear that stellar evolution is universal. It is not just confined to our Galaxy.

Next there is evidence from the various kinds of star clusters. 'Open' clusters, which contain anything from a few hundred members to a few thousand, are evidence, not only of the formation of proto-stars (page 66), but also of the subsequent motion of the cluster's component stars, which will lead to the dispersion of the members – another real change with time. Associations of stars – usually of hot bright ones (classes O and B) – are also evidence of change, since they too disperse in due course. Globular clusters (page 58), on the other hand, seem to keep together. Their old star populations show that they were formed a long time ago and represent an earlier stage in the evolution of the universe, presumably when galaxies like our own were still in the process of condensing into spirals. Then there are the elliptical galaxies themselves. Because they are thought of as being composed of stars formed early on in the history of the universe (page 98), they indicate an earlier phase in its evolution.

Lastly there are the large-scale motions of the galaxies themselves. These motions, known from their redshifts (page 122), are movements in an expanding universe. Such a universe is to be expected from relativity theory. Indeed, when Einstein first formulated his full theory in 1915, an expanding universe was what resulted from the equations he used for expressing the behaviour of the universe on the largest scale. At the time the galaxies were not known to be separate star systems, that only came after the early 1920s, and there could be no idea of a universe expanding out into space. Einstein therefore modified the equations to give a static universe, a universe without any expansion at all. Yet now we see that the evidence for expansion is overwhelming, and once again relativity theory in its original form has received confirmation from observation.

We come then to the conclusion that we are part of an evolutionary universe, a universe that is constantly changing as time passes, and any theory of its origin must take this into account. We cannot merely say that the universe has always existed and will do so for ever without change, though as we shall see in a moment (page 152) there is a theory that comes very near to stating just that.

One way of tackling the problem, and particularly of answering the awkward question: 'How did the universe get there in the first place?' is to have a universe which has always existed but which oscillates – expands and then contracts, and then expands again, and so on. With a theory of this kind it is necessary to explain why the expansion stops after a time and contraction takes over. The present view is that if it does contract, it will be because gravity has taken over. But for gravity to do this there must be sufficient mass in the universe to enable the expansion to be slowed down sufficiently and then to be reversed. The amount of mass in the universe is a thorny problem at the present time and is discussed later (page 160). However, we can say here that, although the matter has not yet been finally settled, the evidence at present does not seem to point to an oscillating universe. Apart from this such a theory would also have to explain why, when it is contracting, an oscillating universe does not shrink down into a giant black hole but begins to expand again instead.

The third possibility is the 'big bang' theory. Here the expansion of the galaxies and of space are traced back to a very dense universe populated by proto-galaxies: The question then remaining is 'What happened before that?' The answer is that the universe began with a great concentration of material, a kind of 'super atom' if you like, which was unstable and broke up. The break up led to the expansion we now observe. Such a big bang beginning can take two forms, a 'cold' big bang or a 'hot' one, and as we shall see (page 154), the results are not quite the same.

left
In time the stars in the constellation Canis Major will have moved so much that the constellation will have changed shape. Sirius, the bright star at the top, is a binary and is itself evidence of evolution.

right
The Pleiades are hot blue-white stars surrounded by gas. They are comparatively young and burn energy at a high rate. That stars of different ages are found in the universe is evidence of evolution.

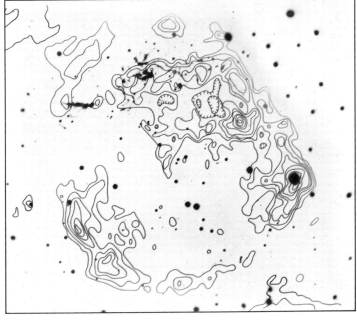

right
A radio image of the supernova remnant Cas A. Not only is a supernova explosion evidence of change but so is the expanding gas cloud shown here.

THE STEADY STATE UNIVERSE

The steady state theory gives a universe that is always the same when looked at as a whole. Yet it does permit some change even on a large scale.

One thing relativity theory makes clear is that there is no special place in the universe which we can think of as the centre of things. Gone are the old ideas that the Earth, or the Sun, is the pivot-point of the universe. Our Galaxy is only one of millions upon millions of others all moving away from each other without any being the centre of the expansion. This means that wherever we are, the universe will appear the same. If the universe was not uniform, at least not on the largest scale, it would not fit the theory of relativity. We would be able to pick out areas of preference and that would spoil the whole principle of relativity – that no observer has a particular place, or 'preferred position' with respect to any other observer. As observation and experimental tests show us that relativity is correct, we must therefore expect a universe which, from a large-scale point of view, is the same to every observer. This basic idea is sometimes known as the 'cosmological principle'.

In the late 1940s and early 1950s an additional factor was raised by Herman Bondi, Thomas Gold and Fred Hoyle in Britain. They said that the universe appeared to be the same from every point in time as well as from every point in space. In other words it did not matter whether an observer viewed the universe now, or in a thousand million years time, he would still see a universe which presented precisely the same appearance. That is, it is not possible to tell either one's whereabouts or at what time one is making observations. This unchanging appearance of the universe in both time as well as space is known as the 'perfect cosmological principle', and the theory of the universe deriving from it is known as the 'steady state' theory.

At this stage you may wonder why anyone ever took the theory seriously, because it seems obvious that the universe is not in a steady state. Indeed, we have just discussed

evidence showing that the history of the universe is an evolutionary one (page 146). The answer is that it depends on how large a sample of the universe we take. For example,

on a small scale we know that stars are continually forming in the spiral arms of our Galaxy, that its central bulge is very active with expanding rings of gas and even, perhaps, a

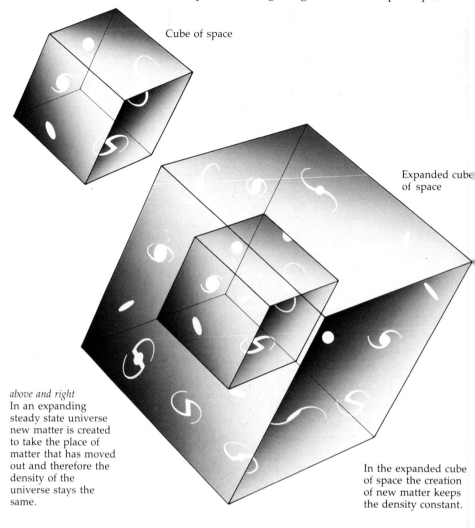

Cube of space

Expanded cube of space

above and right
In an expanding steady state universe new matter is created to take the place of matter that has moved out and therefore the density of the universe stays the same.

In the expanded cube of space the creation of new matter keeps the density constant.

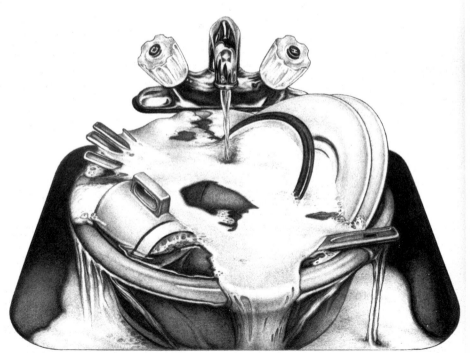

The continuous creation of matter in an expanding steady state universe can be likened to water flowing into a washing-up bowl. If water flows into the bowl at the same rate as it is leaving it, the same volume of water remains in the bowl all the time although the water itself is always changing.

black hole in the centre swallowing stars wholesale. Yet in spite of these minor changes the Galaxy remains substantially the same. And this is true of other galaxies.

Although they have their own individual existences and undergo changes, and even collide and pass through each other, they are still galaxies, and as on a large scale we have a universe of galaxies, so in a sense we can talk of a steady state universe.

However, even if we can think of galaxies as the building bricks of the universe, what about their distribution and their motions? We have found that the majority of galaxies are grouped into clusters, or even superclusters (page 106), so the distribution is not really even; galaxies tend to clump together, at least for a time. However, we can say that, taken as a whole, the universe is a universe of galaxies spread about throughout space, and anywhere we go we should expect to find them, even if the majority are in clusters.

The movement of galaxies presents a more difficult problem. As we know (page 122), the universe is expanding; the galaxies are all moving apart from each other. So the universe is changing with time, and if we take a given volume of space – a cube several megaparsecs in size, for instance – then as time passes it will contain less and less matter. The galaxies within a cube of space will reduce in number as the universe expands. So if we look at that particular volume of space now, and then look at it again in a thousand million years, we shall observe a difference. Does this mean that the steady state theory is wrong, that it does not fit observational evidence?

Surprisingly, there is an explanation that fits the theory, as Fred Hoyle was able to see. A steady state theory can still describe the universe if matter is being created all the time. In that case new matter will replace the material escaping from our cube of space due to the expansion of the universe. The rate of creation does not have to be very large; calculation shows that, on average, there need only be three hydrogen nuclei forming in every cubic centimetre of space during each year. Such a small amount is not directly observable.

The steady state theory was devised at a time when it seemed that every other theory of the universe – including the 'big bang' theories – all gave an age for the universe that was too short. Stars and clusters were known which appeared to have an age far greater than a big bang could give using the then accepted value of the Hubble constant, which was larger than that accepted today. The steady state theory overcame this problem because according to it the universe never had a beginning, any more than it will have an end.

Black holes

White holes

In a steady state universe the balance may be maintained by material being destroyed in black holes and created in 'white holes'. A white hole is notionally a point where material disappearing into a black hole in another universe would enter ours, if such a process existed.

THE MICROWAVE BACKGROUND OF THE UNIVERSE

Observations have now shown astronomers that the steady state theory is not acceptable. The most important evidence against it is the discovery of the microwave background.

The steady state theory was an ingenious interpretation of an expanding universe, and for a time it attracted many able astronomers who saw in it a way out of the problems posed by big bang theories – the sudden appearance of material from which the big bang started and the question of the age of the universe. But gradually, over the years, new measurements of the distances of nearby galaxies have led to a smaller value for the Hubble constant and so a lengthening of the age of the universe. The original need for a steady state theory has gone. Of course, the perfect cosmological principle has its attractions, and the theory still received some strong support until evidence against it became so strong that it had at last to be cast aside.

One observation that makes it very difficult to hold to the steady state theory is the source count of distant radio galaxies (page 124). It is worth looking into this more closely. First of all, if we suppose that all galaxies are equally bright (even though we know that this is not quite true). Then, the strength of the radio signal, S, we actually receive for any source will be related to its distance d and therefore will depend on an inverse-square law (because radiation received varies according to the inverse square of the distance). So for any one source S will be proportional to $1/d^2$. Next let us imagine there is no clustering and that the galaxies are therefore evenly distributed in space (because this makes the arithmetic easier). Then the total amount of radiation will depend not only on the inverse square of the distance of the sources but also on the number of them in a given volume of space and that, it can be calculated, is proportional to d^3. So S is also proportional to d^3. Putting these two facts together S should be proportional to $d^{3/2}$ and wherever we look in the sky we

should observe this relationship.

With optical sources, the intensity of radio signals is affected by the absorption of light by intergalactic and interstellar matter, and the results could therefore not be expected to correspond to the $^3/_2$ relationship. But with radio galaxies, absorption is not the hazard it is with optical galaxies and what is more, it seems that radio-telescopes can delve further into space than optical ones.

Even so observations with radio-telescopes also show up differences from the $^3/_2$ relationship, particularly when we go far back into space and therefore far back into time. It is found that the further we go, the further S strays from the $^3/_2$ relationship, indicating that radio sources become more numerous. There are far more than we should expect on an even distribution, and it has also been found that they

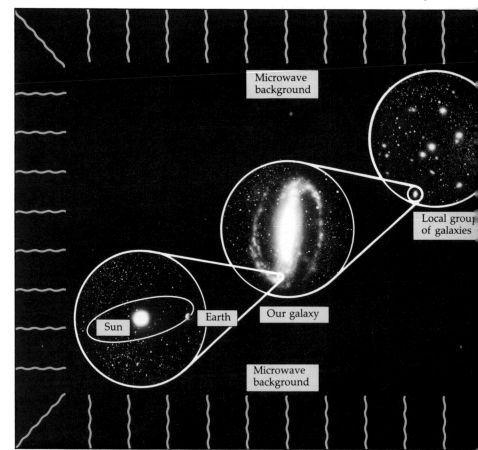

Microwave background

Local group of galaxies

Our galaxy

Earth

Sun

Microwave background

The horn antenna at Crawford Hill was originally built by Robert Wilson (*left*) and Arno Penzias (*right*) to detect radio-noise sources that would interfere with satellite communications systems. When the 3°K background was first discovered it was thought to be due to a design fault in the antenna itself.

outnumber optical sources. Even if we cannot defect all optical sources, nevertheless the difference is extremely marked – at a distance of some 17,000 million light-years there are 100 times more radio sources than optical ones compared with nearby space. This strongly indicates that the situation was different in the distant past. And even further back in time there comes a point when there are almost no radio sources, perhaps because only a few had formed by then.

Another piece of evidence pointing to change with time is connected with QSOs. It now seems almost certain (page 94) that these objects are the central regions of galaxies and that they really are very distant. In consequence it seems that the vast amounts of energy which they display indicate that galaxies were more energetic in the past than they are now. If, therefore, the QSO's large redshifts really do mean great distances, the evidence for change with time is very strong. This is why the QSO redshift distances are often known as 'cosmological', for their interpretation affects our view of the universe.

However, the most telling evidence of all against the steady state theory was the discovery in 1965 of the microwave background of the universe by Arno Penzias and Robert Wilson in the United States. This discovery arose from research which they were doing on the way very short-wave or 'microwave' radio radiation travels through the Earth's atmosphere. As part of their investigations they designed and built a large radio antenna shaped rather like a horn, but no sooner was it completed than they discovered they were receiving radio radiation at a wavelength of 7 cm. They took the antenna to pieces, fitted it out internally with wire to prevent pigeons nesting in it, in case their droppings could have given rise to the microwave radiation, and reassembled it. Still they received microwave radiation at 7 cm. Clearly, it was coming from outside the antenna, not from inside as they had thought.

It was realized that radiation at such a wavelength could come from cool gas in space, but the trouble was that it was some 100 times stronger than expected. An examination was made of the direction from which it was coming, for the antenna was very sensitive to differences in the direction of incoming radio waves, and surprisingly it was found that the radiation was coming equally from every direction. To what could it be due?

If, as physics theory tells us, the universe began with a hot big bang explosion then we should expect to see some of this original gas which has since cooled down. And indeed observations at radio wavelengths between a few millimetres and 1 metre have recorded black-body radiation (radiation from a perfect radiator) of a type which one would expect from a gas with a temperature of 3°K.

The source of such radiation, coming evenly from all over space, cannot be explained on the basis of the steady state theory but only by a hot big bang. Thus the discovery of the microwave background not only disposes of the steady state theory but also actively supports the theory of a big bang origin.

left
Microwave background

Virgo cluster

Microwave background

left
The Earth is orbiting the Sun, the Sun orbits the Galaxy, the Galaxy is a member of the Local Group and is moving with respect to the other galaxies in the Group. The Local Group moves with respect to the giant Virgo cluster of galaxies, and the Virgo cluster itself has a motion of its own with reference to the microwave background. The result of all these motions is to give a Doppler shift to the microwave background radiation as observed from the Earth. This amounts to 500 km per sec. in the direction of the Hydra constellation and is a larger movement than expected.

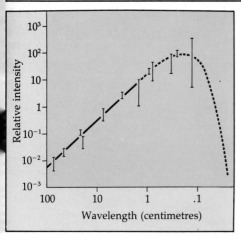

left
Black-body radiation at any particular temperature can be graphed like this. The curve shown here is that of the background radiation discovered by Penzias and Wilson. It was first discovered at the 7-cm wavelength (A) because the apparatus was tuned to that wavelength.

above
In an experiment conducted with high-flying U2 aircraft it was possible to detect the movement of the Earth against the microwave background. From this information it has been calculated that the Galaxy is moving, relative to the background, at a speed of 500 km per second.

THE BIG BANG THEORY

All the evidence available supports a big bang origin for the universe. Recent research has shown that it is possible to work out much that occurred very soon after the beginning.

The basic big bang 'model' of the universe was worked out in the 1920s by two people quite independently, the Russian meteorologist Aleksandr Friedmann and the Belgian mathematician Georges Lemaître. They were able to devise the necessary mathematical expressions to give an expanding or contracting universe, and made it clear that a static universe was out of the question. Their big bang model did not require the continuous creation of matter to keep it going or to account for the evolution of the universe with time.

When Einstein originally devised the equations to express the behaviour of the universe, a mathematical term appeared to which the name 'cosmical constant' was given. Further study showed that this constant represented a force acting on all material in the universe, and that it could take three forms: it could be negative, zero, or have a positive value. If it were negative it would give a contraction, such as would occur in an oscillating universe once the period of expansion was over. If it were zero it would have no effect at all. If it were positive, however, then it would give a force of repulsion, pushing bodies away from each other, in just the opposite way from gravity. If it is indeed positive, the force must be small, so that it does not affect situations in which gravity is the chief force; otherwise we should notice it within the Solar System or in the way binary stars orbit around their common centres of mass. The positive cosmical constant must be small enough so that it only becomes significant when we consider the universe on the largest scale.

A model of the universe using a positive value for the cosmical constant and, incidentally, a larger value than originally used by Einstein in his static universe (page 150), was worked out in detail by Lemaître. His results gave a model in which everything started with a big bang – as a 'super atom' which then broke down, ejecting material outwards. However, this model did not go on expanding continuously. It had a long period during which it was almost stationary, and only continued its expansion when the cosmical repulsion due to the positive cosmical constant took over again.

Today Lemaître's ideas have been supplanted by another big bang theory, even though they do, strangely enough, offer an explanation of Geoffrey Burbidge's discovery that QSOs often have a redshift of 1.95 (page 97). It may therefore be that Lemaître's model could assume greater importance in the future, and if it does we will have to accept the idea that we are living and observing during the almost 'stationary' phase, and that one day, in the distant future, though we do not know precisely when, the universe will begin to expand at a greatly increased rate.

One other factor in the universe which astronomers have taken to be fixed is the 'constant of gravity'. The constant appears in Newton's equation for the force of gravity (F), $F = G \times (m_1 m_2)/d^2$, where m_1, m_2 are the masses of the bodies between which gravity is acting, d is the distance between them and G is the constant. However, it is now realized that G may not be constant at all, but could be changing, growing

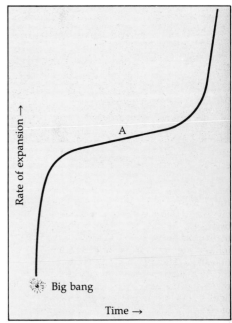

Lemaître's model of the big bang predicts a period (A) during which the universe will expand only very slowly.

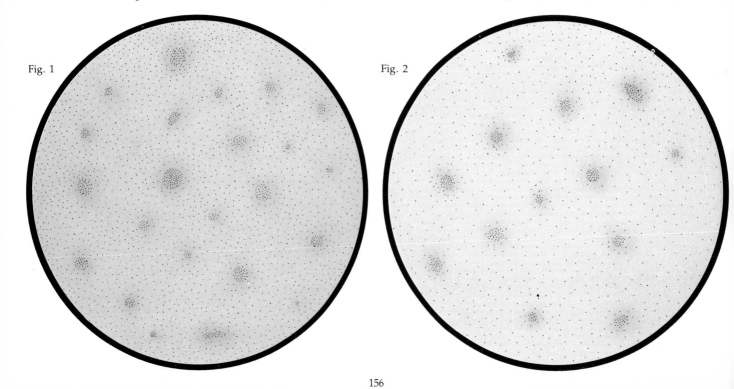

Fig. 1

Fig. 2

progressively less as time goes on. Big bang theories of an expanding universe which take this into account, have now been formulated.

If gravity does decrease with time then we should be able to observe the consequences in the Solar System. For instance decreasing gravity would mean that the orbits of the planets and of their satellites would change with time, so if we calculated when the ancient eclipses of the Sun should have occurred (assuming a constant gravity), we would expect old records to show certain differences; this could be evidence of changing gravity. Also it is now believed that the land masses of the Earth were once all joined

above Total solar eclipses have been noted in ancient records.

below
In the model of the big bang put forward by George Gamow, all matter was in an ionized state for the first 100,000 years and the universe was therefore opaque to light and other forms of electromagnetic radiation at this time (*Fig. 1*). Matter was distributed, broadly speaking, evenly through space, although there were some areas with higher densities. At the end of this period, atoms began to form and the universe became transparent (*Fig. 2*). As time went on the local concentrations of matter formed into proto-galaxies (*Fig. 3*) and ultimately into galaxies (*Fig. 4*).

together but later moved apart. This change could be due to the Earth expanding slightly, which it would do if gravity decreased.

Changing gravity would also cause an alteration in a star's behaviour during the time it is burning hydrogen; if gravity has decreased then the Sun, which is still in its hydrogen-burning phase, should be dimmer now than it was in the past. This would have affected the evolution of life on Earth and the onset of ice ages. Also the whole effect would have been made greater because the Earth's orbit would have been expanding due to decreasing gravity, so enlarging the Sun-to-Earth distance and decreasing the intensity of the light and heat received from the Sun.

As far as our Galaxy is concerned, decreasing gravity means that as we go back in time it too would have been smaller and brighter. And this would apply to every other galaxy as well. The more distant a galaxy is and therefore, the older it is, the brighter it should appear to be in absolute terms. This would have an effect on our measurements of distance and therefore on the Hubble constant. Obviously then if gravity does change with time, it will have important measurable effects on the universe. However, the differences it should cause have not yet been observed for certain. There are differences in old eclipse timings but the matter is still open to debate; this is so, too, for the expansion of the Earth – the drift of the continents could be due to other causes

operating on the Earth's crust. There is possible evidence for the Sun being hotter in the past, but even this is not certain.

The changing gravity model of the universe is due primarily to the work of American cosmologists Carl Brans and Robert Dicke. It describes a relativistic universe but one based on a slight variation of Einstein's theory which Brans and Dicke developed. Gravity changes very slowly in this theory but otherwise its general results are very similar to those of Einstein's. Only very delicate observations will show which fits the facts better, and so far we can come to no firm conclusions. All the same, whether we have a Brans-Dicke universe or not, there seems to be no doubt among astronomers about how it all began: it started with a big bang.

During the last ten years or so, nuclear physicists and astronomers have at last been in a position to work out in some detail what happened during the big bang explosion and are now able to trace events back to within one hundred thousand million million million million millionths of a second (10^{-35} seconds) after the initial explosion. Before this time, the density and temperature would have been so great that it is difficult to work out precisely what would have happened; nuclear physicists are not certain how matter would have behaved under such extreme conditions. However, they do believe that one hundred millionth of a second (10^{-8} seconds) after this time, nuclear particles were created.

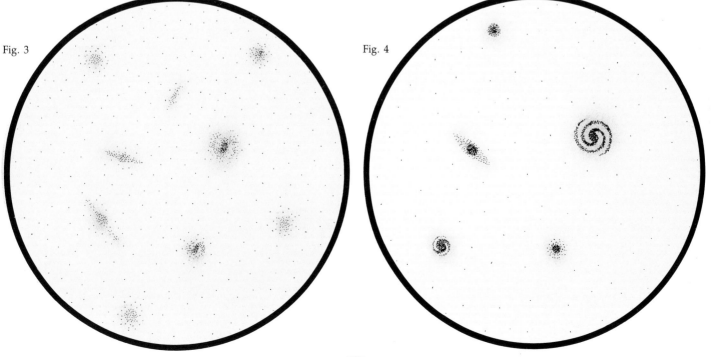

Fig. 3

Fig. 4

The subsequent history of the big bang beginning is based on the idea, first put forward in the United States by George Gamow, Ralph Alpher and Robert Horman, that the whole event took place at a very high temperature; it was a hot big bang. This view has been supported by the later discovery of the background microwave radiation (page 154), though Gamow's belief that all the chemical elements were created during this hot beginning does not seem to be borne out by recent research. The universe does not now appear to have stayed sufficiently hot long enough for the heavier atoms such as carbon and iron to form in this way, and the view now is that all the heavier chemical elements were built up later inside stars.

What, then, are the stages of the hot big bang model that most astronomers think produced the universe? First of all we have the creation of nuclear and atomic particles, as we have just seen, which, like the big bang itself, occurred some 18 to 20 thousand million (18 to 20×10^9) years ago. The belief is that what were formed first were protons, and short-lived particles, as well as their anti-particles. The anti-particles combined with ordinary particles and annihilated one another, generating vast amounts of radiation. This is sometimes known as the 'hadron era' because all the particles created were hadrons.

After one whole second had passed, the big bang entered what is known as the 'lepton era', a period which lasted for a total of something like 60 seconds. Leptons are particles such as neutrinos, electrons, and short-lived particles called muons. They also include the equivalent anti-particles such as positive electrons or positrons. During this single minute the electrons and their anti-particles, the positrons, paired up and annihilated each other, generating radiation as they did so.

There next followed a period, one minute after the big bang itself, known as the 'radiation era'. This period lasted immensely longer than any period met with so far; it is thought to have continued for the next 100,000 years of the universe's existence. But whereas in the hadron and lepton eras nuclear particles were forming and disappearing due to annihilations, this was a more stable period. The first week of this era is believed to have been the time when the nuclear particles joined up to form atoms of deuterium or 'heavy hydrogen' (consisting of one neutron and one proton orbited by one electron) and helium (with two protons, two neutrons and two orbiting electrons). During this period radiation was all powerful and we can visualize it as a time when there were so many photons of radiation that they acted almost like a treacly fluid, slowing down or even stopping the movement of electrons and protons. As time passed, however, differences in density in various parts of the photon fluid built up, some protons and electrons combined and more atoms were formed; these were able to travel through the fluid. Gradually, after one thousand years, matter and not energy came to dominate the scene, though this new era – the 'matter era' – was not fully developed until the universe had reached an age of 100,000 years.

Throughout these eras the temperature of the universe dropped from some 5,000 million degrees K in the first 10 seconds of the universe's life, to 1,000 million K after 100 seconds, and then gradually down to 100,000 K after 1,000 years. Once the matter era had arrived, the matter itself began to fall to a lower temperature than the radiation. The radiation was therefore able to escape; so radiation and matter separated, though this 'decoupling era' only came fully into force some 290,000 years later still. Radiation escaped, atoms moved outwards and after 1,000 or 2,000 million years actual galaxies began to form, some gathering into clusters. Whether or not they did so depended on how unevenly the atoms forming the proto-galaxies were clumped together. Our own Galaxy is believed to have formed from its proto-galaxy some 4,000 million years after the big bang.

The hot big bang theory is certainly an impressive one and seems to take account of most of what we know about the universe. The big bang itself is thought to have started from a singularity in space-time; from, if you like, a black hole. As the 'fireball' expanded outwards so did time and space. The creation of our universe therefore is one of matter, space and time intimately linked together. In consequence there is no meaning to the question 'what was there before the singularity'; time had not begun, nor space either, and the words 'previous' and 'there' have no meaning. But what started the action and triggered the big bang itself is still a mystery.

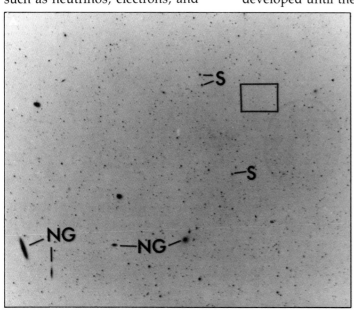

Photograph A shows an area of the sky at the outer edge of the Virgo cluster. It indicates the position of some stars (S) and nearby galaxies (NG). Photograph B is an enlargement of the area boxed in A. It shows the location of a quasar (Q), three faint stars (S) and two primeval galaxies (DG) which were formed soon after the big bang took place.

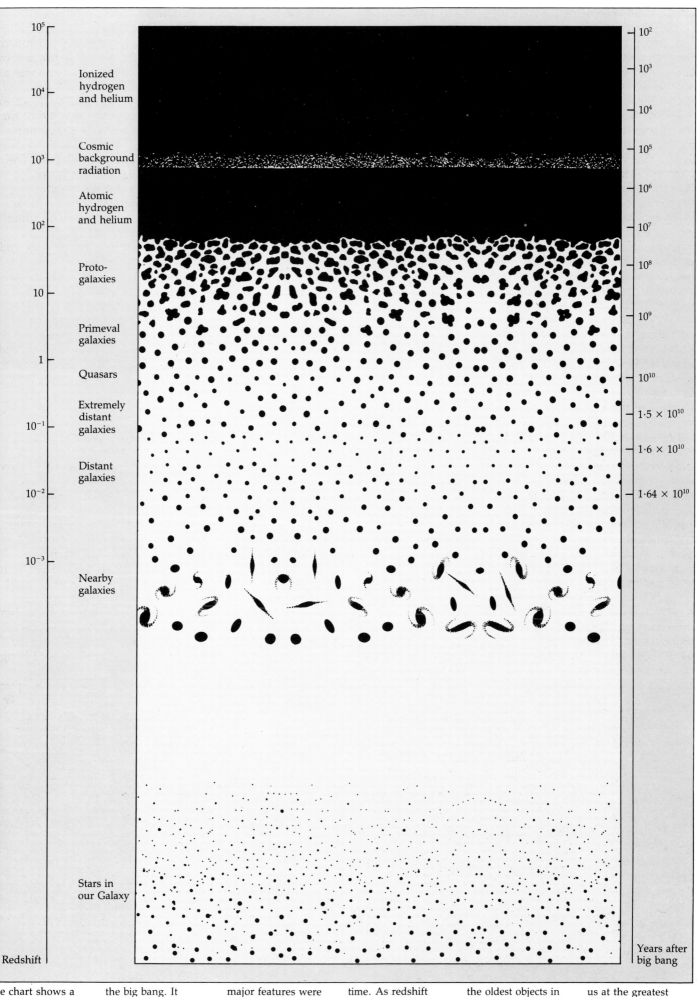

Redshift

10^5
10^4 — Ionized hydrogen and helium
10^3 — Cosmic background radiation
10^2 — Atomic hydrogen and helium
10 — Proto-galaxies
1 — Primeval galaxies

Quasars
10^{-1} — Extremely distant galaxies
10^{-2} — Distant galaxies
10^{-3} — Nearby galaxies

Stars in our Galaxy

Years after big bang

10^2
10^3
10^4
10^5
10^6
10^7
10^8
10^9
10^{10}
1.5×10^{10}
1.6×10^{10}
1.64×10^{10}

The chart shows a timescale of events in the universe since the big bang. It indicates when some of the universe's major features were formed and how redshift changes with time. As redshift corresponds to velocity of recession, the oldest objects in the universe, which are moving away from us at the greatest speed, have the largest redshifts.

WILL THE UNIVERSE STOP EXPANDING?

Is it possible that the universe will, one day, stop expanding and begin to contract? Astronomers can make calculations but are they sufficiently accurate?

We know that the universe is expanding and that it began to do so after the 'big bang' which hurled material outwards into space. Will this material continue to move outwards for ever, or will it, perhaps, gradually slow down until it is no longer rushing off into the depths of space? If so, what will happen then?

To answer this question, let us think what happens when we throw a ball, in particular when we throw a ball upwards. It goes up so far, gradually losing speed, until it comes to the top of its flight; then it falls back again, gathering speed as it drops. The force that stops it going on outwards into space, slows it down and brings it back to the ground is, of course, gravity.

In just the same way, if the universe were to stop expanding, it would be due to gravity. Gravity would cause the galaxies to slow down and then begin to fall back, so that the universe would not only stop expanding, but actually begin to contract. Such an expansion followed by a contraction would mean that we live in an oscillating universe (page 147). Whether the universe will contract one day or go on expanding for ever is an important question for us to try to answer.

First of all, let us examine the problem more closely. What we are trying to do is to find what would be necessary if gravity is to stop the expansion which we observe at present. There is a simple answer. Whether the universe will expand for ever or will one day contract depends on how much mass there is in the universe; in other words, how many galaxies there are and how much other material such as inter-galactic dust there may be. Are there enough galaxies and other material for their gravity to overcome the force of expansion? If there is too little, gravity may slow down the expansion but never by enough to halt it and turn it into a contraction. However, it is not easy to decide how much mass is needed for gravity

to counteract the force of expansion.

If we return for a moment to the example of a ball thrown up in the air, we know that it will drop back to Earth again. But, of course, if it could be thrown fast enough, it would not drop back; it would go out into space. This critical velocity which a ball must reach to go out into space is known, quite simply, as the 'velocity of escape'. If we could throw the ball at a speed of more than 11.18 km per second, it would escape. On the other hand, if we

were on the Moon a speed of only 2.37 km per second would be enough. This is because the Moon has less mass than the Earth. To escape from the Sun, the velocity would have to reach more than 617 km per second because the Sun is so much more massive. When we observe galaxies moving at various velocities, we need to know whether these velocities are greater than the velocity of escape from the entire universe. The answer depends on the mass of the universe, so next we

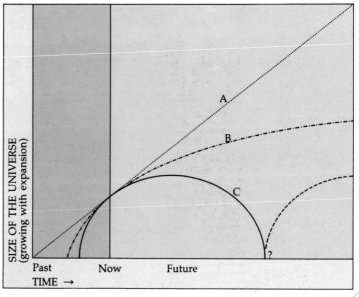

above and right
These diagrams show three possible ways in which the universe may develop. It may go on expanding at the same rate without stopping: this is shown by the straight line (A). If this is the case, any given volume of space (shown here as a cube) just goes on getting bigger as time passes. (The line begins 'before' the instant of the big bang because it is intended to show a regular expansion,

though in reality this would have been faster directly after the big bang.)
But the rate of expansion may slow down. This possibility is shown by line (B). The cube of space grows slowly to begin with; then more slowly. Finally, the universe stops expanding and begins to contract. This is shown by line (C). The cube of space first expands, reaches a peak, and then starts to contract.

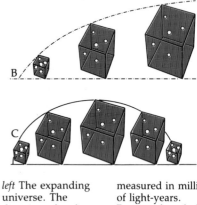

left The expanding universe. The direction of each arrow represents the direction of motion of a galaxy: the length of the arrow is an indication of the galaxy's speed and the concentric circles mark distance

measured in millions of light-years. Because the whole universe is expanding, every observer on a galaxy will see this same picture – to each one every other galaxy will be moving away with a speed depending on distance

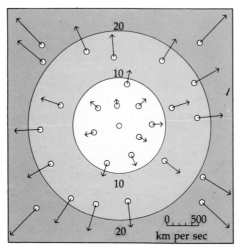

need to discover what astronomers call the 'critical mass'. This is the mass which will give a velocity of escape greater than the speed of even the fastest moving galaxies.

The speed of the fastest galaxies depends on how long they have been travelling; in other words, how long it is since expansion began, or since the big bang occurred. There is some doubt about this; astronomers cannot give an exact figure, but as we have seen (page 146) the generally accepted idea now is that the big

bang occurred about 18 thousand million years ago. Using this as the basis of a complicated calculation, scientists have estimated the critical density as 5 million million million million millionths of a gram (or 5×10^{-30} grams) per cubic centimetre of space. This is very low; it is equivalent to no more than something like three atoms of hydrogen per cubic centimetre, and one is tempted to object that matter in the universe must be far greater than this. Yet the universe is very

large and there are vast tracts of what seems to be empty or almost empty space. Moreover, as we shall see, it is by no means certain that matter in the universe even reaches this critical density. In fact, most of the evidence is to the contrary.

If the amount of mass in the universe manages to reach this critical density or, better still, exceed it, we should be able to gain a clue from observing whether the galaxies are travelling more slowly than they used to and, if so, by how much. The ideal way to measure this deceleration would be to measure the velocity at which a particular galaxy is moving away and then measure it again some years later. This would immediately reveal any drop in velocity. Unfortunately this cannot be done yet, because the gap between one observation and the next would have to be very long (at least a century or two) for the change to be large enough to be measurable. Not long enough has elapsed since the time when scientists were first able to measure the velocities of galaxies.

Nevertheless, there are ways round this difficulty which give us at least an approximate answer. We know that light travels at a constant speed, therefore when we look at distant regions of space we are looking back in time. If we observe a galaxy at a given distance and determine its speed of recession (redshift), then observe another further off and find its redshift, we should discover whether the nearer is slower than we should expect in view of its actual distance and Hubble's law.

However, in practice it is extremely difficult to measure these distances. Their velocity away from us is usually taken as a measure of their distance, and that must not be done here (because in the distant past galaxies may have been travelling at different speeds). What astronomers have to do is to assume that all galaxies of the same type have the same intrinsic brightness, i.e. the same absolute magnitude. Of course they know this will not be exactly so, since some galaxies do not obey this rule, but if enough are measured the results will average out. Again, since this method of calculation looks back in time, some evolution of the stars in the more distant galaxies will have taken place compared with those in the nearer (more recent) ones. However, careful studies of stars indicate that the difference will only amount to a very few per cent drop in brightness even over a million years.

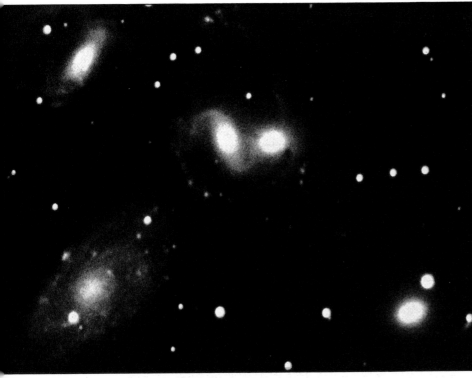

above Stephan's Quintet. A group of five galaxies photographed with the 4 m telescope at Kitt Peak. Notice the faint wisps of material spreading out between the central galaxies and the galaxy in the upper left.

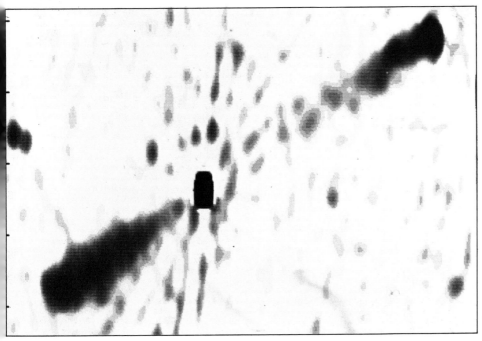

A radio image (based on the intensity of the radio signals received) of the radio galaxy 3C236. It shows a galaxy which seems to be ejecting two vast masses of gas which stretch some 20 million light-years into space – a distance ten times as great as that between our own Galaxy and the large galaxy in Andromeda.

Most galaxies are members of clusters or groups, and sometimes a large galaxy may swallow a smaller one in the cluster (page 107); this means that some large galaxies will change in brightness and size. Nevertheless, if we take all these variations into account and select a large enough sample of galaxies, we can get an idea of the average rate of slowing down. The rate does not seem to be great enough to lead to a contracting universe; galaxies are still moving so fast that it looks as though the universe will always continue to expand. But there is another clue we can use. If we compare the behaviour of distant galaxies with those nearby in our own supercluster (our local group of galaxies, some other small groups and the Virgo cluster) we should expect to see a difference. This is because the amount of matter within our own supercluster is something like 2½ times greater than

the amount outside it. Yet, once again, the deceleration is not sufficient to lead us to think that the universe will contract.

Now let us see what we can discover about the mass of material in the universe that can be observed. If the entire mass of the universe were all concentrated in the galaxies, the task of working out the mass of the universe would not be so difficult. Astronomers would only have to count the number of galaxies in given volumes of space, assess their masses and then, multiplying one by the other, find the total mass in the given volume. Merely dividing this by the volume would give the mass per unit of volume (say, per cubic centimetre) of space. But things are not as simple as this.

We have to take account of the possible existence of black holes and consider how much mass these might contribute. Again, most galaxies are

in clusters, and observations show us that galaxies are often ejecting matter – the galaxy M82 in Ursa Major is a fine example of this – and this matter will be spreading out in space between the galaxies. How much unobserved material is there within a cluster or a group besides that of the galaxies themselves? This is something that must simply be estimated. This can be done by making use of non-visible radiations, especially observations with radiotelescopes. We know that objects like the exploding galaxy Centaurus 'A' are pouring material into space, and other galaxies are also associated with gas streamers; so it seems as though there may be far more matter in space than appears on most photographs. However, if we estimate that what we observe is perhaps no more than a third of all the matter there is, we are still short of material. The mass of the universe

Centaurus 'A'.
This giant elliptical galaxy in the constellation of the Centaur is 16 million light-years away. It has a vast amount of dust and gas around its central regions, and is one of the most powerful radio sources in the sky.

s not great enough to stop expansion, or so it seems.

So far, then, it looks as though there is no doubt about it: the universe will go on expanding. Additional evidence to help us reach a decision can be obtained from the theory of the big bang itself. When the big bang happened, it seems to have been a 'hot' big bang. In this case, protons and neutrons would have come together to form deuterium and helium atoms with a mass of 4. The proportion of deuterium to helium depends upon the density of material in the universe when it was hot enough for this reaction to occur. This density, which can be calculated, will help us to decide whether there is enough mass to stop expansion in the future. In fact estimates show that there is probably too little mass to stop the universe from expanding. These estimates also predict that between 20% and 30% of the original hydrogen should have been converted to helium.

The question now arises as to whether this can be checked by observation. The Orbiting Astronomical Observatory *Copernicus* has found an average deuterium density in nearby interstellar space. From these observations, and by making suitable allowance for some of the deuterium which will have been used up in the stars, it is possible to arrive at an estimate of the overall density.

The result comes out as 40 million million million million millionths of a gram (4×10^{-31} grams) per cubic centimetre. This is a very sensitive test; an error of 1,000 (giving a density of 4×10^{-28} grams per cubic centimetre) would mean an original density in the universe 10 times greater than calculation supposes. So again the evidence indicates that the universe will go on expanding.

What conclusions can we reach about the expansion of the universe? If astronomers' ideas about a hot big bang and what happened during it are correct, then the abundance of deuterium added to the other observational evidence makes it seem certain that the universe will go on expanding. But we must still be a little cautious. Haloes round some galaxies like M31 and our own Galaxy make one wonder whether the mass of the universe has been underestimated. And there may just be a vast number of black holes – not too big and not too small – formed in the early stages of the universe. None have yet been observed though it does seem likely that many large ones have formed since. These would add to the mass, perhaps substantially, and could materially alter the situation.

above The galaxy M82 in Ursa Major. This is connected by a bridge of gas with a neighbouring galaxy M81. M82 looks irregular, but it may be a spiral seen edge-on.

above A close-up of M82 showing filaments of gas. These are the result of an internal explosion. The gas is hot compared with the coldness of interstellar space.

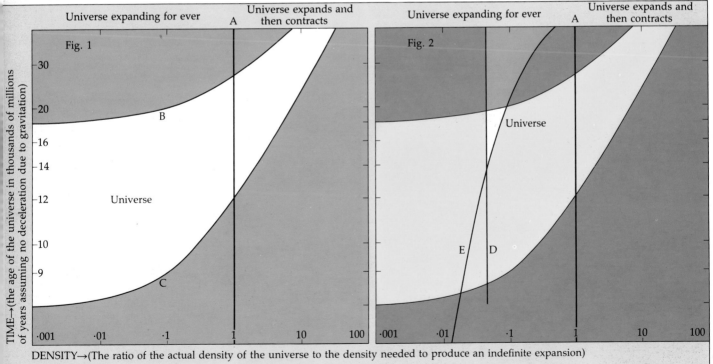

These two diagrams show the evidence for the continued expansion of the universe. In *Fig. 1* the universe may have any age or density that corresponds to values of 'TIME' and 'DENSITY' in the white area. The curved lines B and C are the limits that present knowledge places on these factors. In *Fig. 2* two other limiting lines have been added to those in *Fig. 1*. Investigations of globular clusters suggest that 'DENSITY' cannot be less than D and the amount of deuterium in space, indicates that 'DENSITY' cannot be greater than E. In *Fig. 1* the universe lies on either side of the critical density A and may therefore either expand for ever or eventually contract. However, *Fig. 2* shows that the universe will almost certainly expand indefinitely.

THE END OF THE UNIVERSE

It seems likely that the universe may eventually run out of energy. The stars will cease to shine, galaxies to rotate and human beings to live. Everything will end.

If the big bang theory is correct, and if it is true that the universe will never stop expanding, and if there is no chance of the arrival of new material, as the Steady State theory proposed, then there seems no doubt about it: the universe will end at some time in the future. That time is still a long way off; many thousands of millions of years in the future, but one day it will happen.

The reason why the universe will end is that it will run out of energy. Some time in the distant future it will have used up all the sources of energy that keep it going. This may sound astonishing but it seems to be true, in spite of the fact that the universe contains all kinds of energy.

What do we mean by energy? Essentially energy means the ability to do work. The Sun has energy and the work this energy does is to enable it to shine, to emit heat and other radiation, and to hold the planets and other bodies in the Solar System in orbit around it. Our Galaxy has energy, it does work; it rotates and causes masses of gas to contract and form new stars.

Everything in the universe which radiates energy, undergoes chemical reactions, moves in orbit or takes part in some other motion, or even just exerts a gravitational pull, is doing work and expending energy. But none of this energy is limitless; it has no continual source of supply, and one day it will be used up.

We see this permanent consumption of energy wherever we look at the universe, the most obvious evidence coming from the radiation from stars, nebulae and galaxies. This energy comes from thermonuclear reactions (page 72) where hydrogen is converted into helium, or where more complex processes like the proton-proton chain reaction occur. Once generated, the energy does work in keeping the star from collapsing in on itself and

more work in radiating into space, setting nebulae aglow, making gas emit radio waves, and even reaching our telescopes and generating images that we can observe. Yet one day all the hydrogen will be converted to helium, and other elements of thermonuclear reactions used up. The stars, the galaxies and the nebulae in them will stop shining, and no new stars will be formed.

The planets and their satellites also have energy of their own. Some of this is thermonuclear, though there is not enough to cause them to shine on their own account. Planetary nuclear reactions are what we call radioactivity, and the materials that break up to cause this are heavy elements like uranium and radium. Fortunately for us, the number of atoms of these elements

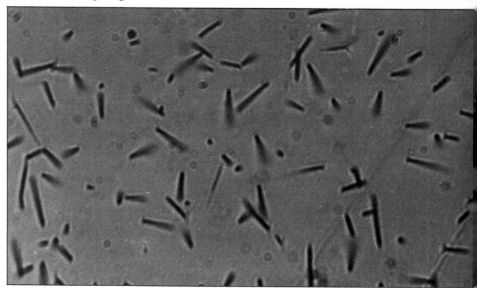

above This ancient meteorite shows tracks formed by particles from a giant nuclear explosion which occurred in our own Galaxy, probably before the birth of the Solar System.

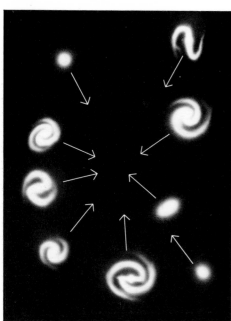

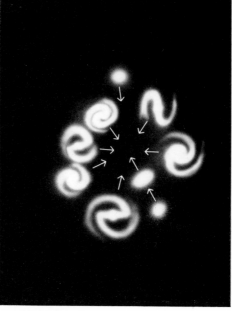

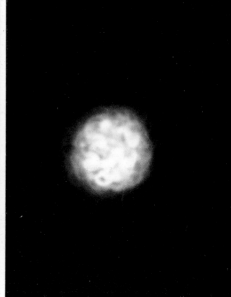

These illustrations show three stages in the contraction of the universe. Galaxies would fall together and also contract in on themselves to form a massive lump of material, which might turn into a gigantic black hole.

that break down at any one time are few, otherwise we should have the equivalent of thousands of atom bombs going off inside the Earth's crust. Yet even at the present slow rate of disintegration, one day the uranium and the radium will have been used up, and this energy source will also have gone. It is as well for us, too, that the Sun is using up its energy in a regular manner, changing its rate of nuclear 'burning' hardly at all. But, of course, this state of affairs will not continue for ever. A time will come when much of the Sun's hydrogen is converted into helium, and it will move over to other reactions, becoming in due course a red giant. When this happens, the Earth will be incinerated and all life on the planet destroyed. Yet at the moment – and for some millions of

years to come – we have a reprieve, though elsewhere in the universe, in our own Galaxy as well as in more distant ones, explosive outbursts of energy are not unusual. In fact, one of the results of modern astronomy has been to show that we live in a very explosive universe in some of whose parts energy is being used up at an alarming rate.

Energy in the universe is not, however, only associated with the burning up of nuclear energy. There is a vast amount of gravitational energy. We can see this kind of energy on Earth in waterfalls and in hydro-electric power schemes. Every time the Sun rises, gravitational energy has been spent making the Earth spin on its axis. One day this energy will be used up; tidal friction between the Earth and the Moon is

causing the Earth's rotation on its axis to slow down.

One day it will become so slow that the Earth will always keep one face turned towards the Moon, and in the very distant future its rotation will cease altogether. But perhaps the Earth will have been burnt up by the Sun before this stage is reached.

The orbital motion of the planets round the Sun is another source of gravitational energy; so too are the orbital motions of all planetary satellites. Yet these will not go on for ever; one day they too will cease. And, on a larger scale, the rotation of our Galaxy and of other galaxies will not go on for ever. Gradually the gas will be used up to form stars, and the galaxies will spin slower and slower until they collapse in on themselves, releasing their final amounts of energy as they do so.

Gravitational collapse is a vast source of energy, but it is not renewable. We can see how powerful it is when we think of collapsed stars and black holes. And once the stars in a galaxy have collapsed and the galaxy itself has stopped rotating there seems no reason why it, too, should not collapse, forming a giant black hole in space. It also seems likely that at this stage – or just before it – those galaxies in groups and clusters will be pulled together by gravity forming huge collapsing masses, really gigantic black holes. This, then, may be how the universe will end, a victim of gravitational collapse. Only if the universe stops expanding and collapses to start a new big bang era will it avoid ceasing to exist.

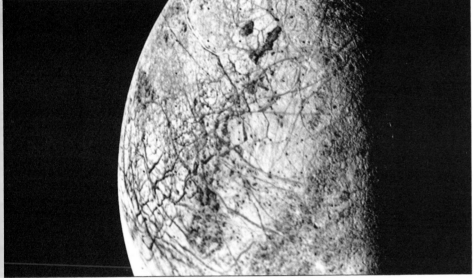

above Europa, the third largest of Jupiter's satellites, has a hard, icy surface. As energy is spent, so all planetary surfaces will cool until their water and gases freeze.

The 'heat death' of the universe. As stars radiate energy into space (*above, left*) so they will all become dimmer and cooler (*above, right*) until no more energy is left and they cease to shine. However, before this final stage happens, stars go through a stage of nuclear disruption (not shown here) so that the 'heat death' (a levelling out of all energy) will be overtaken by gravitational collapse.

THE PAROCHIAL UNIVERSE

Throughout history astronomers have underestimated the size of the universe. Are our views also too parochial and is the universe just part of a system of universes which we cannot observe?

The universe so far described is the universe we can observe. There may be limits to what we can observe, because the further into deep space we go, the faster galaxies and quasars are moving away from us. If we went far enough we should come to a point where they would be travelling with the speed of light, and anything further away would be unobservable. What would this distance be?

As far as we can tell, using a simple 'closed' model of the expanding universe, the exact size would depend on the extent that galaxies and quasars increase their speed with distance; that is on the value we accept for 'Hubble's constant' (page 118). Let us suppose it is 50, which is at the extreme end of the range of values that we think it could possibly have and would give us the largest possible observable universe.

How big, then, is the observable universe when we take 50 as the Hubble constant? You can work out the answer quite simply, especially if you round off the figures, because all we really want is an idea of the size; we do not need to know it to the last kilometre. What the Hubble constant tells us is that for every million parsecs, that is for every 3¼ million light-years, the speed of a galaxy increases by 50 kilometres per second. And as we know that the speed of light is 300,000 km per second, the distance at which galaxies would reach the speed of light is 300,000 ÷ 50, which comes out at 6,000 million parsecs or, in round figures, 20,000 million (20 × 10⁹) light-years. So this is the largest volume of space we could observe in an expanding universe.

What should we see if we looked out as far as this? Should we see galaxies suddenly vanishing into nothingness as they reached the speed of light? Would they look as if they had suddenly been switched off, leaving a blank space where they were shining a moment before? This is possible, though it seems more likely that any blank space we observed would be caused by the fact that we are looking back in time to the moment when the universe began and long before any galaxies had formed.

We should, though, possibly see the state of affairs that existed during the hadron or lepton eras (page 158), though whether any radiation escaped into space then is doubtful; we might just see a dark background. On the other hand, if we could see further still, then we might be in for a surprise.

A time-lapse photograph of a dome at the Anglo-Australian Observatory showing stars of the southern hemisphere sky appearing to rotate round the south celestial pole. Though hundreds and thousands of light-years away these stars are still comparatively close neighbours.

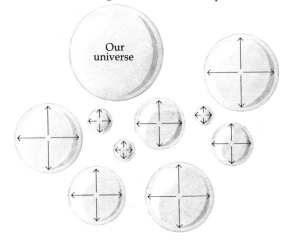

above
Our universe may be an expanding bubble in a far larger universe, composed of many smaller expanding universes.

right
Bubbles generated in boiling water. It has been suggested that the entire universe may be similar – a series of expanding 'bubbles', though not, of course, of water.

When astronomers discuss the universe, they are always thinking about the universe they observe; the universe of galaxies all moving outwards, singly or in groups and clusters. They are discussing the expanding universe that they have been observing for most of this century. But, of course, if we go back in time, we find that astronomers used to think of the universe as much smaller. For back in the past, in the days of the ancient Egyptians and Babylonians four or five thousand years ago, the entire universe seemed to be no more than the dome of the sky, covering the Earth like the dome in a planetarium. The stars seemed at the most some thousands of kilometres away. Then the Greek astronomers, some two thousand and more years ago, thought of the universe as a sphere but still approximately of the same size. Three hundred years ago, Copernicus, who believed the Sun and not the Earth to be the centre of the spherical universe, thought it was much bigger than this, but not until

about 150 years ago did anyone really know the distances of even the nearest stars. Then they found they should be measured in millions of millions of kilometres. But still it was a very small universe, with all the stars together in one large star island.

Not until the 1920's did astronomers discover that our Galaxy was only one of millions of others: only then did astronomy get a really big universe, a universe whose size we have just been calculating. So what history shows us is that, quite properly, astronomers have been cautious and have only come gradually to the idea of a really big universe. But it is useful, now and then, to speculate a little. Of course, we must not speculate too wildly, but it is legitimate for us to ask whether our parochial universe really is all there is in space. We know we are part of an expanding universe, but what if there are other expanding universes?

One possibility that has been suggested is that ours is only one of many expanding universes. In fact

the whole universe has been likened to a boiling liquid, in which new bubbles are continually forming, beginning as tiny centres and then expanding outwards until they burst. Our parochial universe, the one we observe, the one which we find is expanding, is equivalent to just one of these bubbles. All we know about is one tiny part of the whole of the entire universe, one small bubble in a vast cosmos the full extent of which we simply cannot fathom; we cannot even see it. All we can observe is our own expanding bubble; that is what we have been calling the universe, though it is really only a minute fraction of it.

What this view claims is that we are guilty of the same fault as astronomers in past ages when they thought that the entire universe consisted of the Solar System encased in a sphere of stars. We should think large. The real universe may be far bigger than previously thought. This does not mean, of course, that it is really a boiling liquid, and that our parochial universe is no more than a

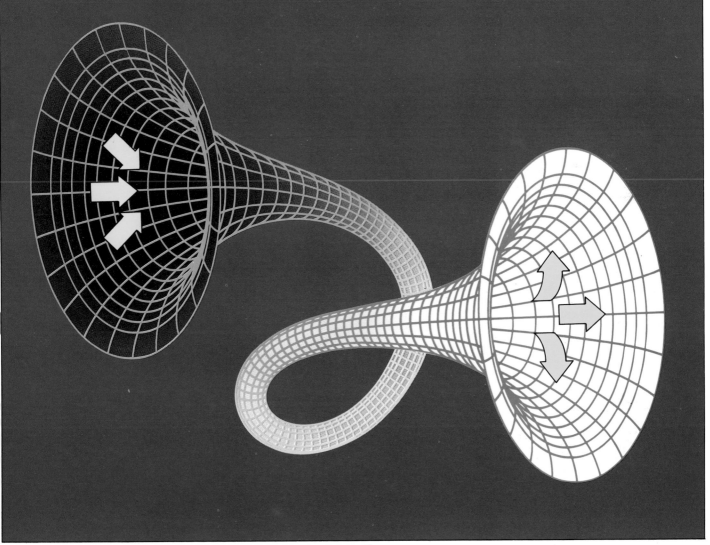

The possible collapse of material into a black hole (*top left*) and its emergence (*bottom right*) into a 'white hole' in another universe or another part of space, travelling through a 'wormhole' in curved space.

bubble of gas – for that is what bubbles in a boiling liquid are. But it does suggest that the cosmos is much vaster than we think, and something of which we have hardly an inkling.

The 'bubble universe' is not the only possible alternative to our parochial universe. There is the quite different idea which we may call the 'wormhole universe'. This is a universe composed of different spaces, of which our own parochial universe is just one. These spaces are connected by special routes nicknamed 'wormholes'. It is not an easy idea to grasp but probably the best way to do so is to consider a black hole. As we know, this is caused by the collapse of a very large body due to gravitation when its atoms and nuclear particles can offer no resistance to the shrinkage. The black hole distorts space and crushes anything falling into it; it squashes things to nothing, into the point in time and space known as a singularity. But does material that falls into it really vanish away? In the universe as we understand it there is a conservation of matter and energy; in other words the total amount of matter and energy is always constant. If matter vanishes away in a black hole is it still conserved? Has it not gone for ever? One way out of the dilemma is to suppose the matter does still exist, but that it moves out from the black hole, through a worm-hole, and into another part of space. Or it could move into another space-time universe altogether.

Is this really possible, or is it just a fantasy? Mathematical studies of space and time do show that this is

possible in theory. Does it happen in practice? The fact of the matter is that we do not know. There certainly seem to be regions in deep space from which material is pouring out into our parochial universe. The jet of material from the active elliptical galaxy M87 is a case in point. Has it come from a 'white hole' connected by a wormhole to a black hole somewhere else? Again there is the strange object SS433 which seems to be throwing out two streams of particles into space. Perhaps this too is material streaming from somewhere else into SS433. And if it is, perhaps that 'somewhere else' is some strange region of space and time, for there is always the chance that such strange regions do exist.

We have already talked about spherical space (pages 44–45) and seen that it is different from flat or

Euclidean space. But there is another alternative to Euclidean space besides spherical space. This is known as 'hyperbolic' space because a piece cut through it has the shape of a curve known as hyperbola. Here the inside angles of a triangle add up to less than 180°. As you can see from the drawing the sides of the triangle look as though they are squashed in, though if you lived in hyperbolic space, you would not notice anything out of the ordinary. The point of mentioning it here is that this kind of space could well be associated with the region near a black hole, so perhaps the region the other side, through the wormhole, is like this too. Perhaps all the space involved with black holes is like this and if we travelled through we should emerge into a region of hyperbolic space.

What we must realize is that

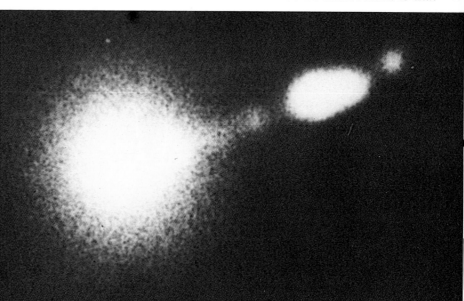

above The elliptical galaxy M87 ejecting a jet of material into space. Studies show that the jet surges out in bursts.

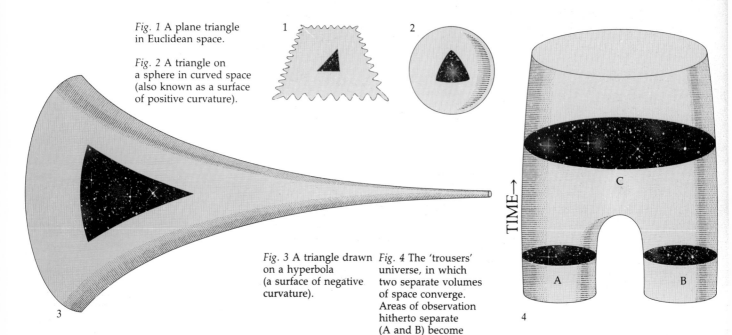

Fig. 1 A plane triangle in Euclidean space.

Fig. 2 A triangle on a sphere in curved space (also known as a surface of positive curvature).

Fig. 3 A triangle drawn on a hyperbola (a surface of negative curvature).

Fig. 4 The 'trousers' universe, in which two separate volumes of space converge. Areas of observation hitherto separate (A and B) become united at C.

TIME →

space in the cosmos, away from our expanding universe, may, if it exists, be different from our own spherical space. And there may be other separate universes which live separate existences for a time. The 'trousers' universe is like this. Suppose we had two regions of space quite separate from each other, each with galaxies, quasars and other objects. We can represent these by the 'legs' of a pair of trousers in a diagram in which time is running from the bottom towards the top of the page. As time passes so we 'move up' the legs until we come to the seat of the trousers. When this happens a galaxy 'A' in one leg which has been quite invisible to observers on a galaxy 'B' in the other leg, can now be seen. If then, while observing very far into space, we should chance to come across a

number of distant galaxies where none had been visible before, instead of having to suppose that these had suddenly been created, we might, perhaps, conclude that the entire universe is shaped after this fashion. Mathematically such a universe is a possibility, though probably not a very likely one.

It has been suggested by some astronomers that the great explosions observed in some galaxies – M87 for example, once again – are due not to material coming in from another universe or some other region of space-time, but to the presence of anti-matter. Nuclear physicists have discovered that, in theory, the nuclear particles we know should also exist in the form of anti-matter, that is to say, as particles with the same mass but with opposite electrical charge. Thus whereas an

atom has a heavy nucleus with a positive electrical charge and lightweight negatively charged electrons orbiting around it, an atom of antimatter would have a heavy nucleus with a negative charge and light orbiting electrons, each with a positive charge. We are also told that if atoms of anti-matter meet atoms of matter there would be an immense explosion.

These theoretical ideas of nuclear physicists are not purely imaginative, because some anti-matter particles have been discovered. When the nucleus of an atom is struck very hard – by a high energy beam of neutrinos for instance – then a matching pair of particles can be ejected, one of matter – the electron – and the other of anti-matter – the positron (which is a positive electron). This process has actually been observed, and it has led some astronomers to suggest there may be a universe of anti-matter, with anti-matter stars and galaxies. So this is yet another possibility. It could explain some of the vast explosive events observed to be happening deep in space, and is another factor that warns us that our present picture of the universe may indeed be parochial.

Bubble universe, distortions of space, anti-matter galaxies, are all speculations. The one thing they emphasize is that we should keep an open mind. We do not know all there is to know about the universe – far from it. It is almost certainly stranger than we know, though probably not stranger than we can ever know.

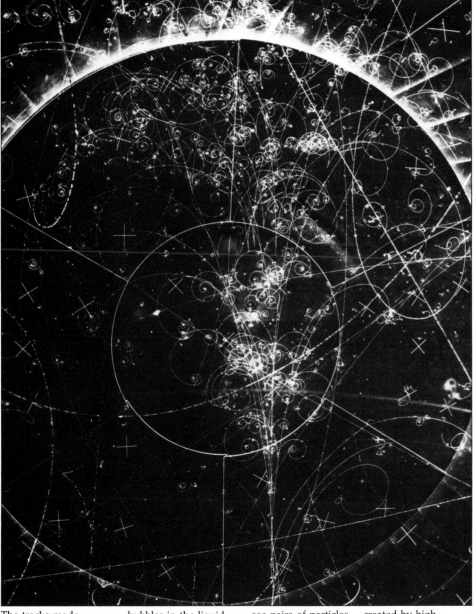

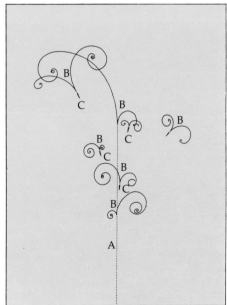

The tracks made by nuclear particles in this bubble chamber becomes visible because they generate tiny bubbles in the liquid inside the chamber. (The liquid contains a mixture of neon and hydrogen.) We see pairs of particles (each containing an electron and its anti-particle, a positron) being created by high-energy neutrinos colliding with particles of the liquid.

The invisible neutron beam (shown as a dotted line) collides at A. Electron/ positron pairs are produced at B. At the points marked C, high-energy but invisible gamma-rays are produced.

CHAPTER 9
THE QUESTION OF LIFE

Are we alone in space or is there a variety of life forms waiting to be discovered? We now know that the universe is made up of the same elements that occur on Earth so the chances of life existing elsewhere are good.

Is the Earth the only inhabited place in the entire universe? The answer to this question is probably 'no'. At present most astronomers think that there is life elsewhere in the universe. But to understand the reasons for this view, we must look in this chapter at the chemical nature of life and examine where it is likely to be found, for it is quite clear that not everywhere in the universe is equally suitable. Two hundred years ago, the great astronomer William Herschel said he believed people were living on the Sun beneath the very bright clouds which he thought covered the whole of the solar surface. We now know that he was wildly wrong; no living thing could exist on the Sun. We can be certain of this because we now know far more about the Sun than Herschel did, or could have done, and because we also know, which he could not, the chemicals of which living things are made.

There is another thing we know about the universe and its contents which has been discovered since Herschel's time, and this is that the same chemical elements exist throughout the whole of space. There are 92 naturally occurring elements and no more. Astronomers and nuclear physicists think there may have been more during the hot big bang stage of the universe, but all of these would have had very short lifetimes before they broke up, and it seems certain they could no longer exist. What this means for the origin of life here or elsewhere in the universe is that it must be based on the 92 elements (actually rather less as we shall see later), all of which are already known to us on Earth. So it would seem that life on Earth can give us very strong clues about the nature of life itself, even in other parts of the universe.

What is life? What is it that makes us call something alive and animate rather than dead or inanimate? Part of the answer seems to be that to be classed as living, material must be able to reproduce its kind. Yet by itself this is not enough; crystals can reproduce, more and more forming in the correct kind of solution at the correct temperature. What we call living things – mammals, fish, insects, plants, micro-organisms like bacteria, and so on – must grow and be responsive to their environment. They must exchange materials with their surroundings – eating, breaking down their food chemically, getting rid of waste products – and yet not be altered by these processes.

When we look around us on Earth, the variety of life we see is enormous. It ranges from creatures as large as the whale, which may

above
An astonishing 'breach' or leap out of the sea by one of the world's largest creatures, the Southern Right Whale (*Balaena australis*).

left
Giant red worms living deep in the hot, sulphur-laden waters near the bottom of the East Pacific Ocean. With a length of some two metres, these extraordinary creatures have no mouths. Instead, they absorb their food, which is made of substances similar to proteins, through their bodies. This unusual way of taking nourishment is found in some sea creatures.

reach a length of 30 metres and weigh 136,000 kilograms (134 tons) to microscopic creatures like bacteria, whose length may be no more than a few thousandths of a millimetre or a virus which may be as small as two hundred thousandths of a millimetre. Plants also show an immense range of sizes, from the sub-microscopic algae, the smallest of which are no more than three thousandths of a millimetre, to giant trees like the redwoods which may exceed 100 metres in height, a difference of 300 million times. And all this life can exist under what seem to us a wide range of conditions – from the freezing wastes of Antarctica to the hot springs of some countries which may reach a temperature of 70°C – though astronomically speaking this is a very limited range indeed.

How did this staggering variety come about? The history of the development of all these many life forms on Earth is something that has intrigued scientists for a long time. For more than a century now, it has been clear that there has been a gradual process of evolution, that animals and plants have developed from very simple living things into the vast range we see all over the world. Of course there are still arguments about how long evolution has taken and about some of the steps along the evolutionary path, but there is no doubt that evolution occurred and is still occurring. Fossils in ancient rocks show us that some different creatures existed in the past. But the fossil record is far from complete, and was never by itself an argument for evolution.

Charles Darwin, who in 1859 put forward the original theory which biologists now study, was himself quite clear on this point. He, as well as biologists today, base their beliefs on other evidence. In the first place selective change is experimentally proved – it can even be man-made, as when special breeds, in many cases new species, of dogs, cattle, crops and other living things are developed. Natural evolutionary changes also exist and have been studied, showing how environment has caused alterations. There is a famous case of a moth whose wing colouration has changed over the last century due to the industrialization of the area where it lives. This is an effect of natural selection. Secondly, studies of the way a species is spread geologically across the world show clearly that there are variations, some of which are large enough to give a new species, though obviously related to the previous one. Thirdly, there are the hereditary factors. These are what determine the type of offspring a plant or an animal will have, so that a dog produces puppies not kittens, a rose makes other roses, not lupins or cornflowers. Careful examination of the way these factors are handed on from parent to offspring give definite evidence of evolution of different species from common ancestors. In other words, all the evidence points to life beginning simply and then developing into more complex forms.

There is good reason to suppose that life will always undergo evolution, wherever it appears in space. Of course it would doubtless evolve into different forms from those we know on Earth, in spite of the great variety of life here, but the chemical basis will be the same, as we shall see.

left
The redwood is the world's largest tree. Redwoods occur naturally only near the coast of California. The largest specimens can reach well over 100 metres in height.

below
An electron-microscope photograph of an adenovirus – a virus that affects the upper respiratory tract (the nose and throat) and sometimes causes conjunctivitis (an eye infection). It is seen here magnified half a million times.

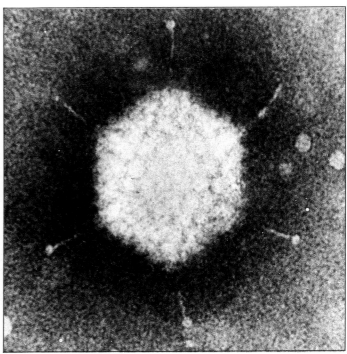

THE COMPLEX MOLECULES OF SPACE

Scientists have argued about whether complex molecules could exist in space itself. With the advent of radio astronomy highly complex interstellar molecules have now been found.

In the Sun, the heat is so great, and the short-wave radiation so strong, that we find atoms appear quite separate from one another. Molecules or groups of atoms cannot hold together – any that were put there artificially would be dissociated at once; broken down into their separate atoms.

What is true of the Sun, however, is not true of all stars. There are a few that are cool enough to let some simple molecules form. Reddish K type stars, whose surface temperatures never reach more than 4230°C, and the cooler red type stars, do have a few molecules among their surface gases. Photographs of the spectra of these stars show dark bands and lines that indicate the presence of molecules. Here, we find molecules of metals with oxygen, i.e. metal oxides, notably the oxides of titanium, scandium and vanadium.

Thus, the red giant star Betelgeuse shows bands of titanium oxide (TiO_2), each molecule of which is a group containing one titanium atom (Ti) with a pair of oxygen atoms (O_2). Also, in the S-type stars, whose temperatures range from about 2700°C down to 1200°C, there are oxides of the heavy metals barium, yttrium and zirconium. In addition, among these stars (classes K, M and S) there are also carbon stars. These are stars whose spectra show the presence of the element carbon, usually in the form of molecules, either molecules of carbon itself (C_2 – i.e. a pair of carbon atoms) or molecules of the cyano group, carbon and nitrogen (CN) and the methyl group, carbon and hydrogen (CH). This is very interesting, because as we shall see (pages 176–179) carbon forms the backbone of all the molecules of living things.

Of course, the molecules of living material are far more complex than the simple oxides of metals, or the pairs of atoms making molecules of carbon, or of the cyano and methyl groups. For large molecules we need somewhere even cooler than the cool K, M and S stars.

If we take the Orion nebula we find cool areas because in some parts there are dark patches where stars are forming. In these cool areas there are molecular clouds. (These also occur in the giant interstellar cloud in the Sagittarius constellation and also close to the centre of our Galaxy, but we shall return to these later.) First of all, let us look nearer home and consider molecules found in comets which, as we have already seen (page 50), spend a great part of their time in the cold and more distant parts of the Solar System.

Observations using optical telescopes with spectroscopes

attached show us that these icy bodies contain some simple molecules. These are the gases carbon monoxide (CO), carbon dioxide (CO_2) and molecules composed of two nitrogen atoms (N_2), water (H_2O), ammonia (NH_3) and methane (CH_4). Space observations made from the Orbiting Astronomical Observatory *Copernicus* show that the deuterium molecule H_2 is also present, although usually in combination with ordinary hydrogen atoms. (This occurrence could not be observed from the Earth because the spectral lines from H_2 only appear in the deep ultraviolet.) In December 1973, when the comet discovered by Lubos Kohoutek appeared, radio-astronomers also took a keen interest

The Orion nebula showing dark patches where there is dust and gas and where interstellar molecules are to be found.

in it, and the observations they made showed some molecules never known before to be associated with comets. These were hydrogen cyanide (HCN) and the more complex molecule methyl cyanide (CH₃CN) previously only observed by radio-telescopes in interstellar space.

We see, then, that comets have molecules in them, one of which is complex enough to have six atoms linked together. This probably means that there are complex molecules, perhaps a great many of them, to be found in the Solar System, and that the Earth is very far from being the one place where they occur. Indeed, we know that, for instance, ammonia, methane and sulphuric

Brook's comet at its last appearance, on October 21 1911. This photograph shows the head of the comet, and it is here that molecules are found.

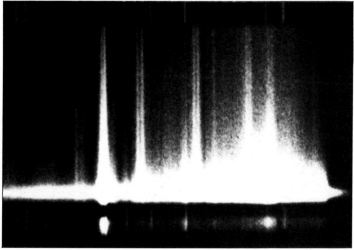

Spectrum of comet Mrkos, which appeared during the late summer of 1957. This shows bands of carbon, cyanogen and ionized carbon monoxide.

acid are among the molecules to be found on some of the other planets.

In interstellar space, a number of molecules have also been discovered among some cool gas clouds. In recent years, especially since 1970, the variety known has increased immensely. Until 1963, however, the molecules that were known were few and simple because the only ones that had been recognized were those visible to optical telescopes. These were the substances cyanogen (CN) and methylidine. This last was found in two forms: straightforward methylidine (CH) and in addition the same molecule but with one of its orbiting electrons (negatively electrically charged particles) missing, giving a positively charged molecule

and thus turning it into a methylidine ion (CH⁺).

The interesting thing about these molecules is that all three of them are carbon compounds. This fact is significant because carbon is such a key substance in the molecules of living material. For this reason the study of carbon substances is also called 'organic chemistry', i.e. the chemistry of chemical compounds connected with living matter.

Once the radio-astronomers had begun to study interstellar material from 1969 onwards, many more molecules were discovered, some of them carbon compounds. At the start, these observations did not seem all that novel or exciting. The first molecule the radio-astronomers came across (in 1963) was hydroxyl (OH) which seemed to be formed from atoms of oxygen (O) and hydrogen (H) carried on dust grains, which, when they bumped into one another, joined up the two atoms into a molecule. This was not a very frequent occurrence, but since there are so many dust grains, quite a number of hydroxyl molecules were formed, certainly enough to give a fairly strong radio signal.

Then, five years later, water vapour and ammonia were detected. But the most surprising and by far the most important discovery was the detection in 1968 of the substance formaldehyde (H₂CO). Here was a really significant carbon compound – the first to contain two heavy atoms (carbon and oxygen). In other words, it was the first compound to have its construction based on these elements rather than on hydrogen. What is more, formaldehyde is an organic substance which takes a very energetic part in chemical reactions, especially with the important constituents of living matter called proteins.

Once water molecules had been found, and formaldehyde had been discovered, radio-astronomers began to look for other complex molecules. First of all, they found formic acid (HCOOH), a molecule made up of no less than five atoms. This acid is produced by some bacteria, though its presence in space cannot be taken to indicate the existence of bacteria, because there are other ways in which it can be formed. Nevertheless, the presence of formic acid does show that there exists complex organic material.

A year later a six-atom molecule was discovered – methyl cyanide (CH₃CN) – and later still seven-atom molecules. These included cyano-diacetylene (HC₅N) and perhaps more significantly the substance methyl alcohol (CH_3OH) sometimes known as wood alcohol or wood spirit. The importance of methyl alcohol is that it is a basic molecule of all kinds of chemical substances. This is the reason why it is used so widely in the chemical industry on Earth, from making dyes to fuelling spacecraft.

Methyl alcohol is a violent poison, causing blindness or death among people unwise enough to drink it. (It is sometimes a product of illicit distillation equipment for making alcoholic drinks.) But its presence led astronomers to wonder whether, perhaps, the safe form of drinking alcohol – ethyl alcohol – was present in space. This is a rather more complex organic molecule which has nine atoms – it is CH_3CH_2OH – and radio observations were first made of it in 1974. Assessments of the quantity available in one large gas cloud have been made and, although it may not be a very scientific way of expressing it, astronomers have found that there is

enough ethyl alcohol present to make 10 thousand million million million million (10^{28}) bottles of whisky. This shows how complex some of the molecules can be, for ethyl alcohol is not the only nine-atom molecule that has been discovered. A similar molecule, ethyl cyanide (CH_3CH_2CN) with CN replacing the OH of ethyl alcohol has also been found.

The next questions – important ones if we are to find out whether there is likely to be living material in space – are to determine the conditions in which these interstellar organic molecules are found, and to discover what we can about the way in which they are formed. The first is easier to answer than the second. The molecules are to be found in gas clouds, but gas clouds by themselves are not a sufficiently suitable environment. The clouds must be cool, and, in particular, they must not be lit by hot bright stars because such stars emit vast amounts of ultraviolet light. It is this ultraviolet light that sets the gas glowing, but such radiation would spell death to

organic molecules. Ultraviolet light carries too much energy with it, and would break up the large molecules into smaller molecules, or, more probably, into separate atoms. X-rays are even more energetic, and so are gamma rays and cosmic rays, so it is clear that the cloud must be cool or at least in a region where the organic molecules can be kept at a lowish temperature. Dust is the ideal protection from heat and radiation. It can mask off undesirable radiation and prevent the breakdown of the more complex organic molecules.

The parts of space where the organic interstellar molecules have been found are all in dust-laden cool areas of clouds. The areas in the gas clouds of the Orion nebula where new stars are being formed have already been mentioned as one place where such molecules are present. So too has the giant dust cloud in Sagittarius; some twelve areas are known in all. All have similar conditions. Every one is, of course, in our own Galaxy, but this is because of problems of observing.

Two organic molecules: formaldehyde (H₂CO) (*left*), and ethyl alcohol (CH₃CH₂OH) (*right*). The atoms are represented by spheres, and the 'stalks' between them represent the chemical forces joining the atoms together.

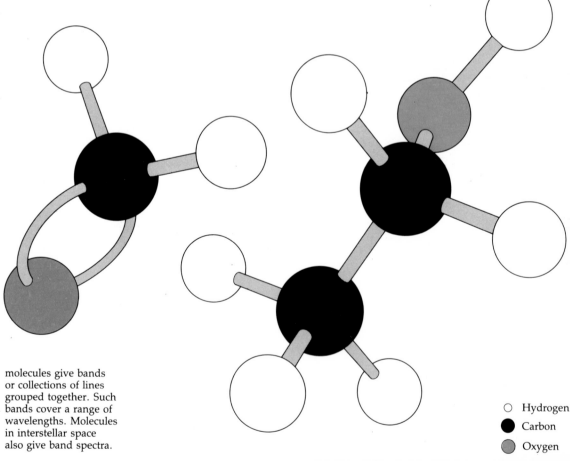

○ Hydrogen
● Carbon
● Oxygen

below Comparison of a spectrum given by atoms (A) with one given by molecules (B). Atoms in the outer layers of a star's gases give dark lines whereas molecules give bands or collections of lines grouped together. Such bands cover a range of wavelengths. Molecules in interstellar space also give band spectra.

A

B

There is absolutely no reason to suppose that things are different in any other similar spiral galaxies. We can therefore conclude that there are organic interstellar molecules to be found all over space.

How are these complex molecules formed? The general idea accepted by astronomers is that, first of all, simple molecules are formed on the dust grains themselves. Then, as the dust grains collide, more elaborate molecules are built up from the simpler ones. Some molecules, too, are ionized, as we have seen in the case of methylidine. These are types of molecules called 'radicals' by chemists because they are a basic kind of chemical root (*radix* means root) which remains unchanged during chemical reactions.

Of course, not all the details of what happens are known precisely, but astronomers have gained further clues by examining what has *not* happened as well as what has. Thus, they have found that the atoms in the molecules are joined only in certain ways; not in all the ways that

are chemically possible. Again, they have discovered that some molecules are missing in space – only one oxide of nitrogen has yet been found – and there do not seem to be any 'ring molecules', which we shall be discussing in the next couple of pages, and which are of particular importance when we come to the molecules of living substances. But the important fact is that complex organic molecules do exist in space.

It has been suggested by a few astronomers that those meteors that are the debris of comets could carry complex molecules, perhaps even living material. This view was originally started by an examination of the Orgeuil meteorite, a meteor that fell on the village of Orgeuil near Toulouse in the south of France in May 1864. When they were carefully examined, fragments of the fall showed the presence of carbon, hydrogen and oxygen. In addition, some of the material seemed to be like peat or the soft brown coal called lignite. Both these substances are the result of pressure and heat on

decayed vegetation. Was the Orgeuil meteorite evidence of living materials elsewhere in space?

Unfortunately, this theory now seems unlikely. A fresh examination of the material in 1962 showed that parts of the meteorite that had been sealed away in a museum had embedded in them particles of a reed plant and of coal. But around them, the meteorite had been very carefully replaced, so that it was clear that these bits had been added *after* the meteorite had landed on Earth. They were part of a hoax. At the time the meteorite fell, great arguments were going on in France among scientists about life evolving from non-living matter – something we now know to be impossible – and these may have been among the reasons for faking the meteorite. So the Orgeuil meteorite is not evidence for the view that living matter does come to Earth with meteorites. The question is still open. If such matter does come, however, it would somehow have to resist considerable heat and ultraviolet radiation.

above Part of the Orgeuil meteorite, which fell in the south of France in 1864. Originally believed to contain particles of living matter, it is now known to have been faked.

left Photograph by the UK Schmidt telescope in Australia of clouds containing interstellar molecules in the region of ρ (rho) Ophiuchi (*top*) and Antares (*bottom left*).

THE COMPLEX MOLECULES OF LIFE

Biochemists can tell the astronomer a great deal about the chemical nature of organic molecules and so help him in his search for alien life.

The substances that compose living creatures are constructed of tiny units or cells. Each cell is surrounded by a wall or skin (usually called a 'membrane') and contains complex chemicals which form the very substance of life. Yet these chemicals are made of ordinary everyday atoms, based on the element carbon. The chemical elements most usually found with the carbon are hydrogen and oxygen, as well as nitrogen, phosphorus and sulphur. In addition there are the radicals, small collections of atoms which, as we saw (page 175), remain unchanged during chemical reactions. All these substances build up molecules— carbohydrates, fats and proteins.

The study of the chemistry of living materials began over 150 years ago when the German chemist Friedrich Wöhler discovered that he could make urea in his laboratory. Urea (H_2NCONH_2) is a substance which is found in the urine of many living creatures, including birds and some reptiles, and also in the blood and in milk. Wöhler's crucial discovery was that he could make urea from the chemical ammonium cyanate. The exciting thing about this was that ammonium cyanate was made of *exactly* the same atoms as urea – in other words, ammonia (NH_3) plus CHNO – yet when used in chemical reactions it behaved quite differently from urea. How was this possible? Wöhler realized that the answer was basically simple: the way the chemical behaved in a chemical reaction was due not only to the atoms of which the molecules were made but also to the way in which they were arranged. By taking molecules of ammonium cyanate, as Wöhler did, and changing the positions of the atoms, you get urea. We now know that urea is not a special case: Wöhler's discovery is true of the chemicals of all living substances. The way the atoms are arranged is vital, as will become clear in a moment, and this is reflected in the way in which chemists write the

formula for urea. H_2NCONH_2 shows that there are two groups of hydrogen and nitrogen – H_2N at one end of the molecule and NH_2 at the other – with one carbon atom and one oxygen atom in the middle. The carbon is the pivot point, the central core of the molecule, as we shall see.

However, many problems still remained. Wöhler had shown that the arrangement of atoms was important as well as the chemical composition. But what types of arrangements were possible? Were there preferred arrangements or not? The next step in discovering this – and thus determining the nature of

organic molecules, the building-blocks of life – came when scientists began to investigate the substance quinine, which is present in the bark of the cinchona tree and is a well-known medicine. Quinine is a very complex substance ($C_{20}H_{24}O_2N_2.3H_2O$) but the English chemist William Perkin found that it was related to aniline ($C_6H_5NH_2$), a product that comes from coal-tar and is thus a result of decaying vegetation. In exploring the relationships between the two, Perkin produced a number of artificial dyes, the first known to man, and made his fortune.

What Perkin had discovered

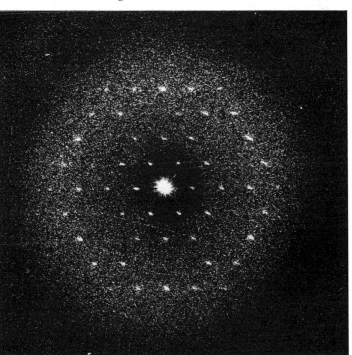

An X-ray diffraction pattern made by a crystal of haemoglutinin, and observed with an electron-microscope (page 8). Haemoglutinin is a protein, taken in this case from the surface of an influenza virus.

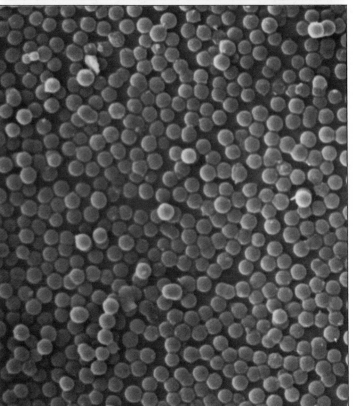

A collection of 'microspheres' of protein-like material which can be produced by heating dry mixture of amino-acids. Under suitable conditions Sidney W. Fox of the University of Miami, who has studied these tiny spherules, has noticed 'growth' or budding with the production of new microspheres. The microspheres have an outside wall or membrane like that possessed by bacteria.

chemically was then followed up by his colleague, the German chemist August Hoffmann, who found that the basis of all the dyes was a substance that he had originally extracted from coal-tar, the chemical benzene. Its formula was easy to write: C_6H_6. The puzzle was to discover how its atoms were arranged. The man who eventually managed to find the answer was another German chemist, August Kekulé von Stradonitz.

Chemical experiments had shown Kekulé that benzene did not behave like a chain molecule (one in which the carbon atoms are in a long chain with the hydrogen atoms sticking out at the sides). But in this case, how were its atoms arranged? One day in 1865, snoozing by the fire, Kekulé suddenly realized that all his experimental laboratory results would be explained if the six carbon atoms were joined together in a ring, with the hydrogen atoms sticking on the outside of the ring, one to each carbon atom. This important discovery – vital in working out the patterns of many molecules needed to make living material – captured the popular imagination. There was even a cartoon to celebrate the discovery, showing six monkeys in a ring, holding on to one another's legs. With Kekulé's discovery, chemists now had the basic patterns for constructing the layout of the atoms in organic chemicals – the ring and the chain.

Biochemists have found that the chemical backbone of all living substances is indeed carbon, but since we are interested in life elsewhere in the universe we should ask whether there is any other chemical element that might replace carbon. We shall see shortly that what we are really looking for is a substance that can act as a backbone for huge molecules containing *thousands* of atoms, and we need something that will manage this without difficulty. In theory, we have 91 other elements from which to choose, but in practice the choice is nowhere near as wide as this. Most are not suitable, for one reason or another, and the only alternative element that would seem to have suitable chain-line properties is silicon, a substance found in rocks and used in making glass.

Silicon can withstand considerable heat, so if silicon-based molecules were the basis of very large complex molecules they might be able to withstand more heat than carbon-based molecules can. Research shows that some silicon chains exist, although not many. But scientists have found that silicon chains are not long enough to make really complex molecules. As soon as very long silicon chains are built up they become extremely brittle and unstable, breaking up of their own accord into simpler molecules.

Strange though it may seem, the only element in the universe that seems to be suitable for making molecules of living things is carbon. Only carbon can make polymers (many-part molecules), substances composed of many small but similar groups of atoms, and found widely in the substances of living material.

We are now at the stage when we can consider the three different kinds of substance that are part of most living things: carbohydrates, fats and proteins. Carbohydrates, as their name tells us, are primarily molecules which are combinations of carbon and a watery part (that is the meaning of 'hydrate'). Some of these are sugars such as those found in honeys and fruits. These are basically what are known as dextrose (grape sugar), fructose and galactose. All three have the same chemical composition ($C_6H_{12}O_6 + H_2O$) and it is the precise way the atoms are

This illustration is based on a nineteenth-century drawing of monkeys forming a benzine ring.

below
A diagram of the benzine ring.

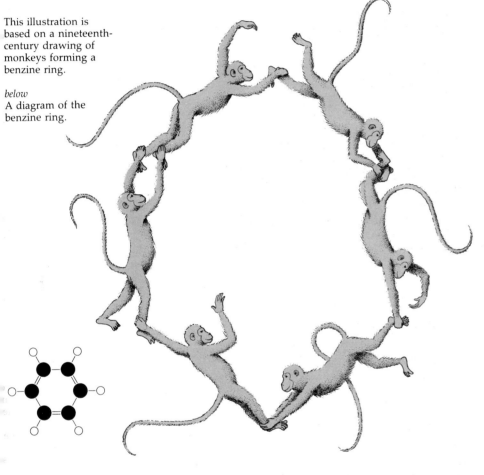

right
A diagram of some carbon and silicon-chain molecules. The carbon ones on the left are stable and can be incorporated into larger molecules. This process is not possible with the silicon-backbone molecules.

○ Hydrogen
● Carbon
◯ Silicon

CARBON COMPOUNDS	SILICON COMPOUNDS
Methane	Silane
Ethane	Di-silane
Ethylene	Does not exist

arranged that determines which particular sugar molecule we find. Detailed research has shown that the sweetness of various sugars depends on the arrangement of the HO groups in the molecule. Some carbohydrate molecules are more complex than others. The ones mentioned so far are called monosaccharides (single sugars), but there are also disaccharides (double sugars), oligosaccharides ('few' saccharides, usually three to six single sugars linked together) and polysaccharides ('many' sugars, which may consist of anything up to 1,000 single sugar molecules linked together), and these all appear in many types. Here we are talking about very large, complicated molecules. They are not, of course, living substances but are used by them as nourishment and provide animals, however small, with energy and help them to form tissue. They must be present for developed life-forms to exist, for they are part of all living cells.

Next we come to the fats, which include oils and waxes. The technical term for them is 'lipids', a word coined from the Greek. Lipids are the molecules which, together with carbohydrates and proteins, form the cells of living material found in animals, plants and micro-organisms. Lipids are all long-chain molecules; they can act as a fuel supply for cells as well as form their own structure. None of the lipids which contain 10 or more carbon atoms in their chains can be dissolved in water (although the shorter ones can) and the molecules of some of them are surprisingly large and heavy. Some lipids have a molecular weight ranging between 2 million and 8 million; compare this with the weight of hydrogen atoms (1.008), carbon (12.01) and oxygen (16).

Lastly we come to proteins, highly complex substances with very large molecules indeed. Proteins contain amino-acids joined together. Amino-acids are acids (there are more than 100 which occur naturally) that incorporate an NH_2 group of three atoms or, in some instances, an NH group; in the latter case, they have a ring structure. Proteins can be broken down into amino-acids by enzymes. Enzymes, so named because they were first discovered in the fermenting cells of the micro-organism we know as yeast (the Greek 'zumos' means 'to leaven'), are themselves a group of proteins that enable chemical reactions to take place in living creatures. These

chemical reactions are known as metabolism and are concerned with the extraction of nutriment from food, the building of bones and tissues, and so on. Without enzymes, living things would die, and in the higher (more complex) animals, special amino-acids known as vitamins are also vital. Admittedly

vitamins are only required in minute amounts but they must be present if life is to continue. Like some enzymes, vitamins act in a special way; they are 'catalysts' whose presence makes various complex chemical reactions possible. Although the vitamins themselves do not take part in the reactions, their presence is

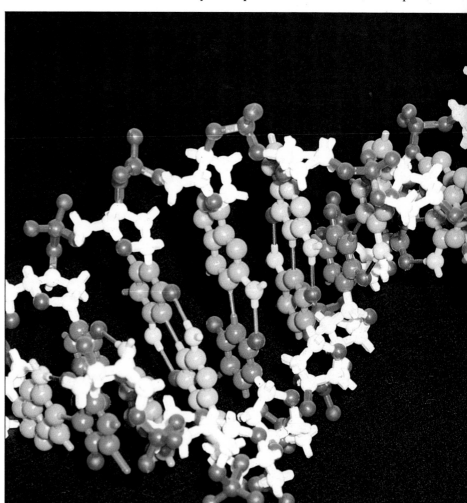

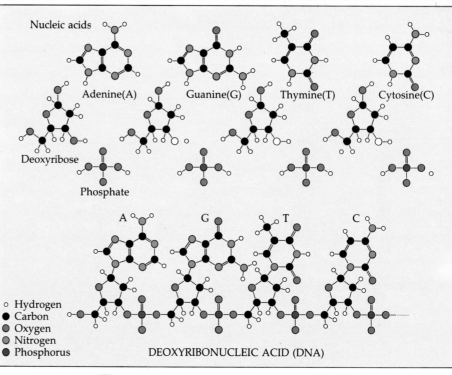

Nucleic acids

Adenine(A) Guanine(G) Thymine(T) Cytosine(C)

Deoxyribose

Phosphate

A G T C

○ Hydrogen
● Carbon
● Oxygen
● Nitrogen
● Phosphorus

DEOXYRIBONUCLEIC ACID (DNA)

...ital. So we see that the whole chemical basis of life and the reactions taking place in living things are very complex indeed.

Protein molecules are very large as well as extremely complex. Their molecular weights are tens of thousands of times greater than hydrogen; for instance, haemoglobin, a substance found in the red blood cells of some higher animals, has a molecular weight of 65,000. But perhaps more significant, from the point of view of life elsewhere in the universe, is the very involved structure of proteins, with their range of atoms joined in long chains and folded over on one another.

Haemoglobin is a typical example of such a molecule.

For life to continue to exist, it must reproduce and we now know that protein molecules are coded so that they will reproduce themselves in such a way that a particular creature or plant has only its own offspring and no other. The code itself is the way the chemicals are arranged within the molecule; the coding is done by special substances known as nucleic acids. These are highly complex substances consisting of chains of ring molecules made up of a phosphorus acid, sugars, and substances called purines and pyrimidines. They are bound to proteins and give gargantuan molecules with weights ranging from 10 million to 100 million times the weight of a hydrogen atom.

There are two kinds of nucleic acids: RNA, or ribonucleic acid, and DNA, or deoxyribonucleic acid. Some RNA acts as a copier of the code given by DNA, but some of it acts as the code itself when it comes to the reproduction of the very tiny, simple organisms known as viruses (page 171) where there is no DNA. In all other living things, from bacteria to the largest plants and animals, DNA is the code carrier. DNA molecules are vast, weighing 120 million times more than a hydrogen atom. The chemicals are arranged in a 'double helix', that is, a structure like a spiral staircase the 'steps' of which are a series of chemical links between the two long strips of the helix. These huge DNA molecules are carried on thin rod-like structures called chromosomes, which divide when cells divide during reproduction. Thus chromosomes, plus DNA molecules, are present in the new cells.

It will be clear by now that the molecules that make up living substances are of immense variety and are far more complex and much larger than interstellar molecules. All interstellar molecules need protection if they are not to be broken down by high-energy radiation (page 174), and the protection needed by the molecules of life is even more stringent. Whereas dust particles alone afford sufficient protection for interstellar molecules, the regions where living things are found are far more restricted. As far as astronomers and biologists can tell at present, life is confined to areas like our Solar System, where planets are orbiting a star that is not too hot and which shines without changing for hundreds of millions of years.

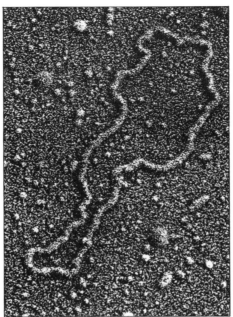

above A photograph through an electron microscope of a DNA plasmid from the *Escherichia coli* bacterium. Plasmids are genetic DNA molecules present in many bacteria.

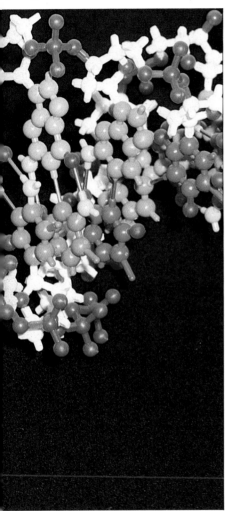

above
A model of a giant DNA molecule. This shows the double helix. (Turn the picture on its side and the 'spiral staircase' structure becomes obvious.) The chemical links – the 'nucleotides' – which form the 'steps' of the staircase, can also be clearly seen.

left opposite
A diagram of part of a DNA molecule and its component parts – deoxyribose and phosphate.

below A view through a microscope of cell division in the Royal Lily (*Lilium regale*).

The chromosones carrying the genetic information have been stained red and show up very clearly.

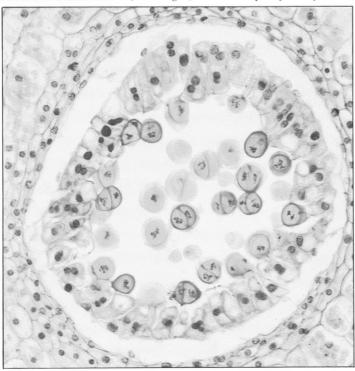

HOW LIFE BEGAN ON EARTH

Of all the planets in the Solar System, our Earth is the only certain abode of life. It seems that life began here just because conditions were right.

We are not certain whether there is life on Mars or indeed anywhere else in the Solar System apart from the Earth. Of course we know that life exists here, but if we are going to try to tackle the question of whether there is life elsewhere in the universe, our first step is to determine how likely it is that living things will appear if conditions are right for them to do so. How did life begin here originally? Did it come from deep space in some form or other, or did it begin on the Earth without any help from outside? And if it did start on the Earth, how, precisely, did it happen? Only if we can find some sort of explanation for these questions can we begin to have an idea of how probable it is that there is life anywhere else in the Solar System, or in our Galaxy, or even in other galaxies.

First of all we know that we are looking for the formation of complex molecules with a carbon backbone, but at the same time we should not lay down precisely what form life itself might take. So what are the possible ways that life forms could have come into being? Could they really have braved the hazards of interstellar or at least interplanetary travel – the intense cold and the damaging effects of very short wave radiation such as X-rays and gamma-rays? Two scientists, Fred Hoyle and Chandra Wickramasinghe, have recently explored this aspect of the problem and have come down strongly in favour of the view that life was brought here from outside. The basis of their idea is that life has come from the complex organic molecules found in some interstellar clouds in our Galaxy (page 172). They suggest that the carriers were comets which, they say, consist largely of this kind of gaseous material. On their journey the comets themselves acted as incubators where possibly bacteria grew, cocooned in gas and so were protected from damaging radiation. If a comet reached the Earth, it would therefore have brought with it the seeds of life.

To Hoyle and Wickramasinghe comets seem to be objects of immense significance; they also believe that comets brought the Earth its atmosphere and its water and, much later, once life was established here, brought virus infections. However, theirs is a minority view, shared by few astronomers and even fewer biologists. But, we do know that the elements for life are present in comets. Also, evidence from fossilized rocks in Greenland shows that microscopic forms of life began only something like 1200 million years after the Earth was formed. To some scientists this seems a very short time for life to have begun without outside help. Yet most biologists still appear to favour an earthbound origin.

If we are to consider how life began on Earth, we must first of all examine the time-scale. All the evidence, including radioactive dating of meteorites, supports the view that the Sun and its planets were formed some 4,500 million (4.5 $\times$ 10^9) years ago. The evidence from the most ancient sedimentary rocks –

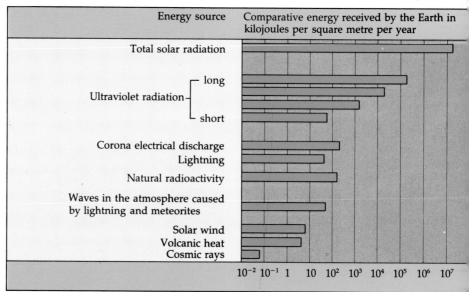

Energy source	Comparative energy received by the Earth in kilojoules per square metre per year
Total solar radiation	
Ultraviolet radiation — long	
Ultraviolet radiation — short	
Corona electrical discharge	
Lightning	
Natural radioactivity	
Waves in the atmosphere caused by lightning and meteorites	
Solar wind	
Volcanic heat	
Cosmic rays	

10^{-2} 10^{-1} 1 10 10^2 10^3 10^4 10^5 10^6 10^7

above A comparison between the amounts of energy received by the Earth from different sources shows that we receive almost 100 times more from the Sun than from any other source. Energy from these sources can be used in chemical reactions.

Lightning is a discharge of electricity in the atmosphere. It seems to have played a part in the formation of life on Earth.

above and right In an experiment carried out in the United States by Miller and Urey in 1953, water was boiled in an atmosphere of hydrogen, methane and ammonia. An electrical spark was passed through the gases, which were now saturated in water vapour. They were then cooled so that the water condensed. After a week, it was found that the liquid in the flask contained many chemicals, commonly found in living organisms.

ocks built up from sediments deposited by lakes, rivers and oceans - shows that many micro-organisms were present something like 3,300 million (33×10^8) years ago. This is how we get the figure of 1,200 million (12×10^8) years for the time it took complex molecules of living things to form. As, in a sense, this is a short time we must therefore ask what could have happened to bring life into being.

At the early stages in the history of the Earth it is more likely that there was very little 'free' oxygen in the atmosphere. This would have been an advantage, because the kind of chemicals from which the molecules of living material would have been constructed would have broken down if oxygen had been free to combine with them. Also without free oxygen, the Earth's atmosphere would have let through almost all the ultraviolet radiation from the Sun, and the energy of this radiation would have helped in building up more complex molecules.

For living substances to form from non-living material four requirements were necessary on the primitive Earth. First, substances such as amino-acids, sugars (page 176) and some other organic molecules, needed to form. Secondly, these materials had to become proteins and nucleic acids. Thirdly, isolated droplets would have had to occur in what has sometimes been called the 'primeval soup', the warm oceans in which we think the amino-acids, proteins and nucleic acids first appeared. Finally these droplets would have needed to contain basic living cells which, in the final stage, would have developed the RNA and DNA (page 178) that would have made it possible for them to reproduce. Once living cells had developed and living creatures had appeared, they would have used the energy in sunlight to split up the molecules of water (H_2O) and to capture carbon dioxide (CO_2) to make glucose ($C_6H_{12}O_6$). In doing so they would have released oxygen and so have changed the Earth's atmosphere to one with free oxygen as it is now, thus destroying the original conditions which had been suitable for their formation.

Really the most crucial question is whether the first stage could have occurred. In the conditions then prevailing could the amino-acids and other basic substances have been built up, and if so, how could this have happened? It has been suggested that ultraviolet energy from the Sun may have been responsible. Among other things this energy would have given rise to giant electrical storms in the atmosphere. Stanley Miller and Harold Urey, at Chicago University in the mid-1950s, built chemical apparatus in which they placed various gases such as hydrogen (H_2), methane (CH_4), ammonia (NH_3) and water vapour (H_2O) which would have been present in the early pre-life or 'prebiotic' stage of the Earth's atmosphere. By subjecting this mixture to artificial lightning flashes, they found that four of the 20 amino-acids usually found in proteins had been formed.

Since the original experiments of Miller and Urey much other experimental and theoretical work has been done. Far more is known about the molecules involved in the later stages of the development of living material and although no one can yet be certain, it does seem highly likely that life began on Earth simply because suitable substances were present in just the right environment.

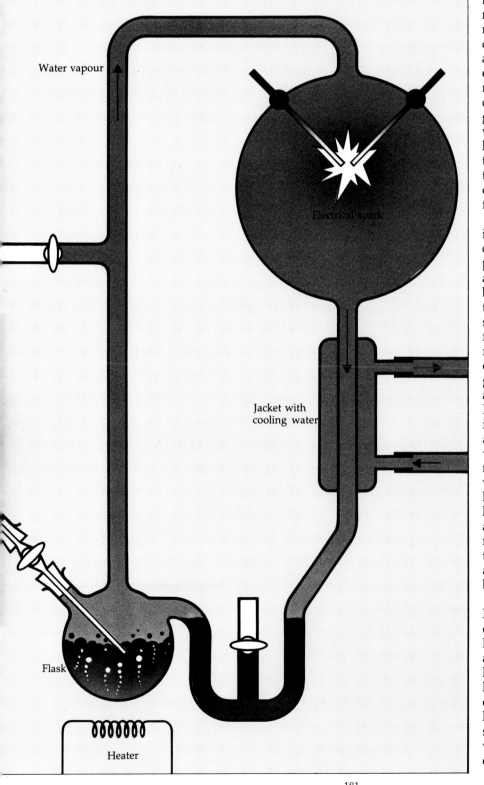

Water vapour

Electrical spark

Jacket with cooling water

Flask

Heater

LIFE IN OUR SOLAR SYSTEM

Is our Earth the only place in the Solar System where there is life? An examination of conditions on the other planets provides an answer.

Assuming that life began on Earth because conditions were suitable, we are bound to ask the question: 'Is there life on any other planet in the Solar System, or even on one of the larger planetary satellites?' We know, of course, that there is no life on the Moon; visits by astronauts have left no doubt on that point. But what about elsewhere? Are there planets which are unsuitable as possible places for life?

Let us start by being clear that we are considering life based on complex molecules with backbones of carbon. What are the requirements of true life-form? As far as can be seen, the presence of water is highly desirable, and possibly even vital. In addition, once life has formed, it needs to have some protection from intense ultraviolet radiation which means that the planet (or satellite) must have an atmosphere. With all this in mind we will consider each planet in turn, beginning with Mercury and moving outwards.

Mercury has virtually no atmosphere, no water and an average surface temperature of 167°C, more than half as hot again as boiling water. But this is an average temperature and under the noonday Sun it becomes much hotter than this because Mercury rotates very slowly. It takes 58.65 days to complete one revolution and therefore there is a large difference between the average and noonday temperature. For these reasons no one expects to find life on Mercury.

Venus was once thought to be a likely place for life of some kind to exist. It is very nearly the same size as the Earth, and about as massive. However, it is much nearer the Sun than we are – a little less than three-quarters of the distance – and therefore receives about twice as much sunlight. This alone would make it very much hotter, but the surface is entirely covered by cloud and this thick atmosphere captures the infrared radiation from the Sun and prevents it from being re-radiated out into space, so creating

an intense greenhouse effect'.

As American and Russian spacecraft have discovered, the surface temperature of the planet is 457°C, more than 2½ times hotter than Mercury. In addition, the atmospheric pressure on Venus is immense – it is 90 times greater than on Earth – and the composition of the atmosphere is very different. The Earth's atmosphere is mainly nitrogen (four-fifths) and oxygen (one-fifth) with some water vapour (one-sixtieth) and a little carbon dioxide (one part in 180). On Venus nitrogen accounts for only about one-thirtieth, and water vapour and oxygen together are found only in traces; 96% of the Venusian atmosphere is carbon dioxide. There are also large numbers of concentrated sulphuric acid droplets; indeed the atmosphere has between 1,000 and 8,000 times more sulphuric acid than the Earth's. The corrosive nature of Venus' atmosphere as well as the very high temperature and the extreme pressure, make it seem quite unsuitable for life. Mars, however, is a different proposition.

Mars is very much colder than the Earth; its surface temperature averages only −55°C, though it gets colder than this at night and much warmer during the day, when it can rise to as much as 50°C above its average temperature. All the same, the planet remains at all times below freezing. The pressure of the Martian atmosphere is low, no more than 0.7% of what we experience on Earth. Mars' atmosphere is mainly carbon dioxide (95%) but there is some oxygen, some water vapour and nitrogen, so in some ways it is more like the atmosphere of Venus than that of the Earth, but it is not

Conceivably life could exist in Jupiter's atmosphere although this may not be very likely. The photograph shows the upper atmosphere near 'Great Red Spot'.

corrosive. There is also some water in the form of ice as well as frozen carbon dioxide.

In spite of its low temperature, Mars has been thought of as a likely abode of life. Seasonal changes on its surface were often interpreted, wrongly as it happens, as evidence of vegetation. In 1976 an American Viking spacecraft landed on the planet to make tests of soil samples in an attempt to determine whether or not life was present. A test was made to see if the soil could take in and use carbon. This would indicate the presence of microscopic forms of life. The test first gave a 'yes' but subsequent tries did not. Then a 'soup,' suitable for supporting microscopic organisms and containing radioactive carbon, was prepared and injected with samples of Martian soil. If micro-organisms existed it was expected that they would 'drink' the soup and 'breathe out' carbon dioxide or carbon monoxide containing the radioactive carbon, which could be detected. In the experiment some carbon dioxide was emitted for a time but the result was thought more likely to stem from a chemical reaction with the soil than to be due to living organisms. In another experiment, the Martian soil, which is quite dry, was first made humid before being added to the soup. Immediately the soil was dampened oxygen was given off – a result not obtained from Earth soils – and when the soup was added, a little carbon dioxide was given off. But this experiment did not answer the question either. Again the carbon dioxide release could have been a chemical effect. So we are not sure about Mars. There could be life of some kind but equally well there could be none. Some biologists would like to test soil samples from the polar caps because water is present there, giving a better chance of finding life. Only a future landing will provide a definite answer.

As far as the much colder outer planets are concerned, these are mainly gaseous and the general opinion is that it is unlikely for there to be life on the solid cores of Jupiter or Saturn. Life floating in their frozen atmospheres does seem possible, though not very likely. But biologists are not certain about Saturn's satellite Titan. It has a methane atmosphere and could, just possibly, support some form of life, cold though it is with a surface temperature of something like −70°C. But only a future space probe can tell us if life really exists there.

above Titan as seen by Voyager 2. It has a diameter of 5,120 km and is the largest satellite orbiting Saturn. Titan has an atmosphere that is more than 90% nitrogen, with methane composing most of the remainder. The molecules formed in Titan's atmosphere maybe similar to those which were in the Earth's atmosphere just before life began.

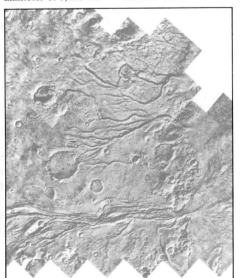

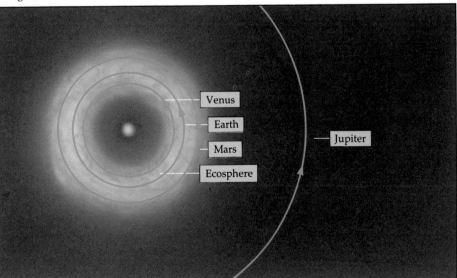

The water courses on Mars, which can be seen in this photograph taken by a Viking spacecraft, show that conditions may have been suitable for life.

Life as we know it on Earth could, in theory, survive in a belt extending from just inside the orbit of Venus to just outside the orbit of Mars. This band, known as the ecosphere, has a range of temperatures that can be tolerated by living organisms. However, evidence of life outside the Earth has so far not been discovered.

SEARCHING FOR LIFE ON OTHER PLANETARY SYSTEMS

In searching for other planets which might have life, we must first examine some suitable nearby stars which may give evidence of planetary systems.

It now seems likely that the Sun and its planetary system were formed at the same time. The planets came out of the 'solar nebula' each condensing from lumps which first formed a proto-planet (page 68). But for life to have formed on any of the planets two basic requirements had to be met. Firstly what resulted, the Solar System, had to be stable; the planets needed to orbit in paths that did not disturb one another, even over a long period of time. Secondly, the central star, the Sun, could not rotate too fast. If it did, it would probably burn up more quickly and would certainly throw off hot gaseous material; this would make it too hot and therefore likely to destroy complex molecules.

Yet when the Sun formed it would have rotated very quickly, as the gas forming it shrank from the proto-star stage down to that of a fully developed star. So it is clear something had to occur to slow the Sun down, and most astronomers are

of the opinion that the Sun passed on some of the energy of its rotation to the rest of the nebula. This explains why the planets orbit round the Sun; if the Sun had retained its high rotation rate then, in due course much, if not all, of the rest of the nebula would probably have fallen into it. But as things turned out, we have a stable planetary system instead.

The requirement of a stable system for the development of life means that we must rule out any planetary systems in orbit round binary or multiple stars. The changing forces operating in such systems would not give a stable result and the radiation received on any planet would vary very much so that no settled life-system could develop. If we are to look for other planetary systems where there is any

chance at all of life existing, we must look at single-star systems.

But what kind of single-star systems should we examine? Are all classes of star equally likely to have planets of the kind we need? A study of the rotations of stars shows that, as a general rule, hot bright stars rotate at a faster rate than cooler yellow and red stars. Because of our requirement that the star should have passed some of its rotational energy on to its planetary system, we should not, therefore, waste time looking at hot bright stars. Rather we should seek stars of classes G, K and M (page 74), though even here we should remember that such older stars may have lost some of their energy of rotation because it has been carried away by their stellar winds (page 70). And we should avoid red giant stars, because if they

The 61-cm refractor at the Sproul Observatory. Much of what we know about Barnard's star and its probable planetary system was discovered using this instrument.

had possessed planetary systems when they were younger, the stars would have by now expanded so much that they would have swallowed up some of their planets and ruined the steady conditions enjoyed by the others.

A last requirement of our survey is that the stars should not be too far away, otherwise we should have difficulty in obtaining evidence of their possessing planetary systems. So let us examine nearby stars, keeping to those which are fairly like our Sun because this will make it more likely that they will have planets suitable for life. G-type stars have a surface temperature about the same as the Sun's and are possibilities, though K-type stars and even some M-type are not too cool. However, it would probably be safer to confine ourselves to G and K, and

thus keep to a range of between 6000°K and 4000°K.

When we look for stars of the right temperature, we find there are seventeen within as short a distance as 4 parsecs (about 13 light-years), though most are multiple systems. For this reason, α Centauri, the nearest, is no use to us, but ε Eridani, at a distance of 3.3 parsecs, is a possibility, even though it is class K and some 1.8 times dimmer than the Sun. The star ε Indi, class K, some 2½ times dimmer still, is another possibility at 3.4 parsecs, so is τ Ceti, a G-type, at 3.7 parsecs, with a brightness about 2½ times less than the Sun. No actual planets have been observed for these stars yet, though the Space Telescope may provide the necessary evidence.

However, direct observation of planets is not necessary, even though

it may be desirable. There is another way of determining the existence of a planetary system orbiting round a star, and that is to determine whether or not the star is moving in a straight line through space. If it has a planetary system then it may appear to have a wobbly path because both the star and its planets will be orbiting round a common centre of mass. Some nearby stars do seem to show such a wobble, though the observations are not conclusive, except in one case, Barnard's star. This is an M-type star some 650 times less bright than the Sun lying at a distance of no more than 1.8 parsecs (5.9 light-years). Barnard's star has a large motion of its own, amounting to no less than 10.3 arc seconds per year, and has been studied carefully for something like 60 years. During this time it has been observed to wobble, that is, to swing regularly either side of its straight path by a few hundredths of an arc second. Very careful study shows that this wobble could be due to the presence of two orbiting planets, one with a period of 11½ years and of about the same size as Jupiter, and the other with a period of 20 to 25 years. This second, more-distant planet, could have a mass of about a half that of Jupiter's. What therefore is certain is that we are not observing a multiple-star system but a star being orbited by planetary bodies. Its discovery, of course, gives us great hope in the case of other wobbling stars and in the belief that there are plenty of other planetary systems.

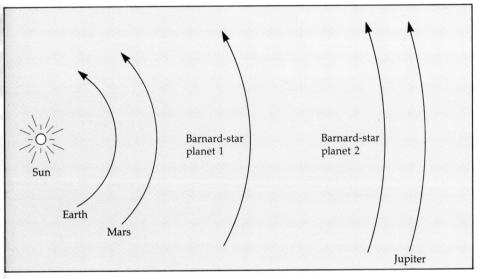

Sun

Earth

Mars

Barnard-star planet 1

Barnard-star planet 2

Jupiter

Observations of Barnard's star over a long period of time have shown that it wobbles from side to side in a predictable way (*right*). This movement is thought to be due to the presence of two large planets positioned in orbits (*above*), that in our Solar System, would lie between those of Mars and Jupiter. A similar wobble pattern has been observed in the movements of ε Eridani (*lower right*). The photographs (*left*), taken at the Lick Observatory, show the change in position of Barnard's Star over a 10-year period.

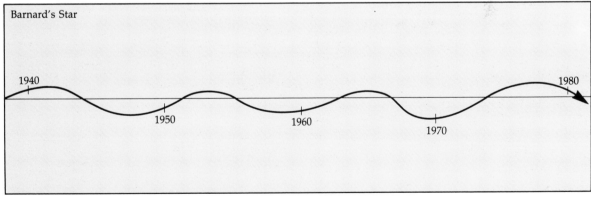

Barnard's Star

1940   1950   1960   1970   1980

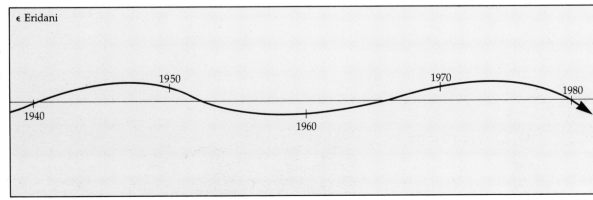

ε Eridani

1940   1950   1960   1970   1980

THE POSSIBILITY OF LIFE IN OUR GALAXY

Considering the nature of our Galaxy and the stars, dust and gas it contains, what chance is there that life lies somewhere else within it?

We have seen that even among a selected list of nearby stars there seem almost certainly to be some which possess planetary systems. Now let us look further afield, not confining ourselves to nearby stars but reaching out to the boundaries of our Galaxy. What are the chances that we shall find life somewhere else in this vast island of stars?

First of all, how many stars are there of the right type to have planetary systems? Our Galaxy is estimated to contain something like 100 thousand million (10^{11}) stars, but not all of these are suitable centres for planetary systems. As we have seen, binary or multiple stars are unsuitable as life-supporting systems, as are very hot bright stars, red giants and supergiants. No planetary system is likely to exist either round a neutron star or a white dwarf, let alone a black hole. How do our figures look if we exclude these?

Astronomers have made estimates of the stars of different kinds and different spectral classes in the Galaxy. Binaries and multiples account for about 70% of the total, but what about the rest? Of the remaining 3×10^{10} probably 15% are white dwarfs and something like 11% are very hot O-type and B-type Population I stars. It also seems likely that 41% are A-type to F-type, and so are rather too hot for our purpose, except possibly for some F-type stars. Nevertheless, this still leaves us with 33% or approximately 10×10^9 (10 thousand million) stars of classes G, K and M, of which the G-type and K-type stars would certainly be suitable. But since we can only make estimates, we should, for safety's sake, err on the side of caution; so let us say there are 10×10^9 suitable stars, and that this total includes also such F-type stars as may have planetary systems in which the outer planets might just support life.

Yet we still have to reduce our figure further because some of the stars we are counting will be giants and supergiants. Let us say that nearly one-third of the stars are of this type (though in doing so we are probably making an overestimate, because most stars seem to cluster round the main sequence of the H-R diagram (page 75) and so are normal size). We are then left with 6×10^9 stars which are likely to have planetary systems. This is still a very large number.

We now come to a stage when we must speculate, and our figures become still less reliable. But if we continue to be cautious, so as not to overestimate how many life-supporting planetary systems there may be, and out of our total of 6×10^9 select only the G types, then our

Part of the great Orion Nebula showing dark clouds of material. There is dust as well as gas here and we know that some of it is carrying complex organic molecules. Perhaps there is also living material on some of the dust grains, and possibly too, stars are being born in this area. It is conceivable that some of these stars may have planets which support life.

figures will not be too unreliable. We now find we are left with, say, 2.75 × 10⁹ or 2,750 million stars. Let us suppose only 75% of these have suitable planetary systems. We then have two thousand million (2×10^9) stars. In our own planetary system only one planet out of a total of nine has life for certain, so let us imagine some planetary systems will not have evolved life at all. Even if we take only one system in ten, that still leaves us with 200 million (2×10^8) stars with planetary systems which may well support life. So on this count alone it would seem likely that we are not alone; even if we reduce this figure by a hundred or even a thousand times it still means life could exist on planets orbiting 200,000 (2×10^5) stars.

Yet planets orbiting round suitable stars may not be the only places where life exists, though they would seem to be the only places where a civilization could develop. We have already seen (page 172) that in some gas and dust clouds, shielded from intense short wavelength radiation (gamma-rays and ultraviolet) and from high-speed nuclear particles (cosmic rays), there are some complex organic molecules. Is it possible, then, that on the dust grains in some of these clouds, protection has been sufficient for even more complex molecules to have been built up, due perhaps to clashes of static electricity generated between dust or gas particles? This is indeed possible, although present knowledge is not sufficient to allow us to be at all certain. Indeed one cannot really say how likely or unlikely it is that some simple life might be floating around in space. Of course, if such clouds are close to or become involved with the formation of a proto-star, which ultimately becomes an ordinary star, any living material would be in danger of being broken up once the star began to shine, unless it happened to lie at the very edge of the dust cloud in which the star forms.

There are parts of the Galaxy in which we would not expect to find life, either on planets or in interstellar dust clouds. Close to the centre of the Galaxy is one such place. If there is a black hole there, then the infalling material would radiate gamma-rays and X-rays strongly thus breaking down any complex molecules. Other active regions in the central bulge of the Galaxy would also seem to be unlikely places for life, again because of the energetic radiation emitted by material there.

There is, of course, the possibility that a few stars in globular clusters might conceivably be of the type to support planetary systems with life. However, most of these stars would be too old for this, and those near the centre of the cluster would be too close together for stable systems to develop. Yet more than 130 globular clusters are known, each containing at least a million old Population II stars, so there might just be life on some stars in them.

Our discussion, therefore, shows us that it is highly likely that there are other places in our Galaxy supporting life, as well as the Earth.

An artist's impression of possible life forms in the atmosphere of Jupiter as conceived by the science-fiction writer, Arthur C. Clarke. He envisages Medusas (giant jellyfish-like creatures) floating in the thick atmosphere. They are here seen defending themselves against attacks from Mantas (more mobile creatures) with A Persid electricity, as certain eels do on Earth today.

LIFE ELSEWHERE IN THE UNIVERSE

As there is life in our Galaxy there is a high chance that it also exists in other galaxies. Some of this life may also have reached the stage of an advanced civilization.

So far we have found that it seems very likely – some astronomers would say almost certain – that there is life elsewhere in our Galaxy. But our Galaxy is only one of many thousands of millions, so, obviously, the chances that there are stars with suitable planets throughout the universe is high. Of course, just as there are many stars in our own Galaxy that are not suitable for life, there are probably some galaxies that are unsuitable too.

The chances of life existing for a long time in active explosive galaxies and on galaxies which have collided with each other must be low. However, galaxies are large, and there could just be a few stars with planets supporting life on even the most active galaxy. It also seems unlikely that QSOs, if they are the centres of galaxies at an early stage of their lives, will have any life-supporting stars. They are probably too young and the intense radiation generated in them too strong to allow the complex molecules of living things to develop. Yet even if we again take a very cautious approach, we should still expect to find the number of galaxies with stars having planetary systems which support life to be high and to number millions, or perhaps even hundreds of millions.

Life may well be universal. Our universe may have living material in abundance in the majority of its galaxies, but what form would such life take? Is it merely to be found as simple uncomplicated creatures such as viruses or micro-organisms or has

it developed into a wide variety of animals? And have any other life-supporting planets evolved perhaps quite different life-forms which are nevertheless intelligent? If they have, what form does this intelligence take? Again somewhere deep in space may there perhaps be civilizations which have developed highly technological societies such as we have now on Earth? Is it possible, even, that such

civilizations could have come and gone? For how long can a civilization last and how soon will it become technically able to communicate across the depths of space, or explore with spacecraft? Would it want to do this? It might be that the cost could be too high or that it would have no wish at all to make its existence known. These are difficult questions to answer, but we must try to do so

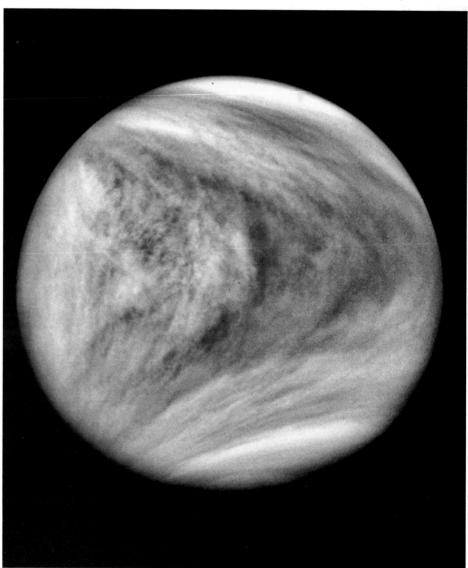

above Venus as observed by the Pioneer Venus orbiter in 1979. The cloud cover, seen here in ultraviolet light, is thick and allows no views of the surface. The orbiter did, however, chart the surface by bouncing radar signals off it. It may be that there was once life on Venus – before it became so hot – and it could be an abode of life in the future. There may be many planets like Venus orbiting stars in space. *below, left and right* A panorama of the surface of Venus, transmitted by the descent module of a Russian spacecraft in March 1982.

if we are to come to any conclusion about the existence of civilized life anywhere else in space.

To begin with let us look at the evolution of life on Earth. As we have seen, Greenland fossils indicate that it probably began as far back as 3,300 million years ago. Yet at that stage, the only living things were micro-organisms, tiny plant-like organisms known as algae, some consisting of no more than one living cell. These were the most primitive forms of life, and gradually more complex life evolved. First there were creatures which could exchange genetic material (DNA); the primitive blue-green algae could not do this but some bacteria could. The next stage was for egg cells and sperm, or fertilizing cells, to form and, after this, came creatures whose bodies were composed of many cells. Changes or 'mutations' in the DNA and the exchange of genetic DNA between parents and offspring gave rise to variety among these creatures and so to a gradual evolution, whereby those best suited to their surroundings prospered.

It is thought that life first began in the primeval 'soup' (page 181) and then developed in the oceans for something like 2,500 million (25 × 10⁸) years before moving out of the sea to colonize the land, 500 million (5 × 10⁸) years ago. For a very long period – from 225 million to 65 million (225 to 65 × 10⁶) years ago, a total of 160 million years – the chief land animals were the dinosaurs. These creatures were reptiles with scaly or horny bodies and some had small front paws rather like hands. It is possible that they might have developed into intelligent animals. Yet 65 million years ago the dinosaurs disappeared, along with a large number of other creatures. Some reptiles survived, it is true, and such mammals as there were remained to evolve further, but the dinosaurs went. What catastrophe caused their disappearance is unknown, though various suggestions have been made. Some scientists believe that it may have been due to a marked rise in temperature, or some lethal epidemic, or even the possibility that the early mammals ate their eggs. On the other hand we know that their disappearance happened at the same time as a period of mountain formation on Earth. The dinosaurs lived on the lowlands and as the mountain chains formed so the lowland areas would have become smaller, and at this same time the climate changed too. Resulting changes in the vegetation may have caused the plant-eating dinosaurs to starve and consequently the flesh-eating dinosaurs which preyed on them also perished.

There is also a possible astronomical explanation for the extinction of the dinosaurs. This

above An eruption of the Prometheus volcano on Jupiter's satellite Io, as photographed by Voyager 1. Because of the low surface gravity on Io (about ¹/₆ of that on Earth), and the speed with which the material is ejected (6 to 10 times that on Earth), it forms a plume. All Jupiter's satellites show different characteristics and emphasize the wide range of conditions there must be on planets and satellites in the universe and the variety of potentially life-supporting bodies there must be throughout space.

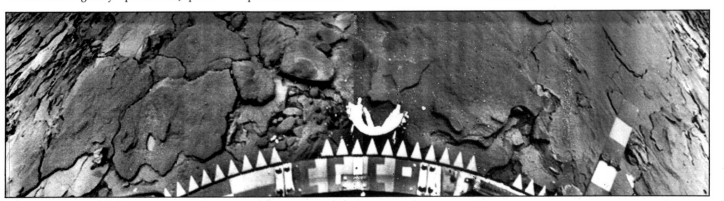

189

supposes that there was a supernova explosion close to the Solar System, within some 3 to 6 parsecs. The explosion would have shot cosmic-ray particles into the Earth's atmosphere, causing some of the free nitrogen in the air to combine with oxygen. As a consequence, the ozone layer in the atmosphere would have disappeared, allowing strong ultraviolet radiation to penetrate to the ground, killing many plants and animals, as well as causing genetic (DNA) changes. These changes would have led not only to the development of new species but also to the loss of many on which the dinosaurs fed. Yet whatever the cause may have been, the age of the dinosaur was over and mammals were able to develop more freely. Even so it was to be another 45 million years before man's immediate tree-living ancestors appeared and not until 17 million years after that did truly man-like creatures – the australopithecines – appear. Although they had small ape-like brains they were able to use simple tools and lived in small groups. There were probably never many of them; perhaps around 125,000 as late as a million years ago.

Human evolution continued, yet not until as comparatively recently as 8,000 years ago did man build his first villages. The fine and elaborate civilizations of Egypt and Mesopotamia arose round the Mediterranean about 4,000 years ago, and only in the last 30 years has Man been technically advanced enough to be able to send messages to any civilization beyond the Earth. With all this in mind we can see that although there has been living material on the Earth for 3,300 million years, no observer from elsewhere in space would have been able to communicate with it until almost the present day. In fact, mankind has had a civilization as elaborate as those which grew up around the Mediterranean for only one millionth of the time life has been here, and there has only been a technically advanced civilization for a tiny fraction of that time. So if there have been advanced civilizations in our Galaxy observing us in the past, they would not have been able to receive messages back. Until fifty years ago no radio response could have been made and if the civilizations had existed millions of years ago, all they would have found was a world occupied by dinosaurs. Of course, such a civilization would find a very different situation now,

but would such a civilization still be in existence?

How long does a civilization last? We cannot answer this question with any certainty. The wonderful ancient Egyptian civilization lasted for only some 3,000 years, but the Chinese civilization, which has already been in existence 4,000 years, still continues. It is possible that with such an advanced civilization as the world now has, it could destroy itself with a nuclear war, and this might apply to any other advanced civilization elsewhere in the universe. But if it did not do so, is there any need to have an upper limit?

It seems highly unlikely that an advanced civilization could continue indefinitely. For instance, there is always the danger that a population would get too large for its planet to support it; emigration to other suitable planets, if they can be found, is a possible escape from this problem. The original civilization would disappear but the newly emigrated civilization could, of course, continue. If, though, the universe does come to an end (page 164) then it will also see the end of all civilizations, wherever they may be. With these different possibilities in mind, some scientists, who have studied the question, give one million years as the average lifetime for a civilization. As the universe is some 18 to 20 thousand million years old, and since our Galaxy and presumably others were formed something like 14 thousand million years ago, there may well have been

The 'open' (Sc-type) spiral galaxy NGC 2997, lying in the southern constellation of Antila, photographed with the 3.9-m Anglo-Australian telescope.

some advanced civilizations in our Galaxy or in some other galaxies in the past. All we can say is that there seem to be no civilizations communicating with us at the present time.

Perhaps there are some civilizations, not ancient but rather like our own, now entering an advanced stage which makes interstellar communication feasible. If there are, can we form any idea of how many? We have seen (page 187) that it is possible that there are at least 200,000 suitable stars in our own Galaxy which might support life. But how can we calculate how many could have advanced civilizations? The American astronomer Frank Drake has devised a formula which gives a figure for the number of civilizations likely to be in existence at any particular time. It takes into account the rate at which suitable stars are formed in our Galaxy, the number of life-supporting planets, where intelligent life develops, the fraction where technology is advanced enough to have developed radio astronomy and so be able to communicate across space, and lastly a factor based on how long any advanced civilization is likely to last. By multiplying these factors together he estimates that one new advanced civilization arises in our Galaxy every 1000 years. With a lifetime of no more than one million years for an advanced civilization, it still means that there are a thousand such civilizations in our Galaxy at the present time. On the other hand if we are pessimistic and think that such a civilization will only last for 100 years before it blows itself to pieces, then the figure alters appreciably, and we become the only civilization of its kind in existence. A more reasonable estimate, however, gives the total number of advanced civilizations in our Galaxy as 150.

Even if our Galaxy has only one advanced civilization, that is ours, then we should reasonably expect this to be the case in many other spiral galaxies. But since it is more likely that there are 150 or let us say more than one hundred such civilizations in our Galaxy alone, the number in the whole universe must, surely, be counted in millions. So it is clear to almost all astronomers that our civilization is not alone, and that there must be others elsewhere in our own Galaxy, as well as on other galaxies which, like ourselves, are probing deep space to discover more about the universe and, perhaps, trying to communicate with us.

A painting of what it might be like to look up at the night sky from a planet orbiting a star that is an outlying member of a globular cluster. The artist has shown life forms on the planet. Some of the strange plants depicted show a resemblance to our earthly mare's tail and to primitive forest plants similar to those of the 'Carboniferous' forests found on Earth some 300 million years ago. Also shown are ruins left by some advanced civilization that now exists no more.

COMMUNICATING WITH OTHER FORMS OF LIFE

With the probability of other civilizations in our Galaxy, communicating by radio and even by spacecraft is possible. The problem is to make ourselves understood.

If there are advanced civilizations besides our own, and it seems highly likely that there are, it is only natural that we should try to communicate with them, and to watch for any signal from them. There are two basic ways of communicating. One is to send messages out in a spacecraft, even in an unmanned one; the other is to send out radio messages and to listen for any radio messages that may be beamed to us.

Spacecraft do not present many opportunities as message carriers at the present time, because most are put in orbit round the Earth or round the Sun. However, the interplanetary probes such as the Pioneers and Voyagers, which have gone out beyond Jupiter, could act as possible couriers to other technologically advanced civilizations. After close encounters with Jupiter or with Uranus or Neptune, they go away into deep space, escaping from the Solar System entirely. Of course, any message they might carry would only be received by a civilization that is advanced enough in space technology not only to undertake interstellar flight itself, but also to detect other spacecraft in flight and to recapture them. But these are not impossible or even improbable requirements; we could reasonably expect such a civilization to be able to do this.

Indeed, the whole thing seems so much within the realms of possibility that the Pioneer 10 spacecraft, which was launched towards Jupiter by the Americans in March 1972, is being used also as a message carrier. After passing close to Jupiter in December 1972 it was accelerated until it reached 11.3 km per second (7 miles per second) and escaped into deep space. The route it is to take will not carry it to the nearest star (α Centauri) but in a direction lying between the Orion and Taurus constellations, because in

above left and right Project Cyclops involves building an array of 1,000 radio-telescopes which will be used to search the universe for the existence of an advanced civilization. The large number of telescopes will have the sensitivity of one

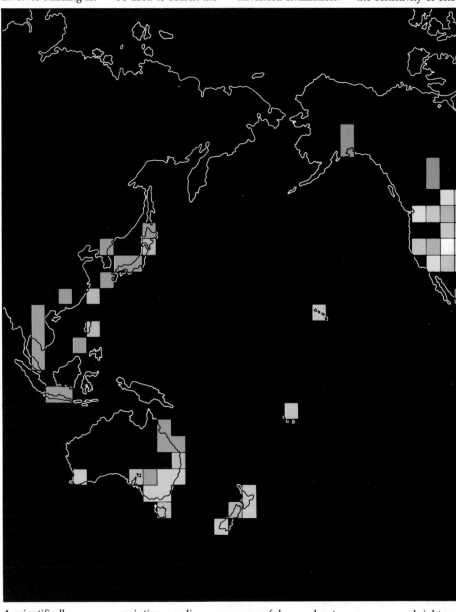

A scientifically advanced civilization pointing a radio-telescope, if it were powerful enough, at the Earth would see some areas brighter than others. This

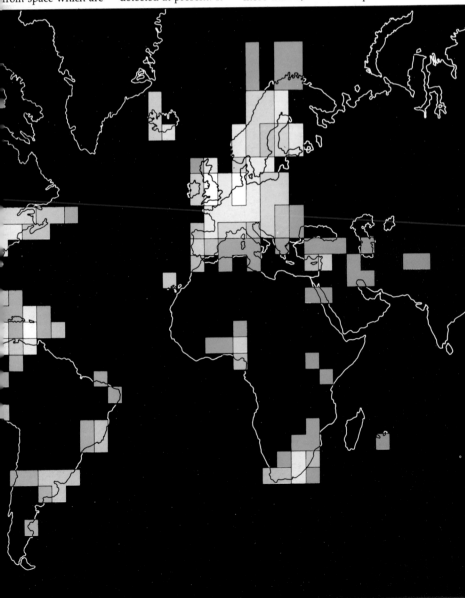

very big disk and will pick up radio signals from space which are far fainter than anything that can be detected at present. It is estimated that Cyclops would cost more than 5,000 million dollars to construct at today's prices.

difference is caused by radio brightness due to transmission of signals from VHF – television and FM – radio stations.

that part of space there seem to be no nearby objects in its path. Consequently it should be more readily detectable by astronomers working in another civilization. However as its velocity is low, a factor that should make its capture easier, the spacecraft will take a very long time on its journey through space, and it is unlikely to reach another civilization for ages. After all it would have taken almost 110,000 years to reach Barnard's star, 1.3 parsecs or 5.9 light-years away, had it been sent off in that direction.

Pioneer 11, another Solar System spacecraft, launched less than a year after Pioneer 10 to make a close approach to Saturn, is also acting as a courier. The spacecrafts Voyager 1 and Voyager 2 also carry messages but in a different form from the Pioneers in the hope of giving further details about our Earth civilization.

Sending messages by spacecraft is a rather primitive way of trying to communicate and it is a one-way system. We shall never know whether another advanced civilization manages to capture one or more of the craft, or whether they are able to read the messages carried by them. It is conceivable that our successors, thousands of generations later, might learn of the event, but by then they will probably have taken more advanced steps to communicate themselves and be using new techniques of space travel.

Another method of getting in touch with other civilizations involves using radio-telescopes to send out radio messages of our own or to listen for incoming signals. As we shall see shortly, quite elaborate messages can be sent and we, for our part, should be prepared to keep an open mind about the possibility of receiving messages ourselves. Any one of the many designs of radio-telescope at present in operation for astronomical research can be used, though some special designs have been produced, none have yet been built. One such scheme is known as 'Cyclops'; it would form a vast circular area, some 10 kilometres in diameter, filled with more than 1,000 separate radio-telescopes, each with a dish 100 metres in diameter. Such an array of separate radio dishes would be equivalent to a single dish 10 km in diameter, and therefore the whole instrument would be extremely sensitive. The project is named after the legendary one-eyed giants of ancient Greece but would look more like a gigantic multi-lensed insect eye than a human one. However, the cost of the project would be very high, at least 5,000 million dollars. Although the instrument could be used for ordinary astronomical research when not being employed to listen for extra-terrestrial messages, there seems no likelihood of it being built by the United States government. Of course, project Cyclops, expensive though it would be, would not cost more than many space projects. However, no government yet seems convinced that communicating with another civilization is important enough to warrant spending so much public money.

Yet a number of attempts have been made to communicate with other civilizations. As long ago as 1960, Frank Drake used a radio-telescope at the National Radio Astronomy Observatory at Greenbank, West Virginia, to listen for signals from two nearby stars. Though he spent a total of 200 hours observing time on the project, he did not receive any messages. This did not necessarily mean that there were no messages to receive; he might have been unsuccessful because of the lack of sensitivity of the equipment he was using, or perhaps the stars he was observing were unsuitable. Since 1973 the project, originally called 'Ozama' after the princess in Frank Baum's story *The Land of Oz*, has been extended. A set of observations has now been made of 500 stars which seem possibly to be centres of planetary systems where life could exist. In this new study, Ozama II, the radio-telescope records are searched by computer for any sign of special signals. None has so far been found.

How seriously astronomers take the possibility of receiving messages from an extra-terrestrial civilization is shown by a discovery made at Cambridge University, England, in 1967. Studies were being made of radio sources in space to see whether or not they 'twinkled'. Twinkling is typical of a source that covers only a very tiny area of the sky. As the various sources were being checked it was discovered that one was emitting pulses at an unusually regular rate, the interval between one pulse and the next being precisely 1.33730 seconds. Once it became certain that the pulses did not come from a man-made source on Earth, it was seriously considered whether, at last, an extra-terrestrial message was being received. The discovery was treated with great secrecy because it was feared that any rumour might

start an undesirable and exaggerated press campaign before the astronomers were certain of their facts. The investigation was therefore code-named LGM (Little Green Men). It was just as well that the Cambridge astronomers were cautious because the source was discovered not to be the only one pulsing regularly and the signal was found not to contain a message. What the astronomers Jocelyn Bell and Tony Hewish had discovered were pulsing neutron stars or pulsars (page 79), not sources of extra-terrestrial intelligence.

The lack of success experienced both by projects in the United States and in the Soviet Union at the present time in receiving messages does not mean that we can turn round and say that there are none. Our receivers may not be sensitive enough and other civilizations may be very far distant, perhaps on the far side of the central bulge of our Galaxy. We must just keep an open mind and examine every radio signal in case it contains some message which we should recognize because of its regular but obviously artificial pattern. For if advanced civilizations are going to communicate with one another, it is no good sending words in any particular spoken language; instead something in the form of a message that a computer can decode will be most likely to have success.

```
00000010101010000000000001010000001010
00000100100010001000100010101100101010101
01010101010010010010000000000000000000
0000000000000011000000000000000000000
11010000000000000000011010000000000000
0000000101010000000000000000001111110
0000000000000000000000000000000001100000
11100011000011000100000000000001111010
00011010001000110000110101111101111111
0111110111110000000000000000000000000000
01000000000000000010000000000000000000
0000000000001000000000000000011111100
00000000000111100000000000000000000000
0011000011000011100010001000000000000
000001000011010000110001110011010111
110111111011111101111100000000000000000
0000000001000000011000000010000000000
1111110000011000000011110000000000110
00000000000000010000010000000010000001
0000000110000001000001100001100000000
1000000000011100010001100100000000000
0110011000000000001100100010011000000
0000100001100010000000100000001000100
00001000001000000011000000001000100000
0000010000001000010000000001000000000
10000010000000010000000010000001000000
0000001100000000000110000000011000000000
0100011101011000000000010000010000000
0000000001000011110000000000000001000
0101110100101101100000100111001001111
1110110001110000011011100000000000010
1000001110110010000000010000001111110
10000010101000011000001000001101100000
000000000000000000000000000000001111000
00010000000000001110101000010101010101
010011100000010101010000000000000000
00100000000000001111100000000000000
0001111111110000000001100000000011100000
00000001100000011000110000000011001100
00000010110000110011000000011001100
001000010100001010001000100100100001
0010001000000100010100010000000000000
0100001000010000000001000000000010100
00000000010010100000000000000011110011
11101001111000
```

left and right
This radio message was beamed from the Arecibo radio-telescope to the globular cluster M13 in 1975. It gave some details of the biochemistry of life on Earth (A), the Earth's population, and the size and shape of human beings (B). The height of a man and the diameter of the transmitting telescope (C) were given in units of the wavelength used to transmit the message. The message was transmitted in binary code. The code (*left*) can be broken by dividing the message into groups of 23 characters and ranging them one below the other. The result (*right*) can be had by making each zero a white square and each number one a black square.

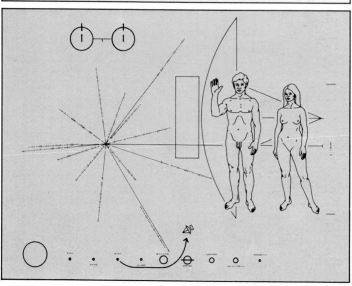

left
The plaque carried by Pioneer 10 indicates what planet the spacecraft came from (*bottom*), when it was launched and the human form in relation to Pioneer itself. The symbols (*top*) give details of the spin of electrons in neutral hydrogen atoms. The radiating lines give frequencies, in binary form of 14 pulsars at the time of launch. The difference in the frequencies when the spacecraft is intercepted will tell when the message was written.

Of course, we do not know what form of computers another technological civilization might have developed, but we can be reasonably certain that they will not only possess such devices, but also that they will use some form of on-off, or 'binary', switching. It is only in this way that devices can be built which will process information quickly and efficiently.

Binary coding is not difficult to understand; it is merely another way of counting and one which ideally fits the on-off switching of computer chips. To see how it works let us take a simple count from zero to ten in the usual decimal system and see how each number is represented in binary. Zero is 0 and 1 is 1 in both systems; it is after this that they differ. The next number, 2 in the decimal system, is 10 in the binary. This is because we change position every two numbers instead of every ten. The decimal number 3 becomes 11 in binary, i.e. 1 in the 'two place' and 1 in the 'one-zero place'. Then 4 is 100 in binary, because we have moved another place to the left again: 5 is 101; 6 becomes 110 and 7 becomes 111; 8 is 1000; 9 is 1001 and 10 is 1010. Of course, for us to do our everyday calculations in this way would be needlessly complicated, but not so if our brains were pocket calculators or computers, because the only things they can recognize are 'on' and 'off'. Zero is 'off', 1 is 'on'; 2 is 'on, off' (10) and 3 is 'on, on' (11). You can follow through the rest yourself up to 10 which is 'on, off, on, off' (1010).

When we use a pocket calculator or a computer for calculating we enter numbers in the decimal system and they are then automatically changed into the binary system. The calculations are all done in binary form, and then converted back into the decimal system for display. But alternatively we could keep to the binary system and present the message as a picture. In fact this is just what a computer does when it produces 'graphics'. It plots graphs or draws pictures which look continuous to us when they are displayed on a screen, but like television pictures, which are made up of lines, these images are made of 'dots', which are electrical 'ons' or 'offs'. So we could send picture-messages to other civilizations using a binary code which we should expect any technically advanced civilization to understand.

In 1974 the giant 305-m (1,000-ft) diameter radio-telescope at Arecibo in Puerto Rico was used to beam a binary picture-message to the globular cluster M13 in Hercules, because it was felt that among its 300,000 stars there might be some which had advanced civilizations. The message, which contained 1,679 consecutive on-offs arranged in groups, gave pictures of a DNA helix, a human being, the Arecibo telescope as well as some atomic details and a map of the Solar System. It will, however, take 24,000 years to reach the cluster.

Similar information has been included on the plaque attached to the radio-antenna supports of the Pioneer 10 and 11 spacecrafts. The plaque, measuring 23 × 15 cm, is made of aluminium and is gold-plated to give it a very long-lasting surface. This too carries binary numbers and a plan of the Solar System, as well as a drawing of a man and a woman and the path of the Pioneer probes. It also carries two drawings of a neutral hydrogen atom, the commonest element in the universe, showing the changing spin of its single electron. The Voyager craft, on the other hand, carry a gramophone disc with playing stylus and instructions for use; the disc contains speech and music. So mankind is certainly trying to communicate with other civilizations, and is still waiting to see if they are perhaps doing the same.

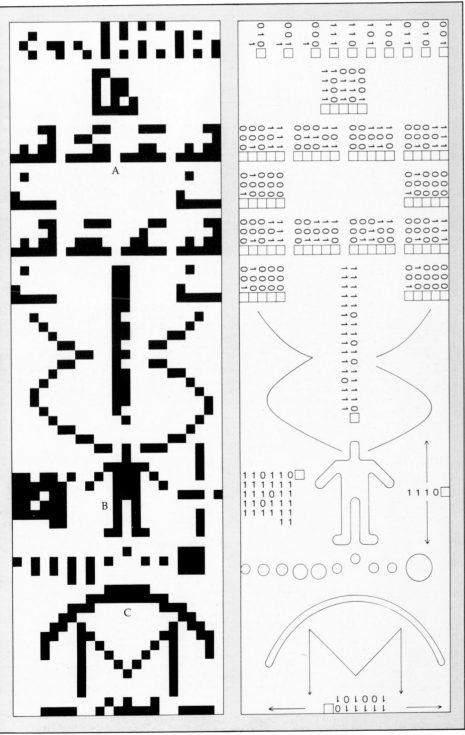

THE END OF LIFE IN OUR SOLAR SYSTEM

Life in our Solar System depends on the Sun maintaining its present size and output of radiation. Any change could be disastrous.

Life on Earth, and life on any other planet in the Solar System – if there is any – has evolved under certain conditions. There are limits to the extremes of temperature, and the amount of short-wave radiation that life can tolerate. Go outside these extremes and many species of animals and plants will die; go too far and life will be destroyed altogether.

Some changes can be accepted; as the history of the Earth shows, our planet has undergone some very striking changes in climate. For example, there have been periods when ice sheets have covered large areas of land; between 570 million and 3 million years ago there were seven or eight ice ages, most occuring either at the beginning or at the end of this period, and also at about 280 million years ago. Also there are places which are now cold or temperate, northern Europe and northern China, for example, that were once hot and semi-tropical. But change within these limits has not destroyed life. It has meant only that some creatures died and others migrated to more suitable surroundings.

This is also true of another change, the gradual lengthening of the day due to the tide-raising power of the Moon dragging on the Earth. Back in Cambrian times, between 570 and 500 million years ago, fossil evidence has shown that the day was only 20.6 hours long. But this is not far enough from our present 24 hours to cause any very great change for living things. Again, though it seems that the ice caps at the north and south poles are shrinking with a consequent rise in the general level of the oceans, this will only cause flooding over part of the land as is happening in some parts of East Anglia in England. Not unless, or until, the caps shrink much further will there by any important changes of climate, and these should not cause an end to life on Earth, but

only shifts of population, both human and animal, and changes in vegetation.

Changes in climate have also occurred on other planets. Mars seems to have had water over its entire surface once upon a time. Evidence from many land formations shows where water flowed on the planet ages ago, and even what seems to be a dried up river bed has been observed. The water probably came from an ice layer melted in the heat of volcanic eruptions. But

because of the lower pressure of the Martian atmosphere, carbon dioxide did not have much of a greenhouse effect (page 182) and so heat was lost. The very cool conditions and extremely low pressure caused the water to evaporate. What water there is now is frozen at the north polar cap; the south pole is mainly composed of frozen carbon dioxide. The Earth is larger than Mars so it has retained more gases and the pressure of its atmosphere is high. Water remains and the balance of

above An impression of what it might be like on Earth when the Sun begins to reach the red giant stage and starts to expand. The increasing heat would cause oceans to evaporate and, as the water level dropped, so new islands would appear in the misty sunlight. Gradually the heat would dry out the land and life would cease.

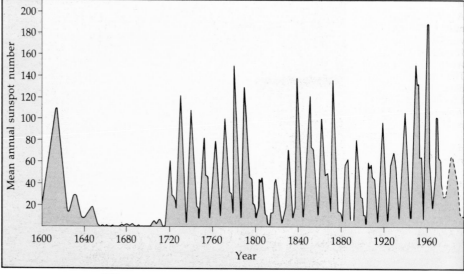

196

gases is helped by the recycling of carbon dioxide, aided by plants. As a result we have a controlled greenhouse effect, and it does not look as though we shall lose our water as Mars has.

Venus is nearer to the Sun than the Earth and is therefore hotter. If the Earth was as near to the Sun as Venus, the Earth too would get very hot because of the greenhouse effect which would be made still greater by the presence of water vapour. It has been suggested that if the Sun were

cooler in the past than it is now, there might have been a time when life could have developed on Venus, only to become extinct later.

This brings us to the question of how stable the Sun is thought to be. We think of it as radiating energy at a constant rate, but is this quite true? Certainly the Sun's total radiation, including the particles it emits as the 'solar wind' (page 70), does vary slightly. We see this variation in the 11-year sunspot cycle, where maximum numbers of sunspots

appear every 11 years or so. However, recent research has shown astronomers that between 1645 and 1715 there was hardly any sunspot activity at all. This 70-year period, often called the 'Maunder minimum' after the British astronomer Edward Maunder who spent his life studying the behaviour of sunspots, is something of a mystery and has not been completely explained. Its effect was, it seems, to cause some slight climatic change throughout the world. Europe suffered very acute winters and the period has even been called the 'Little Ice Age'. The southwest of the United States, on the other hand, experienced drought.

Other recent research appears to show that there may be another change on the way. The Sun does not seem to be emitting as many neutrinos as it should. Nuclear processes in the central regions of the Sun generate neutrino particles – which have no electric charge (hence their name) and weigh nothing, but can react with certain atoms.

In an attempt to detect the rate at which the Sun is emitting neutrinos, vast tanks of perchloroethylene, a substance which reacts with neutrinos, have been built deep underground where they are shielded from all other forms of radiation. The amount of the Sun's radiation leads astronomers to expect a certain number of neutrinos. However, observations have shown far fewer than expected. This could be due to errors in our understanding of what really goes on in the centre of the Sun, or of the rate at which neutrinos combine with molecules of perchloroethylene. But it could be due to a change in the Sun's radiation, the effects of which we have yet to experience. However, no one would expect this to be serious enough to wipe out life although some astronomers believe, that the Sun's radiation is gradually increasing.

Life will only be destroyed on Earth when, in thousands of millions of years, the Sun leaves the main sequence and, with its hydrogen turned to helium ash, expands into a red giant star. Then Mercury will be swallowed up inside the Sun, whose diameter will certainly extend out beyond that orbit. This will signal the end of all life in the Solar System. Any life on planets, swallowed up by the Sun, will be destroyed and any life on planets out as far as Jupiter and beyond will freeze to death as the Sun eventually shrinks to a white dwarf.

above As the Sun continued to expand it would appear ever larger in the sky. Its heat would have completely evaporated the oceans and seas, and would eventually be sufficient to heat the surface rocks so that they became soft and pliable, some, perhaps, even becoming molten. No life would now exist on land or in the sea.

left
A graph of the number of sunspots visible each year from 1645 to 1974 shows well the 11-year cycle. The almost complete dearth from 1645 to 1715, known as the 'Maunder Minimum', is still a mystery.

right
When the Sun becomes a red giant, its diameter will be so great that it will probably exceed 130 million km and stretch out nearly as far as the Earth's orbit.

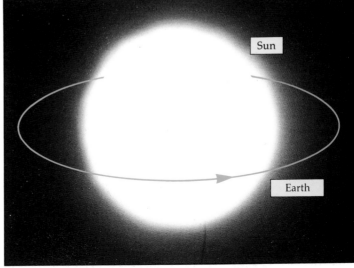

MUST ALL LIFE END?

Life has evolved into advanced civilizations as our universe itself has evolved. But one day the universe will stop developing. Will that mean the end of all forms of life?

It is highly likely that our universe contains other civilizations with advanced technology like our own, or even in a more highly developed state. Yet astronomers do not think that these will last indefinitely. They may destroy themselves with nuclear weapons, for example, or conditions on the planet on which they live may change and become unsuitable for life. We have already seen that planetary conditions can change greatly (page 196) perhaps Venus, and certainly Mars, has altered since they were formed out of the solar nebula (page 68). And on Earth itself the disappearance of the dinosaurs also seems possibly to have been due to some change in conditions, caused perhaps by a supernova explosion not too far away in space. Finally, there is bound to come a time when the parent star of an orbiting planet will become so old that it moves out of the main sequence and begins to expand to become a red giant or even a supergiant. When this happens conditions are bound to change on the planetary system it supports and any advanced civilization would find it hard if not impossible to survive without moving elsewhere in space.

Less highly developed forms of life might well be able to exist on some planets during a star's giant phase. Not, of course, on any planet which is swallowed up by an expanding star, but on those which are far enough out still to exist, and orbit as separate bodies. Of course, it might even be possible during this red giant stage for life to begin on a planet which has previously been too cold for this to have happened before. But such new life would be able to evolve for only a comparatively short time, because no star remains in the red giant phase for anything like the length of time it does in the main sequence, perhaps no more than 1,000 million years at the most. So we should not expect to find an advanced civilization developing.

In due course a star will once again shrink to become either a white dwarf, or, if it is very large, a neutron star or even a black hole. However stars supporting life-bearing planets will probably be rather like our Sun and shrink only to the white dwarf stage. When they do so, their size and output of radiation will have dropped so that they will no longer be able to provide enough energy to support life on any planets still orbiting round them. In brief, every star with a planetary system, on which there is life will one day reach a stage when it can no longer support that life.

We know of the existence of many white dwarfs, and it seems quite possible that some of these may once have been stars with planetary

Dark nebulous material and dust near ρ Ophiuchi. Here some dust grains could just conceivably be carrying actual living material of a simple kind. Yet when the hot stars here cool, and everything becomes dark, even living cells will be frozen before, one day, being ultimately swallowed into a black hole.

systems on which there was some form of life. Some, perhaps, may have once supported a technically advanced civilization. But life has now ceased, as far as these systems are concerned, though this has not meant that life in the universe has ceased. Not only is there life here on Earth but we believe it is highly likely that there is life in other parts of our Galaxy and on other galaxies. Life continues to evolve. What is more, we observe that new stars are still forming in our Galaxy and have every reason to believe this is happening in other galaxies. So new life may be evolving all over the universe. Yet one day this influx of new life will cease.

There will come a time in the distant future when the free gas in our Galaxy has all been gathered into stars. This stage was reached long ago in most elliptical galaxies, and globular clusters are in just the same stage of development. When a spiral galaxy reaches this state, life in that galaxy is finally doomed to extinction. With no new stars forming and the planetary systems supporting life being extinguished one by one as the parent stars near the ends of their lives, all life in the galaxy eventually ceases. Furthermore, we live in a universe in which few if any new galaxies seem to be forming, so there seems no chance that when life is extinguished in one galaxy, there is another new galaxy to take over.

What can a civilization do when faced with the extinction of life in a galaxy? We can conceive that, just possibly, some very advanced civilization, whose technology has progressed much further than our own, might manage to undertake inter-galactic travel, though the vast time-scale involved – millions of years, even travelling just below the speed of light – seems to present an immensely difficult barrier. As one galaxy becomes too old to support life any longer, another, at an earlier stage of development, might just conceivably provide a refuge for such a civilization. But this would only be for a time, because no galaxy will last for ever. One day its stars will die and when all have gone through a white dwarf, or still denser stage, then gravity will take over and it seems that the final result will be a gigantic black hole.

An additional fact is that as expansion continues, so the galaxies will all move further apart. The idea of inter-galactic travel will become increasingly unlikely. There seems, then, to be no escape from the view that all life in the universe will ultimately cease, its remains swallowed up in giant black holes. Of course if the universe does not go on expanding for ever, but does change its expansion into a contraction, then we have an oscillating universe. Once the universe begins to expand again, new galaxies will form, new stars will be born, fresh planetary systems will come into being and, on some, conditions will doubtless be suitable for the complex molecules of life to be put together. Then life will begin all over again, but it will be a new life, with new civilizations. The old life of our present universe will have long since been dead.

An artist's impression of distorted space around a solitary black hole and of material streaming into it. Possibly all planets, all stars, all nebulae, and even all galaxies will end up in a black hole. All life, wherever it might be – on planets or on dust grains – would be swept away into nothingness at the same time.

EMIGRATING INTO SPACE

Whatever the final fate of the universe may be, it is possible that mankind may emigrate into space. There are various ways we could do this, even with present-day knowledge.

With the ability to launch people into space and to bring them back safely to Earth, it is clear we now have the technology necessary for the adventure of colonizing space. We could, within the next fifty years, see a situation where people move out from Earth to live somewhere else. This might be necessary as the Earth's population continues to increase, though it would present no permanent solution to the problem. Space-colonization could take pioneers to places where there are new minerals and other raw materials, and it would be a great adventure which some people would welcome. Such colonization has become more practical since the development of reusable craft like Skylab, because such craft could be used to assemble in orbit the large emigrant spaceships needed. To lift such an emigrant craft away from the Earth's surface might well prove impracticable. Of course, even assembling it in orbit would still be costly, but one day it may be considered worthwhile.

Where could emigrants go? Certainly no other planet in the Solar System has conditions suitable for human beings; Mars is too cold, it lacks water and its atmosphere is too thin and has too little oxygen. Venus is most inhospitable, with its immense atmospheric pressure, its lack of oxygen and corrosive carbon dioxide atmosphere. Mercury is too hot and has virtually no atmosphere, a barren land blasted by ultraviolet radiation, X-rays and cosmic rays that would kill us. The Moon is not as hot as Mercury but it is equally inhospitable, without any atmosphere for protection.

Suggestions have been made about setting up an astronomical observatory on the Moon, with the astronauts living inside artificially constructed domes. But while that might be possible for a few scientists, on a short tour of duty, it would not do for a colony where the numbers of emigrants could total thousands.

However, one of the most astonishing ideas to be put forward in recent years has been that we should modify conditions on some other members of the Solar System to make them suitable for colonization by human beings, so that it would be possible to live on their surfaces just as we do on the surface of the Earth. With the ability to soft-land spacecraft on Mars and Venus and on the Moon we have the technology to visit other bodies and to start making the necessary changes now. But how could we alter the environment of an entire planet?

There is no suggested scheme for modifying Mercury or the Moon. Neither has an atmosphere, and even if it proved possible to take one to them, the Sun's heat combined with their small gravitational pulls would cause it to evaporate into space. To try modifying either body would be a waste of effort. But things are different when we come to Mars; here something could be done to turn it into a habitable planet for human beings, to 'terraform' it. What would be needed is heat. The reason why the rocks on the Martian surface are red coloured is that they have a surface covering of iron oxide, or rust, and if this were heated it would give off oxygen. At the same time a rise in temperature would cause the Martian ice caps to melt, thus increasing the amount of water vapour in the atmosphere. If all this could be done then not only would the content of the planet's atmosphere be altered but also the atmospheric pressure would be increased, and this would also be necessary before the planet could be inhabited.

To heat the surface sufficiently, it has been suggested that a spacecraft could be made to deflect the nucleus of one or more comets so that they collided with Mars, or could force one or more of Jupiter's satellites to drop down large chunks of their icy surfaces on to the planet. The material falling on the planet would cause heating of the surface and would also lead to the addition of some useful vaporized material to the atmosphere. However, any terraforming of Mars would seem to require such a large-scale effort that, if practicable at all, it certainly lies very many years in the future.

By contrast, changing the environment on Venus seems to be far more of a practical possibility. In 1975, the American astronomer Carl Sagan put forward an ingenious suggestion. Considering that the atmosphere of Venus is very thick an

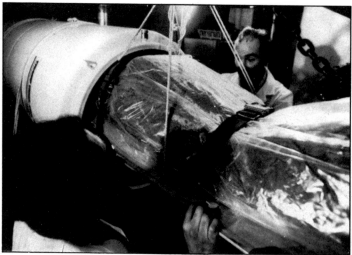

above
The body of someone being guided into a two-patient, vacuum insulated cryogenic storage capsule. The bodily functions of people can be kept from decaying in a deep-freeze. They could thus remain in suspended animation during a long space journey.

right
Space stations at two of the Lagrangian points of the Moon's orbit.

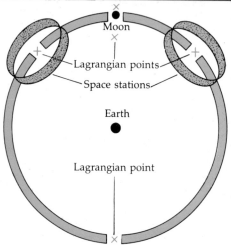

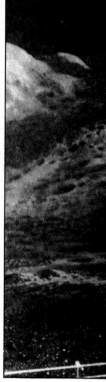

A 'mass-driver' spacecraft for transporting bulk

composed mainly of carbon dioxide, and that the atmospheric pressure has the huge value of 88 kg per square centimetre (over half a ton per square inch), the modifications needed would seem to be immense. And so they are, yet Sagan's suggestion is simplicity itself. He has suggested that algae, a very simple micro-organism, should be dropped into the upper atmosphere of Venus. Once there, they would float in the clouds, and under the bright conditions would begin to photosynthesize. Thus the immediate result of the algae would be to reduce the carbon dioxide in Venus' atmosphere and to replace it with oxygen. In due course the algae would drop down lower in the atmosphere, where they would be burned up in the great heat near the planet's surface. The charring of the algae would release carbon, carbon compounds and oxygen, with the result that all the atmospheric carbon dioxide would ultimately be separated into carbon and oxygen. Any water present would be retained while oxygen would combine with the surface rocks, as clearly happened sometime during the history of Mars. With all the carbon dioxide and some of the oxygen removed from the atmosphere, three things would be likely to happen. In the first place the greenhouse effect would be severely curtailed which would bring about a considerable reduction in temperature. Secondly, because of the absorption of some of the oxygen, Venus' immense atmospheric pressure would be reduced. Thirdly, the presence of oxygen higher up in the modified Venusian atmosphere, would lead to the formation of a layer of ozone, which would absorb the extreme ultraviolet and X-rays from the Sun. Sagan's scheme would, of course, depend for its effectiveness on the algae reproducing themselves while floating in the upper atmosphere at a faster rate than they were being destroyed lower down near the surface.

Of course, terraforming Venus, or Mars for that matter, is no more than theory at present. No experiments have been carried out to prove that the schemes would work in practice. On the other hand, we should realize that changing a planet's environment is not as fantastic as it may sound. Already use of heat by industry and in warming our homes has raised the general temperature of the air over the Earth; the change is only very small but it is enough to cause the general temperature of the polar ice-caps to rise sufficiently to begin a gradual process of melting with a consequent flooding of some land areas (page 196).

Nevertheless some scientists think that a more practical way of emigrating into space would be to construct artificial space colonies – 'man-made biospheres' – and put them into orbit round the Sun. The physical conditions could be specified and kept constant with a certainty that is not yet possible with any terraforming operation on a complete planet.

The orbit adopted for such artificial colonies need not be all that distant, and it is suggested that they should be put into the same orbit as the Moon, moving round the Earth in one of the 'Lagrangian points' on the Moon's orbit. These points, which occur in the orbit of every planet or satellite, were discovered some two hundred years ago by the French mathematical astronomer Joseph Lagrange. He showed that there were five such points in every orbit, equally spaced from each other at 60° intervals away from the orbiting body, where small objects could keep a stable orbit. We can observe such points in Jupiter's orbit where, in spite of the huge mass of Jupiter, minor planets are found to be in orbit. These two 'Trojan' groups lie one 60° ahead of Jupiter's position and the other 60° behind. There are no minor planets at the other three Lagrangian points because the pull of Saturn and the other planets would disturb any bodies orbiting there.

What has been proposed for the artificial space colonies is that they should orbit with the Moon at the Lagrangian point that lies 60° behind the Moon itself. There are good reasons for choosing the Moon's orbit. It is not too far from the Earth to send out construction craft, known as Heavy-Lift Launch Vehicles (HLLVs), and it would be from the surface of the Moon itself that the most of the materials for the colonies would come. For it is suggested that the main bodies of the colonies will be constructed of aluminium, a material that has many properties suited to the job, and is plentiful on the Moon. Some 600,000 tonnes will probably be required for each colony. But an aluminium body has one disadvantage; it will not shield the occupants of the colony from short-wave ultraviolet radiation, X-rays or cosmic rays. As such shielding is vital, it is proposed that it should be

materials which would be needed in building an artificial space colony takes off from the Moon's surface. The craft is propelled by ejecting some of its load; the very act of throwing off the material propels the craft forward through space.

made from lunar rock, probably using the 'slag' left over after the aluminium has been extracted. It is estimated that about 3 million tonnes of slag will be needed to make the shielding fully effective. This is a lot of material but we should remember that it is to be mined from the Moon, where gravity at the surface is only 16 hundredths that of the Earth, so that it will not be as difficult a job to move it as it would be if it were mined on Earth. (The tonnes given above are based on the Earth's scale of weight, under its greater gravitation.) Of course it will all have to be moved some 402,500 km from the Moon to the assembly site (60° behind the Moon's orbital position) but, again, because of the Moon's lower gravity, that will require less energy than would be needed to take the material from the Earth out 384,400 km to that point on the Moon's orbit.

What form will the colonies take, for there could be more than one at this Langrangian point? There are two suggestions, some details of which have been worked out by Gerard O'Niell of Princeton University, New Jersey. The colonies could be shaped either like cylinders or like spheres. In both cases they would have to be kept rotating on their axes to give the inhabitants the effect of living under gravity, as they do on Earth. This is necessary because prolonged exposure to very low gravity weakens the body and, as an artificial colony with a mass of 3½ million tonnes would not have sufficient gravity of its own, it would have to be created artificially. By rotating the colony, the inhabitants

far right
A view inside the torus showing its Earth-like living conditions.

right
A twin-cylinder O'Neill artificial colony. Each cylinder is 6.4 km in diameter, 32 km long and can house 200,000 people. Artificial Earth-like gravity is generated by rotating each cylinder once every 2 minutes.

would experience the so-called 'centrifugal force' pushing them to the inside surface of the cylinder or sphere. This is the same kind of effect you get when a vehicle in which you are travelling goes round a corner very fast. Energy for rotating the colony and for supplying it with power would come from the Sun.

Such colonies would need to be large enough to prevent the inhabitants feeling too cooped up; they would need to be pleasant, comfortable and to give a feeling of security. In the first stage they would probably need to be very like an Earth environment and it is expected that they would contain plants and some animals as well as human beings. The spherically shaped colony, the 'Bernal sphere', named after John Bernal, a British scientist, who made proposals along these lines many years ago, would, it is envisaged, be about 460 metres (500 yards) in diameter.

Another project, though further in the future, is the suggestion for a Space Ark, to carry emigrants on the long journey to some other planetary system, possibly putting the occupants into suspended animation by freezing. This would slow down the ageing process.

But even with such a project as this, life could not be kept going indefinitely; not if our universe becomes no more than a collection of black holes. Unless, of course, astronomers do find there are other universes and discover a way of reaching them, then it might be possible to carry life on for ever. But that is pure speculation at this stage of our knowledge.

The torus or doughnut artificial colony

GLOSSARY

Antimatter: matter which consists of particles that are charged in the opposite way from the matter that makes up the everyday world, but which are otherwise the same.

Asteroid: a small planetary body orbiting the Sun. Most are found between the paths of Mars and Jupiter.

Astronomical unit: the average distance between the Earth and the Sun.

Big bang: the suggested explosive origin of the universe that brought both space and time into being. It is thought to have occurred about 18,000 million years ago.

Black body: a theoretically perfect radiator; a body for which radiation absorbed and radiation re-radiated are identical.

Centre of mass: the average point through which the mass of a body or system of bodies acts.

Cosmology: the study of the nature and origin of the universe as a whole.

Cryogenic: a term used to describe processes which take place at very low temperatures.

Doppler effect: the apparent change in the frequency of light (or other radiation) seen when a source of radiation is moving towards or away from an observer. The Doppler effect accounts for the greater part of all blueshifts and redshifts observed.

Electron microscope: a microscope which relies on streams of electrons rather than light to produce an image.

Globular cluster: an approximately spherical group of stars. Such clusters may contain several hundred thousand stars and are usually found clustered around the central regions of a galaxy.

Graviton: a 'wave-packet' or particle of gravitational energy.

Hadron: a group of sub-atomic particles (those that take part in strong interactions). The group includes protons, neutrons and mesons.

Hubble's law: that the distance of a galaxy from us is directly proportional to its radial velocity.

Hyperbola: a curved line obtained by cutting through both elements of a cone; in other words both the cone itself and its extension beyond its point or apex.

Lagrangian points: six points around an orbit, each 60° apart, at which bodies may circulate without disturbing one another. One such point is always occupied by the primary orbiting body, leaving five remaining points for occupation by other bodies.

Lepton: a group of sub-atomic particles (those that do *not* take part in strong interactions). The group includes electrons.

Local Group: the group of galaxies that contains our own Milky Way Galaxy. It has some 30 members.

Magellanic Clouds: two small nearby galaxies visible from Earth to observers in the southern hemisphere only.

Nutation: a small oscillation which the Earth's axis goes through every 18 years. It is caused by changes in the position of the Moon relative to the plane of the Earth's orbit.

Photoelectric effect: the ejection of electrons by certain metals when light falls on them.

Photon: a 'wave-packet' or particle of light.

Proper motion: the actual movement of a body through space relative to the movement of the background stars.

Proton-proton reaction: a process inside a star whereby hydrogen is converted into helium.

QSO: quasi-stellar object; powerful energy sources of comparatively small size found at great distances.

Radial velocity: the speed at which an object is travelling away from, or towards, an observer.

Radio galaxy: a galaxy which produces large amounts of energy in the form of radio waves.

Redshift: the shift of the lines in a spectrum towards the red end, seen in the light of stars, galaxies and other radiating bodies that are moving away from an observer.

Riemannian space: a form of space used in relativity theory. It conforms to a system of geometry developed in the mid-nineteenth century by Georg Riemann.

Space-time: the combination of space and time in relativity theory. Time is as necessary as any of the spatial dimensions to determine a body's location.

Speckle interferometry: a technique for producing a high-quality image of a star by combining a number of photographs taken with a short exposure time.

Steady state theory: the idea that the universe is both expanding and yet unchanging on the largest scale. To counteract expansion the theory supposes that matter is constantly being created.

Strong interactions: these are the forces which hold the nucleus of an atom together.

Sunspot: a locally cool spot on the surface of the Sun which appears to be less bright than the surrounding area.

Supernova: the vastly energetic explosion of a massive star at the red supergiant stage. A supernova may appear to be brighter than all the other stars in a galaxy put together.

Synchrotron radiation: radiation produced by electrons moving through a magnetic field.

Tangential motion: the apparent motion across the sky or, more precisely, across the celestial sphere, of a celestial body.

Wavelength: the distance between successive crests of a wave. The term applies equally to electromagnetic radiation, waves in the sea and all other wave disturbances.

INDEX

Page numbers in *italic* refer to illustrations, those in **bold** to substantial articles.